Toward a Feminist Philosophy of Economics

Feminist economists have demonstrated that interrogating hierachies based on gender, ethnicity, class, and nation, results in an economics that is less biased and more faithful to empirical evidence than are mainstream accounts.

This rigorous and comprehensive book examines many of the central philosophical questions and themes in feminist economics including:

- history of economics
- feminist science studies
- identity and agency
- caring labor
- postcolonialism and postmodernism

With contributions from such leading figures as Nancy Folbre, Julie Nelson and Sandra Harding, *Toward a Feminist Philosophy of Economics* looks set to become *the* book on feminist economics for some time to come. It will be greatly appreciated by all those interested in gender studies, economic methodology, and social theory.

Drucilla K. Barker is Professor of Economics and Women's Studies at Hollins University, Virginia, USA.

Edith Kuiper is researcher at the Faculty of Economics and Econometrics, the University of Amsterdam, the Netherlands.

Economics as Social Theory

Series edited by Tony Lawson
University of Cambridge

Social Theory is experiencing something of a revival within economics. Critical analyses of the particular nature of the subject matter of social studies and of the types of method, categories and modes of explanation that can legitimately be endorsed for the scientific study of social objects, are re-emerging. Economists are again addressing such issues as the relationship between agency and structure, between economy and the rest of society, and between the enquirer and the object of enquiry. There is a renewed interest in elaborating basic categories such as causation, competition, culture, discrimination, evolution, money, need, order, organization, power probability, process, rationality, technology, time, truth, uncertainty, value, etc.

The objective for this series is to facilitate this revival further. In contemporary economics the label "theory" has been appropriated by a group that confines itself to largely asocial, ahistorical, mathematical "modeling." *Economics as Social Theory* thus reclaims the "theory" label, offering a platform for alternative rigorous, but broader and more critical conceptions of theorizing.

Other titles in this series include:

Economics and Language
Edited by Willie Henderson

Rationality, Institutions and Economic Methodology
Edited by Uskali Mäki, Bo Gustafsson and Christian Knudsen

New Directions in Economic Methodology
Edited by Roger Backhouse

Who Pays for the Kids?
Nancy Folbre

Rules and Choice in Economics
Viktor Vanberg

Beyond Rhetoric and Realism in Economics
Thomas A. Boylan and Paschal F. O'Gorman

Feminism, Objectivity and Economics
Julie A. Nelson

Economic Evolution
Jack J. Vromen

Economics and Reality
Tony Lawson

The Market
John O'Neill

Economics and Utopia
Geoff Hodgson

Critical Realism in Economics
Edited by Steve Fleetwood

The New Economic Criticism
Edited by Martha Woodmansee and Mark Osteen

What do Economists Know?
Edited by Robert F. Garnett, Jr.

Postmodernism, Economics and Knowledge
Edited by Stephen Cullenberg, Jack Amariglio and David F. Ruccio

The Values of Economics
An Aristotelian Perspective
Irene van Staveren

How Economics Forgot History
The Problem of Historical Specificity in Social Science
Geoffrey M. Hodgson

Intersubjectivity in Economics
Agents and Structures
Edward Fullbrook

The World of Consumption, 2nd Edition
The Material and Cultural Revisited
Ben Fine

Reorienting Economics
Tony Lawson

Toward a Feminist Philosophy of Economics
Edited by Drucilla K. Barker and Edith Kuiper

The Crisis in Economics
Edited by Edward Fullbrook

The Philosophy of Keynes' Economics
Probability, Uncertainty and Convention
Edited by Jochen Runde and Sohei Mizuhara

Toward a Feminist Philosophy of Economics

Edited by Drucilla K. Barker
and Edith Kuiper

LONDON AND NEW YORK

First published 2003
by Routledge
11 New Fetter Lane, London EC4P 4EE

Simultaneously published in the USA and Canada
by Routledge
29 West 35th Street, New York, NY 10001

Routledge is an imprint of the Taylor & Francis Group

© 2003 Drucilla K. Barker and Edith Kuiper for selection and editorial matter;
individual chapters the contributors

Typeset in Perpetua by Taylor & Francis Books Ltd
Printed and bound in Great Britain by TJ International Ltd, Padstow, Cornwall

All rights reserved. No part of this book may be reprinted or
reproduced or utilized in any form or by any electronic,
mechanical, or other means, now known or hereafter
invented, including photocopying and recording, or in any
information storage or retrieval system, without permission in
writing from the publishers.

British Library Cataloguing in Publication Data
A catalogue record for this book is available from the British Library

Library of Congress Cataloging in Publication Data
Barker, Drucilla K., 1949–
Toward a feminist philosophy of economics/Drucilla K. Barker & Edith Kuiper.
(Economics as social theory)
Includes bibliographical references and index.
1. Feminist economics. 2. Economics–Philosophy. 3. Women–Economic
conditions.
I. Kuiper, Edith, 1960– II. Title. III. Series

ISBN 0–415–28387–6 (hbk)
ISBN 0–415–28388–4 (pbk)

Contents

List of illustrations   x
Notes on contributors   xi
Acknowledgments   xv

1 Introduction: sketching the contours of a feminist philosophy of economics   1
DRUCILLA K. BARKER AND EDITH KUIPER

PART I
Rereading history   19

2 Into the margin!   21
MICHÈLE A. PUJOL

3 Hazel Kyrk and the ethics of consumption   38
SUSAN VAN VELZEN

4 Feminist fiction and feminist economics: Charlotte Perkins Gilman on efficiency   56
IRENE VAN STAVEREN

5 Beyond markets: wage setting and the methodology of feminist political economy   70
MARILYN POWER, ELLEN MUTARI, AND DEBORAH M. FIGART

PART II
Science stories and feminist economics   87

6 Some implications of the feminist project in economics for empirical methodology   89
JOYCE P. JACOBSEN

viii   Contents

7   Foregrounding practices: feminist philosophy of economics beyond rhetoric
    and realism   105
    FABIENNE PETER

8   After objectivism vs. relativism   122
    SANDRA HARDING

9   How did "the moral" get split from "the economic"?   134
    JULIE A. NELSON

PART III
Constructing masculine/Western identity in economics   143

10 The construction of masculine identity in Adam Smith's *Theory of Moral
    Sentiments*   *145*
    EDITH KUIPER

11 Social classifications, social statistics, and the "facts" of "difference" in
    economics   161
    BRIAN P. COOPER

12 Reading neoclassical economics: toward an erotic economy of sharing   180
    SUSAN F. FEINER

13 The anxious identities we inhabit: post'isms and economic understandings   194
    NITASHA KAUL

PART IV
Beyond social contract: theorizing agency and relatedness   211

14 "Holding Hands at Midnight": the paradox of caring labor   213
    NANCY FOLBRE

15 Integrating vulnerability: on the impact of caring on economic theorizing   231
    MAREN A. JOCHIMSEN

16 An evolutionary approach to feminist economics: two different models of
    caring   247
    SUSAN HIMMELWEIT

17 Domestic labor and gender identity: are all women carers? 266
GILLIAN J. HEWITSON

PART V
Rethinking categories 285

18 Empowering work? Bargaining models reconsidered 287
S. CHARUSHEELA

19 Economic marginalia: postcolonial readings of unpaid domestic labor and development 304
CYNTHIA A. WOOD

20 The difficulty of a feminist economics 321
EIMAN ZEIN-ELABDIN

Index *339*

Illustrations

Table

16.1	Interactions between species (or modes of behavior) classified by advantage or disadvantage to each species	260

Figures

11.1	Population estimates for La Plata Federal Union for the year 1815	169
11.2	Family types in the 1851 British census	172
15.1	The caring situation	236
16.1	Norms and behavior with sluggish norms	254
16.2	Norms and behavior with volatile norms	256
16.3	Populations numbers over time of prey and predator	261

Contributors

Drucilla K. Barker is Professor of Economics and Women's Studies at Hollins University. She is a founding member of the International Association for Feminist Economics and is a member of the editorial board of *Feminist Economics*. Her research interests are in the areas of feminist philosophy and economic methodology. She is currently finishing a book, with Susan F. Feiner, *Liberating Economics: Feminist Perspectives on Gender and the Economy*, to be published by University of Michigan Press.

S. Charusheela is Assistant Professor of Women's Studies at the University of Hawaii at Mānoa. She is an active member of the International Association for Feminist Economics and the Association for Economic and Social Analysis, and works on the intersection between feminism, Marxism, and postcolonial thought. Recent publications include "On History, Love and Politics" (*Rethinking Marxism*, 12(4)), "Women's Choices and the Ethnocentrism/Relativism Dilemma" (in Stephen Cullenberg, Jack Amariglio and David F. Ruccio, *Postmodernism, Economics and Knowledge*, Routledge, 2001).

Brian P. Cooper is Assistant Professor of Economics at the State University of New York at Oswego. He works in the history of economics, and the economics of race, gender, and class. He is currently finishing a book, *Family Fictions and Family Facts*, to be published by Routledge.

Susan F. Feiner is Associate Professor of Economics and Women's Studies at the University of Southern Maine. Her research interests include transdisciplinary examinations of the relationships among psychology, religion, literary criticism, and economics. She is active in economics education, helping faculty integrate questions about race, gender, and equity into the undergraduate economics curriculum. She is currently finishing a book, with Drucilla K. Barker, *Liberating Economics: Feminist Perspectives on Gender and the Economy*, to be published by University of Michigan Press.

Deborah M. Figart is Professor of Economics at Richard Stockton College in Pomona, NJ. Her research on race, ethnicity, and gender issues crosses traditional disciplinary boundaries. Her latest book, with Ellen Mutari and Marilyn Power, is *Living Wages, Equal Wages: Gender and Labor Market Policies in the United States* (Routledge, 2002).

Nancy Folbre, Professor of Economics at the University of Massachusetts at Amherst, is also a staff economist with the Center for Popular Economics. Her academic research explores the interface between feminist theory and political economy. She is the author of *Who Pays for the Kids? Gender and the Structures of Constraint* (Routledge, 1994). Books she has authored for a wider audience include *The Ultimate Field Guide to the U.S. Economy*, and *The Invisible Heart: Economics and Family Values* (New Press, 2001). She is an associate editor of the journal *Feminist Economics*.

Sandra Harding is a philosopher in the Graduate School of Education and Information Studies at the University of California at Los Angeles. She is the author or editor of twelve books on feminist and postcolonial epistemology and science topics. An edited collection, *The Standpoint Reader*, will be published in 2003.

Gillian J. Hewitson is Senior Lecturer at La Trobe University. She researches in feminist economics from a feminist poststructuralist perspective. She is the author of *Feminist Economics: Interrogating the Masculinity of Rational Economic Man* (Edward Elgar, 1999). She is currently working on an annotated bibliography of feminist economics.

Susan Himmelweit teaches economics at the Open University and formerly taught women's studies at the University of Sydney. She is currently engaged in research on the influence of social norms on mothers' decisions about work and childcare as part of the UK Economic and Social Research Council's program on the Future of Work. Her research interests include the economics of care, the gender implications of economic policy, and the effects of taxes and benefits on paid and unpaid caring work. She is a member and former chair of the UK Women's Budget Group, an Associate Editor of the journal *Feminist Economics*, and is an active member of the International Association for Feminist Economics.

Joyce P. Jacobsen is Professor of Economics at Wesleyan University. She is the author of *The Economics of Gender* (2nd edition, Blackwell, 1998), along with a number of articles on sex segregation, labor-force participation, and determinants of earnings.

Maren A. Jochimsen is an expert at the *Bürgschaftsbank für Sozialwirtschaft* in Cologne (Germany), a guarantee bank specialized in the social economy. She received her doctorate in economics from the University of St. Gallen (Switzerland). Her latest research concentrated on the conceptualization of caring in economics and took her as visiting scholar to Cambridge University, Harvard University, and the University of Amsterdam.

Nitasha Kaul has recently joined the University of the West of England in Bristol (UK) as a Lecturer in economics. Her Ph.D. research is in economics and philosophy. Her transdisciplinary interests span feminist, poststructuralist, postcolonial theory, literature, activism, and heterodox economics. Her publications include book chapters and an article in the *Cambridge Journal of Economics*.

Edith Kuiper is researcher at the Faculty of Economics & Econometrics at the Universiteit van Amsterdam. She is Coordinator of the European chapter of the International Association for Feminist Economics (IAFFE–Europe) and was founder and President of the Feminist Economics Network in the Netherlands (FENN). Her research interests are in history and the philosophy of economics. She is co-editor of *Out of the Margin: Feminist Perspectives On Economics* (Routledge, 1995) and author of *The Most Valuable of All Capital: A Gender Reading of Economic Texts* (Thela Thesis, 2001).

Ellen Mutari is Assistant Professor in the General Studies Division at Richard Stockton College. She is co-author of *Living Wages, Equal Wages: Gender and Labor Market Policies in the United States* (Routledge, 2002) and co-editor of *Gender and Political Economy* (M.E. Sharpe, 1997).

Julie A. Nelson is currently at Tufts University, Massachusetts, USA, at the Global Development and Environment Institute. Formerly an Associate Professor of Economics at the University of California – Davis and at Brandeis University, she is co-editor, with Marianne Ferber, of *Beyond Economic Man* (University of Chicago Press, 1993), and author of *Feminism, Objectivity, and Economics* (Routledge, 1996) and many articles.

Fabienne Peter is Assistant Professor of Economics at the University of Basel. Her research explores issues at the interface of economics and philosophy, with particular emphasis on normative theories of social evaluation and on the philosophy of the social sciences. Before joining the University of Basel, she was a Research Fellow at the Harvard Center for Population and Development Studies, where she has worked on equity in health. A collective volume entitled *Public Health, Ethics, and Equity*, jointly edited with Amartya Sen and Sudhir Anand, is forthcoming.

Marilyn Power is a faculty member in economics at Sarah Lawrence College. She has been researching and writing about women and work since 1969. Her most recent publication is *Living Wages, Equal Wages: Gender and Labor Market Policies in the United States* (Routledge, 2002), co-authored with Deborah M. Figart and Ellen Mutari. Currently she is investigating the methodology of feminist political economics.

Michèle A. Pujol was one of Canada's leading feminist economists and a faculty member in the Women's Studies Programme at the University of Victoria. A scholar and activist, she was the author of *Feminism and Antifeminism in Early Economic Thought* (Edward Elgar, 1992).

Irene van Staveren is a lecturer in labor market economics of developing countries at the Institute of Social Studies in The Hague. She won the Gunnar Myrdal Prize 2000 for her dissertation and is the author of *The Value of Economics: An Aristotelian Perspective* (Routledge, 2001).

Susan van Velzen is a political scientist and currently employed at the Dutch Ministry of Finance. She received her Ph.D. in economics from the University of Amsterdam and is the author of *Supplements to the Economics of Household Behavior* (2001).

Cynthia A. Wood is an economist and Associate Professor of Interdisciplinary Studies at Appalachian State University whose publications have appeared in *Feminist Economics and Nepantla: Views from South*. She is currently at work on a book which explores the intersections of critical development studies and postcolonial feminist theory.

Eiman Zein-Elabdin is Associate Professor of Economics at Franklin & Marshall College. Her areas of research are development, postcolonial studies, and gender. She is a former economist with the government of Sudan. She is an editorial consultant for *Explorations in Postcolonial Studies*, published by SUNY Press. She has published in the *Journal of Economic Issues* and the *Review of Radical Political Economics*, among others.

Acknowledgments

In the process of preparing this book, several people and institutions have been important for their intellectual stimulation and support. We are pleased to have this opportunity to thank them explicitly.

We would like to thank Hollins University, the Faculty of Economics & Econometrics of the Universiteit van Amsterdam, and the European University Institute (EUI) in Florence, Italy for providing us with the time, the accommodation, and the inspiring academic environment essential for completing a book like this. We also want to thank the International Association for Feminist Economics (IAFFE) for organizing the yearly conferences and creating the community that provides us with an intellectual home. It helped us to both conceive of this book and to make it a truly international endeavor.

We especially want to thank the faculty (both past and present) of the Women's Studies Program at Hollins for their conversations and inspiration. We also thank Diana Strassmann and Susan Thomas and their friendship and support of this project from the very beginning.

Thanks also to Dawn Lyon of the Gender group of the EUI for organizing many interesting and relevant seminars on feminist theory and research, and giving us the chance to be a part of these discussions. We hope that this book contributes to further integration of feminist economics into feminism and gender studies.

We were very lucky to work with an enthusiastic group of authors, and we thank them for their contributions. The session on this book at the IAFFE conference at Occidental College in Los Angeles in July 2002, in which more than half of all the authors represented in this book participated, showed the richness, liveliness, and importance of the topics involved. We hope and trust that the publication of this book will be a substantial step towards the flourishing of feminist theory in economics. We very much look forward to continuing these discussions.

For their assistance and help of various kinds in the process of preparing the manuscript, we would like to thank Athena Sargent for her friendship and help in the editing process, Joanne Mitchell for her competent secretarial assistance,

Wendela de Vries for her friendship and advice, and Carl Reed for his support and assistance in so many ways.

The authors and the publisher would like to thank the following for permission to reprint material:

"Out of the Margin!" by Michèle Pujol and "Reading Neoclassical Economics: Toward an Erotic Economy of Sharing," by Susan Feiner are both reprinted from *Out of the Margin: Feminist Perspectives on Economics*, edited by Edith Kuiper, Jolande Sap, S.F. Feiner, N. Ott and Z. Tzannatos, Routledge, 1995.

"Holding Hands at Midnight: The Paradox of Caring Labor," by Nancy Folbre is reprinted from *Feminist Economics*, vol.1 no.1. 1995.

Chapter 10 features several quotations from Adam Smith reprinted from the Glasgow Edition of the *Works and Correspondence of Adam Smith: The Theory of Moral Sentiments,* edited by D.D. Raphael and A.S. Skinner (1976) by permission of Oxford University Press. © Oxford University Press 1976.

1 Introduction

Sketching the contours of a feminist philosophy of economics

Drucilla K. Barker and Edith Kuiper

Toward a Feminist Philosophy of Economics is an anthology of essays that sketch the contours of feminist economics and examine the ways in which it can contribute to new and better ways of understanding and practicing economics. By historicizing, theorizing, and critically reflecting on feminist economics, we intend to participate in moving feminist economics out of the margin and into the center: to become economics, unmodified.

Feminist economics is uniquely situated at the intersection of economics, feminism, and philosophy. Scholars are reconceptualizing what economics is, what methodologies are appropriate for feminist research in economics, and what the relationship is between feminist theory and economics. In doing so they inherit both the strengths and the weaknesses of these fields. Feminist economics inherits the prestige and subject matter of economics, along with the problems and paradoxes associated with the scientific aspirations of the discipline. Debates over the truth of assumptions, the importance of statistical evidence, and the role of mathematical reasoning are not eliminated by the introduction of feminist theory. Feminism contributes the powerful tool of gender analysis, along with the contemporary debates in feminist theory regarding the primacy of gender as an analytic category and its relationship to other categories of identity, such as race, class, and sexual orientation. The framework for addressing questions of epistemology and ontology is part of the philosophical heritage of feminist economics, a heritage that includes postmodern and postcolonial thinkers who call into question the very possibility of such concepts. These issues are, broadly speaking, part of the purview of a feminist philosophy of economics.

We understand feminism to be a theoretical and ethical position. The social construction of gender, race, ethnicity, class, sexuality, nation, and other categories of identity is at the heart of contemporary feminist theorizing. Systems of hierarchy and privilege based on them are ethically suspect. Since women's lives differ dramatically depending on various and sometimes contradictory social locations, positing an essentialized, universal subordination of women is no longer tenable. Unstable and shifting as the category "women" is, it nonetheless remains central to feminist theory. It is this instability, and the uneasy alliances created by it, that engenders depth and breadth in contemporary feminist visions.

Gender analysis remains integral to feminist scholarship. Using gender as an analytical category enables feminist economists to theorize persistent and ubiquitous inequalities between women and men that arise from differing social roles and unequal power relations. Since gender is a relational term, referring to the relationship between the social roles of women and men, feminist economics is not only about "women's" economic issues. Rather, economic phenomena associated with women influence economic outcomes for both women and men, albeit in different ways depending on one's social location. Caring labor is a good example. Feminist analyses reveal that, although the provision of caring labor falls most heavily on the shoulders of women, it is crucial to the wellbeing of both women and men. Further, women experience caring labor differently depending on factors such as race, class, and nationality.

Theorizing gender and its intersections with other categories of identity and social location entails taking seriously the philosophical and methodological challenges from post-positivist science studies, postmodernism and postcolonialism. These challenges are significant not only to feminist economists, but to anyone interested in social theory. A feminist philosophy of economics incorporates these issues and philosophical challenges into economics.

What is feminist economics?

A feminist philosophy of economics emerges out of feminist economics, a dynamic and evolving field of intellectual inquiry that challenges traditional economic theory. Many of the central issues in feminist economics, such as women's labor force participation, the wage gap, the value of household labor, and women's role in development, had been of interest to economists for quite a while. These analyses and studies did not, however, question the gender division of labor; nor did they employ gender as a category of analysis (Benería 1995). Feminist economists noticed that absent a gender analysis, economic theories were, and are, linked to masculinist notions of science (J.A. Nelson 1995). Unquestioned and unexamined Western masculine values were deeply ingrained in traditional economic theories about so-called women's issues (Strassmann 1993).

Feminist analysis shows that economics relies on highly gendered and raced metaphors, the most famous of which is *homo economicus*, or the rational economic agent, a conception of human agency that reflects a privileged, masculine worldview. Rational agents have no necessary obligations or responsibilities and interact contractually with others only when it is in their best interests to do so. Moreover, since neoclassical or mainstream economics is defined by its method of analysis rather than by its domain of study – conventional economics generally admits only explanations based on self-interested exchange between rational economic agents – it fails adequately to account for a wide variety of factors germane to women's (and men's) lives (Strassmann 1993). For example, the gendered and raced division of labor is explained in terms of the individual choices of rational agents; the provision of nonmarket, caring labor (such as parenting, caring for the sick, housework, etc.) is either largely ignored or analyzed in the same terms as the provision of paid labor; and the gendered and raced effects of globalization are explained as the natural consequences of differing endowments of skills, technology, and resources.

Feminist economists seek to do better by questioning implicit assumptions about traditional gender roles, and about appropriate race, class, and national hierarchies, thus revealing the biases and distortions in masculinist views of the economy. Feminists also seek to increase the variety of explanations that can count as economics, thus freeing economics from the straitjacket of constrained optimization and formal mathematical modeling. It does this by reconceiving economics in far richer and more visionary ways than the neoclassical paradigm allows.[1]

A feminist philosophy of economics likewise conceptualizes economics as a social institution: it is an integral part of culture, of power relations, and of change. Economics is not an abstract notion; it does not exist without people. Rather, it is a state of affairs, always implicated in global politics, regional interests, and local alliances. As economists, we are part of the picture – we study, write, and teach from interested positions. Such interests are affected by intellectual pleasure, ethical sensibilities, as well as by prestige, uncertainty, and a variety of other institutional constraints. Explicitly recognizing our location ties us concretely to the world and enables us to envision effective strategies for change and new perspectives on economic issues. New visions and strategies need to be located in, and informed by, history, and thus our anthology begins with feminist readings in the history of economic thought.

Rereading history

Originating in Britain, and dominated by men, classical political economy reflected the concerns and perspectives of the emerging industrialist class. This has had an impact not only on economic theory and policy, but also on the writing of its history. The rise of feminist research in the history of economics engendered a growing interest in the neglected work of women economists as well as an examination of the role of women in the work of the classical political economists and of the later economists. A feminist examination of the intellectual history of economics demonstrates the masculinist perspective of economists and, in doing so, fundamentally changes our understanding of the development of economic thought. It regards economics as a social and historical phenomenon and is able to situate the history of thought in a context that provides a broader and richer perspective on contemporary economic issues than is provided by the narrower theoretical framework of today's orthodoxy.

Works such as *Women of Value* (Dimand *et al.* 1995) and *Adam Smith's Daughters* (Thomson and Polkinghorn 1999 [first published in 1973]), have been instrumental in recovering the works of neglected women economists and highlighting the work of prominent ones. Considerations of "women's issues" were not confined only to women economists. Often unstated assumptions about women's appropriate roles in marriage and the family were an integral part of economic theory (Folbre 1992; Forget 1999). In reflecting on these texts, as well as on texts that did not address women's issues explicitly, feminist historians of economics showed how implicit assumptions about gender played an important role in structuring economic arguments (Folbre and Hartmann 1988; Pujol 1992; Justman 1996; Kuiper 2001).

Thus a feminist rereading of history clearly shows that it is not one long, unbroken line of thought – hegemonic, masculinist, and impenetrable – stretching from the past into the future. Rather, it is a history riddled with fissures, contradictions, and dissenting voices. Understanding this aspect of history chips away at orthodoxy by revealing "misattribution of sources and distortion of context" (Dimand *et al.* 1995: 14). Rereading voices from the historical margin is necessary both to producing fuller accounts of intellectual history and to revealing the masculinist bias in economic thought.

Michèle Pujol's *Feminism and Anti-Feminism in Early Economic Thought*, is now a classic in this regard (Pujol 1992). This book anticipates many of the themes found in Part I: recovering the voices of women in economics, understanding the ways that assumptions about gender and the family influence debates about wage setting, and analyzing the raced and gendered discourse of the classical political economists and early neoclassical economists. Thus Part I begins with her.

A popular bumper sticker in feminist circles carries the slogan "feminism is the radical notion that women are human beings."[2] Michèle Pujol's chapter (Chapter 2) demonstrates just how relevant this statement is. Pujol shows that women were not seen as human beings by the early neoclassical economists – Jevons, Marshall, Edgeworth, and Pigou. Rather, they were seen as wives, mothers, and daughters who were economically dependent on male relatives, naturally suited for reproductive rather than productive labor, and economically irrational. These assumptions, which differentiate women from men, rationalize both the exclusion of issues associated with women from neoclassical discourse and the second-class status of women in labor markets. One of the most important contributions of this analysis is to show that these assumptions are not just artifacts of an unenlightened Victorian era, but are necessary to the theoretical consistency of the neoclassical paradigm. Victorian ideology continues to undergird the neoclassical paradigm of the family, especially in the new home economics associated with Gary Becker (Becker 1981).

While Gary Becker may be the father of the new home economics, feminist economists have uncovered its maternal origins in the nearly forgotten work of Hazel Kyrk and Margaret Reid. Reid's work is perhaps the better known among feminist economists, since a special issue of *Feminist Economics* was published to acknowledge and honor her legacy.[3] Less, however, is known about her teacher, Hazel Kyrk, who was nearly lost from the history of economic thought. Susan van Velzen's chapter (Chapter 3) remedies this omission. It provides an overview of Hazel Kyrk's life and work in the field of consumer economics (later to become known as home economics) during the interwar period in the United States. Kyrk's conception of the good life, or what we might today call economic wellbeing, drew heavily on the then thriving pragmatist tradition and led to a conception of economics that considered necessary not only the material aspects of consumer behavior, but the ethical aspects as well. Van Velzen's exposition of the depth and breadth of Kyrk's work demonstrates its continuing relevance to feminist economics and other heterodox economics projects.

Irene van Staveren's chapter on Charlotte Perkins Gilman (Chapter 4) is another contribution to recovering early feminist voices in economics and showing their relevance to contemporary economics. It examines Gilman's conception of efficiency, and uses both literary texts and economic texts to tease out the nuances of her position. Her analysis of Gilman's positions, especially on the relationships among household labor, caring labor, and market labor, is driven by her interest in rethinking them in a contemporary context. It opens up an important space for feminist economists interested in using literary texts in economic analysis, and demonstrates clearly that feminist economics is more than just a criticism of the mainstream. It is an alternative and more humane vision of economics and the economy. Finally, van Staveren shows that reading Gilman's fiction is necessary to fully understand her economics. For feminist economists this should not be too surprising if we accept the proposition that the economy is not radically separate from all other aspects of life, but rather is embedded in them, and that economic wellbeing is tied not only to the material, but to the social, cultural, and political as well.

The last chapter in this section, by Marilyn Power, Ellen Mutari, and Deborah M. Figart (Chapter 5), continues this theme as it analyzes wage setting as a cultural, political, and economic process. The authors show that the neoclassical notion of wages as a price is a relatively recent development. Historically, wages have also been conceived of as a living and as a social practice. In both of these conceptions, wage setting is influenced by considerations of fairness, and such considerations are influenced by gender norms regarding women as housewives and men as wage earners. Power, Mutari, and Figart examine the interaction among these three more or less implicit wage theories in the early twentieth-century debate over minimum wages for women. Their analysis contributes to a disruption of the hegemonic, neoclassical explanation of wages as a price, and it provides feminist economists with historically rooted strategies for confronting the problem of wage inequality.

Science stories and feminist economics

The development of feminist economics can, in part, be characterized as an instance of feminist empiricism. Feminist empiricism has its origins in the work of feminist scholars in biology and related life sciences who recognized that the answers to many questions involving sex and gender reflected a distinct androcentric and/or sexist bias (Harding 1986).[4] Feminist economists, trained in traditional economics, noticed that many questions concerning women's economic lives had not received adequate attention from mainstream economics (Ferber and Nelson 1993; Benería 1995). Moreover, some feminist economists doubted whether these questions were even answerable within mainstream theory (Barker 1999).[5] To them it seemed that, rather than the value-free, objective, scientific enterprise that its practitioners claimed it to be, economics was deeply imbued with values that reflected an elite, masculine worldview.

Revealing these implicit values was a project that was aided and abetted by the early work of Deirdre McCloskey. In the mid-1980s McCloskey mounted a significant challenge to the conventional notions of economic methodology. She argued that methodology, conceived of as a set of rules prescribing what counts as evidence and objective inquiry, ought to be abandoned because it was based on an outdated amalgam of positivism and its various antecedents (McCloskey 1998 [first published 1987]). In this view, economic theories are best understood as metaphors, stories, and conversations, and should be judged according to their rhetorical persuasiveness. At this time, McCloskey did not consider the demographic characteristics of the economics profession and the way those characteristics influence which arguments are likely to be considered persuasive. With the emergence of feminist economics came an interrogation of the shared cultural and social values of economists.

Diana Strassmann's work was particularly influential in examining the link between the demographics of the economics profession and the persuasiveness of economic stories. She argued that economics is an interpretive community whose members are socialized not to question the overarching values of the profession, values that reflected an androcentric and Western perspective on selfhood and agency (Strassmann 1993). Her work is closely akin to that of feminist epistemologists working in the empiricist tradition. They hold that knowledge is not acquired by isolated individuals, but rather by epistemic communities (Longino 1993; L. Nelson 1993). It is within the context of these communities that scientists' observations, theories, hypotheses, and patterns of reasoning are shaped and modified. Alternative points of view are necessary to reveal the influence of unexamined assumptions and shared social values (Longino 1993; Harding 1995). This is no less true of the economics community, an extremely homogeneous community of mostly white, relatively affluent, and mostly male economists.

Feminist economists realize, therefore, that to do economics in ways that are less biased and incomplete requires them to question implicit assumptions, which in turn requires alternative points of view. As the marginalized voices of women and minorities are brought into the profession, the questions, methods, and practices of the profession change as well. Including gender and other markers of identity as categories of analysis, and changing the questions we ask as well as the methods used to investigate them, leads to some very interesting methodological issues and questions.

Joyce Jacobsen's chapter (Chapter 6) asks whether feminist economics has had any impact on empirical work in economics. In answering this question, she develops a taxonomy of the contributions of feminist economics: the treatment of nontradable goods, especially in national income accounting; the measurement of intrahousehold interactions and resource allocation; the measurement of family structure effects on labor market incomes; and the conceptualization of caring work. From this taxonomy she concludes that, despite substantial theoretical and empirical contributions, feminist economics remains marginalized in the profession.

If one takes seriously the traditional values of science, such as open inquiry and the role of evidence in theory choice, then this is a puzzling state of affairs. After all, it has been shown time and time again that feminist economics results in better economics, accounts of the economy that are more theoretically robust and empirically accurate than conventional accounts that ignore gender. So why does feminist economics remain on the margin?

Ironically, at least part of the reason lies in the scientific aspirations/pretensions of mainstream economists. It is certainly true that mainstream economics has been wildly successful in establishing its scientific credentials in the eyes of the academy, the government, and the general public. Serious methodological reflections, however, reveal a huge disparity between the social, cultural, and political authority enjoyed by economics and its manifest failings as a science when evaluated in terms of a positivist or falsificationist philosophy of science (Barker 2003). This view holds that science is a privileged form of knowledge about the world, access to which is predicated on adherence to methodological rules. The application of this view to economics has been dubbed the "received view," by Wade Hands (Hands 2001). The received view has been fatally undermined in contemporary science theory, both by its own internal contradictions and paradoxes, and by the challenges posed by W.V.O. Quine, Thomas Kuhn, and others working in the post-positivist tradition (Kuhn 1996 [first published 1962]; Quine 1953).

Guarding the gates against the feminist philistines will not protect economics from the methodological quandaries of a post-positivist world. Nor will simply adding feminism to economics provide a way of conceptualizing and resolving these quandaries for feminist economics. The task for contemporary science studies and epistemology is to find a middle ground between relativism and objectivism, or, put another way, between the notion of science as a socially constructed activity and science as a rational enterprise (Harding 2001; Longino 2002). The next three chapters address this issue by reconsidering the nature of science.

Fabienne Peter's chapter (Chapter 7) argues for a political philosophy of science, an approach that switches the focus in philosophy of science from knowledge to the practices by which knowledge is produced. Her analysis of existing approaches to the philosophy of economics – in particular the main contenders, rhetoric and realism – demonstrates that they fail to offer an adequate basis for a feminist philosophy of economics because they fail to theorize the social. She offers the notion of practices as an alternative theoretical framework. This does not mean that science reduces to politics, but rather that scientific practices are open to contestation in terms of ethical and democratic principles. How do science practices influence participation in knowledge production? How do social power relations influence knowledge production? What are the goals of science and do science practices advance or retard them? How do feminists resolve the tension between working for acceptance within the current practices of economics and creatively imagining other topics of research and modes of inquiry? These are some of the central questions for a political philosophy of science.

Sandra Harding's chapter (Chapter 8) explores ways to traverse what she terms the relativism/epistemic absolutism debate in ways that preserve the possibility of making rational and objective belief choices. She argues that both relativists and absolutists hold similar views of the relationship between language and the world. Science, in this view, is a set of words or representations of the world, and so the goal of science seems to be accurately to represent nature's order or truth. It is this view of science that raises the fear of relativism. If, however, science is conceived of as a method of inquiry or set of practices, then one can always interrogate these practices in terms of the desirability of their goals and their effectiveness in achieving them.

As Harding points out, this is particularly relevant for feminist economics because of its explicit goals regarding the material wellbeing of women and marginalized groups. In addition, feminist economists take seriously the notion of altering practices in order to conceive of more humane and socially progressive economic policies. Reconceiving women's labor, especially caring labor, is one prominent example of this practice, to which many of the papers in this anthology attest.

Focusing on ontology rather than epistemology is another response to the demise of the received view and the anxieties associated with relativism. This approach is most closely associated with Tony Lawson's critical realist approach (Lawson 1999). Julie Nelson's chapter (Chapter 9) engages with this debate, but changes its terms in a way that is complementary to the work of Peter and Harding.

Nelson argues that the ontology presupposed by the mind/body, knower/known, science/value dualisms permeating modern science may be a misleading assumption. It is an ontology that considers mind and matter as separate, and values and purposes as something that humans impose on a valueless and purposeless external reality. She suggests taking a different perspective – drawing on process ontology, as articulated by process philosophers such as Whitehead – in which events or experiences, rather than matter, are the basic constituents of reality. In this ontology, time and change are crucial; the world is unfinished and evolving. Conceiving of ontology in this way does not preclude doing science – conceived of as methodical inquiry, openness to evidence, and experimentation. As pragmatist philosophers such as Dewey and James pointed out, what it does do is reframe the question of knowledge. Knowledge is not just about things. Rather, knowledge adds to reality. Knowledge production makes a difference in the world. The question becomes: does it make the right difference?

Constructing masculine/Western identity in economics

A long tradition of economists focusing on the behavior of privileged, educated, Western men has had a significant impact on economics. The rational economic agent, the darling of many traditional economists *and* the bane of feminists, rests on an Enlightenment conception of subjectivity. According to this conception, behind the diversity of human experience lies a universal human nature, and the capacity for rationality is an essential part of that nature. Through reason, human beings are able to apprehend natural laws that are objectively true, in the sense that they are equally knowable and binding on every person (Flax 1992). This concept of human nature is the basis for human rights and political autonomy.

There is a long and important tradition in liberal feminism that argues for women's equal rights on the basis that the capacity for reason is common to both women and men. As Genevieve Lloyd persuasively argued, however, this conception of rationality is constituted, in part, by an exclusion of the feminine (Lloyd 1984). Moreover, the liberal subject position is not a neutral position that can be occupied by anyone regardless of the contingent circumstance of identity – gender, race, class, etc. (Hewitson 1999). It is a subject position predicated on a particular identity – that of propertied men of European ancestry – and claims to universality serve to obscure its particular nature.

This is an important question for feminist economics because the liberal subject also provides the basis of its more thinly redefined version: *homo economicus*, or "Max U," as the economist Arjo Klamer once famously dubbed him.[6] It is well established in feminist economics that the concept of rational economic agents is neither gender-neutral (Ferber and Nelson 1993; Strassmann 1993) nor race-neutral (Williams 1993; Grapard 1995), and alternative conceptions of agency have been suggested (Folbre and Hartmann 1988; England 1993). The chapters in Part III of the book continue this tradition, extending the analysis to explicitly include the concept of the economist as a rational and autonomous investigator. They interrogate the ways in which economics, as a set of practices, constitutes gender, race, ethnicity, class, and nation as ideological categories. It examines the ways in which particular representations of women and other social groups come to be accepted as legitimate scientific categories and influence the collection of data and other forms of evidence. Also revealed is the role that these categories play in undergirding mainstream economics.

Analyzing ways in which gender, race, ethnicity, class, and nation are linked to conceptions of identity and their impact upon economics is a transdisciplinary endeavor. Science studies, critical theory, history, psychology, and sociology may all be used to reveal the ways that economics defends a Western, masculinist conception of identity as universal rather than particular. Such revelations open up a space to articulate identity in ways that do not erase difference and rationalize unequal social relations.

The chapter by Edith Kuiper (Chapter 10) is a close reading of Adam Smith's *The Theory of Moral Sentiments*, showing how Smith's notions of gender structure his treatise on men's moral behavior. Tracing the construction of identity through the book, Kuiper shows that Smith carefully distances himself from women and associations with the feminine. Smith conceives of individuals as fundamentally isolated and separate; relations between the self and others are made possible by the imagination. The attainment of masculine identity through self-control and the suppression of feelings is made possible by identification with the impartial spectator – the father within. This is an important instantiation of the Western liberal subject – masculine, self-interested, rational, and separate from others – that becomes central to economic theory. It is also, as Kuiper's chapter points out, a projection of Smith's own self-image – a prescription for the economist as well as for the political and economic subject.

The relationship between the objects of knowledge (the people being studied) and their investigators appears again in Brian Cooper's chapter (Chapter 11). He uses travel stories and conjectural histories from the eighteenth and nineteenth centuries to examine the construction and use of classifications and social statistics in British political economy. Drawing out the ways in which specific notions about the supremacy of Western white men and the British family figure in the development of economic thought, he shows that social statistics are not just descriptive, but prescriptive and aesthetic as well. Social classifications typically reveal as much about their classifiers as they do about the classified, and they have political and economic consequences. Rather than being unchanging and universal, classifications are fluid and contingent, and need to be understood within their particular historical and cultural contexts.

Susan Feiner's chapter (Chapter 12) takes the examination of Western masculine identity in a slightly different direction. She uses it to argue that the appeal of mainstream neoclassical economics is best understood not in terms of either science or politics, but rather in terms of psychology. In this reading, the central metaphor in neoclassical economics is the "market as mother." Using object relations theory, she argues that the symbolic and psychological appeal of its key concepts – exchange, individualism, rationality, and scarcity – lies in the separation anxieties of the Western masculine subject. Feiner's contribution illuminates the specificity of the vision of social relations in neoclassical economics, thus creating a space for alternatives.

Part III concludes with a contribution by Nitasha Kaul (Chapter 13), who introduces notions of identity, agency, and knowledge, and uses them to come to grips with the current state of economics. Instead of engaging in rationalist discussions about the role of assumptions or the success or failure of economics as a science, she engages with the question of emancipation and its links to epistemology. Neoclassical economics is a powerful story for those who see themselves in it. For others, on the outside of these stories, the quest for universally valid, objective knowledge is an epistemically and materially violent exercise. Eloquently, she leads the reader through an amalgam of poststructuralist/postmodern/deconstructive/postcolonial feminist analyses, demonstrating how they can help us to perceive economics as an inherently social and political endeavor, and to analyze its role in the reproduction of today's economic relations.

Beyond social contract: theorizing agency and relatedness

Masculine perceptions of identity, and the focus on activities regulated through the market, linked notions of markets/self-interest/rationality to men and notions of households/relatedness/irrationality to women. Feminist economists both critiqued this dualism and focused their research on economic activities and behaviors associated with women. Discussions of unpaid and domestic work, childcare arrangements, dependency relations, and reproductive labor have always had a prominent place in feminist economics. By now, empirical research on care, as well as theoretical analyses of the care activities – caring labor and care situations – constitute a significant part of feminist economics.

These issues have been examined in relation to women's labor force participation and the gender wage gap by economists using neoclassical and other positivist approaches (c.f. Blau and Ferber 1986; Ott 1992; Jacobsen 1998; Schultz 1995; Gustafsson and Meulders 2000). Others have adopted explicitly feminist perspectives, using gender as a category of analysis and taking the lives and experiences of women as the bases for their work (c.f. Folbre 1994; Himmelweit 1995; Agarwal

1997; Jochimsen and Knobloch 1997; Gardiner 1997). These feminist scholars integrate notions of relatedness, duty, and responsibility into explanations of economic behavior and conceptualizations of the economy. This scholarship demonstrates that the link between women and care and between men and self-interest is fast losing its legitimacy. Feminist economists are rethinking both the meaning of femininity and masculinity, and the link between femininity and women and masculinity and men. The search for an economics that no longer assumes these links is producing new approaches to economics.

Part IV begins with Nancy Folbre's now classic article on the paradox of caring labor (Chapter 14). It provides an early definition of what constitutes caring labor – labor that is undertaken out of affection or a sense of responsibility for other people – and sets the stage for further feminist economic work on the subject. Caring labor is somewhat of a paradox for economists, because it is extolled as important and fulfilling work while at the same time it is devalued economically. In addition, the nature of caring labor constrains its supply, which precludes orthodox economic solutions to shortages. This does not imply that caring labor should not be paid work. Rather, feminist economists need to consider caring labor in terms of both its undervaluation and its unique motivations. Folbre's chapter also points to the importance of not thinking of caring labor as an activity uniquely suited to women. It is learned behavior, and men can learn it, too. She stresses the importance of moving beyond the equality/difference debate and creating public policies that increase the supply of caring labor without reinforcing the sexual division of labor.

Caring labor has proven a rich field for feminist economists, and a substantial literature has now been produced. In Chapter 15 Maren Jochimsen articulates the various ways that care has been conceptualized in the literature. She argues that power and dependency, integral aspects of caring relations, have not been adequately theorized in economics. Jochimsen proposes a theoretical framework that puts caring situations at the center and integrates dependency, relatedness, social norms, and values. Her analysis acknowledges the role of the caregiver, the care receiver, and the resources necessary for caring activities. It also provides a framework for the evaluation of a wide range of caring situations and the various ways these situations can be and are organized.

Susan Himmelweit's chapter (Chapter 16) furthers the feminist economic understanding of the relationship between caring behavior and self-interested behavior. She articulates an approach to economic behavior that is far richer than what is available in neoclassical economic theory, and at the same time demonstrates that that evolutionary theory can be put to good use by feminists. Her explorations of evolutionary theory produce new ways of conceptualizing behavior patterns of both self-interested and altruistic behavior. These explanations use evolutionary theory without resorting to biological essentialism and add an important and powerful methodology to feminist economic research.

Gillian Hewitson's chapter (Chapter 17) explicitly questions this link between women and caring labor. She argues that the link between women, as an untheorized biological category, and care, assumed by contemporary mainstream, non-feminist analyses of caring labor, is similar to feminist analyses that are informed by object relations theory. In both cases women are the altruistic caregivers because the dominant parenting arrangements of Western societies mean that normal feminine identity is one with both the capacity and the desire to care for others. Normal masculine identity, on the other hand, does not have this capacity. Hewitson critiques object relations theory for its assumption of biologically determined complementarity between the sexes, an assumption maintained by the further assumption that gender is social and sex is biological. She advocates a poststructuralist approach that begins with the idea of difference and focuses on identity and embodiment. Such an approach problematizes the "naturalness" of sexual difference, and hence the sex/gender distinction. This approach implies that feminists are not compelled to answer the question of whether all women are carers with a "yes."

Rethinking categories

One of the most significant problematics in contemporary feminist theory is that poor women, especially women of color and women from the global South, continue to demonstrate a deep ambivalence toward feminism. For the majority of the world's poor women, the class oppression created by the underside of globalization – extreme poverty, the feminization of labor, relentless debt burdens, and environmental degradation – is far more devastating than gender oppression.

Feminist economists have long been involved in work on these issues. In the 1970s scholars working in the political economy tradition had already made significant transformative contributions to analyses of women and development, establishing women in development (WID), and, later, gender and development (GAD) as disciplinary fields.[7] This work was motivated by the recognition that gender biases in mainstream development policies increased women's unpaid work and worsened already oppressive and exploitative conditions. Work in this area continues to grow as feminist economists investigate the ways in which unequal gender relations serve macroeconomic objectives and affect international trade and finance (c.f. Grown *et al.* 2000; Benería *et al.* 2000).

The importance and influence of this work are not to be underestimated. Gender is now a part of the accepted vocabulary at the World Bank, the United Nations, and, to a much lesser extent, the International Monetary Fund. As feminist economic work continues to exert an influence on the attitudes and policymaking of these international bodies, it is important to step back and philosophically reflect on it. As many of the articles in this anthology show, the scholarly work we do has consequences and serves particular ends. It is important to be aware that feminism has been used for ends that are antithetical to its stated goals and aspirations. For example, during the nineteenth century feminism was effectively used as a tool in the colonial enterprise. Colonized women were represented as victims of the backwardness and savagery of their own cultures. Freeing them from the oppression of these cultures was a large part of the moral rationale for colonialism (Apffel-Marglin and Simon 1994). Rethinking the categories and concepts that feminist economists use to represent others can help us engage in international and transnational economic work in ways that resist the neocolonial discourse of many of the world's international organizations. It will also facilitate feminist economic practices that are informed by epistemically rich representations of the women and men on whose behalf feminist economists so often speak.

Rethinking the relationship between women's paid employment and empowerment is a good place to start. S. Charusheela's chapter (Chapter 18) critiques the common assumption that paid labor necessarily empowers women. Noting the widespread use of game-theoretic models of intrahousehold decisionmaking by feminist economists, she uncovers their implicit assumptions about the social nature of paid work. These models assume that paid employment has a positive effect on women's bargaining positions in the household and therefore is empowering. Charusheela argues that this experience of paid labor reflects a privileged, white European and US experience, and that the experiences of working-class, ethnic-minority, non-Western immigrant women tell a different story. For them work is not a choice; rather, it is necessary for survival. Moreover, these women enter the labor market on much different terms than their privileged counterparts, and it is their disadvantaged labor market participation as nannies, cooks, maids, etc. that allows other women to enter the empowering world of work in relatively higher echelons of the labor market.

Reconsidering the nature of work is also a theme in Cynthia Wood's chapter (Chapter 19). She argues that, although feminist economists have devoted considerable attention to conceptualizing unpaid labor, this work does not take into account differences between women in the North and women in the South. This first-world bias in the conceptualization of unpaid labor contributes to marginalizing and homogenizing the experiences of women in the South. Although many alternatives to mainstream development have emerged from feminist critiques, Wood argues that feminist analyses of development must also be postcolonial if they are to avoid essentializing women of the South and recreating homogenous models of development based on first-world interests. This project entails understanding that questions about representation, power, and history, so central to postcolonial feminist theory, have material implications and hence need to become topics of conversation in feminist economics.

This is not an easy task, and so it is fitting that this part should conclude with a discussion of the difficulty of a feminist economics. Eiman Zein-Elabdin argues that the project of feminist economic analysis is constantly challenged by the multifaceted nature of domination and difference, which renders a distinct feminist economic subject ultimately ungraspable (Chapter 20). Taking seriously the troubled historical relationship between women's subordination and other historical instruments of domination, such as colonialism, means that feminist economics can only be partially anchored in the plight of women. She suggests that a feminist economic philosophy, if it is to speak to a contemporary global constituency, cannot take European modernity as its starting point. It must transcend both essentialist notions of gender and the implicit assumptions about the inevitability and cultural superiority of industrial modernity, conceive of the economy as culturally instituted habits for material provisioning and accumulation, and recognize the constant transformation of the subject of feminist inquiry. Zein-Elabdin's analysis of material provisioning, sharing and reciprocity, and the predominance of obligation over contract relations in two postcolonial African societies demonstrates the need for such a feminist economic philosophy.

A feminist philosophy of economics?

The astute reader may notice that we have not offered an explicit definition of a feminist philosophy of economics. Rather, we have included diverse essays that illuminate many of the themes constituting such a philosophy. It is an emerging discussion, working toward the construction of a new economics, an economics that allows for an interrogation of hierarchies based on gender, race, ethnicity, class, sexuality, and nation in theorizing and practicing economics. It is a philosophy that welcomes transdisciplinary scholarship and displaces the old theory/practice debate. It is a philosophy that takes seriously the importance of caring labor, while working to displace the dualisms that name it a "women's issue." Finally, it is a philosophy that takes seriously the questions and challenges posed by a recognition of the social nature of science, as well as by postmodernism and postcolonialism. Taking these challenges seriously does not mean giving up the Enlightenment impulse to work toward the social good; nor does it mean giving up the notion of normative epistemology. Normative criteria, however, can no longer be concerned solely with the representational, explanatory, and predictive aspects of science. They must also include considerations of politics, ethics, and culture. Similarly, what constitutes the "social good" can no longer be taken for granted. The social good is always contingent, particular, and open to contestation. The essays in this anthology show that feminist economics, like all knowledge projects, has material and cultural consequences. For these consequences to be socially progressive and consistent with feminist ideals, feminist economics must remain open to evaluation and change. In fact, this would serve as a prescription for economics unmodified.

Notes

1 Julie Nelson's early redefinition of economics as the study of provisioning is an important example of this (J.A. Nelson 1993).
2 This definition is attributed to Cheris Kramarae, author of *A Feminist Dictionary* (1991).
3 See *Feminist Economics* 2(3), 1996.
4 Feminist empiricism soon escaped this neat definition and expanded to include a discussion of the social nature of scientific knowledge, the nature of the knowing subject, and the relationships between science and politics (L. Nelson and Nelson 1997).
5 Marxist economics did not necessarily fare any better, as demonstrated by Heidi Hartmann's classic article (Hartmann 1981).
6 Unfortunately, this caricature is often taken at face value by many mainstream economists.
7 See Irene Tinker (1990) for an overview of WID and GAD.

Bibliography

Agarwal, Bina (1997) "Bargaining and Gender Relations: Within and Beyond the Household," *Feminist Economics* 3(1): 1–51.
Apffel-Marglin, Frédérique and Suzanne L. Simon (1994) "Feminist Orientalism and Development," in Wendy Harcourt (ed.) *Feminist Perspectives on Sustainable Development*, London: Zed Books.
Barker, Drucilla (1999) "Neoclassical Economics," in Janice Peterson and Margaret Lewis (eds.) *The Elgar Companion to Feminist Economics*, Cheltenham and Northampton: Edward Elgar.
—— (2003) "Rethinking Methodology," *Research in the History of Political Economy and Methodology* 21A.
Becker, Gary (1981) *A Treatise on the Family*, Cambridge, MA: Harvard University Press.
Benería, Lourdes (1995) "Toward a Greater Integration of Gender in Economics," *World Development* 23(11): 1,839–50.
Benería, Lourdes, Maria Floro, Caren Grown and Martha MacDonald (2000) "Globalization and Gender," *Feminist Economics* 6(3): vii–xvii.
Blau, Francine and Marianne A. Ferber (1986) *The Economics of Women, Men and Work*, Englewood Cliffs, NJ: Prentice-Hall.
Dijkstra, Geske and Janneke Plantenga (1997) *Gender and Economics: A European Perspective*, London: Routledge.
Dimand, Mary-Ann, Robert W. Dimand and Evelyn L. Forget (eds.) (1995) *Women of Value: Feminist Essays on the History of Women in Economics*, Cheltenham: Edward Elgar.
England, Paula (1993) "The Separative Self: Androcentric Bias in Neoclassical Assumptions," in Marianne A. Ferber and Julie A. Nelson (eds.) *Beyond Economic Man*, Chicago, IL: University of Chicago Press.
Ferber, Marianne A. and Julie A. Nelson (1993) "Introduction: The Social Construction of Economics and the Social Construction of Gender," in Marianne A. Ferber and Julie A. Nelson (eds.) *Beyond Economic Man*, Chicago, IL: University of Chicago Press.
Flax, Jane (1992) "The End of Innocence," in Judith Butler and Joan W. Scott (eds.) *Feminists Theorize the Political*, London and New York: Routledge.
Folbre, Nancy (1992) "'The Improper Arts': Sex in Classical Political Economy," *Population and Development Review* 18(1), March: 105–21.
—— (1994) *Who Pays for the Kids? Gender and the Structures of Constraint*, London and New York: Routledge.
Folbre, Nancy and Heidi Hartmann (1988) "The Rhetoric of Self-Interest: Ideology of Gender in Economic Theory," in Aro Klamer, Donald N. McCloskey, and Robert Solow (eds.) *The Consequences of Economic Rhetoric*, Cambridge: Cambridge University Press.

Forget, Evelyn L. (1999) *The Social Economics of Jean-Baptist Say: Markets and Virtue*, London and New York: Routledge.

Gardiner, Jean (1997) *Gender, Care and Economics*, London: Macmillan Press.

Grapard, Ulla (1995) "Robinson Crusoe: The Quintessential Economic Man?," *Feminist Economics* 1(1): 33–5.

Grown, Caren, Diane Elson and Nilifur Catagay (2000) "Introduction," *World Development: Special Issue on Growth, Trade, Finance, and Gender Inequality* 28(7): 1,145–55.

Gustafsson, Siv and Danièle E. Meulders (eds.) (2000) *Gender and the Labour Market: Econometric Evidence of Obstacles to Achieving Gender Equality*, Basingstoke: Macmillan Press.

Hands, Wade (2001) *Reflections without Rules: Economics Methodology and Contemporary Science Theory*, Cambridge: Cambridge University Press.

Harding, Sandra (1986) *The Science Question in Feminism*, Ithaca, NY: Cornell University Press.

—— (1995) "Can Feminist Thought Make Economics More Objective?," *Feminist Economics* 1(1): 17–32.

—— (2001) "Comment on Waldy's 'Against Epistemological Chasms: The Science Question in Feminism Revisited': Can Democratic Values and Interests Ever Play a Rationally Justifiable Role in the Evaluation of Scientific Work?," *Signs* 26(2): 511–26.

Hartmann, Heidi (1981) "The Unhappy Marriage of Marxism and Feminism," in Lydia Sargent (ed.) *Women and Revolution: A Discussion of the Unhappy Marriage of Marxism and Feminism*, Boston, MA: South End Press.

Hewitson, Gillian J. (1999) *Feminist Economics: Interrogating the Masculinity of Rational Economic Man*, Cheltenham and Northampton: Edward Elgar.

Himmelweit, Susan (1995) "The Discovery of 'Unpaid Work': The Social Consequences of the Expansion of 'Work,'" *Feminist Economics* 1(2): 1–19.

Jacobsen, Joyce P. (1998) *The Economics of Gender*, 2nd edn., Malden and Oxford: Blackwell Publishers.

Jochimsen, Maren and Ulrike Knobloch (1997) "Making the Hidden Visible: The Importance of Caring Activities and their Principles for any Economy," *Ecological Economics: Special Issue: Women, Ecology, and Economics* 20(2): 107–12.

Justman, Stewart (1996) *The Autonomous Male of Adam Smith*, Norman and London: University of Oklahoma Press.

Kramarae, Cheris and Paula A. Treichler (1991) *A Feminist Dictionary*, Urbana-Champaign, IL: University of Illinois Press.

Kuhn, Thomas S. (1996) *The Structure of Scientific Revolutions*, 3rd edn. Chicago, IL: University of Chicago Press; first published in 1962.

Kuiper, Edith (2001) *"The Most Valuable of All Capital": A Gender Reading of Economic Texts*, Amsterdam: Thela Thesis.

Lawson, Tony (1999) "Universalism, Feminism and Realism," *Feminist Economics* 5(2), 25–59.

Lloyd, Genevieve (1984) *The Man of Reason: "Male" and "Female" in Western Philosophy*, Minneapolis, MN: University of Minneapolis Press.

Longino, Helen (1993) "Subjects, Power and Knowledge: Description and Prescription in Feminist Philosophy of Science," in Linda Alcoff and Elizabeth Potter (eds.) *Feminist Epistemologies*, London and New York: Routledge.

—— (2002) *The Fate of Knowledge*, Princeton, NJ: Princeton University Press.

McCloskey, Deirdre (1998) *The Rhetoric of Economics*, 2nd edn., Madison, WN: University of Wisconsin Press; first published in 1987.

Nelson, Julie A. (1993) "The Study of Choice or the Study of Provisioning? Gender and the Definition of Economics," in Marianne A. Ferber and Julie A. Nelson (eds.) *Beyond Economic Man*, Chicago, IL: University of Chicago Press.

—— (1995) *Feminism, Objectivity and Economics*, London and New York: Routledge.

Nelson, Lynn Hankinson (1993) "Epistemological Communities," in Linda Alcoff and Elizabeth Potter (eds.) *Feminist Epistemologies*, London and New York: Routledge.

Nelson, Lynn Hankinson and Jack Nelson (eds.) (1997) *Feminism, Science, and the Philosophy of Science*, Dordrecht, Boston, MA, and London: Kluwer Academic Publishers.

Ott, Notburga (1992) *Intrafamily Bargaining and Household Decisions*, New York: Springer Verlag.

Pujol, Michèle (1992) *Feminism and Anti-Feminism in Early Economic Thought*, Aldershot: Edward Elgar.

Quine, W.V.O. (1953) "Two Dogmas of Empiricism," *From a Logical Point of View*, 2nd edn., Cambridge, MA: Harvard University Press.

Schultz, Paul T. (ed.) (1995) *Investment in Women's Human Capital*, Chicago, IL: University of Chicago Press.

Smith, Adam (1990) *The Theory of Moral Sentiments* D.D. Raphael and A.L. Macfie (eds.) Indianapolis: Liberty Fund.

Strassmann, Diana (1993) "Not a Free Market: The Rhetoric of Disciplinary Authority in Economics," in Marianne A. Ferber and Julie A. Nelson (eds.) *Beyond Economic Man*, Chicago, IL: University of Chicago Press.

Thomson, Dorothy L. and Bette Polkinghorn (1999 [1973]) *Adam Smith's Daughters: Eight Prominent Women Economists from the Eighteenth Century to the Present*, rev. edn., Aldershot: Edward Elgar.

Tinker, Irene (1990) "The Making of a Field: Advocates, Practitioners, and Scholars," in Irene Tinker (ed.) *Persistent Inequalities: Women and World Development*, New York: Oxford University Press.

Williams, Rhonda (1993) "Race, Deconstruction, and the Emergent Agenda of Feminist Economic Theory," in Marianne A. Ferber and Julie A. Nelson (eds.) *Beyond Economic Man*, Chicago, IL: University of Chicago Press.

Part I
Rereading history

2 Into the margin![1]

Michèle A. Pujol

Introduction

The neoclassical economic paradigm is now over 100 years old. Since its inception in the 1890s, it has grown to be the dominant paradigm in economic theory, building its hegemonic power to the exclusion of alternative approaches. I have studied and then taught economics for nearly 25 years now. I had come to economics, as an undergraduate student in Paris, with a lot of excitement and trepidation: that discipline was going to help me understand what was going on in the world. I soon found out that the neoclassical paradigm, while providing some seductive modeling, did not come close to answering the questions I had. But it was only much later, in graduate school, that other questions started coming up. As a woman in the field, I started realizing that my own realities were missing, that they were dismissed or trivialized when issues of women's places in the economy were brought up.

Examining the origins of the neoclassical paradigm, one can identify the Victorian ideology which is at the roots of the treatment of women within it. The founding fathers – Marshall, Pigou, Edgeworth, and Jevons – wrote as one in a voice laden with patriarchal condescension. Unfortunately this attitude towards women has remained virtually the same. Yet simply cataloguing the neoclassical record on the status of women seems increasingly fragmentary: giving voice, again, to "the big men" could not be the sole object of an exploration of the patriarchal bias of neoclassical economics. Two other imperatives emerged:

1 To give voice to women, to feminists, writing on economic matters, asserting their disagreement with the status quo, in society and within the profession; and adding to these the voices of the few male economists approaching "the woman question" with a more sympathetic and innovative outlook.
2 To go beyond a mere history of thought project to challenge the neoclassical monolith by rooting the contemporary feminist critique in the discipline's own history.

This work contributes to the development of a feminist epistemology and ontology. It poses the questions: "Who is writing theory?" "For what purpose?" It also challenges the notion that an epistemology based in the standpoints of women and other marginalized groups[2] in the capitalist/patriarchal system could ever find a place within the neoclassical paradigm.

Such an approach challenges two of the main silencings routinely performed within modern-day neoclassical economics: the erasure of women and feminists both within the paradigm and as voices of dissent, and the dismissal of methodological critics of the paradigm. I will note here that the second erasure is explicit, while the first is still implicit only. It is relevant to mention, in this respect, that my book (Pujol 1992) has been criticized so far, not so much for its feminist stance and its challenge of the erasure of women and feminists in the discipline, but for daring to criticize the neoclassical paradigm, to suggest that it is flawed. These flaws can be seen more clearly when we analyze the five elements which characterize neoclassical views of women:

1 All women are married, or, if not yet, they will be. Similarly, all women have or will have children.
2 All women are (and ought to be) economically dependent on a male relative: father or husband.
3 Women are (and ought to be) housewives, their reproductive capacities specialize them for that function.
4 Women are unproductive (whether absolutely or relative to men is not always clear) in the industrial workforce.
5 Women are irrational, they are unfit as economic agents, they cannot be trusted to make the right economic decisions.

Through all these elements women are constructed as different from the norm (men). All the above characteristics together contribute to rationalizing women's exclusion from the public realm of economics: the market. These characteristics are seldom openly and clearly stated by economists. They fall within what economists call "unstated assumptions" (even though there is so little awareness of their existence). And because they are unstated it is not entirely easy for women in the discipline to put a name on the source of our malaise. And I quote here my own inner voice: my voice, the "I" I am using here, a scary thing to do (there is no I in my book). I am doing it because it is necessary for us, women/feminist economists, to use our own voices, to claim the right to do so. As Diana Strassmann and Livia Polanyi say, in economics

> direct voices have seldom been female voices, seldom been voices on the margin, seldom been voices not legitimated by the mainstream of power and control...until women speak their own thoughts and experiences in their

own voices and legitimate their speech by the authority of their own histories and experiences, we will not have a truly feminist economics.

(Strassmann and Polanyi 1992: 13–14)

Let us remember, as feminist economists, that the personal is political and the political is economic. As a woman, as a feminist, as a lesbian, and as a survivor within the discipline of economics, my identity and the experiences I have encountered in this discipline for 25 years inform my analysis of economic theory.[3]

We turn, now, to an examination of the work of the early neoclassical economists to show how these five unstated assumptions have been used consistently,[4] and contrast them with the actual situation of women and with feminist economic analyses of women's situation.

Women as married and dependent

The first two characterizations, that all women are married or are to be married,[5] and its immediate corollary that they are the economic dependants of men, invariably inform neoclassical discussions of women's labor force behavior and, beyond that, of any economic activity in which they might be engaged. This sets the stage for questioning women's presence in the labor market or for refusing to take this presence seriously. Women, being supported, have no reason to be in the labor market. The concerns they might have – particularly for higher wage levels and for access to employment – can be and have been dismissed as inconsequential. By contrast, men's presence in the labor force has never been questioned by neoclassical economists.[6]

This characterization leads economists to see women as non-autonomous agents. For Pigou, the main determinant of (all?) women's labor supply is their husbands' labor income (Pigou 1960: 565–6). In modern/Beckerian neoclassical economics, women seek employment as the result of a "household decision" (Becker 1981a). One can wonder if, in neoclassical economics, the decision to seek employment is an individual decision for women. Clearly such an approach allows us to avoid asking why women continue to supply their labor when their wages are so low; such a decision might reflect an individually non-optimal use of their productive abilities; and women are not allowed by market conditions to optimize returns to their human capital investment.

Women's presence in the labor force is not seen as a contribution to economic welfare; it is instead problematized as threatening severe negative consequences for national welfare and "household utility." Edgeworth warned with alarm that large numbers of women in the workforce would bring a "depression or debacle of industry," a "debacle, ultimately ruinous alike to wealth and family life" (Edgeworth 1922: 436; 1923: 493). Marshall, Jevons and Pigou all expressed concern for the impact of employment on women's household duties and on infant mortality rates (Marshall 1930: 685, 198; Jevons 1904; Pigou 1960: 187).

Ironically, the solutions to these "problems" proposed by the heretofore "free market" economists relied on draconian interventions in existing labor market conditions. Marshall supported the Factory Acts (1930: 198, 751); Edgeworth argued for the maintenance of barriers to women's entry into occupations (1923: 490–4). Jevons was more severe, advocating legislating the complete exclusion of mothers of children under the age of 3 from factories.

In the same vein, where Pigou advocated state intervention to correct market failure in the labor market, women were explicitly exempted.[7] Marshall, Pigou, and Edgeworth were all either against legislating minimum wages for women, or against minimum wages set at the same level as men's. None of them supported equal pay for equal work legislation. These economists' opposition to women's employment went hand in hand with their support for both preserving men's privileged access to employment and an enhanced male pay packet such that all men, whether married or not, could earn a "family wage" (Edgeworth 1923). Such proposals, if implemented, would have removed what they saw as the main cause of women's labor force participation: their need to earn complementary family income.

We can find direct parallels in the contemporary neoclassical treatment of women's labor force participation. Since Mincer's (1962) seminal article, the focus has been on married women's labor supply. The main question has been "Why are these (married) women in the labor force?" and not the appropriate pay scale, working conditions, or utilization of their human capital investments. Hence (all) women's waged employment is constructed as problematic, their human capital investment behavior as anomalous (see Mincer 1962; Mincer and Polachek 1974, 1978; Sandell and Shapiro 1978; Mincer and Ofek 1979). Thus the New Home Economics is a rationale for (all) women's "specialization" in reproduction and housework as opposed to income-earning employment (see Becker 1973, 1976, 1981a; Schultz, 1974).

By implicitly generalizing from married women to all women, the existence and the needs of women who are not attached to men are denied, and the "norm" of women's economic dependence is ideologically reinforced by both contemporary (Mincer, Polachek) and early neoclassical economists (Marshall, Pigou, Edgeworth, Jevons). One has to look hard to find references to single women, or to no-longer-married women, let alone to lesbians – whom economists must never have heard of.[8]

Yet the actual situation of women differed substantially from the view proffered by the neoclassical economists. In nineteenth- and early twentieth-century England a substantial proportion of women were and remained unmarried (Bodichon 1859: 28), and among those who married, full economic support by husbands was often far from the more distressing reality (Cadbury *et al.* 1906;

Smith 1915; Rathbone 1917, 1924). Women, both married and unmarried, were present in the labor force in large numbers (Scott and Tilly 1978). These facts were reported and documented by feminists, who often used them as a basis for their demands for the means to economic independence for women: access to jobs, education, professional employment, and equal pay (Bodichon 1859; Fawcett 1892, 1916, 1918; Webb-Potter 1914, 1919).[9] The so-called "family wage" was described by Eleanor Rathbone (1917, 1924) as an inadequate mode of support for families, and, furthermore, as a completely ineffective mode of income distribution.[10] The issue of the degree to which women supported themselves and their dependants was hotly debated and the object of contradictory empirical claims.[11]

Feminist writers who discussed issues of women's economic status, in the pages of the *Economic Journal* and elsewhere, provided ample documentation and analysis to contradict the assumptions and normative reasoning of neoclassical economists. Economic historians such as Alice Clark (1968; first published 1919), Edith Abbott (1910), Georgiana Hill (1896), Elizabeth Hutchins (1915), and Ivy Pinchbeck (1981) documented the work and economic contributions of women, from the middle ages to the late nineteenth century. The research team of Edward Cadbury, M. Cecile Matheson and George Shann published an extensive sociological study of working women in 1906; the Fabian Women's Group's survey of *Wage-Earning Women and their Dependants* in 1915 (Smith 1915) was corroborated by Hogg's study published in *Economica* in 1921.

Indeed, these studies documented the ongoing productive role of women, married and not married, and their contribution to their own support, the support of their dependants, and to the overall economy. In the pages of the *Economic Journal*, Ada Heather-Bigg argued that it was not women's work, but their earning of an income, which was objectionable to the opponents of women's employment. She clearly perceived that the overwork of women was of no concern to patriarchal ideologues, but their fear of women's access to economic independence was, to quote her colorful words, "the veriest scooped-out, sheet-draped turnip that ever made a village dolt take to his heels and run" (Heather-Bigg 1894: 55).

Feminists writing on these issues pointed out the necessity of women's employment as a source of economic support for themselves and others, thereby challenging the "family wage" and "pin money" doctrines. They argued and empirically demonstrated that there was no such thing as universal support of women by men, that men's earnings were insufficient to support their families, and that women contributed a high proportion of subsistence needs out of their meager earnings and hard work. Out of these observations arose serious challenges to some of the justifications for existing labor market conditions.

Feminists saw the Factory Acts as discriminatory restrictions to women's entry into the labor market. They denounced them as protecting the "monopoly" of men over some occupations (Bodichon 1859; Taylor 1970; Mill 1965, 1970; Fawcett 1916, 1918; Webb-Potter 1914, 1919) and the license of employers to exploit (Smart 1892). The "family wage" ideal was also seen as a protection of male privilege, of men's right to a job and to a pay check whether or not they had a family to support. Furthermore, it reinforced their power in the home (Rathbone 1917, 1924).[12] Policy proposals to exclude women from the labor force were denounced by feminists as a means to disempower women, to thwart their efforts to organize, and as an encouragement to employers to exploit them (Smart 1892; Webb-Potter 1919; Fawcett 1918).

Women as mothers

Characterizing all women as married or to be married goes along, in the writing of the early neoclassical economists, with the third characterization of seeing them as mothers whose duty is to properly raise children and carry out related housework. Any other occupation was seen as interfering with this obligation and therefore causing major losses in economic and general welfare. Marshall maintained that (all) women's employment "tempts them to neglect their duty of building a true home, and investing their efforts in the personal capital of their children's character and abilities," and insisted on the necessity of their presence in the home (Marshall 1930: 685, 721). He asserted that the "degradation of the working classes varies almost uniformly with the amount of rough work done by women," and, more particularly, with mothers losing their "tender and unselfish instincts" due to "the strain and stress of unfeminine work" (*ibid.*: 564).

Pigou advocated shorter workdays for women to provide them with "opportunities for better care of their homes" (Pigou 1960: 463). He believed that "a woman's work has a special personal value in respect of her own children" (*ibid.*: 188), which led him to assign women to the home in his blueprint for economic welfare. Jevons asserted that "there are no duties which are more important in every respect than those which a mother is bound by with regard to her own children" (Jevons 1904: 166). He also proclaimed "the right of the infant to the mother's breast" (*ibid.*: 171). Women's rights are never mentioned in such fashion.[13]

Marshall, Pigou, and Jevons' advocacy of full-time domesticity for mothers was based entirely upon alarmist accounts of high infant mortality in districts where women could find industrial employment (Marshall 1930: 198, 529; Pigou 1960: 187; Jevons 1904: 153). Other factors which might have caused high infant mortality, particularly starvation-level wages and the resulting unsanitary living conditions in working-class households, were not investigated.

In fact, the evidence cited did not support the economists' claims regarding the negative effects of mothers' employment, but it was authoritatively dismissed anyway. Jevons, for example, attempted to explain away the case of Liverpool, which held "the place of dishonour," with the nation's highest infant mortality rate *although there were no women-employing industries in Liverpool!* Liverpool was an "anomaly" due to its population mix (Jevons 1904: 153–4). In similar fashion, Pigou invoked *ceteris paribus* reasoning in his attempts to dismiss the annoying evidence that working mothers provided a remedy to poverty and infant mortality:

> The reality of this evil [working mothers' alleged neglect] is not disproved by the low, and even negative, correlation which sometimes is found to exist between the factory work of mothers and the rate of infant mortality. For in districts where women's work of this kind prevails there is presumably – and this is the cause of women's work – great poverty. This poverty, which is injurious to children's health, is likely, other things being equal, to be greater than elsewhere in families where the mother declines factory work, and it may be that the evil of the extra poverty is greater than that of the factory work. This consideration explains the statistical facts that are known. They therefore, militate in no way against the view that, *other things equal*, the factory work of mothers is injurious.
>
> (Pigou 1960: 187)

Reasoning like this was used effectively to depict women who cared for children as criminals. Mothers who sought employment "and go earn good wages in the mills" (Jevons 1904: 166), along with the wet and dry nurses who provided childcare for the employed mothers, were held directly responsible for the death of children. Curiously, these women were not perceived by neoclassical economists as economic agents who exercised rational decisionmaking under the specific constraints they faced.

Furthermore, working mothers were described as acting unnaturally. Jevons compared them unfavorably to female animals: "The very beasts of the field tend and guard their whelps with instinctive affection. It is only human mothers which shut their infants up alone, or systematically neglect to give them nourishment" (*ibid.*: 166). Casting employed mothers in such a light was obviously meant to generate public outrage and gain support for restrictions on their employment.

The economists' prescriptions were outright punitive. Jevons stated: "I will go so far as to advocate the *ultimate complete exclusion of mothers of children under the age of three years from factories and workshops*" (*ibid.*: 167–8; emphasis in original). He proposed to fine the husbands and employers of the derelict mothers, as well as the nurses. Mothers were not treated as responsible agents. Instead, they were patronized, and economists attempted to reinforce their dependency by making their husbands and employers answer for their actions. Pigou and Marshall also advocated the prohibition of employment for mothers. But, while Marshall showed no concern for how this might affect the income of working-class households and women's ability to feed their children, Pigou proposed some form of state-funded "relief to those families whom the prohibition renders necessitous" (Pigou 1960: 188).

The argument about mothers' nurturing instinct (although it was found lacking by economists) and of the special value of their reproductive work towards their own children was used to reject all other solutions, particularly that of day nurseries, which could provide adequate childcare (Jevons 1904: 164–5). While he acknowledged that factory-supervised *crèches* observed in France "have produced most beneficial results," Jevons supported the idea only as a transitional measure for the period of adjustment to the new regime of employment prohibition. As for relief, it was to be provided only to "widows and deserted wives," to be "employed" by the state "as nurses to their own children" (*ibid*: 169). Hence, a sexual division of labor which served patriarchal interests and kept women in the domestic sphere, without access to an independent income source, was assumed to be "natural." As an element of nature, it could then become the "logical" basis for policy prescriptions.

Whereas the proposed policy of prohibition of employment targeted specifically the mothers of young children, the economists cast a wider net to ensure the domestification of women in general. In particular, they uniformly supported the Factory Acts – Jevons praised them as "one of the noblest products of legislative skill and patience" at the end of his article on "Married Women in Factories" (1904: 172). The status quo of below-subsistence wages was also seen as inducing domesticity among women in general. Marshall explicitly opposed a rise in women's wages, which he claimed to be detrimental to the performance of their domestic duties (Marshall 1930: 685). More generally, Marshall, Pigou, and Edgeworth's opposition to equal pay, to minimum wages for women, to access to industrial training were all intended to keep women dependent and domestified.

The strange paradox is that women do not seem to want to do what is claimed to be "natural" to them; they have to be coerced onto that path. In the name of their "natural duties," women were kept away from making their own decisions. Severe legislation to keep them in the home was proposed as the panacea for the "evil" of infant mortality. Jevons evoked idyllic images of "the wife…a true mother and a housekeeper; and round many a Christmas table troops of happy, chubby children," which would miraculously appear once the legislator speeded up what he saw as a process of evolution whereby "the manufacturing population would become fitted to its environment" (1904: 171–2). Meanwhile, as working-class women were to be coerced into the dependent reproductive role, their economic contribution to their family and to society as a whole was to be further denied and made invisible: their work, although seemingly essential, would receive no economic return or recognition.[14]

Contemporary neoclassical economists reveal an intimate commitment to nineteenth-century patriarchal ideology by their continued reliance upon the assumption that women are naturally suited for reproductive work. The new home economics takes this further and insists that women have a "comparative advantage" in the performance of mothering and household duties. Not only does this "scientific reasoning" reinforce the dominant sexual division of labor within the home and in society, it also bolsters the human capital school's circular explanation of women's lower wages: since women earn less than men, it is to their advantage and the advantage of their families for them to remain specialized in reproductive work. Women's assumed "comparative advantage" in nurturing is used to privilege their contribution to the human capital of others (husband, children) over maximizing returns to their own human capital (Becker 1973, 1976, 1981b; Mincer and Polachek 1974; Schultz 1974).

All this fails to address the reality of women's "double workday" and the oddity of the lack of monetary return for the activities in which women have a "comparative advantage." We can see that, in spite of greater sophistication and more complex mathematical expression, very little change in either assumptions or reasoning has occurred since Marshall. Now, as then, this economic "logic" tends to justify and maintain a status quo of female dependence, domesticity, and "specialization" in reproductive work.

Feminists of the first wave of the women's movement opposed the existing barriers to women's access to the labor market. They denounced the Factory Acts (Bodichon 1859; Taylor 1970; Mill 1965, 1970; Strachey 1969), as well as trade boards and trade union restrictions on women's entry and access to skills and apprenticeship (Fawcett 1892, 1916, 1918; Webb-Potter 1914, 1919). However, in the feminist economic writings I studied, I did not find anyone directly taking on the infant mortality argument of the neoclassical economists. But, as I have already mentioned, a number of studies documented the extent of income-earning support generated by working women.[15]

Eleanor Rathbone, however, focused specifically on the economic position of working-class mothers in post-World War I England. She criticized the ideologies of the "family wage" and of the male breadwinner as utterly flawed representations of the income-earning reality of working-class households and as an inadequate income-distribution system (Rathbone 1917: 62). She developed a proposal for a "motherhood allowance," where mothers would receive from the state an independent income to provide for the subsistence needs of their children. Whereas she supported the position that mothers should stay home to take care of their children, she maintained that their reproductive work must receive the economic recognition of a specific income payment. She rejected the situation where mothers were the dependent victims of a patriarchal order. Her mother's allowance system proposed providing mothers with an independent, state-funded income, recognizing their role and their work in the household, and generating economic support for children independent of the sometimes uncertain labor market earnings of men.

The economists of the time did not sanction Rathbone's proposals. As has already been mentioned, Pigou endorsed state allowances only in the case of widows, with the express purpose of keeping them domesticated and dependent on the state. He did not favor schemes which would recognize mothers' reproductive work economically while ensuring them access to an independent income. Edgeworth opposed motherhood allowances after applying a strict economic cost/benefit analysis to them (Edgeworth 1922: 450–3), and he was not willing to recognize that, in a wider social welfare approach, the balance might tip in their favor (Edgeworth 1923: 494).[16]

Productivity

The fourth assumption, that of women's low industrial productivity, is pervasive in the early [and late] neoclassical economists' writings. For instance, women were repetitively characterized as unskilled and "low grade workers" by Pigou (1960: 607, 723). Pigou never demonstrated this and never stopped to wonder about employers' continued demand for women's labor, particularly in specific "women's" industries.[17] The argument that women receive low wages as a result of low productivity is also reinforced by the assumption of perfect competition in the labor market. Given this assumption, women's low wages are seen as "proof" of their low productivity. Yet the absence of a necessary correlation between women's wages and productivity is paradoxically confirmed by Pigou. He argued that women's wages should be pegged at a presumably "fair" market-determined level even when their productivity should warrant a higher wage (Pigou 1960: 566–70).[18]

The views of neoclassical economists were contradicted in their days by the more realistic observations and theories of first-wave feminists. Mill (1965) and Fawcett (1892, 1916) put forward a theory of non-competing groups which provided an alternative to the neoclassical unified labor market. The concept of crowding, which has today become an accepted approach to labor markets, was first developed by Bodichon (1859), Fawcett (1892, 1916), Smart (1892), Cannan (1914), and Beatrice Webb-Potter (1914, 1919). As early as 1859, Bodichon identified institutional and customary barriers to women's entry into industry. This analysis was refined by Taylor (1970) and Mill (1965, 1970), Fawcett (1892, 1916), and Webb-Potter (1914, 1919). Others developed a "customary wage" approach whereby customs and tradition were greater determinants of women's wages than actual productivity (Marshall and Marshall 1881; Smart 1892). Discrimination between the sexes in the form of a dual system of women's subsistence wage and men's "family wage" was another approach proposed by Smart (1892), Rathbone (1917, 1924), and Webb-Potter (1914, 1919). William Smart's 1892 comprehensive and incisive critique of the economists' use of the law of demand and supply to justify women's low wages is just as relevant today, and testifies to the ossification of the discipline.[19]

It is interesting to see how the biases of the neoclassical economists were reasserted in spite of these other approaches and in spite of their own acknowledgement of less than competitive conditions in the labor market. Edgeworth listed three reasons why the labor market is not competitive: employers' power, their preference for hiring men even at a productivity disadvantage, and trade unions' interference (Edgeworth 1922: 439). Yet he asserted:

> I submit as an *inference based on general impressions and ordinary experience* that, even if all restrictions on the competition between male and female workers were removed we should still find the average weekly earnings of the former to be considerably higher.
> (Edgeworth 1922: 442; emphasis added)

Here, against all precepts of positivist science, assertion prevails over evidence and proof.

Pigou's suggestions on the problem of non-competing markets for women workers was to keep them such. In contrast, where men receive wages below the value of their marginal product Pigou recommended state intervention to raise these wages to their efficiency level. No such solution was proposed in the case of women, as their wages were decreed "fair" if they corresponded to what women were "paid elsewhere," regardless of their actual productivity level. Pigou forgot his usual efficiency concerns, and used instead the apparently solicitous argument that higher wages would deter employers from hiring women and thus harm women's position in the labor market (Pigou 1960: 569–70). Reading on, we find out, however, that he was a lot more concerned with employers' access to a supply of cheap female labor than with women's employment opportunities (*ibid.*: 600–2).

The belief that women have low industrial productivity did not lead to proposals to raise productivity levels via either training or education. The neoclassical economists saw such schemes as wasteful, since they believed that women should not remain in the labor force, that their dependent status removed all motivation for productivity improvement, or that women's unproductivity is irremediable (Pigou 1960: 616). In a nutshell, any proposal to improve women's wage-earning capacity, whether through increased skills and training, through wages reflecting more adequately women's actual productivity, or through equal pay (and in some cases minimum wages) measures, were opposed (Edgeworth 1922, 1923; Pigou 1960, 1952; Marshall 1930: 715).

Such measures were seen as harmful to the market, to employers, and to overall economic welfare. Edgeworth believed they could cause a "debacle of industry," or, worse, men's rights to jobs and their status as breadwinners might be challenged (Edgeworth 1922, 1923). Pigou saw such measures as threatening to harm general welfare by "divert[ing] women into industrial activity away from home-making, child-rearing and child-bearing" (Pigou 1952: 224–5), and as unnecessary because women do not need higher labor income, being dependants and only temporarily present in the labor market.

Once again we see direct parallels with contemporary human capital theory: the market is assumed to be both perfect and infallible in its determination of wages which truly reflect productivity; women's lower employment income is therefore attributed to their own choice in human capital investment and choice of low-productivity occupations. Any legislative approach (pay equity/comparable worth, affirmative action) will only create market imperfections and jeopardize women's chances in the labor market (Killingsworth 1985).

These positions are directly opposed to feminist analysis of women's labor force situation and to feminist economic policy recommendations.[20] What is so striking is the neoclassical economists' heavy reliance on their patriarchal bias rather than on theoretically and methodologically sound approaches to support their policy recommendations. The pervasiveness of this bias raises the question of whether feminist ideas and approaches can ever gain a place within the paradigm. To date, feminist critiques of human capital theory and of the new home economics have largely been ignored.

Rationality

The four assumptions/characterizations discussed above are closely linked. They reinforce each other and contribute to a specific construction of women by the early neoclassical economists. Through their combined effects (in theory and policy) women are seen as occupying a radically different place in the capitalist economy than men, who are conversely constructed as "rational economic men."[21]

In neoclassical economics, men are autonomous, independent individuals, while women are dependants who cannot stand on their own. Women are always defined as members of family units, as wives, daughters, mothers. Men make economic decisions based on their own needs, and their own abilities and options; they circulate freely in the market sphere. In contrast, women have limited access to the market and even more limited access to their own utility-maximizing decisionmaking. Even in the single example Marshall uses where women are seen to skillfully exercise such decisionmaking, by stretching (i.e. "maximizing the allocation" of) the meager household budget (Marshall 1930: 195–6),[22] it is not their own utility which is maximized, but that of the household.[23] Where men may choose across an array of occupations, women are assigned to a single one: motherhood.

In this construction, women lack access to the conditions required to act freely and rationally in the capitalist marketplace. The complete absence of these conditions for women is mirrored in the monopoly exerted over them by men – a means by which the masculinity of homo economicus is erected. Women's condition is closest to that of the pre-capitalist serfs or slaves, whose lives are determined and whose decisions are made by someone else: husband, father, guardian. Is this not why Jevons proposes to fine husbands when women break the law?[24]

But are women's economic actions really so different? Do they not seek employment to support themselves and their families? Do they not respond to the economic incentive of starvation and poverty (their own and their children's) by seeking employment? And do they not try to make the best of the limited opportunities offered by the labor market? But, given the misogyny of neoclassical economists, we are not surprised to see women blamed for competing against each other and driving down their own wages (are men ever chastised for competing against each other?). Viewed from a feminist standpoint, it is obvious that women's behavior is rational despite the incredible restrictions they continue to face.

Women are seen as irrational, not because they act against the laws of economic rationality, but because they are not allowed to act rationally, or because they act in contravention of the roles that are prescribed as "natural" for them. Taking this further, it seems that women's access to economic rationality is perceived as a threat to the economy and to society. Marshall, Jevons, Edgeworth, and Pigou share this view, and it leads them systematically to oppose attempts by women to claim an equal economic status and to create for themselves the conditions for that status.

Conclusion

Approaches to women in neoclassical economics have not changed much since the founding of the paradigm in the last decade of the nineteenth century. The men who wrote then and the many men and women who write from this perspective today share a common commitment to a methodology which is imbued with patriarchy, sexism, and misogyny. As in the early days, women and feminists are excluded from developing or establishing alternative theoretical approaches. Our words are not heard within the "malestream" of the discipline. Can neoclassical economics be cleansed of its patriarchal bias so that it can open its eyes to the methodological flaws resulting from its ingrained sexism? With the authors of other papers in this collection, I want to suggest that the very logic, rhetoric, and symbolism of the paradigm may be inseparable from the five sexist assumptions I have discussed here. Neoclassical economics has a history of stifling feminist approaches. We cannot wait for it to change. We must transcend it.

Notes

1. I gratefully acknowledge the support of Brook Holdack and the invaluable editorial help of Susan Feiner.
2. On standpoint theory, see, in particular, Nancy Hartsock (1983, 1991).

3 Just as your experiences and identity shape your analyses.
4 I will focus on the following early neoclassical works: A. Marshall's *Principles of Economics* (1930), W. S. Jevons' 1904 article "Married Women in Factories," A.C. Pigou's *The Economics of Welfare* (1960), and F. Edgeworth's two articles "Equal Pay to Men and Women for Equal Work" (1922) and "Women's Wages in Relation to Economic Welfare" (1923).
5 This goes back to the origins of patriarchal thought: Vicki Spelman, in *Inessential Woman*, discusses how, for Aristotle, women were acknowledged only if they were wives of citizens. All other women simply did not exist (Spelman 1988: 45–7).
6 Their only worry is where it is deemed insufficient, e.g. in discussions of the Poor Rates' impact on the (male) supply of labor.
7 See his discussion of unfair wages (Pigou 1960: 549–70).
8 Widows – with children – are the only women not dependent on a male breadwinner who have elicited some interest. Pigou specifically devises state welfare schemes to keep them away from the labor force, staying home to reproduce the next generation, and to keep them economically dependent – on the state (Pigou 1960: 722–3).
9 In the Cambridge degree controversy, the argument used by Marshall to oppose women's admissions was his *belief* that most (90 per cent) female students would marry and consequently not require the economic independence provided by a degree. On the opposite side of the controversy, E.M. Sidgwick documented, in a statistical study of families from which students would be drawn, that the marriage rate would be under 50 per cent (McWilliams-Tullberg 1992: 24).
10 On the "Family wage," see also Land (1979/80), and Barrett and McIntosh (1980).
11 Two studies by Ellen Smith (1915) and M.H. Hogg (1921) show a high rate of self-support among women workers (85 per cent in Smith's study), and additionally they show that one in three working women fully or partially supported dependants besides themselves. By contrast, Seebohm Rowntree and Frank Stuart (1921) found that only 12 per cent of working women supported dependants. The latter study, in spite of its dubious methodology, was used by Edgeworth to dismiss women's contribution.
12 Note that Edgeworth's reply to the feminists in 1923 does not contradict this analysis, but instead reasserts men's rights in the labor force as a rationale for unequal pay.
13 This position is by no means unique to the early neoclassical economists. We find it expressed by the feminist Mill (1965, 1970), who argued against married women's employment, and by Marx (1967) and Engels (1968), who saw the employment of married women as harmful to the living conditions and the autonomy of the working class.
14 Both Marshall (1930: 79–80) and Pigou (1960: 32–3) prescribe the outright and unjustified exclusion of women's contribution from national income accounts (see Folbre 1991; Pujol 1992).
15 Similarly, today feminist studies point out how much worse poverty statistics would be without women's income contribution.
16 Interestingly, one of Edgeworth's arguments in favor of the status quo is the "seriously deleterious" effect that "relieving the average house-father from the necessity of providing necessaries for his family…would remove a great part of his incentive to work" (1922: 453). It becomes clear, here, that constraining women to economic dependence on their husbands provides the further economic benefit to the nation (to capital) of increasing and stabilizing the male supply of labor.
17 This contradiction was acknowledged by Edgeworth (1922: 437).
18 See Pujol (1992) for a more detailed analysis of the approaches of Marshall, Edgeworth, and Pigou to the issue of women's productivity and wages.
19 With thanks to Susan Feiner for this assessment.
20 See, for instance, Hartmann (1976), Phillips and Taylor (1980), Treiman and Hartmann (1981), England (1982), Bergmann (1986), Blau and Ferber (1986), Folbre and Hartmann (1988), Waring (1988), Ferber and Nelson (1993).
21 An important element of the different construction of women and men by the neoclassical economists lies in their assigned relationship to the market. See Grapard (1993) and Hewitson (1993).

22 Curiously, this is the only instance where women are allowed access to training (in home economics).
23 Here, we can see the close connection between the early neoclassical economists and the new home economics.
24 For a full discussion of these dichotomies, see Folbre and Hartmann (1988), McCrate (1991), and Nelson (1992, 1993).

Bibliography

Abbott, E.G. (1910) *Women in Industry*, New York: Appleton.

Barrett, M. and M. McIntosh (1980) "The 'Family Wage': Some Problems for Socialists and Feminists," *Capital and Class* 11, summer: 51–72.

Becker, G.S. (1973) "A Theory of Marriage: Part I," *Journal of Political Economy*, July/August: 813–46.

—— (1976) "Altruism, Egoism and Genetic Fitness: Economics and Sociobiology," *Journal of Economic Literature* XIV(3), September: 817–26.

—— (1981a) *Treatise on the Family*, Cambridge, MA: Harvard University Press.

—— (1981b) "Altruism in the Family and Selfishness in the Market Place," *Economica* 48: 1–15.

Bergmann, B. (1986) *The Economic Emergence of Women*, New York: Basic Books.

Blau, F. and M. Ferber (1986) *The Economics of Women, Men, and Work*, Englewood Cliffs, NJ: Prentice-Hall.

Bodichon, B.L. Smith (1859) *Women and Work* (American edn.), with an introduction by C.M. Sedgwick, New York: C.S. Francis & Co.; English edn. (1857), London: Bosworth & Harrison; reprinted in C.A. Lacey (ed.) (1987) *B.L. Smith Bodichon and the Langham Place Group*, New York and London: Routledge & Kegan Paul.

Cadbury, E., M.C. Matheson and G. Shann (1906) *Women's Work and Wages: A Phase of Life in an Industrial City* (American edn. 1907), Chicago, IL: University of Chicago Press.

Cannan, E. (1914) *Wealth: A Brief Explanation of the Causes of Economic Welfare*, London: P.S. King & Son.

Clark, A. (1968) *The Working Life of Women in the Seventeenth Century*, London: Routledge & Sons; first published in 1919.

Edgeworth, F.Y. (1922) "Equal Pay to Men and Women for Equal Work," *Economic Journal* XXXII, December: 431–57.

—— (1923) "Women's Wages in Relation to Economic Welfare," *Economic Journal* XXXIII, December: 487–95.

Engels, F. (1968) *The Condition of the Working Class in England*, Stanford, CA: Stanford University Press.

England, P. (1982) "The Failure of Human Capital Theory to Explain Occupational Sex Segregation," *Journal of Human Resources* 17: 358–70.

Fawcett, M. Garrett (1892) "Mr. Sidney Webb's Article on Women's Wages," *Economic Journal* II, March: 173–6.

—— (1916) "The Position of Women in Economic Life," in W.H. Dawson (ed.) *After-War Problems*, London: Allen & Unwin.

—— (1918) "Equal Pay for Equal Work," *Economic Journal* XXVIII, March: 1–6.

Ferber, M. and J. Nelson (eds.) (1993) *Beyond Economic Man: Feminist Theory and Economics*, Chicago, IL: University of Chicago Press.

Folbre, N. (1991) "The Unproductive Housewife: Her Evolution in Nineteenth Century Economic Thought," *Signs* 16(3), spring: 463–84.

Folbre, N. and H. Hartmann (1988) "The Rhetoric of Self Interest: Ideology and Gender in Economic Theory," in A. Klamer, D. McCloskey and R. Solow (eds) *Consequences of Economic Rhetoric*, Cambridge: Cambridge University Press.

Grapard, U. (1993) "How to See the Invisible Hand, or From the Benevolence of the Butchers' Wife," paper presented at the Conference Out of the Margin, Feminist Perspectives on Economic Theory, Amsterdam, June.

Hartmann, H. (1976) "Capitalism, Patriarchy, and Segregation by Sex," *Signs* 1(3): spring: 137–69.

Hartsock, N. (1983) *Money, Sex and Power*, Boston, MA: Northeastern University Press.

—— (1991) "The Feminist Standpoint Revisited," paper presented at the International Political Science Association, Buenos Aires, July.

Heather-Bigg, A. (1894) "The Wife's Contribution to Family Income," *Economic Journal* IV, March: 51–8.

Hewitson, G. (1993) "Deconstructing Robinson Crusoe," paper presented at the Conference Out of the Margin, Feminist Perspectives on Economic Theory, Amsterdam, June.

Hill, G. (1896) *Women in English Life from Medieval to Modern Times*, London: R. Bentley.

Hogg, M.H. (1921) "Dependants on Women Wage Earners," *Economica* January: 69–86.

Hutchins, E. L. (1915) *Women in Modern Industry*, London: G. Bell.

Jevons, S. (1904) "Married Women in Factories," *Methods of Social Reform and Other Papers*, London: Macmillan.

Killingsworth, M.R. (1985) "The Economics of Comparable Worth: Analytical, Empirical and Policy Questions," in H. Hartmann (ed.) *Comparable Worth: New Directions for Research*, Washington, DC: National Research Council.

Land, H. (1979/80) *The Family Wage*, Eleanor Rathbone Memorial Lecture, Liverpool University Press.

McCrate, E. (1991) "Rationality, Gender and Domination," Working paper, Women's Studies Program and Department of Economics, University of Vermont.

McWilliams-Tullberg, R. (1992) "Mary Paley Marshall, 1850–1944," unpublished ms.

Marshall, A. (1930) *Principles of Economics*, 8th edn., reprinted, London: Macmillan; Guillebaud edn. (1961), London: Macmillan.

Marshall, M. Paley and Marshall, A. (1881) *The Economics of Industry*, 2nd edn., London: Macmillan.

Marx, K. (1967) *Capital*, vol. 1, New York: International Publishers.

Mill, J.S. (1965) "Principles of Political Economy, With Some of Their Applications to Social Philosophy," in J.M. Robson (ed.) *Collected Works of John Stuart Mill*, II and III, Toronto: University of Toronto Press.

—— (1970) "The Subjection of Women," in A.S. Rossi (ed.) *Essays on Sex Equality*, Chicago, IL: University of Chicago Press.

Mincer, J. (1962) "Labor Force Participation of Married Women: A Study of Labor Supply," *Aspects of Labor Economics*, Princeton: NBER.

Mincer, J. and Ofek, H. (1979) "The Distribution of Lifetime Labor Force Participation of Married Women," *Journal of Political Economy* 87(1), February: 197–201.

Mincer, J. and Polachek, S. (1974) "Family Investment in Human Capital and the Earnings of Women," *Journal of Political Economy* 82(2), pt. 2, March/April: S76–108.

—— (1978) "Women's Earnings Reexamined," *Journal of Human Resources* 13(1), winter: 118–34.

Nelson, J. (1992) "Gender, Metaphor and the Definition of Economics," *Economics and Philosophy*: 103–25.

—— (1993) "The Study of Choice or the Study of Provisioning? Gender and the Definition of Economics," in M. A. Ferber and J. A. Nelson (eds.) *Beyond Economic Man*, Chicago, IL: University of Chicago Press.

Phillips, A. and B. Taylor (1980) "Sex and Skill: Notes Towards a Feminist Economics," *Feminist Review* 6: 79–88.

Pigou, A.C. (1952) *Essays in Economics*, London: Macmillan.

—— (1960) *The Economics of Welfare*, London: Macmillan; first published in 1920.

Pinchbeck, I. (1981) *Women Workers and the Industrial Revolution, 1750–1850*, London: Virago.

Pujol, M. (1992) *Feminism and Anti-feminism in Early Economic Thought*, Aldershot: Edward Elgar.
Rathbone, E. (1917) "The Remuneration of Women's Services," *Economic Journal* XXVII, March: 55–68.
—— (1924) *The Disinherited Family: A Plea for the Endowment of the Family*, London: Edward Arnold & Co.
Rowntree, Seebohm B. and Stuart, F.D. (1921) *The Responsibility of Women Workers for Dependants*, London: Clarendon Press.
Sandell, S.H. and Shapiro, D. (1978) "An Exchange: The Theory of Human Capital and the Earnings of Women: A Reexamination of the Evidence," *Journal of Human Resources* 13(1), winter: 103–17.
Schultz, T.W. (ed.) (1974) *Economics of the Family, Marriage, Children and Human Capital*, Chicago, IL: University of Chicago Press.
Scott, J. and Tilly, L. (1978) *Women, Work and the Family*, New York: Holt Rinehart & Winston.
Smart, W. (1892) "Women's Wages," *Proceedings of the Philosophical Society of Glasgow* XXIII: 87–105, Glasgow: J. Smith & Son.
Smith, E. (1915) *Wage-Earning Women and their Dependants*, on behalf of the Executive Committee of the Fabian Women's Group, London: Fabian Society.
Spelman, E. (1988) *Inessential Woman*, Boston, MA: Beacon Press.
Strachey, R. (1969) *The Cause*, Port Washington, New York: Kennikat Press.
Strassmann, D. and Polanyi, L. (1992) "Shifting the Paradigm: Value in Feminist Critiques of Economics," unpublished paper presented at the first Conference of the International Association for Feminist Economics, August.
Taylor, H. (1970) "The Enfranchisement of Women," in Alice S. Rossi (ed.) *Essays on Sex Equality*, Chicago, IL: University of Chicago Press.
Treiman, D. and Hartmann, H. (1981) *Women, Work and Wages: Equal Pay for Jobs of Equal Value*, Washington, D.C: National Academy Press.
Waring, M. (1988) *If Women Counted*, San Francisco: Harper & Row.
Webb-Potter, B. (1914) "Personal Rights and the Woman's Movement, V. Equal Remuneration for Men and Women," *The New Statesman*, August 1: 525–7.
—— (1919) "Minority Report," War Cabinet Committee on Women in Industry, Cmd 167, London.

3 Hazel Kyrk and the ethics of consumption[1]

Susan van Velzen

Introduction

She approached consumer theory as a theory of human behavior. She argued that goods and services are no end goal, but merely instrumental in the production of welfare. She stressed the importance of what goes on in the household as a field worthy of economists' attention. And she emphasized the importance of conceptualizing the consumer not in a timeless and spaceless world, but as a human being with a past and a social context. Because of this, some say that – writing in the first half of the twentieth century as she did – she "was a pioneer in the field of consumer economics," "broadened the economics curriculum to include consumer topics," "established Chicago as the premier university for the study of family and consumer economics," and that her contribution to economics was "great" and "significant."[2]

Most economists, however, say nothing about her. When asked who best fits the above description of a Chicago pioneer approaching consumer theory as a study of human behavior, Nobel Prize winner Gary Becker would come to their minds, were it not for the fact that he is not a she, nor writing in the first half of the twentieth century. Some of the more well read may come to think of Margaret Reid, female, a Chicago economist and one of her students, now recognized as "one of the pioneers in several areas of consumer and household behavior" and "the mother of home economics."[3] But they hardly ever mention her.

This chapter is about Hazel Kyrk and her approach to consumer theory. Even without having to qualify her contributions as "great" or "significant," the almost total lack of consideration of her work seems uncalled for and stands in the way of any serious discussion of its contribution to the history of economics. To be sure, there are some references to Kyrk's work and life. Three biographical articles make interesting reading,[4] and Mary Hirschfeld's (1997) more theoretical article provides noteworthy thoughts on what she labels Kyrk's feminist methodology. However, none of these contributions aim to provide a more comprehensive discussion, and they cover either none or only part of her work in economics. The aim of this chapter is to put Hazel Kyrk's nearly forgotten work and life back on economists' maps and to further contribute to current feminist economic research on the history of economic thought. To accomplish this, this chapter continues in the following section (pp. 39–44) with a brief biographical sketch and a synopsis of Kyrk's approach to consumption theory. The section on the border between home economics and economics (pp. 44–6) continues with a description of Kyrk's life, while the section "Kyrk's approach compared" (pp. 46–50) compares Kyrk's approach to other approaches to consumer behavior. The chapter then concludes (pp. 50–2) and suggests the further study of Kyrk's main contribution: the weaving of pragmatist ethical thought into the economics of consumer behavior.

Towards *A Theory of Consumption*

From Ohio to Chicago

Hazel Kyrk was born in Ashley, Delaware County, Ohio (US) on 19 November 1886.[5] She was the only child of Elmer Kyrk, a laborer, and Jane Kyrk, a housewife, who died when Kyrk was 3 years old. After graduating from high school at the age of 17, Kyrk enrolled at Ohio Wesleyan College in 1904. She was self-supporting and earned her living working as a mother's helper in the home of one of the economics professors at the college, Leon Carroll Marshall, who was soon to move to the University of Chicago to become dean of the College of Commerce and Administration (now the Graduate School of Business). In 1908, two years after Marshall's move, Kyrk also moved to Chicago, again worked for the Marshall family and enrolled at the University of Chicago, where she obtained her B.A. in Economics in 1910. She enrolled as a graduate student at the Department of Political Economics during the fall term of 1910, combining her studies with teaching jobs at Chicago and several other colleges.

In the academic year 1918–19, while teaching at Oberlin College, Kyrk was granted leave to finish her thesis. However, she instead decided "to join the war effort" (Nelson 1980: 405). President Woodrow Wilson, who in 1917 had finally declared it time for the United States to enter (what is now known as) World War I, argued that the world had to be "made safe for democracy." Kyrk, it seems, was one of the many people Wilson's principles strongly appealed to. In 1918 she followed her Ph.D. advisor James Alfred Field on a Mission of the War Shipping Board to London, where she worked as a statistician for the American Division of the Allied Maritime Transport Council. In 1919 she returned to her teaching work and finished her thesis.

In 1920, the year in which American women obtained the right to vote and a peak year in terms of the percentage of Ph.D. dissertations in economics by women,[6] Kyrk, at the age of 33, received a doctor's degree magna cum laude for her thesis "The Consumer's Guidance of Economic Activity," later published as *A Theory of Consumption* (1923). The book is written from a welfare perspective and is fundamentally concerned with the prevention of what Kyrk labels "waste" of productive resources. This concept of "waste" includes the more common notions of uneconomical use of productive resources as well as ineffective and inefficient use. In addition, however, it includes two ethical notions not usually considered in the economic literature on welfare. First, it includes the notion of distributional flaws such that resources are used to fulfill the not-so-urgent whims and fancies of some, while the urgent needs of others are not met. Second, it includes the notion of waste when "unwise" ends are fulfilled while "wise" ends, ends that lead to "the good life," are not. Kyrk argues that, if one is concerned with human welfare, an important question to ask is how best to prevent *all* these manifestations of waste. It is the desire to answer this question which forms the motivational force behind Kyrk's theory and which makes her theory worthwhile for those interested in heterodox methodological frameworks.

A Theory of Consumption

Kyrk's *A Theory of Consumption* is a survey of the problems consumers face in working out their own concept of welfare. The survey is divided into two parts. In the first part Kyrk focuses on "economic factors" that influence the degree of waste involved in consumption. She specifically focuses on economic factors that get in the way of consumers' effective freedom of choice. Kyrk's experience in World War I had convinced her that, except in the direst of circumstances, those interested in human welfare should not focus on the success or failure of social engineering. Instead, they should focus on whether "in choosing the instruments of material life" consumers are able to use their formal freedom of choice to work out their *own* concept of welfare. She argues that, unless there is a clear-cut and definite primary social need to which all others are subordinated, freedom of choice is to be preferred above authoritative control. We cannot determine for others how they can best determine "the good life," simply because we do not all agree on what the good life is. And, even if we did, authoritative control remains problematic. Neither we nor our experts know all there is to know about how to attain the good life as we can only discover this along the way, living, seeking, and growing. This stance, combined with the turbulence of the industrial times at the beginning of the twentieth century, led Kyrk to focus on the question of whether and to what degree consumers' freedom of choice is actually "real freedom, the effective exercise of the power which has nominally been granted" (Kyrk 1923: 42).

One obstacle to real freedom, she reasons, is "the preparation of senseless luxuries whilst there is need for more bread." To prevent this type of waste, society has to establish "a minimum of consumption requirements" which guarantees everyone "the material basis for a civilized healthy life." Without it, no distribution of resources can be optimal. According to Kyrk, here lies the real difficulty for public policymakers in non-war times. For although from a welfare perspective there is no need to define the good life, one cannot avoid reaching some kind of agreement as to what constitutes the very *minimum* of consumption requirements. Thus, Kyrk argues, there is a clear role for science to help formulate these basic needs, and for public policy to guarantee their provision.

Another type of waste may result if consumers encounter producers who are tempted to defraud them "by short measure, or downright misrepresentation." At the beginning of the twentieth century, the separation of production and consumption had led to an increasingly complex market with an increasing amount and diversity of goods. It was a time of "industrial turmoil," with big business enthusiastically awaiting the Roaring Twenties. With all those changes and more to come, the question of to what degree this mass of products satisfied or would satisfy the wants of the mass of consumers popped up in the minds of some observers, including Kyrk's. And thus Kyrk, in line with Woodrow Wilson's policy to develop rules for "fair competition" and a "Magna Carta" for labor, suggests another reason for state intervention, i.e. the prevention of fraudulent practices and the misuse of monopoly power, the prohibition of misstatements of facts, and the provision of information such as "quality stamps."

The first part of Kyrk's thesis concludes that real freedom of choice does not imply no state intervention at all. Interventions are necessary to guarantee the provision of basic needs and "fair competition." However, Kyrk warns that these interventions alone are not enough to prevent all manifestations of waste. Clearly, she argues, there are obvious limitations upon the state's scope to protect consumers from errors of judgement, and it is this type of waste she focuses on in the second part of her thesis.

The second part of *A Theory of Consumption* focuses on the way social factors such as customs, traditions, and conventions influence the effectiveness of consumers' power of choice. Arguing against the marginal utility school, with its "demonstrably false ideas on human behavior" and its lack of interest in "consumers' attitudes which lie back of choice" (Kyrk 1923: 17), Kyrk reasons that:

> A complete theory of consumption cannot take [consumers' attitudes, preferences, and purposes] for granted and ask merely how adequate is the mechanism through which they are carried out, but must undertake the analysis of the forces which called them into existence and which strengthen or change them.
>
> (Kyrk 1923: 131)

Thus she embarks on an explanation of the valuation process, applying concepts derived not only from economics, but from cognitive theory and social psychology as well. Kyrk especially makes use of the ideas of pragmatic philosopher and educator John Dewey, and describes the valuation process as a process of "making practical judgments," a "constant attempt of human interests to realize themselves through the means at hand." Values are merely instrumental in this process and valuable objects are objects which are "good for something." Kyrk focuses in *A Theory* on "economic values," values in the context of scarcity, which, through moral choices between different ends, are arranged in "scales of values," a qualitative ordering of preferences for goods and services, identifying what are "necessities" and what are "luxuries." These values, to be sure, are not the result of merely individual processes, resulting in separate and distinct universes for each individual. Individuals have a past and a social context, and do not make value judgments in a timeless and spaceless world. What is good is pointed out by others and accepted by us because we are social animals. Therefore, "judgments of value are thoroughly social in process" (*ibid.*: 169).

This pragmatic approach to the valuation process leads to a clear angle for further analysis, because

> [J]ust as in the realm of ethics we find moral values organized in elaborate codes of rights and duties, so in the realm of economic values, we find standards of consumption, organized systems of the essential, the proper and the required.
>
> (Kyrk 1923: 170)

These standards are what consumers deem to be "minimum requirements for a 'decent' living." By the time consumers are grown adults, they govern their consumption patterns with "a considerable degree of force and binding power." In order to understand where our attitudes, preferences, and purposes come from, a large part of Kyrk's *A Theory* is consequently devoted to the study of these standards of consumption.

First, Kyrk discusses how these standards, which vary "from period to period, from country to country and from class to class," come into existence. She argues that individuals' range of choice and concepts of what is and what is not essential are always bound by the existing state of the arts and sciences, and by the resources available in their time and place. One cannot have what does not exist, and "invention is the mother of necessity." And as income and price levels differ between social groups, so do their standards of consumption. In addition, she argues, in line with Thorstein Veblen's argument in *A Theory of the Leisure Class* (1899), that differences in cultural legacy ensure that even with the same economic resources at hand standards of living differ and furnish us with different symbols of status and achievement or ways to "keep up appearances."

Second, Kyrk discusses how and in what direction our standards change. For, although standards do constrain consumers' freedom of choice, they also evolve, thanks to our creative impulse. She quotes Dewey's colleague James Tufts to illustrate her point of view:

> [Choice] represents not merely a process of evaluating ends which match actually defined desires, but also a process in which the growing self, dissatisfied with any ends already in view, gropes for some new definition of ends that shall better respond to its living, creative capacity.[7]
>
> (Kyrk 1923: 246)

This "growing self" gropes by means of experimentation, and the more favorable the circumstances, e.g. a personal inclination to innovation or a large amount of contact and communication with others, the more it does so. The direction this groping takes is determined by our "tentative working concept" of what constitutes a high standard. Because it is "the business of intelligence to give life as a whole some coordination and plan," our values are "formed into scales of higher and lower" and tentatively systematized to give us some direction in which to lead our lives. It is this concept of a high standard which allows us to distinguish wise from unwise choices and to order our lives according to some plan.

Finally, having studied the origins and change in our consumption standards, Kyrk returns to the main question of her thesis and concentrates on waste due to mistaken judgements. Kyrk's main worry is that consumers resolve choice situations by reference to the value standards they bring with them in a specific situation, without re-evaluating these standards and critically examining them. Instead of evaluating whether products have instrumental value for consumers in terms of their own interests and purposes, consumers may take the easy way and simply purchase more of the same, or superlatives in quality. Furthermore, consumers may follow traditions or customs not only when circumstances call for traditions or customs, but also when these are outdated, pointless, or even harmful. Or they may follow the elite, not only when the elite engages in truly worthwhile activities, but also when it engages in "conspicuous consumption" and leisure with no value to the good life at all.

How to prevent this type of waste? Kyrk clearly does not want to prescribe some sort of recipe for the good life and ends with some pragmatic suggestions. Thus, she argues that education, time, and experimentation are necessary to increase consumers' self-reliance, ability to discriminate, and independence of judgement, and to allow them, aided by impartial inquiry and practical science, to engage in critical analyses of their own standards.

> This is the business of human intelligence – to criticize and to remake human valuations. Our valuations come to us in large part ready-made; our attitudes and reactions follow established behavior patterns. But life upon the level of intelligence means that we examine and, if necessary, remake our valuations. This is the scientific spirit applied to life; this is scientific knowledge and human experience applied directly to the problems of living.
>
> (Kyrk 1923: 287–8)

And she also urges consumers – again aided by advice "upon the whole art of living from sages of the past and present" – to try and formulate "the good life," to give ample thought to the ends to be promoted through the consumption of goods and services, and to analyze their standards of living in terms of the fundamental values sought and secured. Kyrk concludes *A Theory of Consumption* hoping for "a higher level of human life":

> What must be guarded against in the spending of a surplus is its disbursement in an irrational imitation of the mode of living of a class of a high social grade, or in other ways requiring no time or thought. If instead, this expenditure is the expression of individual interests and tastes, native or acquired, if it is the tentative reaching out of new impulses for realization through economic goods, there is hope that the direction of the developing standard will be toward a higher level of human life.
>
> (Kyrk 1923: 293)

The borderland between home economics and economics

Kyrk obtained her doctorate at a time when it was not that uncommon for women to secure such a degree. At the same time, however, Kyrk was also looking for a career in academia. To secure that *was* uncommon for women.[8] Although Kyrk was awarded the Hart, Schaffner & Marx Prize in 1921,[9] and although her former employer, Marshall, appears to have been especially supportive in her quest for an academic position, it took several years to find a suitable one. It was only in 1925, after some odd jobs and a short stint at Iowa State College, that Kyrk seemed to settle down when Chicago offered her a job: at her own university, close to her mentor Marshall, and with the prospect of an appointment not only in home economics but in economics, her own field of study, as well.[10] It was at Chicago that Kyrk really started to develop what Marshall called "the borderland between economics and home economics,"[11] both through her Ph.D. students, such as Day Monroe and Margaret Reid,[12] and through her own academic work. Kyrk's most well-known work to result from this is her second major publication, *Economic Problems of the Family* (1933), an outgrowth of a course introduced at the University of Chicago in 1925 and one of the major textbooks used at that time for courses in consumer economics.

Economic problems of the family

Kyrk herself summarizes the contents of the 500-odd pages of *Economic Problems of the Family* as "an analysis of [the] economic position [of American families] in terms of incomes, prices and standards of living" (Kyrk 1953: v). The work describes the economic situation of American families in the 1920s, the years characterized by both a consumption boom and a substantial increase in the numbers of gainfully employed women. It is structured around the "economic problems of families," i.e. around problems incidental either to direct production, to earning, or to spending of money (Kyrk 1933: 41). The topics discussed cover a broad range, from the future of household production, the complexities of the income concept, to problems associated with inflation, monopoly power, and the risks of disability. The book can be interpreted as a practical attempt to further the insights formulated in *A Theory of Consumption*. It analyzes minimum standards of consumption and the public policy necessary to ensure that all attain those minimum standards, and presents a wealth of both quantitative and qualitative information to allow consumers to analyze critically their existing standards.

In one example, Kyrk analyzes whether families are able to attain a "minimum of consumption requirements." Referring to Engel's family expenditure studies and Sydenstricker and King's work on the expenditure of South Carolina mill families in 1916–17, she considers the possibilities of constructing (what we now refer to as) equivalence scales and focuses on ways to define "the minimum tolerable level" of living, "a measuring stick, a standard that will not vary from class to class but that will represent common requirements…a minimum standard below which no family should fall" (*ibid.*: 198–9).

Another example relates to above-minimum standards, when she discusses the waste which may result from traditional norms and customs if these prevent women with "too little housework" in their "deserted workshop" from finding (part-time) employment. Kyrk lists numerous factors which may explain why Veblen's "ladies of leisure" are such not by choice, but because they cannot do much else, for example because of employers' hostile attitudes, the difficulty of combining paid work with household work, etc. She discusses possible solutions, such as contracting out part of the household work, "an equal sharing of the household activities by husband and wife and other members of the family in proportion to their ability," and "the abandonment of family life in independent households" (*ibid.*: 106–7).

Kyrk ends *Economic Problems* with chapters on the importance of setting one's own standard of living to determine the "good life." Again, her treatment of this issue is similar to, but also more practical and detailed than, her treatment in *A Theory*. For example, in *Economic Problems* she actually provides a list of "wise uses of time and money" – not as a prescription to govern expenditure, but in the hope that "each family may attempt such an analysis."

From Chicago to Washington, DC

From the middle of the 1930s on, Kyrk's work gradually shifted from the academic area towards the area of public policy, a shift which coincided with a shift in the political landscape and the beginning of the Roosevelt era. Kyrk's involvement with the New Deal started in the summer of 1937, a year after the publication of Keynes' *General Theory*, when she worked at the US Bureau of Human Nutrition and Home Economics in the Department of Agriculture. Here she contributed to the Consumer Purchaser Study, with publications on family housing and facilities, and family expenditure on housing and household operation. This work led to her appointment, in 1943, as chair of the Consumer Advisory Committee to the Office of Price Administration (OPA) and, in 1947, as chair of the Technical Advisory Committee of the Bureau of Labor Statistics, a committee which undertook to formulate the City Worker's Budget, an attempt to estimate the content of a "modest but adequate level of consumption" and for more than thirty years the "yardstick for measuring the economic health of American families and for setting levels of income tax exemption."[13]

In 1952 Kyrk, who had obtained full professorship in 1941, retired, leaving behind a revised and extended version of *Economic Problems*, now entitled *The Family in the American Economy*.[14] One year later Ohio Wesleyan College – the university where Kyrk started as a student herself in 1904 – honored her with the degree of Doctor of Humane Letters, citing her "accomplishments as an inspirational teacher, as a scholar who made 'unusual and outstanding contributions to the field of home economics', and as a government advisor" (Beller and Kiss 1999: 12). By that time Kyrk had moved to Washington, DC, "the center of much of her professional activities apart from the University of Chicago and the home of many of her friends" (Reid 1972: 186), a move symbolizing the change in focus from the pure academic work at Chicago in the early period to the more policy-oriented work from the 1930s on. On 6 August 1957, having been in ill health for two years, Kyrk died of a stroke while vacationing in Brattleboro, Vermont. She was buried in Ashley, Ohio, her birthplace.

Kyrk's approach compared

Despite the early praise for her *A Theory of Consumption* and the wide use of the several editions of *Economic Problems of the Family*, Kyrk's approach to consumer and household studies did not attract a large number of followers. The lack of such a following does not make it easy to give Kyrk's work a proper place in the history of economics. Hardly any systematic thought has been given to this issue, and, with some notable exceptions, such as Heidi Hartmann's (1974) and Mary Hirschfeld's (1997) work, most references to Kyrk's work are confined to the remark that Kyrk contributed "greatly" to consumer and household economics. To more fully understand the nature of Kyrk's work and to add to the few strands that are available, it is necessary to qualify this "great contribution" and discuss the relationship between Kyrk's work and that of some of her contemporaries.

Kyrk and the early home economists

An important characteristic of Kyrk's approach is her belief that consumption is important as an economic activity, and should thus be studied. Of course, Kyrk and her students were neither the first nor the only writers to address the specificities of consumption, household work, or, more generally, "woman's work." In particular, the work of the "early home economists," such as Catherine Beecher, Ellen Richards and Christine Frederick, resembles that of Kyrk.[15]

Home economics can be traced back to Catherine Beecher, who provided a wealth of technical details regarding the efficient management and performance of household labor in her *Treatise on Domestic Economy* (1841). With it, she also spread her Victorian view on domesticity, which held as ideal the woman who, educated in "domestic economy," presided over a cultured, well-managed household. Some decades later, it was Ellen Richards who really established the field. Writing during the Progressive Era, Richards politicized Beecher's domesticity concept, expanding women's political power to "that larger household, the city." She also emphasized women's new role as consumers, and focused on economic and social issues instead of housekeeping and decoration. And having in mind a professional field for educated women, she emphasized the role of experts. In the 1920s the emphasis in home economics changed again. It lost its focus on social and economic issues, and returned to Beecher's ideal household as the very specific and concrete realm of women's moral authority. Experts remained important, however, and scientific management, already popular for shops and workplaces, gained particular popularity. This was in no small part thanks to Christine Frederick, who stereotyped female consumers as "essentially emotional, intuitive, and hence malleable" (Goldstein 1997: 276), and saw it as her task to try and upgrade women's workplace by scientific management and invention.

When Kyrk started to teach home economists in the 1920s, most of her colleagues were infatuated with the Frederick approach to home economics, and were trying to construct a rationalized, scientific discipline. Kyrk explicitly set her work apart from that of the more dominant home economists of her time.[16] In the preface to her *Economic Problems*, she warns her readers:

> In no respect can the book be considered a manual of "whats" and "hows" for the home-maker. Nor should the title "Economic Problems of the Family" be construed as "Home Economics" in the broad sense, covering technical and practical questions of nutrition, child care, care of the house and selection of clothing, furniture and household equipment. The problems dealt with are "economic" in the academic sense of that term.
>
> (Kyrk 1933: xix)

Kyrk's work shows more overlap with that of Richards. Both stress the need to include economic and social issues in home economics, and both discuss social reform issues. However, other characteristics of Richards' work are more similar to Beecher's and Frederick's work than to Kyrk's. Whereas Richards argues explicitly from the perspective of women's moral authority on household matters, Kyrk focuses on these matters as economically important activities that might be organized along different lines. And whereas Richards and the other early home economists in the main focus on education for girls and women, Kyrk explicitly stresses the relevance of the field for both women and men (cf. Kyrk 1933: xix). And finally, although both Richards and Fredericks as well as Kyrk favor the application of "the scientific method," Kyrk's approach differs markedly from that of these early home economists. They mean to carve out a niche for scientifically trained expert women, who could serve housewives or larger communities with their knowledge, and prescribe what they ought to do. Kyrk, on the other hand, refers to the scientific method in a Deweyan way, and urges all consumers, women and men alike, to "apply the scientific spirit to life" and make their *own* valuations.

It is because of all these differences that Kyrk's work can be clearly distinguished from that of the early home economists, despite their shared interest in consumer and household issues. In fact, Kyrk helped to establish a new line of research for home economists, and shifted them away from the earlier focus on household management towards economics (cf. Yi 1996).

Kyrk and the institutionalists of the early 1900s

Other important characteristics of Kyrk's work are her preference for a reality-based approach, her focus on the endogeneity of preferences, her skepticism regarding reliance on marginal utility approaches to explain economic behavior, and her emphasis on the role of institutions as opposed to free markets in allocating resources efficiently. These are characteristics she shares with representatives of the institutional school, the dominant approach of economic thought in the United States in the first decades of the previous century (cf. Reder 1982). Kyrk's work is especially related to the works of Thorstein Veblen and Wesley Mitchell.

With Veblen, Kyrk shares an almost anthropological interest in "the world behind the demand curve." She frequently refers to his *A Theory of the Leisure Class* (1899). And Kyrk's fear of uncritical, unintelligent copying of the consumption standard of the upper class was no doubt inspired by Veblen's argument that pecuniary emulation, or "keeping up with the Joneses," had become a dominant motive in society. However, Kyrk's work is not a mere copy of Veblen's work. More than Veblen, Kyrk is not only concerned with the question of *why* consumers behave as they do, but also with how they *should* behave, and uses his analysis to point to, for example, waste involved in a thoughtless "emulation of the rich." Also, Kyrk is not as antagonistic to business as Veblen is. Whereas Veblen conceptualizes businessmen with their profit motive as saboteurs of the economic system and suggests they should be replaced by disinterested, benevolent engineers, Kyrk views businessmen and the profit motive as essential forces in the productive process, which in the proper institutional setting may be conducive to the generation of welfare. And, with few exceptions, she rejects social engineering.

With Mitchell, Kyrk shares an interest in the analysis of the specific characteristics of consumption activities as compared to market activities, and can be said to be among the first to put what was traditionally seen as women's work on the agenda of economists (cf. Yi 1996: 28). For example, like Mitchell in "The Backward Art of Spending Money" (1912), Kyrk points to the typical family organization of the household; to the slow development of scientific techniques which prohibit an efficient, Taylorlike organization of consumption; to the lack of a common denominator to equate money costs and the ends of consumption; and to the lack of a clear specification of these ends of consumption. Again, however, Kyrk does not simply summarize Mitchell's work. Rather, together with her students, she extends it and provides a comprehensive, detailed survey of the many aspects of consumption, and collects figures about consumption levels and family expenditure. She also goes on where Mitchell stops. Because, where Mitchell (1912: 281) concludes his "The Backward Art" observing that "there is a scheme of values embodied in every housewife's work, whether she knows it or not," and seems to accept that some "will ever continue to accept uncritically the scale of conventional values which their day and generation provides ready-made," Kyrk is concerned with mapping out this scheme of values and making people aware that it *can* be changed. She suggests ways to improve what Mitchell labeled "a backward art," not only by discussing more technical aspects related to the consumption process, but also, following Dewey, by urging and helping consumers to reflect critically on their consumption behavior. It is this characteristic of Kyrk's approach that led Hirschfeld (1997: 207) to remark that Kyrk writes from a "conversational or democratic stance," as if her main purpose is to provide information to individuals in the economy which they can then use for their own ends.

Kyrk and Dewey's ethical thought

Kyrk's approach then, it can be argued, is even more philosophical than institutional, and it is because of the incorporation of Dewey's ethical thought that her theory stands out as it does. A study of Kyrk's work reveals many Deweyan elements. Thus, Kyrk agrees with Dewey's view on the instrumentality of values, on the impact of the social context on values, and on the temporality of values. And, like Dewey (and Tufts), Kyrk argues that consumers do not simply satisfy given wants, but organize their lives around working concepts of a high standard of living.

Kyrk's concomitant focus on the importance of experiments as ways to enhance the valuation process is also typically Deweyan, as is her tireless stress on the importance of critical reflection as opposed to rule-of-thumb practice. And though neither Dewey nor Kyrk is very specific as to what the "scientific spirit applied to life" would entail, both hint that it involves an inventory of possible responses to a new choice situation, as well as the formulation and testing of hypotheses as to the sort of standard one would attain and the sort of person one would become if one committed oneself to any of the responses which are prima facie good.[17]

Similarly, Kyrk's stress on the importance of effective freedom of choice and the market mechanism as a means to guarantee this freedom is comparable to Dewey's stress on the importance of democracy to further human welfare. No one can critically reflect *for* consumers. Both Dewey and Kyrk argue that people need a command of resources such that basic needs are met. Second, they argue that legal or social obstacles should be removed to strengthen our effective freedom of choice, and suggest that all should be educated so as to be able freely to grow and develop as human beings.

This leads to a last major parallel, i.e. the emphasis on the importance of education not as a lesson in "whats and hows," but as a lesson in using one's own inventiveness and creativity. Neither Kyrk nor Dewey denies the importance of passing on knowledge; nor do they hold that any type of socialization is bad. On the contrary, human beings are social animals, and it would be foolish to assume there are such things as true, "uncontaminated" individual preferences. Still, both argue that, once consumers have received a basic stock of information to work with, a Deweyan type of education is essential because it enables consumers to learn through experience and in communication with others.

Kyrk's approach to consumer theory, then, is especially of interest because of its attempt to extend the institutional approach and weave Dewey's pragmatist philosophical ideas into the economics of consumer behavior. It focuses around the concept of the good life, and on the role of consumers, economists, and philosophers in trying to attain it. The result is an ethical underpinning to consumer theory, and an approach which shares some elements with Frank Knight's philosophical work in his Harvard Lectures, *Ethics and the Economic Interpretation* (1922) and *The Ethics of Competition* (1923), both of which may be interpreted as similar pragmatic conceptualizations of the valuation process.[18]

Conclusions

To summarize Hazel Kyrk's contributions to consumer theory from a feminist and heterodox economics perspective, several aspects of her work seem especially notable and worthwhile.

First, Hazel Kyrk contributed considerably to the development of the borderland between economics and home economics. She was one of the first to study explicitly the concrete activities of consumers at a time when these were hardly considered legitimate objects of study for economists and were considered women's domain. In her day she was remarkably modern, with her non-essential view on gender relations, pointing out time and time again that gender relations are not fixed and *can* be changed. Today her work is still interesting reading for feminist economists studying, for example, the concept of full income, the difference between household and market production, and the redistribution of paid and household work.

Second, together with contemporaries such as Veblen, Mitchell, and Dewey, Kyrk was among the first to argue for a broadening of the social and psychological basis of consumer behavior, and extended her theoretical framework to give a less abstract, more realistic – some might say more feminist – account of human choice behavior. Today, Kyrk's observation that economics needs to take serious notice of the advances in sister sciences such as psychology and other social sciences still rings true, despite the considerable advances in mainstream economics since the 1920s and the increasing number of interdisciplinary challenges to the mainstream approach to consumption.[19] And in fact her approach to consumer theory may even regain importance due to our increasingly rich characterizations of economic agents. This trend may lead back to the early institutionalist approaches, which contain refreshing "new" statements of by now well-known phenomena such as habit formation, bounded rationality, cognitive dissonance, and reference drift.

Finally, Kyrk also was among the first, if not *the* first, to explicitly formulate a theory of consumption linking pragmatist ethical thought to economics and to argue that – in order to be able to make *any* welfare statements – economics needs an ethical underpinning. It is mainly because of these characteristics that her work differs fundamentally from the more recent work of new consumer theorists such as Gary Becker, Kelvin Lancaster, and Richard Muth.[20] Like Kyrk, these economists conceptualize goods as instrumental and agree that habit, customs, traditions, and other social aspects need to be incorporated into any valid theory of consumption. However, because they all explicitedly aim to incorporate the influence of the social context into a marginal utility framework they are unable to capture the tentative, dynamic aspects of choice behavior. Nor do they give specific attention to ways of strengthening consumers' valuation process, because, whereas Kyrk seriously doubts that people act "rationally," these economists usually simply assume that they do. And they also do not allow more ethical questions to be addressed, because their "thin ethics" leaves the big question of the recipe for the good life to one side and defines right action as that which maximizes whatever happens to be selected as a goal (cf. Cottingham 1998: 43).

Kyrk's approach might better be compared to more recent heterodox approaches, for example, those of Chicago philosopher Martha Nussbaum or Cambridge economist Geoffrey Hodgson.[21] In her *Women and Human Development*

Nussbaum (2000), building on Amartya Sen's capability concept, argues for an ethical underpinning to all thought about development planning and public policy. In ways comparable to Kyrk's approach, she focuses on basic human capabilities, a social minimum beneath which truly human functioning is not available to citizens. Hodgson focuses on the good life, and in his *Economics and Utopia* (1999) pictures a utopia of "a learning economy," which can be compared to Kyrk's dynamic welfare approach with its focus on the importance of a Deweyan type of education. Kyrk's focus on pragmatist ethical issues ties in with this and other recent work on ethics and consumption, and is a considerable contribution to current discussions in feminist and heterodox economics.

Those who knew Hazel Kyrk and her contributions to economics remember her as a "pioneer" and "a wonderful person" who contributed greatly to economics. When interviewed in 1994, Josephine Staab, one of Kyrk's doctoral students from 1945–7, remembered her thus:

> A pleasant person, a person that was easy to talk with and encouraging in terms of helping you plan your work. First of all she tried to educate you.... So that you had a background of information to deal with. Then she tried to stimulate your thinking and serve as a catalyst to bring you into experimenting on something new. But she also had very firm standards. She was assertive. She challenged. She accepted no foolishness.
>
> (Staab, as quoted in Beller and Kiss 1999: 11)

This description seems especially apt as a characterization not only of Kyrk's approach to teaching, but of her work as well. For it uses only a few sentences to name the central ingredients of Kyrk's recipe for both good teaching and the good life: education, critical thinking, experimentation, and high standards. It is these constituent elements of Kyrk's approach to consumption that deserve further serious consideration, both in relation to their place in the history of economics, and in relation to more contemporary work in ethics and economics on the quest for the good life.

Notes

1 This chapter is a shortened version of "The Consumer and the Good Life: Hazel Kyrk's Ethical Approach to Consumer Theory" (see van Velzen 2001: 9–66). Many thanks to Mary Morgan, Laurie Philips, and Debra Levine and colleagues.
2 See Reid (1972), Hartmann (1974), Nelson (1980), Hirschfeld (1997), Beller and Kiss (1999); also Yi (1996).
3 On Reid, see, for example, a special issue of *Feminist Economics* 2(3), 1996.
4 See Nelson (1980), Lobdell (2000), Beller and Kiss (1999).
5 The biographical information is taken from Reid (1972), Nelson (1980), Beller and Kiss (1999), as well as from Kyrk's own resumes in her Biographical File, Department of Special Collections, Joseph Regenstein Library, University of Chicago.
6 See Forget (1995: 26).

7 Tufts' quote is taken from his contribution, "The Moral Life and the Construction of Values and Standards," in a volume of Dewey *et al.*, *Creative Intelligence: Essays in the Pragmatic Attitude* (1917).
8 See Rossiter (1982: 50); also R. Dimand (1995: 9).
9 Kyrk received this prize for her thesis, and shares this honor with, for example, Frank Knight and later Nobel Prize winner Simon Kuznets.
10 Actually, it took some time for this joint appointment to materialize, and it was only in 1928 that Kyrk was given a joint appointment with her original department.
11 In a letter to Kyrk, dated March 24, 1924 (Department of Special Collections, the Joseph Regenstein Library, University of Chicago, Marshall's papers, Box 16, Folders 9 and 10).
12 Day Monroe, Kyrk's first student, received the degree of Doctor of Philosophy for her *Chicago Families: A Study of Unpublished Census Data* (1932). Margaret Reid was the first woman economist to become a Distinguished Fellow of the American Economic Association (in 1980), and is well known for her thesis *The Economics of Household Production* (1934).
13 See Reid (1972), Nelson (1980), and Beller and Kiss (1999).
14 In response to great demand, in 1967 the University of Chicago Press published a revised version that incorporated new findings and descriptions of institutional changes (Reid 1972; cf. Beller and Kiss 1999).
15 See, for example, Matthews (1987), Apple (1997), and Stage (1997) on the history of home economics.
16 See also Beller and Kiss (1999), and Thorne (1995: 69).
17 Neither Kyrk nor Dewey paid a lot of attention to the ways individuals might go about this in practical terms. Discussing Dewey, Welchman (1995: 177ff.) takes up the challenge and tries to spell out what procedures individuals ought to use. On Kyrk's more practical attempts, see a short note in *Economic Problems* (1933: 393 ff.).
18 As I briefly mention in van Velzen (2001), without apparently having been aware of each other's efforts, both Kyrk and Knight appear to have been working more or less simultaneously on similar approaches to combining ethics and economics, Knight focusing on production, Kyrk on consumption.
19 See, for example, Crocker and Linden (1998) and the references mentioned there.
20 See Becker (1965), Lancaster (1966), and Muth (1966).
21 For more contemporary work on ethics and consumption, see Crocker and Linden (1998).

Bibliography

Apple, Rima D. (1997) "Liberal Arts or Vocational Training? Home Economics Education for Girls," in Sarah Stage and Virginia B. Vincenti (eds.) *Rethinking Home Economics: Women and the History of a Profession*, Ithaca, NY: Cornell University Press.

Becker, Gary, S. (1965) "A Theory of the Allocation of Time," *Economic Journal* 80, 200: 493–517.

Beecher, Catherine E. (1941) *A Treatise on Domestic Economy, for the Use of Young Ladies at Home, and at School*, Boston, MA: Wm. A. Hall & Co.

Beller, Andrea H. and D.E. Kiss (1999) "On the Contribution of Hazel Kyrk to Family Economics," paper prepared for presentation at the Society for the Advancement of Behavioral Economics meetings, Exploring the Reorientation of Economics, San Diego, California, June 12–14.

Cottingham, John (1998) *Philosophy and the Good Life: Reason and the Passions in Greek, Cartesian and Psychoanalytic Ethics*, Cambridge: Cambridge University Press.

Crocker, David A. and Toby Linden (eds.) (1998) *Ethics of Consumption: The Good Life, Justice and Global Stewardship*, Lanham: Rowman & Littlefield Publishers, Inc.

Dewey, John *et al.* (1917) *Creative Intelligence: Essays in the Pragmatic Attitude*, New York: H. Holt & Co.

Dimand, Mary-Ann, Robert W. Dimand and Evelyn L. Forget (1995) *Women of Value: Feminist Essays on the History of Women in Economics*, Aldershot: Edward Elgar.

Dimand, Robert W. (1995) "The Neglect of Women's Contributions to Economics," in Mary Ann Dimand, Robert W. Dimand and Evelyn L. Forget, *Women of Value: Feminist Essays on the History of Women in Economics*, Aldershot: Edward Elgar.

Forget, Evelyn L. (1995) "American Women Economists, 1900–1940: Doctoral Dissertations and Research Specialization," in Mary Ann Dimand, Robert W. Dimand and Evelyn L. Forget, *Women of Value: Feminist Essays on the History of Women in Economics*, Aldershot: Edward Elgar.

Goldstein, Carolyn M. (1997) "Part of the Package: Home Economists in the Consumer Products Industries, 1920–1940," in Sarah Stage and Virginia B. Vincenti (eds.) *Rethinking Home Economics: Women and the History of a Profession*, Ithaca, NY: Cornell University Press.

Hartmann, Heidi Irmgard (1974) "Capitalism and Women's Work in the Home, 1900–1930," unpublished dissertation, Yale University.

Hirschfeld, Mary L. (1997) "Methodological Stance and Consumption Theory: A Lesson in Feminist Methodology," in John B. Davis (ed.) *New Economics and Its History*, Durham: Duke University Press.

Hodgson, Geoffrey M. (1999) *Economics and Utopia: Why the Learning Economy Is Not the End of History*, London: Routledge.

Knight, Frank H. (1922) "Ethics and the Economic Interpretation," *Quarterly Journal of Economics* 36: 454–81.

—— (1923) "The Ethics of Competition," *Quarterly Journal of Economics* 37: 579–624.

Kyrk, Hazel (1923) *A Theory of Consumption*, London: Sir Isaac Pitman & Sons, Ltd.

—— (1933) *Economic Problems of the Family*, New York: Harper & Brothers Publishers.

—— (1953) *The Family in the American Economy*, Chicago, IL: University of Chicago Press.

Lancaster, Kelvin J. (1966) "A New Approach to Consumer Theory," *Journal of Political Economy* 74(2): 132–57.

Lobdell, Richard A. (2000) "Hazel Kyrk," in Robert W. Dimand, Mary Ann Dimand, and Evelyn L. Forget (eds.) *A Biographical Dictionary of Women Economists*, Cheltenham: Edwin Elgar.

Matthews, Glenda (1987) *"Just a Housewife": The Rise and Fall of Domesticity in America*, Oxford: Oxford University Press.

Mitchell, Wesley C. (1912) "The Backward Art of Spending Money," *American Economic Review* 2: 269–81.

Monroe, Day (1932) *Chicago Families: A Study of Unpublished Census Data*, Chicago, IL: University of Chicago Press.

Muth, Richard F. (1966) "Household Production and Consumer Demand Functions," *Econometrica* 34(3): 699–708.

Nelson, Elizabeth (1980) "Hazel Kyrk," in Barbara Sicherman and Carol Hurd Green, with Irene Kantrov and Harriette Walker, *Notable American Women: The Modern Period. A Biographical Dictionary*, Cambridge, MA: Belknap Press of Harvard University Press.

Nussbaum, Martha C. (2000) *Women and Human Development: The Capabilities Approach*, Cambridge: Cambridge University Press.

Reder, Melvin W. (1982) "Chicago Economics, Permanence and Change," *Journal of Economic Literature* 20: 1–38.

Reid, Margaret G. (1934) *The Economics of Household Production*, New York: John Wiley & Sons.

—— (1972) "Miss Hazel Kyrk," in Marie Dye (ed.) History of the Department of Home Economics, University of Chicago (Chicago: University of Chicago Alumni Association, 1972). Typescript in the Archives of the Department of Special Collections, Joseph Regenstein Library, University of Chicago.

Rossiter, Margaret W. (1982) *Women Scientists in America: Struggles and Strategies to 1940*, Baltimore, MD: Johns Hopkins Press.

Stage, Sarah (1997) "Ellen Richards and the Social Significance of the Home Economics Movement," in Sarah Stage and Virginia B. Vincenti (eds.) *Rethinking Home Economics: Women and the History of a Profession*, Ithaca, NY: Cornell University Press.

Stage, Sarah and Virginia B. Vincenti (eds.) (1997) *Rethinking Home Economics: Women and the History of a Profession*, Ithaca, NY: Cornell University Press.

Thorne, Alison Comish (1995) "Women Mentoring in Economics in the 1930s," in Mary Ann Dimand, Robert W. Dimand and Evelyn L. Forget, *Women of Value: Feminist Essays on the History of Women in Economics*, Aldershot: Edward Elgar.

van Velzen, Susan (2001) *Supplements to the Economics of Household Behavior*, Amsterdam: Thela Thesis.

Veblen, Thorstein (1899) *A Theory of the Leisure Class*, New York: Macmillan.

Welchman, Jennifer (1995) *Dewey's Ethical Thought*, Ithaca, NY: Cornell University Press.

Yi, Yun-Ae (1996) "Margaret G. Reid: Life and Achievements," *Feminist Economics* 2(3): 17–36.

4 Feminist fiction and feminist economics
Charlotte Perkins Gilman on efficiency[1]

Irene van Staveren

> [B]oth in life and in art the values of a woman are not the values of a man. Thus, when a woman comes to write a novel, she will find that she is perpetually wishing to alter the established values – to make serious what appears insignificant to a man, and trivial what is to him important.
>
> (Virginia Woolf 1998 [1958]: 51)

Introduction

This essay explores the extent to which a reading of feminist literary texts might contribute to feminist economic analysis. The exploration rests on the assumption, defended by various literary critics and economists (Nussbaum 1990, 1995; Gagnier 1991; Henderson 1995; Woodmansee and Osteen 1999), that fiction has epistemological value for the social sciences, including for the analysis of economic behavior.[2] Ulla Grapard and Gillian Hewitson demonstrated the significance of a feminist economic analysis of literary sources to economics (Grapard 1995; Hewitson 1999). Their work on the *Robinson Crusoe* story, a literary text widely referred to in economics, reveals the gendered dualisms and raced metaphors embedded in it. As a part of this emerging tradition, I will suggest some ways to use feminist literary texts as possible epistemological sources for feminist economics.[3]

The author to be focused on here is the American writer Charlotte Perkins Gilman (1860–1935). She published pamphlets and poems, studies in social sciences and novels, an autobiography, and many articles in magazines. Because of this diverse legacy, different groups of readers are familiar with different parts of her work. Among feminists she is known for her fiction, which examines women's position in American society around the turn of the past century, and also for her radical feminist and social ideas on social change. Feminist literary critics have discussed her literary work at great length (see, for example, Golden 1992; Hedges 1992; Gough and Rudd 1998), while feminist social scientists engaged with her non-fiction (see, for example, Hayden 1981; Karpinski 1992). Her impact was substantial. As one of her biographers puts it:

She offered a perspective on major issues of gender with which we still grapple: the origins of subjugation; the struggle to achieve both autonomy and intimacy in human relationships; the central role of work as a definition of self; new strategies for rearing and educating future generations to create a humane and nurturing environment.

(Lane 1990: 3–4)

While her book *Women and Economics*, published in 1898, was a bestseller and appreciated by a wide public, economists have paid only marginal attention to it (Pujol 1992). Grapard (2001) provides us with a persuasive explanation for its exclusion from the canon in economics. She argues that in addition to the more obvious reasons, such as the radical proposals for social change and Gilman's lack of academic training, the gender analysis behind her evolutionary theory did not fit with the core assumptions of economic theory at the turn of the nineteenth century. Gilman rejected the assumptions that women are naturally confined to the domestic sphere, and that this sphere has no economic value and is instead the site of moral values defined as feminine. It is, however, Gilman's economic analysis of this feminized domestic sphere, its economic benefits as well as the limitations it brings for women's economic position, which is significant for feminist economic analysis today.

Several economists have indeed recognized the value of Gilman's work for today's analysis of women's economic position and wider economic issues. O'Donnell (1994), Sheth and Prasch (1996), and Grapard (2001) have discussed Gilman's analysis of the household and the gender division of labor, mainly focusing on *Women and Economics*. Dimand (1995) gives a broader overview of Gilman's contribution to economic thought, including a discussion of her views on the market and on externalities, and referring to a variety of Gilman's publications, fiction as well as non-fiction.

Another reason to choose Gilman for a discussion on feminist fiction and feminist economics is that she wrote and successfully published in both genres, and dealt with similar issues across these genres. In a comparative analysis of the styles of Charlotte Gilman and Thorstein Veblen, Margaret Lewis and David Sebberson (1997) note the absence of a strict demarcation between a factional style in the one genre and a literary style in the other, and point out that the literary rhetorical strategy which Gilman employs in her economic books contributes to the significance of her economic writings. They argue for both Veblen and Gilman that "the very rhetoricality of Gilman's and Veblen's work is actually constitutive of their theories and the ways in which they theorize economics: it is their rhetorical sensibilities that create their understanding of economics, not stand in the way of them" (Lewis and Sebberson 1997: 418).

The choice to discuss Charlotte Gilman here may not be very surprising, given the themes, variety, and style of her writings. The choice for a particular concept to be discussed in both genres might not be difficult either, at first sight: the household, the gender division of labor, women's economic position, these are all subjects discussed at great length by others who have analyzed either Gilman's economic work or her literary texts, or both. For this paper on feminist economic methodology, I structure my discussion of her work around a core economic idea, economic efficiency. Of course, I am well aware of the fact that Gilman did not use the concept of efficiency as economists do today. But reading her economic works one notes a concern with issues and arguments that are clearly related to a broader view of efficiency, such as a full use of one's human capabilities for men and women alike. She demonstrates a rich understanding of efficiency, which goes beyond the idea of the optimal use of resources through markets. Instead, Gilman seems to understand efficiency in terms of self-realization in life, including one's capacity for affection and cooperation. O'Donnell (1994), Dimand (1995), and Grapard (2001) have also noted Gilman's holistic view of efficiency, in particular in relation to much of women's unpaid labor in the household, which Gilman considered as inefficient: "The home is marked by inefficiency, waste and sometimes damaging child rearing practices because it forces all women, irrespective of interest and talent, to focus exclusively on their prescribed tasks as wives and mothers" (Grapard 2001: 270).

On the other hand, she also argues that labor undertaken for intrinsic motivations such as love and duty can be more efficient. In this essay I show how a reading of both her economic texts and her literary texts sheds light on this seeming contradiction in Gilman's holistic view of efficiency.

Feminist economic views on efficiency

Before I go to Gilman's texts for a reading of her ideas on efficiency, it may be useful first briefly to outline current feminist concerns with the concept. These concerns start with a critique of the standard notion of efficiency in welfare economics, as Pareto optimality. Vilfredo Pareto (1848–1923) was a contemporary of Gilman and was the creator of the definition of efficiency that is still dominant today. His definition claims to be a purely technical device to calculate the welfare optimum of an economy in terms of production. In this definition, the allocation of resources in the economy is such that no one can be made better off without someone else being made worse off. This optimum level of gross domestic product (GDP) is understood to reflect the maximum possible level of output with given resources, generated by perfectly competitive factor markets and product markets.

In the 1930s and 1940s Margaret Reid, an economist,[4] showed her disappointment with the characterization of efficiency as maximum production, calling it "a very meagre goal" (Reid 1943: 7). She pointed to the imperfections of real markets as well as inequalities that may create distributive inefficiencies. In fact, Reid proposed an alternative, and much more intuitive, definition of efficiency as the minimization of waste, a definition that built on the concerns of her teacher, Hazel Kyrk.[5] This can include waste of productive resources, as well as waste in production processes and distributive waste (for example through demerit goods or a very unequal distribution of consumption). Reid thus recognized that Pareto optimality is not a value-neutral concept. As Drucilla Barker has shown, the value-ladenness of efficiency has only become more concealed over time (Barker 1995). Moreover, she argues that the hidden values in the dominant efficiency concept have crucial gender dimensions. First, the concept excludes unpaid production from its calculations, which is largely unpaid caring labor carried out by women. Second, it assumes a masculine stereotype image of autonomous agents, who do not take one another's wellbeing into account insofar as this does not add to their own utility, and whose utility cannot be compared and hence cannot be traded off for the sake of more equity and/or more efficiency. This leads her to ask an important question about efficiency: "efficient for whom?" (Barker 1995: 36).

In the new home economics, associated with Gary Becker,[6] efficiency is an important concept and is tied to the idea of perfectly functioning markets. In a household bargaining model exercise, Braunstein and Folbre (2001) challenge the position put forward in home economics that the gender division of labour in which men specialize in the labor market, where male wages are higher than female wages, and women specialize in housework is necessarily efficient. They show that gender biases create hierarchies, which can lead over time to inefficiencies in household production, resulting in a loss of production. They conclude that "[s]tatic efficiencies, such as the sexual division of labor, may give rise to dynamic inefficiencies, as when patriarchal property rights constrain changes in that division by conferring power in the household" (Braunstein and Folbre 2001: 40). A similar result is obtained by Darity (1995) in a model of an agriculturally based economy in sub-Saharan Africa in which the gender division of labor assigns women to the unpaid production of food for the family and men to the production of marketable crops for cash earnings. Men's cash-crop production depends partly on labor input by women. But if women are not allowed to share in the earnings that men receive from the sales of these cash crops they may well decide to withdraw their labor from men's land, which will lead to a waste of resources, and hence an inefficiency.

Since in practice the received notion of efficiency relies exclusively on measuring market production and ignores unpaid production, it denies a trade-off between the market economy on the one hand and the unpaid care economy on the other hand. As Elson (1995) argues, women produce human resources at home which have value for the labor market but also beyond the labor market. Moreover, she argues that a so-called efficiency gain in the market, by downsizing services such as healthcare, shifts healthcare burdens to the care economy, without the benefits of economies of scale and professionally trained staff, most probably resulting in an inefficiency for the economy as a whole.

In an attempt to redress such problems, Nelson (1996) has proposed an alternative way to evaluate economies based on the notion of provisioning. She argues that economics should be concerned with how humans try to meet their needs for goods and services: "Economic provisioning and the sustenance of life becomes the centre of study, whether it be through market, household, or government action, or whether it be by symmetric exchange, coercion, or gift" (Nelson 1996: 36). This harks back to Reid (1943), who noted that nonmarket production does not need to be less efficient than market production, as she demonstrated for the case of subsistence agriculture in the US. Following up on Reid, Elson, and Nelson, I have elsewhere proposed the notion of "meaningful efficiency" as an endogenous balance in production that reduces waste in the market, by the state, and in the care economy (van Staveren 2001: 166). The balance is a contextual one, depending on trade-offs (substitution) and positive externalities (complementarity) between these three domains of production.

In conclusion of this section, it becomes possible to distinguish two major feminist concerns with efficiency: efficiency as beyond maximum market production but concerned with waste, and efficiency of nonmarket production. Below, the discussion of Gilman's work will follow these two concerns.

Efficiency as the minimization of waste

In *Women and Economics*, as well as in a less known but equally interesting text about women's economic position, *The Home* (published in 1903), Gilman assesses the gender division of labor in the household as a social construct arising from society's ideas on proper roles for men and women. This social construct relies on biological stereotypes of male and female roles, she notes, and not on the actual and far more equal division of labor between males and females that can be found in other species. Compared to these species, human beings waste talents and skills by assigning each sex to a strictly demarcated sphere of life. In *Women and Economics* Gilman's rhetorical question makes it clear that mothers have far more capabilities than they need for motherhood: "Does the human mother, by her motherhood, thereby lose control of brain and body, lose power and skill and desire for any other work?" (Gilman 1920: 19). Nevertheless, she states, women are kept from the labor market, which is deprived of women's contribution – in fact, a waste of human resources: "When women stand free as economic agents, they will lift and free their arrested functions, to the much better fulfillment of their duties as wives and mothers and to the vast improvement in health and happiness of the human race" (*ibid.*: 241). On the other hand, Gilman notes that the lack of proper education for women reduces their efficiency as housewives. As Grapard notes, Gilman recognizes the costs implied in this waste, costs like endangering the health of the family when women with only limited education are made responsible for important household consumer decisions and home production (Grapard 2001: 276). Moreover, as

Gilman notes in *The Home*, domestic labor is very time consuming, leaving women with no time for work outside the household, even limiting the time that mothers spend with their children (Gilman 1972: 95–7). This observation points to her analysis of the method of household production as being far from efficient.

Another source of inefficiency is that domestic labor tends to take up much more time than comparable work in the labor market. Gilman contrasts the production method of women in domestic work with that of men in industrial labor, noting that "she toils on forever in the same primitive industries. He…splits his task into a thousand specialties, and invents countless ways to lighten his labors" (Gilman 1920: 132). Dimand notes another example of this contrast in Gilman's magazine *The Forerunner* (Dimand 1995). In this example Mary, a young widow with a child, runs a profitable boarding house. One of her tenants is Jane, who after a few years tells Mary that she loves her and wants to live together with her and support her. Thereupon Mary stops running her boarding house and only keeps house for the apartment she shares with Jane and her child, while Jane has to work longer hours to support not only herself but also Mary and her child. The result is inefficient, as Gilman explains, because the housekeeping in the building no longer has economies of scale, nor does it earn an income, and the income earned by Jane is less than the two incomes Mary and Jane earned before. As Sheth and Prasch have observed, Gilman's solution to the inefficiencies of women's household production lies in professionalizing and socializing this production into "institutions requiring specialized domestic labor such as communal kitchens and day-care centers, [which] would be accessible at an enhanced quality to all citizens and all children" (Sheth and Prasch 1996: 330). In the case of childcare, Gilman asks: "Cannot the mother love it while the nurse takes care of it?" (Gilman 1972: 340). And for the preparation of dairy products or in cooking, for example, she suggests in *The Home* setting up community cooperations (*ibid.*: 110). Such arrangements outside individual households will enable gains from specialization by professionals, as well as economies of scale.

In *Women and Economics* and *The Home*, Gilman regards the gender division of labor in the household as a double source of waste: a waste of human resources, limiting allocative efficiency, as well as a waste of time through the "primitive" production method in households. This characterization of inefficiency as waste goes beyond the strictly economic meaning, since Gilman not only points to a loss in market production and in the low quality of household production, but also emphasizes women's loss of self-realization. It is in her literary work, however, she furthers our understanding of this holistic view of inefficiency as waste, in particular in a short story published in 1899, *The Yellow Wallpaper*. This well-known short story can be understood on a variety of levels. For the purposes of this essay I confine my discussion to its economic implications.

The Yellow Wallpaper introduces a young couple with a baby renting a house during the summer holidays. The woman is suffering from depression and her husband is a physician – he advises her to rest. Throughout the holiday John forbids his wife to do anything, providing a nurse for the baby. Charlotte Gilman herself had no positive experiences with this rest cure, nor had some other patients who did not accept the Victorian ideals for women of the time.[7] The wife feels that the rest cure is not of much help. She would rather like to work, to spend her energy outside the house, to do something productive: "Personally, I believe that congenial work, with excitement and change, would do me good" (Gilman 1995: 3). This gives a more personal meaning to what Gilman expressed in her economic texts about the limitations of being a housewife: "The housewife does not bring out our humanness, for all the distinctive lines of human progress lie outside" (Gilman 1972: 217). It seems that restricting the woman to the house does not help her to feel better – the story indicates that it even makes her suffer: "John does not know how much I really suffer. He knows there is no reason to suffer, and that satisfies him" (Gilman 1995: 6).

In her economic texts Gilman suggests that not only do women lack humanness by being excluded from the labor market, but also men lack humanness by being excluded from caring in the home: "Pride, cruelty, and selfishness are the vices of the master" (Gilman 1920: 338). In the story, John, the husband, completely relies on his formal medical knowledge and ignores the subtle signals of his wife's illness as these do not fit with his view. His pride, in the end, helps to lead to the wife's cruel fate, which begins with her visions at night in the pattern of the wallpaper. She distinguishes a female figure in it, trying to get out: "The front pattern does move – and no wonder! The woman behind shakes it!" (Gilman 1995: 15).

At the end of the story she helps the woman to keep her freedom, from the patterned wallpaper. She tears the paper from the walls and happily creeps over the floor, satisfied with the thought that she has helped to release the woman from behind the bars. But the end is tragic as well, since the protagonist has slid from a postpartum depression into a serious state of psychic disorder.

The rest cure in *The Yellow Wallpaper* might be understood as a metaphor for women's confinement to the home, as criticized so forcefully by Gilman in her economic texts. The metaphor shows not only that the gender division of labour implies a waste of human resources for the labor market and in household production (the wife was not allowed to go out and work and they needed to hire a nurse for the baby), but that it is also detrimental to women's self-realization. Victorian gender roles, when carried to their logical conclusion, create suffering, a loss of self, and, in the end, a loss of humanness for women. Thus, Gilman shows the ethical meaning of the characterization of inefficiency as waste. In *The Yellow Wallpaper* the waste caused by the rest cure is not ethically neutral, but a vice rather than a virtue as held in Victorian ideology on women's proper roles. The inefficiency is not just a technically sub-optimal level of production, but extremely harmful for women's mental and physical wellbeing.

Efficiency of nonmarket production

For Gilman, the household is not only a site of consumption, but of economic production as well, an insight later elaborated on by both Reid and Becker. In *The Home*, Gilman characterizes the household as an economic as well as a familial institution, producing goods and services leading to "genuine economic value" (Gilman 1920: 13). In *Women and Economics* and in *The Home*, Gilman characterizes efficiency as resulting from a combination of subsistence production and market production, rather than from market production alone. Contrary to market production, Gilman notes that the incentives for household production are found in "duty, love, and necessity" (Gilman 1972: 104), in particular duty (Gilman 1920: 14–15), motives that she regards as stronger than the motive for income earning. Duty demands an effort based on some principle that one is expected to obey – freely or under coercion. Love, an intrinsic motive behind unpaid household labor and childcare, is again different from self-interest, but also different from duty (van Staveren 2001; also Folbre and Hartmann 1988). Love does not seek to maximize individual satisfaction; nor does it follow (with or without coercion) an agreed principle – love cannot be ordered. The love which urges one to undertake unpaid household work and childcare is a very personal incentive that stems from responsibility, affection, and personal commitment to those to whom the love is given. Gilman notes that together duty, love, and necessity – the homebound incentives of women's household production – result in high labor productivity: "So the housewife struggles on, too busy to complain; and accomplishes, under this threefold bond of duty, love, and necessity far more than can be expected of a comparatively free agent" (Gilman 1972: 104). It is in the productivity resulting from these motives, Gilman suggests, that household production is efficient. The intrinsic motivation results in low transaction costs: there is no shirking, and no time and money is wasted on sales or negotiation. Moreover, the intrinsic motivation of household production also leads to what Reid later distinguished as distributive efficiency, since it leads to the supply of goods and services that neatly match household members' needs, in particular needs that markets cannot fulfill, such as needs for love, comfort, and bonding. Gilman recognizes the process behind the distributive efficiency of household production: "The wife and mother…constantly ministers to the physical needs of her family with ceaseless and concentrated intensity" (Gilman 1920: 120).

Gilman's insight into the particular qualities of household production originating from intrinsic motivation rather than from money incentives is an attractive argument for considering nonmarket production as more efficient than is assumed in Pareto optimality, which solely depends on market production. Various economists today have also discovered the economic benefits of intrinsic motivation, notably Frey (1997). However, Gilman's argument on the efficiency of household production seems to contradict her view as discussed in the previous section, and of household production as a *waste* of human resources, time, and quality. This paradox is not resolved in her economic texts.

At this point, therefore, I propose to shift our focus to Gilman's literary imagination on nonmarket production. We find this in *Herland*, a utopian novel published in 1915.

Herland takes Gilman's critique of Victorian gender roles further, envisaging a completely different life for women, in an imagined country without men. In *Herland* three American men discover a country where, as the story goes, only women live.[8] Terry is sure that "we mustn't look for inventions and progress; it'll be awfully primitive" (Gilman 1979: 8). When they noticed the high quality of the roads, with hard manufactured layers and perfect gutters, Terry sneered: "No men, eh?" (*ibid.*: 18). But their fantasy about natural male superiority did not last for long. They were captured and provided with a private interpreter/teacher. Gradually, the men learned about the highly developed economy of Herland, and were surprised to find neither competition nor even markets. They could not understand how the Herland economy could function as well as it did without competition:

> We rather spread ourselves, telling of the advantages of competition: how it developed fine qualities; that without it there would be "no stimulus to industry." Terry was very strong on that point.
>
> "No stimulus to industry," they repeated, with that puzzled look we had learned to know so well. "*Stimulus? To industry?* But don't you *like* to work?"
>
> "No man would work unless he had to," Terry declared.
>
> "Oh, no *man*! You mean that is one of your sex distinctions?"
>
> "No, indeed!" he said hastily. "No one, I mean, man or woman, would work without incentive. Competition is the – the motor power, you see."
>
> "It is not with us," they explained gently, "so it is hard for us to understand. Do you mean, for instance, that with you no mother would work for her children without the stimulus of competition?"
>
> No, he admitted that he did not mean that. Mothers, he supposed, would of course work for their children in the home; but the world's work was different – that had to be done by men, and required the competitive element.
>
> (Gilman 1979: 60)

No such distinction existed in Herland. Instead, in the Herland economy work is considered an integral part of life and its citizens appear to thrive on a "conscious effort to make it better" (*ibid.*: 76), an effort that appears pleasurable in itself: "We have pride enough in our work" (*ibid.*: 76). In other words, in the Herland economy work is not a disutility, as it is depicted in the men's world's economics or in the work/leisure trade-off integral to contemporary interpretations of economic efficiency. Herlanders recognize the value of work in itself, and appear intrinsically motivated, as Gilman had argued in her economic work about the motives women have for their caring labor in households. But in Herland there is no individual household production, nor a gender division of labor between housework and market work. Herland is populated with women only, and the economy is not structured as a dichotomy between market and home, but as a well-functioning arrangement of community production. Herlanders think in terms of their community, not in terms of individual benefit, and carry out production cooperatively, in groups of women, each specialized in a few tasks.

This system of production appears to hold a middle ground between household production, on the one hand, and market production, on the other hand, since it combines intrinsic motivation in a community of people with the benefits of professional education, specialization of tasks, and economies of scale. Specialization is also applied, for example, in childcare, and its high quality is happily accepted by mothers: "For the child's sake, she is glad to have for it this highest care" (*ibid.*: 83). But the Herlanders are aware of the risks of over-specialization. Children are educated in more than one profession, since too much specialization limits the benefits of education, is their conviction: "When one settles too close in one kind of work there is a tendency to atrophy in the disused portions of the brain. We like to keep on learning, always" (*ibid.*: 105). And by sharing knowledge widely throughout their community, through a system of lifelong learning, it costs "no waste of time or strength" (*ibid.*: 105).

The novel *Herland* seems to solve the paradox found in Gilman's economic texts. The novel shows how nonmarket production can be efficient when it is carried out outside individual households and without the artificial construct of a gender division of labor between household and market production. Where production is organized in community-based cooperatives, reaping economies of scale and employing professionally trained labor for a variety of specialized tasks, and relying on the intrinsic motivation of workers, there is no longer a trade-off between the efficiency of market production and inefficiency of home production. The meaning and the organization of nonmarket production are very different from how we know them in our economy, and, as Gilman tries to show in her novel, result in higher levels of wellbeing. The novel not only illustrates Gilman's ideas in her economic texts on the value of nonmarket production, but effectively makes the case for a holistic understanding of efficiency. The Herland economy exhibits both allocative efficiency through specialization and economies of scale, and distributive efficiency through intrinsic motivation rather than the profit motive, ensuring that what is wanted and needed is what is produced. Moreover, the Herland economy expresses dynamic efficiency to a much larger extent than market economies, since the diversification of production reduces uncertainty and risk, and the high levels of trust and responsibility among producers and consumers reduce the occurrence of economic crises while limiting the incidence of negative externalities such as pollution.

Reading across feminist genres

My readings of *The Yellow Wallpaper* and *Herland* as samples of Gilman's literary texts can contribute to a feminist understanding of efficiency. *The Yellow Wallpaper* makes clear that efficiency is not a morally neutral concept: waste of human resources does not only lead to sub-optimal levels of production but may in the end lead to a loss of humanness. While *Herland* shows that nonmarket production may be more efficient than market production when it is *not* located in households and *not* organized through a gender division of labor, Gilman's literary texts make clear that efficiency and equity should no longer be understood as trade-offs as in Pareto optimality, but as positively related: the more equity, the more efficiency, and, conversely, the less equity, the less efficiency. In *The Yellow Wallpaper*, gender inequality in the household, expressed by the metaphor of the rest cure, eventually leads to the waste of a human life, whereas in *Herland* the lack of gender inequality and the absence of a dichotomy between the market and the household lead to static and dynamic efficiency gains.

How is it that feminist literary imagination contributes to feminist economic analysis? Why can we not find it all just in the economic texts? Why might we want to read feminist literature? Well, I think that without *The Yellow Wallpaper* and *Herland* feminist economic analyses of Gilman's ideas on the gender division of labor and nonmarket production would have paid less attention to the ethical meaning of efficiency and to the various efficiency gains inherent in the community-based cooperative production proposed by Gilman. In other words, it is the reading of Gilman's literary texts that fruitfully demonstrates her holistic view of efficiency. To paraphrase Woolf's assessment on women's values as compared to men's values, quoted at the start of the chapter, Gilman's fiction makes serious what appears insignificant to Pareto optimality, and trivial what is to it important. That is, she showed that efficiency is not about maximum market production but about the ethically relevant notion of waste in all spheres of production, market and nonmarket ones. Her literary works have shown this through the rich context they provide, expressed in thick descriptions of persons, situations, and events. As Nussbaum (1995: 64) has argued about the epistemological value of reading literature, literary imagination reveals actors' emotions and motivations behind courses of action. It also brings in a community's social, cultural, and political values, showing how these guide and constrain behavior, and draws the reader's attention to the vulnerability of human life, showing how uncertainty impacts upon people's behavior.

Hence, the added value of fiction to economics lies in these three characteristics. The value of literary imagination seems even more important for *feminist* economic analysis, given the fact that feminist economists challenge the standard notion of economic motivation embodied in the idea of rational economic man, the assumption of the value neutrality of core economic concepts, and the assumption of perfect markets with perfect foresight. In conclusion, feminist literary imagination enables feminist economists to engage with the meaning of economic analysis deriving from the specific context in which a particular economic phenomenon, activity, or concept is situated.

Notes

1   The author would like to express her gratitude to the editors of this volume for their patience and continuous support, without which this paper would not have materialized.
2   At the same time, economists are discovering literary techniques for economic analysis. They have introduced methods of literary analysis such as a concern with language, metaphor, stories, and historical narratives (McCloskey 1985; Klamer *et al.* 1988; Lavoie 1990; Henderson *et al.* 1993; Brown 1994; Henderson 1995).
3   I am aware of the many pitfalls inherent in such an attempt. As the editors of an important volume on the intersections between literature and economics conclude about such interdisciplinary research, it is not at all easy to find the right balance between the two disciplinary sides (Woodmansee and Osteen 1999). This essay is clearly the work of an economist.
4   For an overview of Reid's work and influence, see a special issue of *Feminist Economics* dedicated to her (vol. 2, no. 3, 1996).
5   See Chapter 3 for a discussion of Hazel Kyrk's concept of waste.
6   See, for example, Becker (1981). For feminist critiques and evaluations, see, for example, Ferber and Greene (1983), Folbre (1996), Agarwal (1997), and Woolley (1996).
7   As Golden explains: "Although Mitchell's Rest Cure was in accordance with the most advanced neurological thinking of his day, in modern eyes it can be read as an attempt to reorient women to the domestic sphere (and away from influences of their changing world) so that they could fulfill their most important role in society: to bear and rear children" (Golden 1992: 146).
8   It should be noted that Gilman explicitly points out that they are of European origin. Her progressive attitude toward gender does not, unfortunately, extend to race and ethnicity.

Bibliography

Agarwal, Bina (1997) " 'Bargaining' and Gender Relations: Within and Beyond the Household," *Feminist Economics* 3(1): 1–51.

Barker, Drucilla K. (1995) "Economists, Social Reformers, and Prophets: A Feminist Critique of Economic Efficiency," *Feminist Economics* 1(3): 26–39.

Becker, Gary (1981) *A Treatise on the Family,* Cambridge, MA: Harvard University Press.

Braunstein, Elissa and Nancy Folbre (2001) "To Honor and Obey: Efficiency, Inequality, and Patriarchal Property Rights," *Feminist Economics* 7(1): 25–44.

Brown, Vivienne (1994) "The Economy as Text," in Roger Backhouse (ed.) *New Directions in Economic Methodology*, London: Routledge.

Darity, William (1995) "The Formal Structure of a Gender-Segregated Low-Income Economy," *World Development* 23(11): 1,963–8.

Dimand, Mary-Ann (1995) "The Economics of Charlotte Perkins Gilman," in Mary-Ann Dimand, Robert Dimand and Evelyn Forget (eds.) *Women of Value: Feminist Essays on the History of Women in Economics*, Aldershot: Edward Elgar.

Elson, Diane (ed.) (1995) *Male Bias in the Development Process*, 2nd edn., Manchester: Manchester University Press.

Ferber, Marianne and Carole Greene (1983) "Housework vs. Marketwork: Some Evidence How the Decision Is Made," *Review of Income and Wealth* 29(2): 147–59.

Folbre, Nancy (ed.) (1996) *The Economics of the Family*, Elgar Reference Collection, International Library of Critical Writings in Economics, vol. 64, Cheltenham: Edward Elgar.

Folbre, Nancy and Heidi Hartmann (1988) "The Rhetoric of Self-Interest: Ideology and Gender in Economic Theory," in Arjo Klamer, Deirdre McCloskey and Robert Solow (eds.) *The Consequences of Economic Rhetoric*, Cambridge: Cambridge University Press.

Frey, Bruno (1997) *Not Just for the Money: An Economic Theory of Personal Motivation*, Cheltenham: Edward Elgar.

Gagnier, Regenia (1991) *Subjectivities: A History of Self-Representation in Britain 1832–1920*, Oxford: Oxford University Press.

Gilman, Charlotte Perkins (1920) *Women and Economics. A Study of the Economic Relation between Men and Women as a Factor in Social Evolution*, 9th edn., London: Putnam's Sons; first published in 1898.

—— (1972) *The Home: Its Work and Influence*, Urbana, IL: University of Illinois Press; first published in 1903.

—— (1979) *Herland*, with an introduction by Ann Lane, New York: Pantheon Books; first published in 1915.

—— (1995) *The Yellow Wallpaper and Other Stories*, edited by Robert Shulman, Oxford: Oxford University Press; first published in 1899.

Golden, Catherine (1992) "'Overwriting' the Rest Cure: Charlotte Perkins Gilman's Literary Escape from S. Weir Mitchell's Fictionalisation of Women," in Joanne Karpinski (ed.) *Critical Essays on Charlotte Perkins Gilman*, New York: Prentice-Hall.

Gough, Val and Jill Rudd (1998) *A Very Different Story: Essays on the Fiction of Charlotte Perkins Gilman*, Liverpool: Liverpool University Press.

Grapard, Ulla (1995) "Robinson Crusoe: The Quintessential Economic Man?," *Feminist Economics* 1(1): 33–52.

—— (2001) "The Trouble with Women and Economics: A Postmodern Perspective on Charlotte Perkins Gilman," in Stephen Cullenberg, Jack Amariglio, and David Ruccio (eds.) *Postmodernism, Economics and Knowledge*, London: Routledge.

Hayden, Dolores (1981) *The Grand Domestic Revolution: A History of Feminist Designs for American Homes, Neighborhoods, and Cities*, Cambridge, MA: MIT Press.

Hedges, Elaine (1992) "'Out at Last?' 'The Yellow Wallpaper' After Two Decades of Feminist Criticism," in Joanne Karpinski (ed.) *Critical Essays on Charlotte Perkins Gilman*, New York: Prentice-Hall.

Henderson, Willy (1995) *Economics as Literature*, London: Routledge.

Henderson, Willy, Tony Dudley-Evans and Roger Backhouse (1993) *Economics and Language*, London: Routledge.

Hewitson, Gillian (1999) *Feminist Economics: Interrogating the Masculinity of Rational Economic Man*, Cheltenham: Edward Elgar.

Karpinski, Joanne (ed.) (1992) *Critical Essays on Charlotte Perkins Gilman*, New York: Prentice-Hall.

Klamer, Arjo, Deirdre McCloskey and Robert Solow (eds.) (1988) *The Consequences of Economic Rhetoric*, Cambridge: Cambridge University Press.

Lane, Ann (1990) *To Herland and Beyond. The Life and Work of Charlotte Perkins Gilman*, Charlottesville, VA: University Press of Virginia.

Lavoie, Don (1990) *Economics and Hermeneutics*, London: Routledge.

Lewis, Margaret and David Sebberson (1997) "The Rhetoricality of Economic Theory: Charlotte Perkins Gilman and Thorstein Veblen," *Journal of Economic Issues* 31(2): 417–24.

McCloskey, Deirdre (1985) *The Rhetoric of Economics*, Madison, WI: University of Wisconsin Press.

Nelson, Julie (1996) *Feminism, Objectivity and Economics*, London: Routledge.

Nussbaum, Martha (1990) *Love's Knowledge: Essays on Philosophy and Literature*, Oxford: Oxford University Press.

—— (1995) *Poetic Justice: The Literary Imagination and Public Life*, Boston, MA: Beacon Press.

O'Donnell, Margaret (1994) "Early Analysis of the Economics of Family Structure: Charlotte Perkins Gilman's Women and Economics," *Review of Social Economy* 52(2): 86–95.

Pujol, Michèle (1992) *Feminism and Anti-Feminism in Early Economic Thought*, Aldershot: Edward Elgar.

Reid, Margaret (1943) *Food for People*, New York and London: Wiley and Chapman & Hall.

Shell, Marc (1978) *The Economy of Literature*, Baltimore, MD: John Hopkins University Press.

Sheth, Falguni and Robert Prasch (1996) "Charlotte Perkins Gilman: Reassessing Her Significance for Feminism and Social Economics," *Review of Social Economy* 54(3): 323–35.

van Staveren, Irene (2001) *The Values of Economics: An Aristotelian Perspective*, London: Routledge.

Woodmansee, Martha and Mark Osteen (1999) *The New Economic Criticism*, London: Routledge.

Woolf, Virginia 1998 [1958] "Women and Fiction," in Deborah Cameron (ed.) *The Feminist Critique of Language: A Reader*, London: Routledge. Reprinted from Virginia Woolf, *Collected Essays*, Vol. II. London: Hogarth Press, 1966.

Woolley, Frances (1996) "Getting the Better of Becker," *Feminist Economics* 2(1): 114–20.

5 Beyond markets

Wage setting and the methodology of feminist political economy

Marilyn Power, Ellen Mutari, and Deborah M. Figart

Understanding gender wage inequality is obviously of great importance to feminists. Feminist political economists can build on past economic theorizing, but need to break new ground to achieve sufficient complexity and depth of analysis. Much existing economic wage theory is overly simplistic, ahistorical, and deterministic. Wage setting, though, is a deeply political and cultural, as well as economic, process. As such, the process of wage setting is something that must be studied at the meso (organizational, institutional) and macro levels as well as the micro.

By recognizing that wages serve multiple functions and contain multiple meanings, we can better grasp the complexity of wage-setting processes. Specifically, wage bargains are affected by culturally and historically specific notions of fairness. These interpretations of fairness are gendered, as for example the dominant belief in many different cultural contexts for much of the twentieth century that men deserved to earn a family wage, while women needed, at most, to support only themselves (see Kessler-Harris 1990; Agarwal 1997). Further, women's primary responsibility for social reproduction has been almost entirely privatized, making it difficult for them to compete on equal terms in the labor force. This organization of paid and unpaid labor, often referred to as the male breadwinner family, is a social construction, rather than the manifestation of ahistoric individual preferences or comparative advantage. A feminist approach to political economy is attentive to the way meso/social institutions, including the organization of families, have contributed to wage setting and thus to the gender-based wage gap.

A feminist political economy approach to wage setting must address both the mechanisms of wage setting and the relation of wages to well-being on a societal (or macro) level.[1] Feminists view theoretical work as aiding in the construction of an egalitarian economic system in which human well-being and social provisioning are central priorities. Feminist theorizing thus does not shy away from value judgments. In Lourdes Benería's words, feminist political economy advocates "people-centered development" (Benería 1999: 77), in which markets are subordinated to the goals of true democracy. As Benería describes this endeavor, it "implies placing issues of distribution, inequality, ethics, the environment, and the nature of individual happiness, collective well-being, and social change at the center of our agendas" (*ibid.*: 77). Similarly, Amartya Sen (1999) interprets development as the process of increasing human capabilities, defined as the achievement of individual freedom. Freedom, for Sen, means the availability of good choices one can really make. Adequate income is necessary – although not sufficient – for the achievement of human freedom so described. Wage labor is a key means of attaining such income. Nevertheless, evaluations of well-being must take into account non-waged as well as waged labor, and interrogate differences in well-being by gender, class, race, age, and other factors.

In our study of key legislative struggles over wages in the twentieth century United States (Figart *et al.* 2002), we attempted to convey the complex and historically situated process of wage setting through an examination of the wage theories expressed by the central actors in the debates. We found that the academics, social reformers, and politicians involved in policy debates have held a range of assumptions about the process of wage setting in general and, in particular, of what constitutes a fair wage for women and men. Their different understandings of fair wages become articulated as these groups participate in specific negotiations and struggles over wages. We categorize these implicit wage theories as *wages as a living*, *wages as a price*, and *wages as a social practice*. These three views of wage setting contain within them assumptions about the economic and social functions that wages play within a market economy. The outcome of any specific policy debate (over, for example, minimum wages for women or the definition of equal work) can be seen as reflecting the relative success and interpretation of each of these three faces of wages.

In what follows we will provide a brief examination of the theoretical bases for wages as a living, a price, and a social practice. We will then provide an illustration of the interaction among these three implicit wage theories in the debate over minimum wages for women in the United States in the early twentieth century. We will end by suggesting that this complex and non-deterministic view of wages can provide feminist political economists with a deeper and more historically rooted strategy for confronting the problem of wage inequality.

Wages as a living: lessons from classical political economy

We will begin our discussion of the three faces of wages with wages as a living, because it was chronologically the earliest of the three theoretical views. From the writings of Adam Smith until the mid-twentieth century, economic theorists frequently employed institutional and cultural analyses (as, of course, institutional economists continue to do), and considered community well-being a valid subject for economic interrogation. Many heterodox economic theorists, as well as political activists advocating wage regulations, have continued this tradition. This living-wage approach is consistent with the feminist understanding of economics as the process of provisioning, or, as we prefer, social provisioning (Jennings 1993; Nelson 1993; Power 2001). While "provisioning" could be understood as the individual (or family) project of getting a living, *social* provisioning reflects the interdependent nature of human survival. It is a set of social activities, rather than individual choices, the ways a society organizes itself to produce and reproduce material life.[2]

Theories based on what we term wages as a living were common among classical economists, who used the concept in both an analytic and a normative sense. The basis of wages is the production and reproduction of the working class through the provision of sufficient income to ensure their survival both individually and over generations. Adam Smith (1937), for example, in his chapter "On Wages," provided a rich and complex story of wage setting involving market forces and active class struggle between workers and employers. But subsistence, Smith argued, was necessarily the floor below which wages could not fall if the economic and social health of the nation were to continue. Without living wages, "it would be impossible for (the worker) to bring up a family, and the race of such workmen could not last beyond the first generation" (*ibid.*: 68). To this practical argument, Smith offered an ethical one:

> No society can surely be flourishing and happy, of which the far greater part of the members are poor and miserable. It is but equity, besides, that they who feed, cloath, and lodge the whole body of the people, should have such a share of the produce of their own labour as to themselves be tolerably well fed, cloathed, and lodged.
>
> (Smith 1937: 79)

Note that the subsistence wage in Smith's view was a family wage, sufficient for the working class in total to maintain its numbers over generations.

Karl Marx, in Volume I of *Capital*, also argued that wages had a basis in the subsistence of working-class families "in order that this race of peculiar commodity-owners may perpetuate its appearance in the market" (1967: 172).[3] While Smith sometimes identified the subsistence wage as socially determined and at times appeared to view it as a biological minimum, Marx was clear that wage setting was a social process. The exact amount considered sufficient to reproduce the workers' labor power over time would depend on the historically specific standard of living for the working class. Marx had little illusion about the tendency of employers to drive down the standard whenever possible. The relative bargaining power of different classes was therefore an important factor influencing wage levels.

The view of wages as a living is, of course, by no means confined to the writings of the classical economists. It has also served to animate social movements. A living wage was articulated as a goal of the U.S. labor movement and social reformers in the late nineteenth and early twentieth centuries (see Glickman 1997). The family wage was initially viewed as an "American Standard of Living" that was the prerogative of native-born white male workers. But contemporary living-wage movements expand the demand for living wages to other constituencies, including solo-mother families, ultimately challenging the priority placed on the male breadwinner family (Figart *et al.* 2002). The current living-wage movement in the United States has its political base in the strong and widespread public indignation that low-wage workers earn less than enough to support their families even for full-time work (Pollin and Luce 1998; Ciscel 2000; Figart *et al.* 2002: ch. 9). Basic needs budgets, developed by economists and reformers to illustrate the inadequacy of the current U.S. minimum wage, not only graphically demonstrate the shortfall, but provide a useful forum for discussion of what the minimum adequate standard of living should be (see for example, Renwick and Bergmann 1993; Ciscel 1999; Bernstein *et al.* 2000; Pearce and Brooks 2000). Contemporary living-wage advocates in the United States often define it as a gender-neutral family wage, sufficient to support family of three (Figart 2001). Others argue for a lower standard, supplemented by a larger social wage in the form of state-provided services and supplemental income (Himmelweit 1995; McLaughlin 1995; Ciscel 2000).

Wages as a price: valuing the work performed

While classical political economists recognized that markets played a role in wage setting, we have seen that they viewed subsistence as the central organizing principle for wages. Neoclassical economics, emerging in the late nineteenth century, made the market the primary – indeed, almost exclusive – basis of their wage theories. In explaining the wage gap between men and women, neoclassical economists stress the role of differences in human capital, especially those due to labor force attachment. Such analyses presume that wages are based upon productivity, and productivity is primarily the outcome of worker characteristics. The mechanism for assuring that wages reflect productivity is markets, markets that are impartial and therefore indifferent to the gender or race-ethnicity of the worker. Government intervention in labor markets can only distort micro-optimal outcomes, causing inefficiency and raising costs.

Early neoclassical economists tempered their theories of market wages with normative policy prescriptions based on notions of fairness. John Bates Clark, for example, one of the founders of the marginal productivity theory of wages, searched for "natural laws" of income distribution within the logic of the market (Clark 1965: v). Nevertheless, in a reluctant endorsement of (very limited) minimum-wage regulation, Clark argued for the moral responsibility of providing a living for workers: "If in every large city thousands of persons must continue to work hard and get less than a living, the fact is an indictment of civilization" (Clark 1913: 289). Historians of economic thought refer to the years in the twentieth century between the two World Wars as the period of "Interwar Pluralism"

(Morgan and Rutherford 1998), during which neoclassical economics, Marxian economics, and the emerging institutionalist economics coexisted in dialogue, and even collaboration.

From mid-century on, economists' stories about wages increasingly emphasized the necessary equivalence of exchange between the value of the work performed and the wage received. Fairness was defined purely in terms of commutative justice – that is, an equal exchange between two parties. Such approaches treat wages primarily as a type of price. For neoclassical economists and those endorsing their worldview, market mechanisms – the laws of supply and demand – were the most efficient and objective means of ensuring the equivalence of exchange, or the right price. In contrast, management consultants, industrial relations specialists, and neoinstitutional economists looked to job-evaluation systems and other wage-setting practices within firms to determine the relative value of different jobs and to compensate them fairly. In the context of these two versions of wages as a price, fairness became separated from measures of well-being. Prior understandings of economic activity as a process of provisioning gradually faded into the background.

Challenging the neutrality of market mechanisms and existing administrative practices, feminists in the mid- to late twentieth century nevertheless adapted to the constraints imposed by market discourse. Movements for equal wages (equal pay for equal work and comparable worth) strategically adopted this language of equal productivity and fairness in exchange, asserting that women's work was equal to men's. But their success in contesting market outcomes was limited. As Ellen Mutari and Deborah Figart note, faith in the market as "the best arbiter of wages" gained strength in the relative stagnation of the 1970s and the resurgent conservatism of the 1980s. By the 1990s arguments in favor of flexibility and deregulation of labor markets were firmly entrenched in both the United States and in Europe. Strategies to narrow the wage gap, including pay equity policies, were aggressively impugned by pro-market advocates (Mutari and Figart 1997: 691–3).

Wages as a social practice: integrating gender theory

Historically, debates over wage theory have largely concentrated on the tension between wages as a living and wages as a price. Economists have not developed theoretical discussions of social practices. For this concept, feminist political economists must look to the rich literature of feminist gender theory (Figart *et al.* 2002: ch. 4). Practice theory has been elucidated by gender theorists such as R.W. Connell, in his books *Gender and Power* (1987) and *Masculinities* (1995), and Sherry Ortner, in her book *Making Gender* (1996).[4]

In practice theory, gender is treated as an "organizing principle" of social structures rather than simply a characteristic of individuals (Glenn 1998: 33). According to practice theorists, gender relations are continually reproduced or transformed through a series of social practices. Social practice is not, however, comprised of random or purely individual acts. Human agency is constrained by the prevailing social order but is also capable of remaking these structures, although not according to an underlying narrative or historical trajectory. Practice theory is thus an attempt to reconcile structure and agency as influences on gendered outcomes.

Wages are a social practice when they are used to enforce implicit beliefs about the ordering of society by factors such as race-ethnicity, class, and gender. They serve as a means of establishing and reinforcing what men and women should be doing and how they should live. Although policymakers and other economic actors have not used the term "social practice," they have overtly advocated setting wages in order to enforce particular gender norms. Historically, for example, as in the case discussed below, men's wages were supposed to enable breadwinning, and women's wages were supposed to promote, not inhibit, their work as mothers.

The social practice approach is different from introducing gender and race-ethnicity into wage setting specifically in the context of a theory of wage discrimination. Of course women and racial-ethnic minorities experience discrimination. The limitation of both mainstream and heterodox theoretical accounts of discrimination, however, is that they treat wage differentials as simply distortions of market wages. Wages as a price remains the primary focus. Associating gender and race-ethnicity solely with discriminatory processes assumes that basic wage-determination models remain unchanged. Discrimination becomes a special case of market failure.

In contrast, the underpinning of feminist political economy is the belief that gendered relations in society have fundamental effects on wages as well as other economic outcomes. Therefore, we propose to treat the organization of gender, race-ethnicity, and class segments through social practices as integral to wage setting.

An application of the three faces of wages

Wages as a living, a price, and a social practice have all been active forces in wage setting in the United States. As we examined a range of movements over wage regulation in the twentieth century, we found that the relative weight given to each of these perspectives varied according to the economic and political climate of the times. In what follows we recount the early twentieth-century debates over minimum wages for women, with particular emphasis on contemporaneous living-wage arguments. These arguments, based on what was called "parasitic industries analysis" are worth examining in some depth because they may be an effective component of a feminist economic paradigm based on social provisioning and people-centered development.

The discussion of minimum wages for women in the early twentieth century also illustrates a period in which economic actors were not self-conscious about articulating the assumptions about gender that influenced wage setting. A legally sanctioned division between women (and children), who were protected by the state, and men, who were supposed to negotiate their own wage bargains, institutionalized gendered wage-setting processes. Once gender-specific minimum-wage laws were accepted as a social practice, social reformers, politicians, and employers argued with wage boards over how much a woman "should" be paid based upon how she should live. In particular, debate centered over whether her pay should be sufficient to enable her to live independently of her family or whether women should be discouraged from living apart from a family, supported by a male relative.

Parasitic industries and the rationale for living wages

In the late nineteenth century British Fabian socialists Sidney and Beatrice Webb provided a very influential critique of low-wage employers, which was adopted by U.S. reformers in their attempts to raise wages for women. In their book *Industrial Democracy* (1920) and other writings, the Webbs argued that capitalism was an inefficient economic system, in part because it fostered employers who paid less than living wages. Echoing Smith and Marx, a living wage was defined as a wage that would support workers "unimpaired in numbers and vigor, with a sufficient number of children to fill all vacancies caused by death or superannuation" (Webb and Webb 1920: 751). A farsighted employer would want to pay this wage, recognizing that living wages would "increase the activities and improve the character" of workers so as to "heighten the faculties and enlarge the enjoyments of the community as a whole" (*ibid.*: 703). In essence, the Webbs were bypassing questions of micro-efficiency and making Benería's "people-centered development" the criterion for the success of their proposals. The implication was that this was a macro-efficient outcome with benefits for most members of the society.[5]

Micro-efficiency was not a concern for the Webbs at least in part because they argued that the normal state of the market was not perfect competition, but combination. Wages were indeterminate outcomes of bargaining between workers and capitalists, in an environment where unorganized workers were severely disadvantaged both by their desperate need of income and by their lack of knowledge of employers' economic conditions. In this institutional environment, workers would try to maintain a floor on wages based on customary notions of fairness, but unscrupulous employers would often succeed in driving wages down even below the level necessary for "physiological efficiency" (*ibid.*: 721).

While all unregulated industries faced competitive pressure to pay wages below customary subsistence, some trades became *parasitic*, paying wages so low that the labor process could only continue because of a bounty or subsidy from some other source. Workers could be subsidized by poor relief from the state, or their earnings could be supplemented by the surplus incomes of other family members. This latter case was particularly common, the Webbs argued, in the case of children or women, who were paid too little to survive without the financial help of their families (*ibid.*: 750). In the worst cases the "subsidy" took the form of robbing workers of their future health and productivity, with the expectation that they would simply be replaced by new sources of labor.

Parasitic industries were a threat to society as a whole, not only because they paid their workers too little for their own health, but also because they drained resources from other, more productive trades. Because they received a subsidy from other workers, from the state, or from their workers' future productivity, the parasitic trades employed labor at less than its true social cost, and as a result had little incentive to increase their workers' productivity through better organization or technological improvements. These "sweated" trades expanded at the expense of self-supporting industries, with negative effects on national productivity. Legislation requiring these employers to pay a living wage would force them to find more effective methods of production. Some sweated trades might fail or leave the country, but this would allow the capital and labor they had employed to be redistributed to more profitable uses. Because mandating a living wage would raise efficiency on this broader level, it would benefit the entire community.

Gendering the living wage

The Webbs' parasitic industries argument was gender-neutral, although, as we have seen, they acknowledged that women and children were the most vulnerable to employers paying substandard wages. During the Progressive Era in the United States, this parasitic industries argument became explicitly gendered. The Progressive Era (approximately 1900–20) saw the emergence of a social reform movement that institutionalized some of the first labor regulations in the United States. Passed at the state, not federal, level, these regulations included minimum wages, maximum hours, restrictions on night work, and bans on child labor. With the exception of the child labor bans, the legislation was gender-specific. Minimum-wage laws, aimed at women in sweated trades, were passed by fifteen states and the District of Columbia between 1912 and 1923. In 1923 the Supreme Court declared the District of Columbia's minimum-wage legislation unconstitutional, effectively ending the enforcement of minimum wages for women in most states. Given the extremely brief life span of this legislation, little can be concluded about its overall effectiveness. However, the debates surrounding the setting of the wage floors are interesting for what they reveal about the accepted roles of women in the labor force and in the family, and about the state of theorizing on wages. The policies promoted living wages while serving as a gendered social practice.

Social reformers employed the Webbs' parasitic industry analysis (with or without explicitly citing their work) to argue that raising wages would lead to increased productivity both through the effects on workers' health and through the impetus to technological innovation (Holcombe 1912; Seager 1913; Millis 1914; Hutchinson 1919; Seligman 1926; Wolman 1924). The economist Emilie Hutchinson asserted that "[a]n industry that pays its workers less than a living wage is a positive detriment to the community against which the community protects itself by erecting a standard of wages for industry to observe as a condition of its survival" (Hutchinson 1919: 82). Hutchinson and other reformers asserted that legislating living wages was justified to "safeguard the welfare of the community" (ibid.: 83), even if the result was higher prices for the consumer. Virtually all American economists writing on minimum wages for women were in support of the policy, although not all endorsed the parasitic industry arguments (Prasch 1998; Power 1999).

Most of the opposition came from employer groups, who used arguments based on wages as a price, claiming that interference with free-market forces in the setting of wages would lead to unemployment and bankruptcy. Proponents of minimum wages agreed that less efficient employers would be driven out of business, but this was to be desired because they were a net drain both on the community and on more productive businesses. Maud Swartz of the Women's Trade Union League strongly expressed this sense of the priority of community over industrial interests at a 1923 Women's Bureau conference:

> Will a living wage…tend to close down certain industries in the United States? Yes and no. We will not deny that it will tend to close down the industries that prosper purely on low standards…. They are nothing but people who are living on the bounty of the Nation…. It is not only other industries and other workers who are supplementing these people, but the vast aggregate of charitable organizations that are maintained throughout this country, and into which millions of public and private funds are poured yearly. Therefore we say that, yes, it will force out the inefficient businesses; it will force out the inefficient employers. And I say God speed the day!
> (Swartz in Women's Bureau 1923: 80–1)

The reasons social reformers focused on protective legislation for women (rather than gender-neutral policies) during this period were largely pragmatic and strategic. Factory investigations by networks of social reformers and other studies of working conditions had shown that women were the lowest-paid workers, and that their wages frequently left them in desperate circumstances. Women working in the sweatshops were usually young, often recent immigrants to the United States, and almost entirely non-unionized. They were perceived by reformers as too young, timid, and uninformed to bargain effectively. Further, their ability to command a living wage was impeded by social norms that work was a temporary interlude before marriage. As Hutchinson expressed it:

> What can be said of the bargaining power of the individual in such a group of young, inexperienced, untrained, shifting workers whose wage work is regarded by themselves and every one else as something to be done in the years between leaving school and getting married?
>
> (Hutchinson 1919: 83)

Under such conditions, Hutchinson continued, "the employer may practically dictate the wage rate" (*ibid.*: 83). Echoing her concern, the National Consumers' League, one of the chief architects of state minimum wage policies, asserted that without societal intervention "there is no limit beyond which the wages of women may not be pressed down" (Nathan 1926: 26–7).[6]

For many labor reformers, gender-specific legislation was appropriate, not simply pragmatic. Women were seen as essentially different from men in their natures, in their appropriate economic and social roles, and even in their consumption needs. For others, laws covering women provided an opening for the idea of broader labor legislation, a strategy that Katherine Kish Sklar has described as using gendered policies as a surrogate for class policies (Sklar 1995: 41). Supreme Court rulings had essentially ruled out protection for men as interfering with their freedom of contract. In contrast, for a short time the Court allowed the possibility of protection for women, accepting a legal argument that the state had an overriding concern to preserve their reproductive health (see, for example, Hart 1994). In borrowing against the future health of the women they employed, sweatshops were affecting the ability of these women to fulfill their presumed future role as "mothers of the race." Clearly this view of women as needing protection because of their biological functions was a double-edged sword, improving the lives of women working in sweatshops while perpetuating the idea of innate gender difference.

Implementation and social practice

Unlike the federal minimum-wage floor passed in 1938, earlier state minimum-wage regulations were administered by wage boards, which set minimum rates for a specific industry. The process was quite laborious, as each separate regulation required lengthy and often acrimonious hearings. During this implementation phase debate centered on the appropriate living standard to be embodied in the wage. The split was between those arguing for a wage based on a woman's costs within a family circle and those arguing for a wage that would support her alone. Reformers argued that the true measure of a living wage must be its sufficiency for the health and decency of a woman living independently from her family – that is, in the parlance of the day, a woman "adrift." To pay any less than this, they argued (echoing the Webbs' analysis), would be to allow the employer a subsidy from the wages of other family members.

Employers countered that young women workers largely lived at home and needed only to cover their own expenses within the family group. They opposed wages in excess of these costs, citing the "economies of family life." Reformers had a rejoinder: if the true costs of a woman living with her family were calculated – including her portion of the support of her mother's housekeeping labor – the economies of family life all but vanished, and her living wage would be little less than a woman living independently (see Hutchinson 1919: 47; Douglas 1920: 246). Few voices argued for a family wage for women, although researcher-advocate Mary Van Kleeck (1919) was one.[7] In fact, this possibility never received serious consideration, again reflecting that wages, as a social practice, signaled the proper societal role for women.

Significantly, despite the lobbying of employers and their awareness that most women workers in fact lived with their families, state wage commissions in all cases adopted the woman living independently as the standard for determining a living wage, endorsing the principle that the community needed to be protected from parasitic employers (Women's Bureau 1928: 75). But having adopted this general principle, state commissions still faced considerable disagreement about what, exactly, comprised a decent and acceptable standard of living. Wage boards generally included representatives of labor, employers, and the public. These three groups not surprisingly often had conflicting views on this question. In their search for an "objective" basis for a minimum decent cost of living for working women, wage boards commissioned detailed budget studies. These budgets, and the arguments within the boards about them, reflected the fundamental subjectivity of the figures debated. In the words of the National Consumers' League activist Elizabeth Brandeis, employers on the boards:

> usually questioned the inclusion of many items such as laundry or vacation or "party dress" or "best hat".... How much is necessary to spend on a dress or a coat which is to last two years? Which is the least for which a healthful lunch can be bought?
>
> (Brandeis 1935: 525)

In the end the rate arrived at almost always involved a compromise, one in which rates were frequently set below the estimated cost of living (*ibid.*: 527). The Women's Bureau commented wryly: "It seems probable that constant repetition of the phrase 'economies of family life' has influenced these determinations, even when official statements maintain that all workers should be self-supporting" (Women's Bureau 1928: 75).

Social practice based on race also played a role in the determination of living wages. African-American women were largely excluded from state minimum-wage legislation, since the occupations in which they most frequently worked, domestic labor and agricultural labor, were exempted from coverage. This exclusion seemed unproblematic to many reformers, who saw it as natural for occupations in which "the character of the relationship between employer and employee would seem to make enforcement of a minimum-wage decree by a State commission difficult, if not impossible" (Women's Bureau 1928: 15). The exclusion of occupations held by African-American women was also indicative of the *absence* of a perceived social interest in their mothering role. As noted by historian Eileen Boris, the exclusion of jobs held by women of color from protective legislation "suggests how the term 'mother'…referred to white women" (Boris 1993: 234). It was the white race whose social reproduction was at stake in these early attempts at labor legislation. Further, although African-American women did work in laundries, a sector that was often covered by the minimum-wage laws, at least in one case, in Washington DC, minimum rates for laundry workers were set substantially below the rates for other industries in which white women predominated (see Hart 1992).

Conclusion

Feminists and labor reformers of the Progressive Era incorporated parasitic industries analysis into their arguments for a living wage for both pragmatic and ethical reasons. It was of considerable value as a counter to the narrow, unidirectional, marginal productivity argument of neoclassical economics that asserted that women in the sweatshops were earning what their labor was worth (wages as a price) and raising wages could only do harm. By highlighting the social costs of low wages, parasitic industry analysis broadened and enriched wage theory, emphasizing the present and future costs to the community of paying less than a living wage even when that wage was fair by the neoclassical definition. In addition, these arguments were appealing to minimum-wage proponents because they implied a harmony of interest between low-wage women workers and the expanding middle class, potentially widening the base of political support for minimum wages. Because the analysis claimed that higher wages would result in improved productivity and would lessen pressures on employers of higher-wage workers and on the public to subsidize the sweated trades, it could be used to enlist the self-interest of middle-class members of the community on the side of low-wage workers.

As became clear in the process of setting actual rates, seemingly objective arguments for a living wage left much room for disagreement about the exact *level* of wages necessary for social provisioning, a debate that was explicitly gendered. While wage boards appeared to accept the principle that the wage must be enough to support a woman independently from her family, in practice they set wages somewhat below their own calculations for the necessary level. Both the substance of the debates and the implicit message of these below-living-minimum wages suggest that the setting of actual minimum wages served as a social practice. Women wage earners (especially white women) should earn enough to live in very modest decency without having to resort to immoral behavior, but not so much that they would be tempted to prefer wage labor to their true callings as mothers. Bargaining power and prevailing social norms helped define what constituted living wages.

For contemporary feminist political economists, the parasitic industries argument may suggest that ethical arguments for advancing women's status, while fundamental, are not enough. Jane Humphries and Jill Rubery argue that proponents of equal opportunity for women must address the orthodox economic argument that policy intervention to legislate equal opportunity interferes with competitiveness, and hence is inefficient (Humphries and Rubery 1995: 1). The parasitic industries analysis attempted to make efficiency-based rather than values-based arguments. But the definition of efficiency used was not microeconomic profit maximization. Rather, the Webbs focused on community well-being and the maximization of human potential to, in the Webbs' words, "heighten the faculties and enlarge the enjoyments of the community as a whole" (Webb and Webb 1920: 703). This definition of efficiency redirects attention from profitability to social provisioning as the goal of economic activity, a view very much in keeping with feminist writings. Thus, while efficiency-based arguments should not be considered a substitute for arguments based on principles of equality and human well-being, parasitic industries analysis suggests ways in which the concept of social efficiency can aid in the furthering of feminist goals. Such arguments can supplement alternative visions of how gender and race-ethnicity should be organized.

The notion that wages are usually set solely through the market, and that attempts to establish a living wage are therefore a violation of normal market processes, flies in the face of historical evidence. Our investigation of wage regulations over the course of the twentieth century in the United States, including the example of state minimum-wage laws discussed here, reveals that wages consistently derived from a process of cumulative causation. Markets matter, but so do the relative powers of contending interests and cultural understandings of what constitutes a living. Rather than an impersonal narrative of demand functions and supply functions, wage setting is a human story. The agency of human actors attempting to steer the interaction of the state, economic relations including markets, and families in order to produce certain defined outcomes is at the heart of the process of wages setting.

If economic theory is going to be a positive force in the twenty-first century, in our collective struggle for human well-being within the United States and across the globe, it is going to have to replace its emphasis on mechanistic modeling with a holistic, humanistic, and (for economists used to tidy models) frighteningly messy and non-deterministic methodology. Economists can find inspiration in their classical roots, in the works of institutionalist economists, and in the writings of feminist theorists and progressive social scientists for this challenging and exciting enterprise.

Notes

1 We use the term "feminist political economy" in preference to "feminist economics" to emphasize the importance of moving beyond the narrow boundaries of current mainstream economics to incorporate the insights of heterodox economists, feminist theorists, and other social theorists. The search for complex answers requires a widening, rather than a narrowing, of the scope of inquiry.
2 In a social provisioning approach, the criterion for evaluating public policy is whether it contributes to "social efficiency." Social efficiency is defined by Jane Humphries and Jill Rubery as the success of an economic policy at maximizing human potential at a societal level (Humphries and Rubery 1995: 11).
3 For Marx, workers owned only their labor power, or ability to labor; this is the commodity that they had to sell in order to survive.
4 Practice theory has its roots in existentialist thought and in recent work by Pierre Bourdieu, Anthony Giddens, and others.
5 Malcolm Sawyer elaborates on the concept of macro-efficiency. He questions the neoclassical assumption that micro-efficiency will necessarily lead to macro-efficiency. Sawyer points out that there can be numerous efficient macroeconomic outcomes to microeconomic choices. For example, markets could be equally likely to clear if a disadvantaged group is given little training and placed in low-wage jobs, or given high levels of training and placed in high-wage jobs. He notes that "[h]ow this group actually fared would depend on previous history," which for women would include "centuries of patriarchy and exclusion from positions of status." In such cases, "there is no reason to think that the actual equilibrium reached (if indeed it is an equilibrium) is in any sense the best" (Sawyer 1995: 38).
6 The National Consumers' League, for example, introduced the principle of living wages for women in retailing in the 1890s. They declared that consumers had a duty to insist that women workers who produced the wares they purchased had been paid enough to live in decency and respectability (Nathan 1926: 26–7).
7 Van Kleeck was an investigator with the Russell Sage Foundation, researching the conditions of women workers in New York sweatshops and producing books and testimony that were influential in the establishment of protective legislation for women. She was appointed head of the Women in Industry Service (the precursor to the Women's Bureau) when it was formed in July 1918.

Bibliography

Agarwal, Bina (1997) " 'Bargaining' and Gender Relations: Within and Beyond the Household," *Feminist Economics* 3(1): 1–51.

Benería, Lourdes (1999) "Globalization, Gender and the Davos Man," *Feminist Economics* 5(3): 61–83.

Bernstein, Jared, Chauna Brocht and Maggie Spade-Aguilar (2000) *How Much is Enough? Basic Family Budgets for Working Families*, Washington, DC: Economic Policy Institute.

Boris, Eileen (1993) "The Power of Motherhood: Black and White Activist Women Redefine the 'Political,' " in Seth Koven and Sonya Michel (eds.) *Mothers of a New World: Maternalist Politics and the Origins of Welfare States*, New York: Routledge.

Brandeis, Elizabeth (1935) "Labor Legislation," in John R. Commons (ed.) *History of Labor in the United States, 1896–1932*, New York: Macmillan Company.

Bruegel, Irene and Diane Perrons (1995) "Where Do the Costs of Unequal Treatment for Women Fall?," in Jane Humphries and Jill Rubery (eds.) *The Economics of Equal Opportunity*, Manchester, UK: Equal Opportunities Commission.

Ciscel, David H. (1999) *What is a Living Wage for Memphis?* Memphis: University of Memphis, Center for Research on Women.

—— (2000) "The Living Wage Movement: Building a Political Link from Market Wages to Social Institutions," *Journal of Economic Issues* 34(2): 527–35.

Clark, John Bates (1913) "Minimum Wage," *Atlantic Monthly* 112 (September): 289–97.

—— (1965) *The Distribution of Wealth*, New York: Augustus M. Kelley; first published in 1899.

Connell, R.W. (1987) *Gender and Power*, Stanford, CA: Stanford University Press.

—— (1993) "The Big Picture: Masculinities in Recent World History," *Theory and Society* 22: 597–623.

—— (1995) *Masculinities*, Berkeley, CA: University of California Press.

Douglas, Dorothy W. (1920) "The Cost of Living for Working Women: A Criticism of Current Theories," *Quarterly Journal of Economics* 34(1): 225–59.

Figart, Deborah M. (1997) "Gender as More Than a Dummy Variable: Feminist Approaches to Discrimination," *Review of Social Economy* 55(1): 1–32.

—— (2001) "Raising the Minimum Wage and Living Wage Campaigns," in Mary C. King (ed.) *Squaring Up: Policies to Raise Women's Incomes in the United States*, Ann Arbor, MI: University of Michigan Press.

Figart, Deborah M., Ellen Mutari and Marilyn Power (2002) *Living Wages, Equal Wages: Gender and Labor Market Policies in the United States*, London: Routledge.

Glenn, Evelyn Nakano (1998) "Gender, Race, and Class: Bridging the Language–Structure Divide," *Social Science History* 22(1): 29–38.

Glickman, Lawrence B. (1997) *A Living Wage: American Workers and the Making of Consumer Society*, Ithaca, NY: Cornell University Press.

Hart, Vivien (1992) "Feminism and Bureaucracy: The Minimum Wage Experiment in the District of Columbia," *Journal of American Studies* 26 (Part 1): 8–17.

—— (1994) *Bound by Our Constitution: Women, Workers, and Minimum Wage Laws in the United States and Britain*, Princeton, NJ: Princeton University Press.

Himmelweit, Susan (1995) "A Critique of the Concept of the Value of Labour-Power," Working Paper, Milton Keynes, UK: Open University.

Holcombe, A.N. (1912) "The Legal Minimum Wage in the United States," *American Economic Review* 2(1): 21–37.

Humphries, Jane and Jill Rubery (1995) "Introduction," in Jane Humphries and Jill Rubery (eds.) *The Economics of Equal Opportunities*, Manchester, UK: Equal Opportunities Commission.

Hutchinson, Emilie Josephine (1919) *Women's Wages: A Study of the Wages of Industrial Women and Measures Suggested to Increase Them*, New York: Longmans, Green & Company.

Jennings, Ann L. (1993) "Public or Private? Institutional Economics and Feminism," in Marianne A. Ferber and Julie A. Nelson (eds.) *Beyond Economic Man: Feminist Theory and Economics*, Chicago, IL: University of Chicago.

Kessler-Harris, Alice (1990) *A Woman's Wage: Historical Meanings and Social Consequences*, Lexington, KY: University Press of Kentucky.

LaRossignol, James E. (1917) "Some Phases of the Minimum Wage Question," *American Economic Review* 7(1): 251–74.

McLaughlin, Eithne (1995) "Gender and Egalitarianism in the British Welfare State," in Jane Humphries and Jill Rubery (eds.) *The Economics of Equal Opportunities*, Manchester, UK: Equal Opportunities Commission.

Marx, Karl (1967) *Capital*, vols. I–III, New York: International Publishers; first published 1867.

Millis, H.O. (1914) "Some Aspects of the Minimum Wage," *Journal of Political Economy* 22(2): 132–59.
Morgan, Mary S. and Malcolm Rutherford (eds.) (1998) *From Interwar Pluralism to Postwar Neoclassicism*, supplement to vol. 30 of *History of Political Economy*, Durham, NC: Duke University Press.
Mutari, Ellen and Deborah M. Figart (1997) "Markets, Flexibility, and Family: Evaluating the Gendered Discourse Against Pay Equity," *Journal of Economic Issues* 31(3): 687–706.
Nathan, Maud (1926) *The Story of an Epoch-Making Movement*, New York: Doubleday, Page & Company.
Nelson, Julie A. (1993) "The Study of Choice or the Study of Provisioning? Gender and the Definition of Economics," in Marianne A. Ferber and Julie A. Nelson (eds.) *Beyond Economic Man: Feminist Theory and Economics*, Chicago, IL: University of Chicago Press.
—— (1996) *Feminism, Objectivity and Economics*, London: Routledge.
Ortner, Sherry B. (1996) *Making Gender: The Politics and Erotics of Culture*, Boston, MA: Beacon Press.
Pearce, Diana and Jennifer Brooks (2000) *The Self-Sufficiency Standard for the City of New York*, New York: Women's Center for Education and Career Advancement.
Pollin, Robert and Stephanie Luce (1998) *The Living Wage: Building a Fair Economy*, New York: New Press.
Power, Marilyn (1999) "Parasitic-Industries Analysis and Arguments for a Living Wage for Women in the Early Twentieth-Century United States," *Feminist Economics* 5(1): 61–78.
—— (2001) "A Social Provisioning Critique of the Personal Responsibility Act: Developing a Feminist Political Economic Methodology," Sarah Lawrence College, Bronxville, NY, unpublished ms.
Prasch, Robert (1998) "American Economists and Minimum Wage Legislation During the Progressive Era: 1912–1923," *Journal of the History of Economic Thought* 20(2): 161–75.
Renwick, Trudi J. and Barbara R. Bergmann (1993) "A Budget-Based Definition of Poverty," *Journal of Human Resources* 28(1): 1–24.
Sawyer, Malcolm (1995) "The Operation of Labour Markets and the Economics of Equal Opportunities," in Jane Humphries and Jill Rubery (eds) *The Economics of Equal Opportunities*, Manchester, UK: Equal Opportunities Commission.
Seager, Henry R. (1913) "The Theory of the Minimum Wage," *American Labor Legislation Review* 3 (February): 81–115.
Seligman, Edwin R.A. (1926) *Principles of Economics*, 9th edn., New York: Longmans, Green & Company.
Sen, Amartya (1999) *Development as Freedom*, New York: Alfred A. Knopf.
Sklar, Kathryn Kish (1995) "Two Political Cultures in the Progressive Era: The National Consumers' League and the American Association for Labor Legislation," in Linda K. Kerber, Alice Kessler-Harris, and Kathryn Kish Sklar (eds.) *U.S. History As Women's History*, Chapel Hill, NC: University of North Carolina Press.
Smith, Adam (1937) *An Inquiry into the Nature and Causes of the Wealth of Nations*, New York: Modern Library; first published 1776.
Van Kleeck, Mary (1919) "Federal Policies for Women in Industry," *Annals of the American Academy of Political and Social Science* 81: 87–94.
Webb, Sidney and Beatrice Webb (1920) *Industrial Democracy*, London: Longmans, Green & Company.
Wolman, Leo (1924) "Economic Justification of the Legal Minimum Wage," *American Labor Legislation Review* 14 (September): 226–33.
Women's Bureau, U.S. Department of Labor (1923) *Proceedings of the Women's Industrial Conference*, Bulletin No. 33, Washington, DC: U.S. Government Printing Office.
—— (1928) *The Development of Minimum Wage Laws in the United States, 1912–1927*, Bulletin No. 61, Washington, DC: U.S. Government Printing Office.

Part II
Science stories and feminist economics

6 Some implications of the feminist project in economics for empirical methodology[1]

Joyce P. Jacobsen

I describe myself as a "fence-sitter" when it comes to feminist economics – an early joiner of the International Association for Feminist Economics (IAFFE) who has participated regularly in its sponsored paper-presentation sessions and other activities, but who has reserved judgment on what exactly constitutes feminist economics. This is to a large extent because I am by professional and personal inclination an empiricist. I prefer to wait until a large enough corpus of publications amasses, written by persons who purport to be feminist economists and/or published in a feminist-labeled journal such as *Feminist Economics*, at which point I can analyze the papers with regard to topics, techniques, and results and thereby determine inductively what feminist economics apparently is.

It may be too early to apply this inductive technique; *Feminist Economics* has so far (as of early 2002) produced seven years' worth of articles. However, many IAFFE members were at work well before 1995, and continue to publish in many outlets, turning out refereed articles, essays in edited volumes, monographs, and consultancy reports in alarming numbers. Also it seemed reasonable that I should at least start to formulate an opinion (which could subsequently be updated as the feminist economics publication project continues into the foreseeable future). Therefore I determined to attempt my empirical project at this possibly premature moment, with the goal of formulating partial answers to two questions: What scholarly contributions can so far be attributed to the feminist project in economics? Has the feminist project affected the methodology that some economists have used in performing empirical research? At the end of this paper I also offer my thoughts regarding the (partial) answer to a third, related question: How might the feminist project have greater effect on the methodologies generally used in empirical economics research?[2]

I utilize the following strategy in developing this essay: First, consider ways in which feminism might affect empirical work in economics. Second, armed with ideas of what to look for, look for examples of ways in which feminist economics has had an effect on empirical work in economics. Third, present concrete examples of these ways, using a small number of topics that have been developed relatively extensively by feminist economists. Fourth, consider measures of overall impact and discuss possibilities for further dissemination of the methodologies utilized by proponents of the feminist economics project. My observations are by no means meant to be definitive; rather, they are meant to provoke discussion (particularly among similarly situated fence-sitters) towards arrival at an understanding of what feminist economics is and what its implications are for empirical methodology.

The feminist economic project: a response to "perceived inadequacies" in economics

The need to have an economics that is explicitly labeled as feminist arises, at it has in other disciplines, as a response to the lack of something in the economics discipline as it currently exists. Ferber and Nelson, in their ovular work *Beyond Economic Man* (1993b), group responses to perceived inadequacies in the academic disciplines into five categories: "affirmative action," "feminist empiricism," "feminist 'difference,'" "feminist postmodernism," and "feminist constructionism." Given space constraints, I comment only on the elements of this taxonomy that relate to empirical methodology.[3]

Note that affirmative action could be construed in two senses. One is to ensure that there are sufficient female economists to enable their potentially alternative ways of viewing and studying economic phenomena to be represented in the profession's output (more broadly characterized than in this essay as teaching, consulting, research, holding decisionmaking positions in business and government, and making department-building decisions like hiring and tenure). Affirmative action is important because appropriate scientific practices, topics, and methods are developed in epistemological communities.[4] Numerous feminist philosophers of science have argued that diverse epistemological communities are desirable (cf. Harding 1986; Longino 1993; L.H. Nelson 1993; Tuana 1992). Diversity is desirable because, as Longino explains, "social values and interests can become enshrined in otherwise acceptable research programs.... As long as representatives of alternative points of view are not included in the community, shared values will not be identified as shaping observation or reasoning" (1993: 112).

The other sense of affirmative action is to focus on the subjects being studied and ask whether topics relevant to women are given sufficient attention by economic researchers. Feminist economics can draw attention to economic phenomena that are germane to women's lives, both through example – choosing subject matters for research that are in underattended to areas of relevance to women – and through exhortation – urging other researchers, both feminist and non-feminist, to do the same. This attention would potentially ensue from having more diverse scientific communities, although this is neither a necessary nor a sufficient condition.

Taken in either of these senses, the affirmative action response implies no particular empirical methodology as different from the mainstream, but only allows for the possibility that something different might arise through greater representativeness of persons and/or topics. It is an empirical question whether greater diversity within the scientific community does lead to either a greater diversity of topics studied or alternative methodologies.

The second response category of feminist empiricism, as Ferber and Nelson (1993b) state, is an attractive option to many empirical economists. Harding (1986: 24) is credited with first using the term "feminist empiricism" to describe a type of feminist science practice. Feminist scientists, mainly in biology and other life sciences, held that androcentric bias in science was not the result of the scientific method, but rather the lack of adherence to existing methodological norms. Similarly, in economics the problem is not with economics per se, but rather that economists do not adhere to their own methodological precepts. Hence economic theory itself may not be intrinsically patriarchal and therefore methodologically suspect from ground zero, and so it can potentially be extended in nongendered ways.

One suspects that most economists would agree with the view that economic research could be greatly improved if all practitioners "tightened up" on their research practices in ways that are already known (and often well known). These include considering alternative hypotheses explicitly, subjecting results to multiple robustness tests (including alternative estimation techniques), attempting to replicate results to the extent possible using additional data (including cross-cultural and cross-temporal data), and making their data and programs readily accessible to other researchers. In addition, a majority of both male and female economists likely find the framework that they work within (whether neoclassical or an alternative framework such as institutional, ecological, radical, or post-Keynesian) to be, if not exactly above suspicion, at least serviceable on a day-to-day basis. In this view, no new empirical methodology is required.

However, if the very underpinnings of economics are deeply gendered, then developing a gender-bias-free economics requires more than closer attention to scientific method. Ferber and Nelson argue in favor of feminist constructionism, which "would consider the intertwining of the social construction of gender and the social construction of science" (1993b: 9). This calls for a different methodological approach towards empirical work. While this construct is less than fully worked out in their book (1993a), it is quite similar to the broader conception of feminist empiricism advocated by Helen Longino (1993), Nancy Tuana (1992), and Lynn Hankinson Nelson (1990).

In this broader view the demographics of science communities are crucial because "what constitutes evidence for a claim is not determined by individuals, but by the standards a community accepts" (L.H. Nelson 1990: 248). So clear grounds for evaluation can still be determined as community standards; and if the community is sufficiently inclusive (with sufficiently empowered subgroups that can make their dissenting views heard), then there will be general agreement that these standards are appropriate. Hence the affirmative action emphasis on the importance of inclusive scientific community reappears with theoretical justification. Feminist constructionism can be seen as a call for gender, as well as other potentially relevant categories of identity such as race, ethnicity and class, to be considered in the construction of both communities and evidentiary standards.[5]

While feminist epistemology and philosophy of science articulate the broad methodological contours of the feminist economics project, this work does not provide concrete prescriptions for how these concepts work in practice.[6] The next stage of feminist methodological work needs to include the formulation of a framework that will demonstrate specifically feminist methods for feminist research. Hands dismisses the interpretation of methodology as the study of methods, or what he calls "lower-case-m methodology" in favor of defining economic methodology as "the interpenetration of economics and science theory" (2001: 3, 7). But in order to have an effect at the practitioner level discussions of methodology have to move from Methodology to methodology.

As a solid step in this direction, Woolley (1993) has written a paper with relatively concrete prescriptions. She lists six feminist challenges to economics:

1   to develop models to explain and evaluate endogenous preference changes;
2   to allow that people may make systematic mistakes;
3   to correct mistaken stylized facts;
4   to incorporate both men and women into economic analysis;
5   to find out what shapes the institutions which privilege or disadvantage women;
6   to develop a better economic model of caring and reproductive activity.

Institutionalists, behavioralists, and neo-neoclassical economists might protest that members of their ranks have already made these various points. Hence, they might question whether feminist economists have contributed anything new, other than to group these critiques together, and then to find particular examples of where endogeneity, mistake-making, and institutions matter in the context of making women visible, i.e. in the context of finding cases where the issues matter disproportionately to women. Alternatively, if gender is a fundamental organizing principle of institutions, feminist insights are crucial to how institutionalists, behavioral economists, and neo-neoclassical economists carry out their research agendas.

Even if all feminist economics has done is to add additional voices to those already in the profession who were clamoring for attention to particular under-utilized modeling strategies, that would be a valuable function. However, I think feminist economics has done more than that.

Consider, for example, two practices that characterize much of feminist economic research. The first is the stress on considering distributional effects between demographic groups. The second is the emphasis on empiricism, on uncovering what economic agents actually do, rather than asserting that they act in particular ways that are consistent with economic theory and building policy prescriptions on a theoretical rather than an empirical base. These practices are also not unique to feminist economics. Yet both can have a particular twist in the way they are carried out by feminist economists.

Some might consider detailing differential effects of policies optional; feminist economists (including myself) tend to argue that it is almost always important, in particular with differential effects by gender or sex. Distributional effects might always be of interest in and of themselves, but others might prefer them only in the context of answering a particular research question. But gender differences can matter not only in detailing distributional patterns (i.e. equity), but also in pointing out ways in which efficiency can be affected. For instance, Elson (1991) and Agarwal (2001), among others, have argued that including women in decisionmaking processes leads to additional information that is valuable in making better allocational decisions. Hence, focus on the distribution of decisionmakers as well as on the distribution of outcomes.

The second point, seeing what economic agents (firms etc.) actually do instead of what they do in a theoretical framework, is a matter of sound scientific practice (even if it goes against the way economics is practiced by many researchers). For example, Julie A. Nelson (1995: 121) argues that Polachek (1995) confuses possession of a set of theories about how firms *might* work under restrictive assumptions with possession of knowledge about how firms *do* work as real institutions populated by real human beings. The advantage of trying to see what is actually happening rather than what we think should happen is often obvious to empiricists, but also hopefully stimulates further/alternative theorizing by theorists.

An approach requiring that data analysis be done without a strongly held prior belief works particularly well in analyzing frameworks where we know (by our own discipline-internal standards) that competition and profit-maximization are not reasonable premises. For example, consider Kim's (2000) study of the California civil service wage-setting process. Even though government employers supposedly take account of "prevailing market wage" in setting government pay rates, this does not lead to gender-neutral outcomes. Kim shows the many places in the wage-setting process where supposed neutrality and "letting the market rule" break down.

With their emphasis on empiricism, the new subfields of behavioral economics and experimental economics seem like areas that would be open to feminist economists. Somewhat surprisingly, behavioral economics appears rather resistant, with few studies focusing as yet on gender differences. In experimental economics, however, increasing attention is paid to how subjects' gender can affect experimental outcomes, with some theoretical justification of these differences (cf. Andreoni and Vesterlund 2001; Croson and Buchan 1999; Eckel and Grossman 1996, 1998; Saad and Gill 2000; Schubert et al. 1999).

Why bother with new approaches?

What are the potential payoffs to new thinking? In the case of feminist economics as applied to empirical work they have been threefold: identification and development of new topics as fair game for economists to study; uncovering of new dynamics for theoretical amplification and better accordance with empirical patterns; and bringing new facts to light, particularly ones that are in contrast to conventional economic thinking. All of these events can be seen (relatively uncontroversially) as legitimate scientific advance, and are consistent with the expanded definition of feminist empiricism.

In order to make these points more concrete I present below short examples regarding four topics in which I argue that feminist economists have advanced the discipline in these three ways. The first topic is treatment of nontradeables in general, and specifically in national-income accounting. The second is measurement of intrahousehold interactions and resource allocation. The third is measurement of family-structure effects on labor-market outcomes. The fourth is the conceptualization of caring work. The astute reader will point out correctly that these four topics are interrelated. Nevertheless, articles generally focus on one or two of these areas rather than all four, and therefore can be used as exemplars for one area at a time.

Treatment of nontradeable goods

The importance of considering nontradeables (i.e. goods with limited marketability, in the limiting case only usable by the person who produces them and in the broadest case not exportable outside the country) and time spent in producing them is a recurrent theme in feminist economics (cf. Aslaksen 1999). Waring's influential book *If Women Counted* (1988) focused attention on the shortcomings of the national-income accounting systems used throughout the world, in particular their failure to account for value produced in nontraded activities, particularly household activities and subsistence production. Measurement of nontradeables has become an increasing focus within the development economics literature, and also within the economic history literature. It is also beginning to enter the statistics systems in a number of countries and at the international level – witness ongoing efforts to measure unpaid work by Australia (Australian Bureau of Statistics 2000) and Canada (Statistics Canada 2002), as well as treatment of this issue in the United Nations Development Programme *Human Development Report* for 1995 (UNDP 1995: ch. 4).

An excellent example of the feminist economic expanded focus leading to a revision of the conventional wisdom that nontradeables can be ignored can be found in Wagman and Folbre (1996). In their study, they create an alternative measure of gross national product (GNP) that includes a measure of nonmarket household services. They then compare per-capita GNP growth for this augmented GNP measure to the traditional GNP measure for the United States from 1870 to 1930. This demonstrates that including nonmarket household services in GNP leads to a substantially different story about the trajectory of economic growth. For example, there is a decline in the growth rate from 1890 to 1910 rather than the increase found for the standard GNP measure.

Additional work has considered current estimates of the size of the nonmarket sector for a number of developed countries (Aslaksen and Koren 1996; Ironmonger 1996), finding it to be a significant proportion of augmented GNP. This has implications not only for long-term measures of economic growth, but also for variations in economic activity across the business cycle. For instance, Madrick (1997) hypothesizes that the United States' economic performance since the early 1970s, a period in which women moved increasingly into paid work, has been particularly prone to mismeasurement.

This nonmeasurement of nontradeables is no less of a problem in the developing-country context; indeed it is likely much more of a problem given the potentially larger proportions of augmented GNP produced in subsistence production and informal-sector production as well as in household. For instance, Cloud and Garrett (1996) highlight the specific problem of undermeasurement of household human capital production by estimating the value of labor in the nonmarket activity of "production and maintenance of human capital" for 132 countries. Benería (1992, 1999) has documented the increased efforts in the international statistical community towards achieving more accurate measures of these sectoral activities. She and others have argued, in a series of influential papers published in special issues of *World Development* (Çagatay *et al.* 1995; Grown *et al.* 2000), that accurate measurement of these sectors is necessary for good design of macroeconomic policy.

Intrahousehold dynamics and resource allocation

While this topic has been a standard one for feminist economists (cf. J.A. Nelson 1989), the growing number of articles in this area evidences a rising level of interest in intrahousehold dynamics and intrahousehold resource allocation. Again, many of these articles appear in the development economics journals and focus on different consumption both among adults and among boys and girls (in the latter context with particular attention paid to health and education outcomes). For instance, the World Bank's recent report *Engendering Development* discusses all the recent articles that test whether or not the household acts as a single unit (2001: app. 4).

Feminist economists have been critical instigators in exploring what types of inequality might exist and why they matter, as well as what phenomena we might wish to explain and whether existing analytical tools are sufficient for exploring these phenomena (cf. Seiz 1999 on the use of game theory and bargaining models in this context). For instance, Woolley and Marshall (1994) consider both intra-household inequality in money incomes and inequality in control over household resources. Control is measured in two ways: first, as control over the management of household finances and, second, as influence over household decisionmaking. This way of conceptualizing inequality emphasizes the dynamics of how inequality can be perpetuated. Feminist economists have also expanded the discussion on household bargaining and outcomes by delineating both the wide range of factors that can affect control (Agarwal 1997) and the wide range of issues over which one might see bargaining occur (cf. Agarwal 1997 on family land, subsistence within the family, and social norms; Ott 1995 on birth control).

To give an example of how this line of work can overturn conventional wisdom, consider that most empirical studies of poverty assume implicitly an equal sharing of resources between all household members. There is a growing body of research indicating that this assumption is not realistic (Findlay and Wright 1996; Cantillon and Nolan 2001) and that in particular differential ownership of property by gender leads to differential returns by gender even when property rights are expanded to the lower classes (Agarwal 1994). These authors' findings suggest that if there is significant intrahousehold inequality of this type, then conventional methods of poverty measurement are likely to lead to a serious underestimate (overestimate) of the incidence and intensity of female (male) poverty.

Effects of family structure on labor-market outcomes

As certain types of family and household structures have become more predominant, including single-parent-headed households, cohabitation, and dual-earner couples, increased interest has been paid by economists and other researchers to the effects of family structure on a variety of outcomes, including labor-market measures, consumer expenditures, and macroeconomic variables. Again, this is a topic of both early and continuing interest to feminist economists (cf. Strober 1988). I recently surveyed a number of such papers that attempt to measure the effects of family structure (including marital status, presence of children and other dependents, and whether or not one's spouse works) on labor-market outcomes (including earnings and hours worked for pay) (Jacobsen 2002).

Family structure does turn out to have measurable effects in many ways one would expect, such as a negative effect of children on both earnings and hours worked for pay by women. It also has effects that are harder to explain, such as the wage premium that married men appear to receive relative to both cohabiting and noncohabiting unmarried men (Stratton 2002). Netz and Haveman (1999) argue convincingly for inclusion of family-structure variables as standard controls or predictors in numerous types of studies (e.g. unemployment duration) besides those that focus on hours and earnings effects. Another interesting dynamic is the effect of family structure from one's childhood continuing to affect current outcomes. This is well established in a developing-country context, given that children have differential access to human capital based on birth order, the gender composition of their family and the number of siblings (cf. Garg and Morduch 1998). But measurable effects also occur in developed countries, such as women from small families working less when young and more when older (Kessler 1991).

In addition, recent work has considered how attitudes regarding the role of family in one's life (i.e. the importance of marriage and family vs. one's career) can affect outcomes. Interestingly, Cappelli, Constantine, and Chadwick (2000) find that placing a high priority on family is linked to higher earnings for men, but has no effect for women's earnings. This is a provocative line of research that will hopefully be developed further.

Caring labor

Research that focuses on "caring" and "caring labor" brings together interests in all three of these areas. Caring labor is often unpaid labor. Both input (time spent in productive labor within and without the household) and output (time and money) allocation among household members (and between members of separate households connected often by familial ties) can be explained as the outcome from an intrahousehold resource allocation problem. The supply of (and demand for) caring labor, in both the paid and unpaid sector, is determined in part by family structure.

I mention this topic separately from the above three discussions not only because it does combine the three earlier topics, but also because feminist economists appear to have been especially effective in advancing the research agenda in this area – witness the United Nations Development Programme *Human Development Report* for 1999. It addresses, within the broader context of the impacts of globalization, the importance of "caring labor – the task of providing for dependents, including children, the sick, and the elderly" (UNDP 1999: abstract). The World Bank has also begun to use this concept in its publications (e.g. World Bank 2001).

This degree of attention to a prime feminist concept is satisfying, given that a number of prominent feminist economist theorists (witness Folbre 1995, 2001; Himmelweit 1995, 1999; J.A. Nelson 1999; see also Chapters 15–17 in this volume) have written on care and caring labor in an economic context. The notion that this type of labor is different, both in terms of the motivation for doing it and the type of output that it produces, is an important stimulant for further theoretical and empirical research.

How could the feminist economic project have more of an impact on economic practice?

In each of the above cases I have argued that feminist economists have contributed by either researching new topics, expanding theory (thereby generally leading to recommendations regarding new avenues for empirical work), or considering new variables and linkages between variables. They have also suggested that new types of data be collected and thereafter incorporated into an augmented statistical framework. And, notably, some of the people working in these areas do not consider themselves (or at least do not explicitly label themselves) feminist empiricists even as they have expanded the realm that the economics community deems "worthy" of study. This would include many persons working in the field of population and family economics, and household economics (cf. Grossbard-Shechtman 2001 for a discussion of the intellectual roots and disciple patterns in this area). Hence the feminist economic project is succeeding on some fronts in creating a more inclusive scientific community that is open to feminist contributions.

But while the above examples illustrate some research topics where feminist economists have been critical in either defining, expanding, or redefining the topic, there are still numerous subfields in economics where feminist economics has had virtually no impact, even within labor economics and development economics, the two fields where arguably the greatest notice of feminist critiques of the ways of doing business has occurred. Albelda (1995) demonstrated the relatively small impact of feminism on the economics profession, including results from a survey of economists that indicated a low perception of impact both on economics in general and on specific subfields. More recently, Long and Woolley (2002) find that books by feminist economists are infrequently cited, even by other feminist economists. To the extent that it is desirable to expand the feminist economic project to these other fields, one question is how to undertake this expansion.

In looking to the history of empirical methods in economics for ideas of how best to propagate practice, it turns out that there has been surprisingly little systematic study of the spread or diversity of empirical techniques in economics. My study of current and past practice in labor economics (Jacobsen and Newman 2002) regarding whether or not gender and race are modeled explicitly in empirical work shows widespread exclusion of women and nonwhites from data samples and a failure to investigate gender and racial differences even in the 1990s.[7] In the course of this study we also noted the rapid rise of the use of the technique of multiple regression (concurrent with the rise in availability of first mainframe-computing time and then personal computers), and have also commented in previous work about the relative lack of use of novel data sources in economics as compared to other social scientists (Jacobsen and Newman 1997). But we are far from developing a theory of what propagates and what does not in social science practice, although the feminist philosophers of science have something important to say about why certain types of practices, even though deemed desirable in the abstract, may be resisted.

In order to encourage further thought into methodology and the spread of potential best (or better) practices, including in particular those that are feminist economist in nature, I suggest the following three-part program to be followed by all those dedicated to furthering this plan:

1 Creation of a framework that indicates what empirical practices are feminist in nature, and why they are preferred practices (even for non-feminists). This task is larger than I am able to undertake in this essay, and needs to be more committee based in nature (following some of the prescriptions for community-building as suggested in Longino 1993), although I have pointed to some such practices and features.

    Note that developing a set of good practices does not require a complete reinvention of empirical method. As MacDonald (1995: 175) points out: "feminist economists are borrowing methods from the other social sciences, including survey research, case studies and participant observation." A short exploration section in *Feminist Economics* highlighted some feminist economists' use of qualitative research techniques brought over from other social sciences, including focus groups (van Staveren 1997; Esim 1997) and in-depth interviews (Olmsted 1997).[8] We need not reinvent the wheel even to this extent. Rather than having to spend additional time (often after receiving one's formal graduate training) learning additional skills, work in teams with other researchers.[9] Just as we consider a good academic committee to be constituted with voices from all areas of the academic disciplinary spectrum, one might want a good paper to be at least checked over by members of other disciplines.

2 Consideration of what incentives exist or might exist for encouraging researchers to consider their methodological choices. Again, I do not have a full plan worked out here. I do have some ideas, including perhaps foremost among them not being too picky about author labeling. Blank (1993: 138) mentions that a number of economists already try to do what the authors in *Beyond Economic Man* are calling for. She cites the examples of neighborhood effects (as a way to link cultural and economic factors) and work on immigration looking at ethnic differences between different immigrant groups. She argues that the researchers working on those topics would not define

themselves as feminist economists, yet the approaches seem consistent with the desire expressed in *Beyond Economic Man* for more inclusive models of economic behavior. Blank extends a challenge: "I would like to see those who want to pursue feminist models evaluate this existing literature and indicate how they would alter or add to it, or present their own examples of good feminist economic research" (*ibid.*). Forbearance in rushing to label people as being from one or another school might enlist more allies for support of feminist economic good practice.

3   Following good practice ourselves. Easier said than done, of course, particularly when there is one or another pressing deadline like the tenure clock or an overdue research report. However, the four topical areas I discussed above are all areas in which researchers have followed good practice and have come up with important contributions. Hence perhaps I was overly pessimistic before when I said it was hard to ascertain feminist empirical practice without explicit self-aware references to such practice. To the extent that feminist empirical practice is good practice, we have numerous examples already waiting.

Notes

1   Comments on earlier versions of this paper by Drucilla Barker and Edith Kuiper are gratefully acknowledged.
2   In posing these latter two questions specialists in economic methodology may already be protesting that I am focusing on methods rather than methodology (see Hands [2001: 3] for a discussion of this potential distinction). I would argue that if discussions of economic methodology have no obvious prescriptive relationship to economic empirical method, then they are doomed to irrelevancy in terms of both the performance *and* the interpretation of empirical economic research.
3   The interested reader should refer to Ferber and Nelson (1993a), Kuiper *et al.* (1995), J.A. Nelson (1996), and Hewitson (1999) for a full explication of these alternatives.
4   For instance, Longino states: "scientific knowledge is constructed not by individuals applying a method to the material to be known but by individuals in interaction with one another in ways that modify their observations, theories and hypotheses, and patterns of reasoning" (1993: 111).
5   I am indebted to Drucilla Barker for pointing out that Ferber and Nelson's feminist constructionism can be construed as a variant of Tuana's and L.H. Nelson's version of feminist empiricism.
6   This reflects the fact that contemporary epistemology has moved away from the notion of epistemology as a prescriptive endeavor, and has moved toward either naturalized epistemology or a sociology of knowledge approach. See Hands (2001) for an in-depth discussion.
7   This is not to say that simply paying attention to gender is sufficient methodological improvement in many contexts. For instance, Badgett (1995a) points out that focusing on gender alone is inadequate for discussing the economics of sexuality because of important differences between "gender" and "sexuality" as analytical categories. For instance, she shows (Badgett 1995b) that gay and bisexual male workers earned substantially less than comparable heterosexual male workers, but that it is not as clear whether lesbian and bisexual women earn less than heterosexual women. Redmount (1995) provides the particularly provocative idea of attempting to treat gender endogenously (one could then measure the earnings penalty, say, for being a "womanly" woman), although she does not appear to have followed up on this idea as yet.

8 The organizer/editor of this explorations section commented in her introduction that the "papers do not cover the wide span of issues or methods we were hoping to have addressed" (Pujol 1997: 120). This likely indicates the tentative nature of such techniques infiltrating the profession at large, as well as the difficulty in coming up with truly novel practices that fit economics research situations.

9 On the other hand, considering alternative methodologies for approaching research problems probably does require economists to read more widely afield than they currently tend to do. This is not a trivial task given the amount of material there is to read already, the amount that becomes available every year (and the difficulty there is in identifying what is available, even with the helpful resources of internet-accessible bibliographic databases), and the amount of time the average economist has to devote to reading, given the multiple demands on our time. But, at least in the early stages of this project, someone has to be out there reading and conciliating these materials. Apologies are due to all readers who, by this point in the essay, have found that I have not cited your relevant paper or mentioned the research topic that you work on.

Bibliography

Agarwal, Bina (1994) "Gender and Command over Property: A Critical Gap in Economic Analysis and Policy in South Asia," *World Development* 22(10): 1455–78.

—— (1997) "'Bargaining' and Gender Relations: Within and Beyond the Household," *Feminist Economics* 3(1): 1–51.

—— (2001) "Participatory Exclusions, Community Forestry, and Gender: An Analysis for South Asia and a Conceptual Framework," *World Development* 29(10): 1,623–48.

Albelda, Randy (1995) "The Impact of Feminism in Economics – Beyond the Pale? A Discussion and Survey Results," *Journal of Economic Education* 26(3): 253–73.

Andreoni, James and Lise Vesterlund (2001) "Which is the Fairer Sex? Gender Differences in Altruism," *Quarterly Journal in Economics* 116(1): 293–312.

Aslaksen, Iulie (1999) "Gross Domestic Product," in Janice Peterson and Meg Lewis (eds.) *Elgar Companion to Feminist Economics*, Cheltenham and Northampton: Edward Elgar.

Aslaksen, Iulie and Charlotte Koren (1996) "Unpaid Household Work and the Distribution of Extended Income: The Norwegian Experience," *Feminist Economics* 2(3): 65–80.

Australian Bureau of Statistics (2000) "Unpaid Work and the Australian Economy 1997," occasional paper no. 5240.0.

Badgett, M.V. Lee (1995a) "Gender, Sexuality, and Sexual Orientation: All in the Feminist Family?," *Feminist Economics* 1(1): 121–39.

—— (1995b) "The Wage Effects of Sexual Orientation Discrimination," *Industrial & Labor Relations Review* 48(4): 726–39.

Benería, Lourdes (1992) "Accounting for Women's Work: The Progress of Two Decades," *World Development* 20(11): 1,547–60.

—— (1999) "The Enduring Debate Over Unpaid Labour," *International Labour Review* 138(3): 287–309.

Blank, Rebecca M. (1993) "What Should Mainstream Economists Learn from Feminist Theory?," in Marianne A. Ferber and Julie A. Nelson (eds.) *Beyond Economic Man: Feminist Theory and Evidence*, Chicago, IL: University of Chicago Press.

Çagatay, Nilüfer, Diane Elson and Caren Grown (1995) "Gender, Adjustment and Macroeconomics," *World Development* 23(11): 1,827–26.

Cantillon, Sara and Brian Nolan (2001) "Poverty Within Households: Measuring Gender Differences Using Nonmonetary Indicators," *Feminist Economics* 7(1): 5–23.

Cappelli, Peter, Jill Constantine and Clint Chadwick (2000) "It Pays to Value Family: Work and Family Tradeoffs Reconsidered," *Industrial Relations* 39(2): 175–98.

Cloud, Kathleen and Nancy Garrett (1996) "A Modest Proposal for Inclusion of Women's Household Human Capital Production in Analysis of Structural Transformation," *Feminist Economics* 2(3): 93–119.

Croson, Rachel and Nancy Buchan (1999) "Gender and Culture: International Experimental Evidence from Trust Games," *American Economic Review* 89(2): 386–91.

Eckel, Catherine C. and Philip J. Grossman (1996) "The Relative Price of Fairness: Gender Differences in a Punishment Game," *Journal of Economic Behavior & Organization* 30(2): 143–58.

—— (1998) "Are Women Less Selfish Than Men? Evidence from Dictator Experiments," *Economic Journal* 108(448): 726–35.

Elson, Diane (1991) "Male Bias in the Development Process: An Overview," in D. Elson (ed.) *Male Bias in the Development Process*, Manchester: Manchester University Press.

Esim, Simel (1997) "Can Feminist Methodology Reduce Power Hierarchies in Research Settings?," *Feminist Economics* 3(2): 137–9.

Ferber, Marianne A. and Julie A. Nelson (eds.) (1993a) *Beyond Economic Man: Feminist Theory and Evidence*, Chicago, IL: University of Chicago Press.

—— (1993b) "Introduction: The Social Construction of Economics and the Social Construction of Gender," in Marianne A. Ferber and Julie A. Nelson (eds.) *Beyond Economic Man: Feminist Theory and Evidence*, Chicago, IL: University of Chicago Press.

Findlay, Jeanette and Robert E. Wright (1996) "Gender, Poverty and the Intra-household Distribution of Resources," *Review of Income & Wealth* 42(3): 335–51.

Folbre, Nancy (1995) "Holding Hands at Midnight: The Paradox of Caring Labor," *Feminist Economics* 1(1): 73–92.

—— (2001) *The Invisible Heart: Economics and Family Values*, New York: New Press.

Garg, Ashish and Jonathan Morduch (1998) "Sibling Rivalry and the Gender Gap: Evidence from Child Health Outcomes in Ghana," *Journal of Population Economics* 11(4): 471–93.

Grown, Caren, Diane Elson and Nilüfer Çagatay (2000) "Growth, Trade, Finance, and Gender Inequality: Introduction," *World Development* 28(7): 1,145–56.

Grossbard-Shechtman, Shoshana (2001) "The New Home Economics at Columbia and Chicago," *Feminist Economics* 7(3). 103–30.

Hands, D. Wade (2001) *Reflection Without Rules: Economic Methodology and Contemporary Science Theory*, Cambridge: Cambridge University Press.

Harding, Sandra (1986) *The Science Question in Feminism*, Ithaca, NY: Cornell University Press.

Hewitson, Gillian J. (1999) *Feminist Economics: Interrogating the Masculinity of Rational Economic Man*, Cheltenham and Northampton: Edward Elgar.

Himmelweit, Susan (1995) "The Discovery of 'Unpaid Work': The Social Consequences of the Expansion of 'Work,'" *Feminist Economics* 1(2): 1–19.

—— (1999) "Caring Labor," *Annals of the American Academy of Political & Social Science* 561: 27–38.

Ironmonger, Duncan (1996) "Counting Outputs, Capital Inputs and Caring Labor: Estimating Gross Household Product," *Feminist Economics* 2(3): 37–64.

Jacobsen, Joyce P. (2002) "How Family Structure Affects Labor Market Outcomes," in Emily P. Hoffman and Jean Kimmel (eds.) *The Economics of Work and Family*, Kalamazoo: W.E. Upjohn Institute.

Jacobsen, Joyce P. and Andrew E. Newman (1997) "What Data Do Economists Use? The Case of Labor Economics and Industrial Relations," *Feminist Economics* 3(2): 127–30.

—— (2002) "Do Women and Non-economists Add Diversity to Research in Industrial Relations and Labor Economics?," *Eastern Economic Journal*, forthcoming.

Kessler, Daniel (1991) "Birth Order, Family Size, and Achievement: Family Structure and Wage Determination," *Journal of Labor Economics* 9(4): 413–26.

Kim, Marlene (2000) "Employers' Estimates of Market Wages: Implications for Wage Discrimination in the U.S.," *Feminist Economics* 6(2): 97–114.

Kuiper, Edith and Jolande Sap, with Susan F. Feiner, Notburga Ott and Zafiris Tzannatos (eds.) (1995) *Out of the Margin: Feminist Perspectives on Economics*, London and New York: Routledge.

Long, David and Frances Woolley (2002) "Feminist Economics and Disciplinary Transformation," working paper.

Longino, Helen E. (1993) "Subjects, Power, and Knowledge: Description and Prescription in Feminist Philosophies of Science," in Linda Alcoff and Elizabeth Potter (eds.) *Feminist Epistemologies*, London and New York: Routledge.

MacDonald, Martha (1995) "The Empirical Challenges of Feminist Economics: The Example of Economic Restructuring," in Edith Kuiper and Jolande Sap, with Susan F. Feiner, Notburga Ott and Zafiris Tzannatos (eds.) *Out of the Margin: Feminist Perspectives on Economics*, London and New York: Routledge.

Madrick, Jeff (1997) "Why Mainstream Economists Should Take Heed," *Feminist Economics* 3(1): 143–9.

Nelson, Julie A. (1989) "Individual Consumption Within the Household: A Study of Expenditures on Clothing," *Journal of Consumer Affairs* 23(1): 21–44.

—— (1995) "Comments on Chapters by Polachek, Ott, and Levin," in Edith Kuiper and Jolande Sap, with Susan F. Feiner, Notburga Ott and Zafiris Tzannatos (eds.) *Out of the Margin: Feminist Perspectives on Economics*, London and New York: Routledge.

—— (1996) *Feminism, Objectivity and Economics*, London and New York: Routledge.

—— (1999) "Of Markets and Martyrs: Is It OK to Pay Well for Care?," *Feminist Economics* 5(3): 43–59.

Nelson, Lynn Hankinson (1990) *Who Knows: From Quine to a Feminist Empiricism*, Philadelphia, PA: Temple University Press.

—— (1993) "Epistemological Communities," in L. Alcoff and E. Potter (eds.) *Feminist Epistemologies*, London and New York: Routledge.

Netz, Janet S. and Jon D. Haveman (1999) "All in the Family: Family, Income, and Labor Force Attachment," *Feminist Economics* 5(3): 85–106.

Olmsted, Jennifer C. (1997) "Telling Palestinian Women's Economic Stories," *Feminist Economics* 3(2): 141–51.

Ott, Notburga (1995) "Fertility and Division of Work in the Family," in Edith Kuiper and Jolande Sap, with Susan F. Feiner, Notburga Ott and Zafiris Tzannatos (eds.) *Out of the Margin: Feminist Perspectives on Economics*, London and New York: Routledge.

Polachek, Solomon W. (1995) "Human Capital and the Gender Earnings Gap: A Response to Feminist Critiques," in Edith Kuiper and Jolande Sap, with Susan F. Feiner, Notburga Ott and Zafiris Tzannatos (eds.) *Out of the Margin: Feminist Perspectives on Economics*, London and New York: Routledge.

Pujol, Michèle (1997) "Introduction: Broadening Economic Data and Methods," *Feminist Economics* 3(2): 119–20.

Redmount, Esther (1995) "Toward a Feminist Econometrics," in Edith Kuiper and Jolande Sap, with Susan F. Feiner, Notburga Ott and Zafiris Tzannatos (eds.) *Out of the Margin: Feminist Perspectives on Economics*, London and New York: Routledge.

Saad, Gad and Tripat Gill (2000) "Gender Dynamics in the Ultimatum Game: An Evolutionary Psychology Perspective," working paper.

Schubert, Renate, Martin Brown, Matthias Gysler and Hans Wolfgang Brachinger (1999) "Financial Decision-Making: Are Women Really More Risk-Averse?," *American Economic Review* 89(2): 381–5.

Seiz, Janet A. (1999) "Game Theory and Bargaining Models," in Janice Peterson and Meg Lewis (eds.) *Elgar Companion to Feminist Economics*, Cheltenham and Northampton: Edward Elgar.

Statistics Canada (2002) "Households' Unpaid Work: Measurement and Valuation," catalogue number 13–603E, No. 3.

Stratton, Leslie S. (2002) "Examining the Wage Differential for Married and Cohabiting Men," *Economic Inquiry* 40(2): 199–212.

Strober, Myra H. (1988) "Two-Earner Families," in Sanford M. Dornbusch and Myra H. Strober (eds.) *Feminism, Children, and the New Families*, New York: Guilford Press.

Tuana, Nancy (1992) "The Radical Future of Feminist Empiricism," *Hypatia* 7(1): 100–14.

UNDP (United Nations Development Programme) (1995) *Human Development Report 1995*, New York and Oxford: Oxford University Press.

—— (1999) *Human Development Report 1999*, New York and Oxford: Oxford University Press.

van Staveren, Irene (1997) "Focus Groups: Contributing to a Gender-Aware Methodology," *Feminist Economics* 3(2): 131–5.

Wagman, Barnet and Nancy Folbre (1996) "Household Services and Economic Growth in the United States, 1870–1930," *Feminist Economics* 2(1): 43–66.

Waring, Marilyn (1988) *If Women Counted: A New Feminist Economics*, San Francisco, CA: Harper & Row.

Woolley, Frances R. (1993) "The Feminist Challenge to Neoclassical Economics," *Cambridge Journal of Economics* 17(4): 485–500.

Woolley, Frances R. and Judith Marshall (1994) "Measuring Inequality Within the Household," *Review of Income & Wealth* 40(4): 415–31.

World Bank (2001) *Engendering Development*, New York: Oxford University Press.

7 Foregrounding practices
Feminist philosophy of economics beyond rhetoric and realism[1]

Fabienne Peter

> One cannot not be politically and epistemically engaged.[2]

Introduction

Feminist economics is concerned with the many ways in which economic life is shaped by gender as well as other significant categories of identity. Its goal is to reveal the gender-blindness of existing economic analysis, and to bring into the debate issues which have previously been ignored. Developing alternative theories to address these issues has revealed that the existing tools of economic analysis do not lend themselves well to the kinds of questions that feminist economists address. The attempt to explain the impact of gender on the economy thus often goes hand in hand with a theoretical inquiry into the gendered nature of these tools.[3]

Because of the stake feminist economics has in economic methods themselves – not just in their application – it has from the beginning displayed great affinity with epistemology and philosophy of science. The traditional – positivist – philosophy of economics, still endorsed by many practicing economists, insists on the separability of facts from values and on the objectivity of scientists. It is incompatible with feminist economics for two reasons: First, feminist economics does not conceal its affinities with the political goal of improving the status of women and other social groups; second, feminist philosophy of science and feminist epistemology suggest that economic methods and theories should themselves be understood as the product of gendered social and scientific norms and practices. Scientific knowledge is socially constructed, and facts and values are never radically separate.

Attempts in contemporary philosophy of economics to replace Popperian epistemology are dominated by rhetoric (McCloskey 1985) and scientific realism (Lawson 1997; Mäki 1992a, 1993a). Rhetoric and realism propose different avenues for rethinking the practices of economists. Deirdre McCloskey rejects all appeals to epistemological rules, as economics, like all "science," cannot be more than a conversation. The realists, too, are critical of the positivist preoccupation with epistemology, but for a different reason. They try to move into the foreground ontological reasoning – reasoning about the nature of the (social) world and human beings and its consequences for the production of knowledge – which has been neglected as a result of positivism's preoccupation with epistemology.

Each of the three principal proponents – McCloskey, Uskali Mäki, and Tony Lawson – has in one way or another engaged with feminist economics, arguing that his or her respective proposal is able to accommodate the issues feminist economists are concerned with. Are their suggestions satisfactory? Does a *feminist* philosophy of economics have anything to contribute that is not already covered by, or at least derivable from, some approach or other of contemporary mainstream philosophies of economics? This paper will scrutinize the claims of McCloskey and the realists, concluding that none can fully meet the exigencies of feminist economics. Nevertheless, there are elements in each approach that pick up central concerns of feminist economics. It will thus be useful to clarify just how far either rhetoric or scientific realism can take us towards a feminist philosophy of economics and where it will be necessary to reach further.

I shall argue that McCloskey's deflationary account of the process of scientific knowledge production, which views scientific knowledge in principle as on a par with other forms of knowledge, has some promise for a feminist philosophy of economics. But McCloskey is overly optimistic about the self-regulatory potential of economic discourse (see also Strassmann 1993). The scientific realists, having similar reservations, warn of the dangers of a relativistic account of economic knowledge. Many feminist economists would agree. For, as Janet Seiz (1995) argues, feminist economics needs to identify a way of doing scientific inquiry which avoids the respective dangers of disempowering relativism and of fallacious immunization from contestation. The realists claim that ontological reflection, properly conducted, can avert the dangers of relativism. But their solution may not be "no strings." It can come at the price of a reified notion of scientific knowledge – a notion of the process of scientific knowledge production that is impervious to, and set above, other cognitive processes.

The dilemma between relativism and reification of scientific knowledge – or between science as "social" and as "rational" (Longino 2002) – not only affects economic methodology but is well known in recent (post-Kuhnian) philosophy of science. Under the labels of "social epistemology" and "science as practice," however, perspectives have started to emerge that theorize more carefully the social nature of scientific inquiry and its implications for the production of knowledge and the status of science.[4] Many of these perspectives, developed out of an engagement with social studies of science, depart from the preoccupations of classical epistemology with truth, justification, and rational beliefs. They focus instead on how ethical and political values influence belief formation, judgments of what constitute important topics of inquiry, and the processes of knowledge evaluation.

It is not surprising that these approaches have been championed, not last, by feminist epistemologists and philosophers of science. Feminists are well aware of the pervasive influence of social power relations – be they based on gender or on other distinctions – on people's agency and social institutions. For many, scientific inquiry is no exception. Working in the spirit of Kuhnian theories of scientific inquiry, they see science as a "value-based enterprise" (Rorty 1979: 342).[5] What is of principal interest to me in this paper is how feminist epistemologists and philosophers of science have expounded the problems of claims to sovereignty in all their variations – be they based on epistemic privilege or social privilege, thus bringing to the fore the role of democratic ethics and politics in scientific inquiry.[6] I shall argue that a feminist philosophy of economics that is able to deal with the way social power relations influence the process of economic inquiry will have the form of a *political philosophy of science*, inspired by the analogies of problems in theories of scientific inquiry to those encountered in democratic theory. To do this, feminist philosophy of economics has to go beyond both rhetoric and realism.

A final word is necessary about how I understand the feminist project. There are, of course, many interpretations of what feminism is about. I interpret feminism as part of a broader social movement, nourished from many sources, that is oriented towards more radically democratic societies. I see the feminist project as an invitation to rethink established constructions of meaning – including its own past constructions.[7] I would not, therefore, expect feminism to be a coherent project with a singular political aim (i.e. to improve "women's" lives). From such an interpretation of feminism follows a perspective on feminist philosophy of economics that points beyond standpoint epistemology and that is not limited to the contribution that "thinking from women's lives" can make to economics (Harding 1995). This broadening of perspective is necessary, I believe, because standpoints do not account for much of what constitutes legitimate knowledge claims; nor is it helpful to base a theory of how knowledge claims should be validated on a priori fixed distinctions – such as gender standpoints – as these very distinctions are, not last, a product of processes of knowledge production.

Rhetoric, realism, and feminist economics

Let me start with a brief review of the main positions spanning the field of mainstream philosophy of economics and their claims to feminist economics.

McCloskey attacks the "party line" – positivist – methodology, which many economists still invoke to legitimize their work. She dismisses the methodological rules to which economists appeal as irrelevant and mistaken, on the grounds that they paint a mistaken picture of how economic knowledge actually gets produced. From the perspective of the rhetoric approach, economics is – and should not aspire to be anything other than – an ongoing conversation. For McCloskey, the still common appeal to methodological rules is purely rhetorical, having no effect other than to induce in scientific discourse an inappropriate slant. Such rules arbitrarily constrain the free flow of economic discourse by excluding certain forms of argumentation and privileging others – not requiring of them any further substantiation. McCloskey urges economists to become aware of their discursive strategies, and make full use of the argumentative force of language rather than limit themselves to a jargon that is falsely believed to convey scientific status.

What determines the acceptability of arguments – be it in science or in other social spheres – is the *persuasion* of the participants in the conversation (McCloskey 1985: 44). According to McCloskey's broad understanding, "[a]ll that moves without violence…is persuasion, *peitho*, the realm of rhetoric, unforced agreement, mutually advantageous intellectual exchange" (1994: 41). It follows that the criteria by which theories are assessed are necessarily contained within and emerge from the discourse itself – outside of discourse, there is no "safe metalinguistical level" (*ibid.*: 201). McCloskey thus advocates a deflationary conception of science – a conception where scientific knowledge is on a par with other forms of knowing.

With one exception, McCloskey's argument is directed against any rule-bound methodology (in economics and in science in general), which would be imposed on the scientific discourse from outside (McCloskey 1985: ch. 2). The exception is what she calls *Sprachethik* – a framework of moral rules of polite respect that should guide all conversations. These norms are necessary to ensure that persuasion is genuine and not coerced.[8]

On various occasions McCloskey has intervened on feminist economics. In her contribution to *Beyond Economic Man* (McCloskey 1993), she concedes that neoclassical economics is prone to androcentric biases, but sees this as a result of adhering to a fantasy of "hard" science. Awareness of rhetoric, McCloskey suggests, could correct such biases (and improve economics overall).[9]

The deflationary account of science McCloskey suggests is probably the most attractive feature of the rhetoric approach for feminist economists. It undermines attempts to put economists' understanding of society a priori above that of other groups – in academia and elsewhere – and to devalue dissenting voices within economics as unscientific. Yet some caution is in order. Diana Strassmann's examination of the discursive practices of economists (Strassmann 1993) casts doubts on McCloskey's conception of science as a self-regulatory process – a "free marketplace of ideas" – among groups of peers.

The conclusion the realists draw from Strassmann's argument is that the assessment of economic discourse and of knowledge claims cannot function when viewed as entirely contained in scientific discourse itself. In a nutshell, the realist approach emphasizes that to make sense of the endeavor of economics as a science, economics has to be understood as an attempt to represent and explain economic reality, to discover truth about entities that exist independently of scientific theories. This is not to say that scientific realists, as Mäki rightly stresses, have to believe that a theory is "a literally true story of what the world is like," as Baas van Fraassen (1980: 8) claims. What matters is that they aim for truth, even if there is no certainty to be had whether or not truth is discovered. So let us take a closer look at Mäki's and Lawson's versions of scientific realism.

In one strand of his work, Mäki examines the philosophical foundations of rhetoric and presents a rereading of rhetoric which would be compatible with realism (e.g. Mäki 1993a). Mäki agrees with McCloskey in seeing rhetoric as related to persuasion, but disagrees on the role of the aim to represent the world and the search for truth in scientific inquiry. Mäki critiques what he interprets as McCloskey's conflation of truth and justification, as well as her collapsing of the representational and the rhetorical functions of language (Mäki 1993a: 36f.). Mäki (1993a) is working towards an understanding of economics which does not ignore the representational functions of language. Rejecting persuasion of the participants in the economic discourse as the only criteria, he advocates a correspondence theory of truth.[10]

This aiming at truth, at saying something about how the world really is, anchors economic discourse. But how should this anchoring be understood? The answer hinges on the role Mäki attributes to ontology in economic explanations. He develops this through a taxonomy of the role of assumptions in economic models and theories. Mäki (1994) distinguishes between "core" assumptions and "peripheral" assumptions. The former constitute the theory, while the latter help to make the theory more easily tractable. An example of a core assumption is the hypothesis that individual behavior corresponds to the maximization of utility. Core assumptions are often selected in terms of what are believed to be the essential elements of the economic activities to be explained. They are, moreover, often believed to be at least partially true. Peripheral assumptions – which may well be false – may then be introduced to bring into sharper relief those features of the world that are believed to be essential. Together, such assumptions thus contain ontological claims, and these claims account for the substance of economic theories – for what economic theories are all about.[11] Since there need not be consensus on such assumptions within the discipline of economics, Mäki's taxonomy of assumptions illuminates why debates which have their origins in disputes about core assumptions tend to be the most divisive.

Mäki's account of the influence of ontological considerations on the content of economic discourse is no doubt echoed in certain efforts of feminist economists. Consider the following passage from Strassmann, which generalizes the problems feminist economists encounter when trying to change the terms of economic discourse:

> Difficulties linked to the core assumptions will be extremely hard to change because of the identification of economics as an approach that uses those

assumptions. Because any account of the world is constructed on the basis of a partial perspective, standard economic accounts do more than just leave out other voices. They create a conceptual framework for organizing an understanding of the world in which some features are prioritized over others.

(Strassmann 1993: 64)

Although Strassmann is not advocating realism, from the passage quoted, Mäki's analysis of the ontological underpinning of economic theories seems to be quite compatible with work done in feminist economics. Whereas McCloskey's rhetoric framework has to treat all debates as in principle on a par, Mäki's combined approach offers a starting point for a critical examination of the substance of ongoing debates in economic discourse. In contrast to the positivist method, it is open to debates about the ontological foundations of economic methods. Accordingly, it can accommodate the feminist critique of neglect of gender relations in economics as one contribution to the more general debate about how the world should be accurately represented. Yet, if feminist economists critique certain assumptions of mainstream economics as being androcentric, they probably intend to say more than simply: "We (feminist economists, women, women from my cultural background) have a different view of essential features of the world than you guys." They see the neglect of gender relations in economic analysis not just as a simple oversight, but as a structural feature that shapes – among other things – economic discourse. Mäki's detached analytical framework for assessing economic discourse does not provide a space for the political and ethical dimensions of such criticism. It seems as if the possibility of substantial engagement with economic discourse – which Mäki finds lacking in McCloskey's rhetoric approach – is bought at the price of reinstating a (positivist) conception of rational science that stands above political and moral struggles.

The final approach to consider is Lawson's critical realism. Lawson explicitly advocates his philosophy as offering a backing for heterodox economics, including feminist economics. Compared to Mäki's version of realism, critical realism makes more prescriptive use of ontology: ontological reasoning is not merely invoked as a way to capture what are believed to be essential features of the world, but linked to the question of scientific success. More specifically, critical realism takes as its starting point the success of the scientific method in the natural sciences, which is believed to be possible only with a particular ontology of the natural world. In what concerns economics, critical realist analysis sees current economic practices as relying on a flawed social ontology and puts forward an alternative ontological theory which economists should take into account if they want their discipline to become a successful science. Lawson's argument for critical realism in (feminist) economics hinges on the possibility that a philosophy that accounts for the success of the natural sciences can also be put to good use in economics – and make it more successful than it currently is (Lawson 1997: 52).[12]

Critical realism is realistic about causes. This is to say, it postulates as objects of scientific inquiry the mechanisms, structures, etc. which operate hidden from our immediate experience, but whose effects we perceive. It believes that the objects of scientific inquiry in both the social sciences and the natural sciences are "structured" (not reducible to "correlations about surface phenomena") and "intransitive" (they are effective independently of our knowledge of them) (Lawson 1997: 20ff.). There is, however, an important difference between the natural sciences and economics and other social sciences. Regarding the social world, Lawson sees human beings as acting within social structures without being fully determined by them. It follows that social structures are constantly reproduced and/or transformed by human actions. Lawson stresses that in this respect the conditions for the social sciences are different from those for the natural sciences, as in the social world it holds only to a certain extent that the mechanisms and structures underlying our social world exist without our knowledge of them – in the natural world, in contrast, mechanisms and structures operate independently of our knowledge of them. The social world is more dependent on consciousness than the natural world, its underlying structures and mechanisms can be changed when knowledge of them is available, and, without society, social structures and processes vanish too. Given that social science can achieve knowledge about the otherwise hidden forces underneath social phenomena, it is able to aid processes of social change towards commonly desired goals. The term *critical* realism has been chosen to underline this potential of social science (Lawson 1997: 158).

In a recent article in *Feminist Economics* Lawson (1999) argues that critical realism champions feminist standpoint epistemology – the examination of how thinking based on women's lives transforms the production of economic knowledge. For critical realists, the way to discover and explain a mechanism at work in an open social world, Lawson suggests, is by following something akin to the methodology of controlled experiments in medical research. By contrasting two or more situations or populations which are equal in most aspects but show different outcomes according to some factor, one obtains hints about underlying mechanisms that can account for the observed differences. Given that what is perceived as an interesting contrast depends on one's own position in society, critical realism requires different standpoints.

Lawson also sees critical realism as compatible with the political goals of feminist economics – to make economic research useful for the emancipatory goals of feminism. Lawson describes feminism as oscillating between the difficulty of assuming shared interests among women and the threat of losing its very object. He applauds feminist theory for successfully challenging falsely universalist assertions, but echoes the familiar warning against relativism. Lawson claims that critical realism can offer an alternative to this relativist picture of difference and more difference by positing a common human nature, which creates the theoretical possibility of speaking meaningfully of shared interests of particular social groups.

Lawson's critical realism brings to the philosophy of economics an explicitly political orientation – something I identified as missing from the other two approaches. It has the further merit of engaging with feminist epistemology, trying to show that it can be made compatible with scientific realism. But there is a fundamental mismatch with feminist economics here too. Even more manifestly than in Mäki's approach, critical realism relies on a reified conception of scientific knowledge. This is to say that it presumes that scientific processes of knowledge production are inherently superior to other forms of knowledge and knowledge production. Since the methods of scientific inquiry are believed to be a tool for uncovering those hidden social structures that drive social phenomena, science itself and processes of scientific knowledge production are a priori excluded as fields of inquiry, as a social phenomenon on a par with others. As a philosophy of feminist economics, critical realism is thus overly uncritical about science.

Legitimacy *interruptus*: neglecting social influences on knowledge

I have contrasted rhetoric and realism with regard to their implications for how processes of knowledge production and the assessment of knowledge claims should be understood and evaluated. McCloskey wants to eliminate all a priori boundaries between science and other forms of discourse – in particular, methodological rules which lay down what is to count as scientific knowledge. The thrust of her argument is that as long as rules of individual good conduct (the norms of *Sprachethik*) are respected the machinery of scientific inquiry will work at its best. Biases in economic knowledge based on social prejudices and exclusive social practices – for example those related to gender – will, eventually, be corrected by the force of better arguments.

Mäki and Lawson fear that this conception does not offer sufficient safeguards against arbitrariness and, ultimately, relativism. Mäki warns of uncontrolled social influences which cannot be checked by McCloskey's criterion of persuasion as long as the formation of peer groups is not questioned. Although both Lawson and Mäki invoke realism, they emphasize that ontological reflection cannot, by itself, discriminate among competing explanations. At this level, the realists recognize the role of discourse.[13] They presume, nevertheless, that the extra-discursive existence of the objects of scientific inquiry provides an additional constraint, necessary to ensure the rationality of scientific discourse.[14] In this quasi-positivist move, both Mäki and Lawson conjure up the rationality of scientific processes of knowledge production – their superiority to political processes – as necessary to check illegitimate social influences.

This dilemma is not peculiar to economic methodology. The heated debates between, on the one hand, those with a background in post-Kuhnian social studies of science and, on the other, those with a background in traditional philosophy of science have been dubbed the "science wars" of today.[15] It can be argued, however, that the alleged dichotomy between relativism and rationalism, or between the social and the rational (Longino 2002), obstructs a more productive thinking about processes of knowledge production and the assessment of knowledge claims. What is called for is a more adequate theorizing of social influences on the production of knowledge.[16]

Post-Kuhnian social studies of science have cast serious doubt on inherited understandings of scientific knowledge production and of science itself. They have exposed the inseparability of scientific knowledge from social values and practices. While some social studies of science – those which are part of the so-called "strong programme" – have suggested that all scientific knowledge is a result of specific interests of particular groups (Barnes 1977), the literature on "science as culture and practice" that has developed since is more nuanced. They keep the focus wide enough to describe and theorize the multitude of channels through which processes of knowledge production are imbued with social factors – insisting on the inescapable presence of social influences on all forms of science and on the recognition that not only "bad" science is affected by social values and practices, but "good" science too. It follows that trying to protect scientific inquiry from social influences is not only impossible, but misleading. The question is, rather, which social influences help scientific inquiry and which hinder it (Harding 1991).

In reaction to such insights, the project of epistemology has undergone a profound change. No longer confined to establishing rational, asocial, and ahistorical criteria to define knowledge, social epistemology has taken it as its task to analyze and interpret claims to knowledge. As Elisabeth Anderson defines it:

> Social epistemology is the branch of naturalized epistemology that investigates the influence of specifically social factors on knowledge production: who gets to participate in theoretical inquiry, who listens to whom, the relative prestige of different styles and fields of research, the political and economic conditions in which inquirers conduct their investigations, the social settings in which they interact with the subjects of study, their ideological commitments, the availability of models and narrative forms in the culture that can be used to structure scientific observation and explain phenomena, and so forth.[17]

The social factors Anderson lists are both internal and external to science. Internal factors affect the way scientists interact with each other and their relationship to what they study. External factors shape what scientific inquiry is understood to be and the political and economic context in which it is conducted. Feminist philosophers of science and epistemologists have played a vital role in this renewal of the projects of epistemology, as the gendered character of social norms and practices and of the political and economic organization of society is an important social factor that influences scientific inquiry, both from within and from outside.

This transformation of the project of epistemology and the awareness of social influences on knowledge production suggests that the relativism/rationalism dichotomy can be bridged. Failing to respond to the challenges raised by social influences on scientific knowledge is what creates the trap of the dichotomy between relativism and rationalism. And this is indeed what is happening in contemporary economic methodology. While the issue of social influences on knowledge production is touched upon, its implications – in particular for the question of how knowledge claims should be assessed – are insufficiently spelled out. What is missing in both rhetoric and realism is a more critical and progressive engagement with epistemology. Epistemological issues and the potential of a renewed project of epistemology are marginalized as a result of Mäki's and Lawson's goal to shift emphasis away from epistemology towards ontology and of McCloskey's fear that epistemology is inevitably tied to the positivist approach. From the perspective of feminist economics, this situation is unsatisfactory.

Economic knowledge and epistemic democracy

What, now, could be the elements of a feminist philosophy of economics? First, and most obviously, the engagement with feminist social epistemology is crucial. Feminist economists have from the beginning addressed epistemological issues, which are widely acknowledged as an important tool for tackling the exclusion of feminist concerns from mainstream economics. Rather than a set of a priori rules, epistemology should be conceived of as a critical inquiry into the processes of scientific knowledge production and the content of scientific claims to knowledge, contributing to the redress of hegemonic tendencies in processes of knowledge production (Flax 1981; L.H. Nelson 1995).

Next, feminist philosophy of economics – together with feminist philosophy of science more generally – has to show that accepting that the practices and values constituting scientific inquiry cannot be insulated from broader social practices and values does not condemn one to judgmental relativism, i.e. to the view that there can never be any standards by which claims to knowledge can be evaluated. Harding (1991) has, in this context, proposed the notion of *strong objectivity*. Whereas the received view treats scientific objectivity as independent from the observing scientist(s), her criterion is one of epistemic inclusiveness. The criterion she proposes for the assessment of knowledge claims is stronger than the received criterion of objectivity in the sense that it is not limited to a narrow conception of scientific practices. Instead, strong objectivity extends to "the macro tendencies in the social order, which shape scientific practices" (Harding 1991: 149), and thus includes the examination of the influence of social values and practices on who gets to participate in scientific inquiry, on how topics of research get selected, and on the content and results of scientific research. Harding asks that instead of calling for the elimination of all values,

> the sciences need to legitimate *within scientific research*, as part of practicing science, critical examination of historical values and interests that may be so shared within the scientific community, so invested in by the very constitution of this or that field of study, that they will not show up as a cultural bias between experimenters or between research communities.
> (Harding 1991: 14f.)

If Harding stresses that such critical examination has to take place *within* scientific inquiry, she rejects the often-made objection that such a view amounts to subjecting scientific inquiry to external political control. Accepting that scientific inquiry, scientific practices and values cannot be insulated from broader social practices makes the received view of science, according to which scientific inquiry is – and has to be – sharply distinguished from politics and ethics, seem inadequate. If internal and external social influences on scientific inquiry intertwine, trying to make a distinction between what is properly called "scientific" and what is a "political" or an "ethical" question becomes an impossible task.

Political and ethical dimensions are manifest not just in epistemology, but in ontological reasoning as well. The realists are right to stress that specific ontological assumptions underlie different theories and different epistemologies. But ontological reasoning should not – contra the realists – be seen as a way out of ethical and political conflicts in scientific inquiry. As Harding has warned in her recent comment on Lawson's critical realism, according to Thomas Kuhn's account of the scientific process "to give up one theory for another can be to 'switch worlds' – to exchange ontologies" (Harding 1999: 130), something that established scientists will be reluctant to do. Harding argues that insofar as feminist scientists follow Kuhn's account it will be important to pay attention to "the way that ontologies are imbedded in moral and political projects" (*ibid.*). And she adds that, for this reason, "it requires a lot more than just 'clear thinking' to dislodge such ontologies from their status as obvious" (*ibid.*). Far from denying the deep impact of ontologies on scientific explanation, Harding draws attention to how addressing them may open additional political divides. This criticism targets Lawson's optimism about how, if social scientists could settle on "the" one appropriate ontology, scientific inquiry could be directed at the pursuit of universally shared values. It also constitutes an objection to Mäki's approach to realism, as it casts doubts on Mäki's belief that ontological reflection will safeguard economic discourse from social influences and biases.

Nevertheless, Harding's suggestion to avoid ontological realism for strategic reasons cuts too short and so does her attempt to settle the question of the legitimacy of knowledge claims on the basis of a notion – objectivity – inherited from the foundationalist epistemology of positivism. As Jane Flax (1981: 1,013) pointed out already in the early eighties:

> In philosophy, being (ontology) has been divorced from knowing (epistemology) and both have been separated from ethics and politics. These divisions were blessed by Kant and transformed by him into a fundamental principle derived from the structure of mind itself.
>
> (Flax 1982: 1,013)

The switch of focus in philosophy of science from knowledge to the practices by which knowledge gets produced underlines the inseparability of knowing from being. According to Joseph Rouse's definition, "practices are not just agents' activities but also the configuration of the world within which those activities are significant" (1996: 133). In scientific practices epistemic elements (the search for knowledge) are thus intertwined with ontological elements – premises about reality which make these practices meaningful. It is not necessary, however, to assume a fixed ontology, given prior to the production of scientific knowledge. Karen Barad's (1998) notion of "agential reality" considers being itself – just as knowing too – as something that is "continually reconstituted through…material-discursive intra-actions" (Barad 1998: 104).[18] From a perspective based on practices, we can see that feminist economists should understand their work as doing more than providing additional knowledge claims based on the standpoint of "women." They should aim at something other than Harding's "strong objectivity" – the coming together of knowledge claims from different social standpoints. The goal, instead, becomes to identify and change the practices – both within and outside of science – that lead to the exclusion of feminist concerns from the production of scientific knowledge.

If my analysis of mainstream philosophy of economics and of developments in philosophy of science more generally is correct, something like a *political philosophy of science* is called for.[19] By drawing attention to the political I do not intend to suggest that everything scientists do is to be interpreted directly in terms of their political interests. Nor am I advocating subjecting every move of scientists to political control. Given that "[o]ne cannot *not* be politically and epistemically engaged" (Rouse 1996: 257; emphasis mine), I have in mind, instead, the inherent contestability of processes of scientific knowledge production. Ideally, how scientific practices constrain participation in epistemic processes, the goals of scientific inquiry, what count as appropriate questions, as good arguments, etc. should all be questions open to continual contestation. Moreover, since what have traditionally been conceived of as internal and external factors intertwine in these scientific practices, space for contestation should be accommodated both within a scientific discipline and in the exchange between scientists and the "general public."

If the production of knowledge is viewed as a social process, inherently tied to ethics and politics, the assessment of knowledge claims raises issues of legitimacy similar to those that political philosophy and political theory deal with. The problem is not only pressing for the philosophy of economics, but stands at the heart of recent developments in philosophy of science in general. Definitive answers are, not surprisingly, still missing, and I am not able to provide one either. I thus have to limit myself to drawing attention to a few important elements of such a political philosophy of science.

First, social influences on the production of knowledge should not be seen as a foundational problem for scientific inquiry, but one concerning their practices. In other words, rather than worry about how social influences would affect received views of truth, justification, and objectivity, the challenge lies in rethinking the legitimacy of knowledge claims in ways that take into account the inherent political and ethical aspects of processes of knowledge production. The bearing of gender and other aspects of social identity, as well as the power relations embodied in them, on processes of scientific knowledge production is one example. The emphasis that is placed in feminist economics on criticisms of mainstream economics may be explained as a struggle over access to epistemic practices. Since feminists find it impossible to address issues of concern to them in the dominant practices of the economic discipline, they have tended to prioritize the critical examination of the principles upon which they operate.

In a discipline such as economics, where there is little space for self-reflection, this strategy bears the danger of placing feminist scholarship distinctively outside of the dominant discourse (shaped by the already included) and thus of further contributing to the marginalization of feminist scholarship. The problem is best illustrated in comparison to McCloskey's rhetoric of economics. Requiring persuasion only from within the current economic profession gives undue weight to the status quo and, more importantly, does not provide the tools for a broader inquiry into questions such as whose beliefs count, whose experiences are reflected, what sorts of interests influence the scientific discourse and how, etc. One of McCloskey's main arguments against conditions on scientific discourse other than the rules of *Sprachethik* is that they will inevitably become rigid over time. Discursive practices do, however, have an equal tendency to become rigid and thus – by way of the view of the world they entail – lead to discrimination against some forms of reasoning.

A political philosophy of science thus calls for more than rules of individual good behavior, as, even if no one acts consciously in an exclusionary way, social practices may still lead to such effects.[20] Ulla Grapard (2001) illustrates the problem of exclusion with the example of the fate of Charlotte Perkins Gilman's work. Grapard closes her analysis with the following warning:

Working within neoclassical economics, many liberal feminists have uncritically absorbed the methodological stand of their non-feminist colleagues. Many have been told by teachers and advisers to stay clear of controversial political issues if they want to establish themselves in the profession. But – as I have argued here and as much of the work of feminist economics has shown – a conformist methodology or research agenda has not historically been a guarantee for inclusion.[21]

Instead of fighting for acceptance within current practices – which may well be futile – the goal would be to creatively imagine alternative topics of research and modes of inquiry which have the potential to stimulate more contestation within economics about what constitutes legitimate and illegitimate epistemic practices.[22]

The vision for such a political philosophy of science is one of intellectual pluralist democracy, a process that draws its moving energy from continuing contestation of established scientific practices. Realizing this vision is, of course, full of challenges, not least because it will not be sufficient to give access to the excluded on the terms of the included. Many feminist economists will have experienced the inadequacy of proceeding in this way. A similar problem is encountered in the political sphere. If deliberative democracy is understood as limited to "rational" public deliberation, where rationality is defined in terms of the included, forms of reasoning that differ from this norm will continue to be silenced (Sanders 1997). What is at stake for feminist economists, therefore, is to contribute to the transformation of the terms of economic inquiry and to bring to bear previously excluded practices. It is not unlikely that feminist economists will not have to pursue this on their own, but will be able to forge alliances with others – researchers in economics and in other disciplines, as well as people outside of academia.

Notes

1 I am most grateful to Drucilla Barker for very helpful comments and editorial suggestions. I also benefited from the comments on an earlier version of this paper received at the History of Economics Society annual conference in Greensboro in 1999.
2 Rouse (1996: 257).
3 See, for example, Folbre and Hartmann (1988), J.A. Nelson (1992, 1996), Seiz (1992, 1995), Strassman (1993), Strober (1994), Barker (1995); for a comprehensive overview over the development of feminist economics, see Hewitson (1999).
4 Cf. the contributions in Pickering (1992), Galison and Stump (1996), and in Biagioli (1999); Rouse (1987, 1996), Longino (1990, 2002), and Fricker (2000).
5 See also Kuhn (1977, ch. 13).
6 Harding, for example, points out that feminist standpoint epistemologies do not sanction all types of political and ethical influences on scientific inquiry, but "only *prodemocratic* ethics and politics" (2001: 512). She adds that "such ethical and political considerations are invoked because they have scientific value, though of course that is not the only value they are recognized to have" (*ibid.*).

7 Cf. Butler (1990).
8 McCloskey lists the following norms: "don't lie; pay attention; don't sneer; cooperate; don't shout; let other people talk; be open-minded; explain yourself when asked; don't resort to violence or conspiracy in aid of your ideas" (1985: 24). She claims that the idea of *Sprachethik* is borrowed from Habermas, but this is a rather sloppy reading of Habermas. For an analysis of this issue, see Mäki and Vromen (1996).
9 McCloskey writes:

> Men and women already must use a wide and conjective rhetoric in doing economics, but are not aware of it. If they became aware of it they would do their economics better and keep their tempers better. They could speak then in their own voice but with a tolerant confidence, without shouting or sneering. And perhaps they could speak better in the voice of the other, too.
>
> (McCloskey 1993: 90)

10 Mäki defines it as follows: "The truth of a statement S consists in its correspondence with objective (i.e. S-independent) reality" (1993a: 28).
11 Mäki calls this the "method of isolation" – see, for example, Mäki (1992a).
12 Lawson wants "to use philosophy to investigate the possibility of economics as social science. Specifically…to use it to assess the scientific possibilities for, or scientifically of, actual economic practice" (1997: 45). Lawson's critical realism is developed in conjunction with Roy Bhaskar's (1989) philosophy of transcendental realism for the natural sciences. For a more extensive review of critical realism, see Peter (2001).
13 As Lawson points out, to expect more from ontological reasoning would amount to an "ontic fallacy," the pendant to the "epistemic fallacy" of positivism (Lawson 1997: 33; Bhaskar 1989: 157f.).
14 See Lawson (1997: 246); Mäki (1992b, 1993b).
15 Cf. the title of the volume edited by Ross (1996).
16 For arguments along these lines, see Harding (1991), Rouse (1996), Fricker (2000), and Longino (2002).
17 Anderson (1995: 54). Naturalized epistemology no longer views epistemology as a branch of philosophy, but instead as a branch of the empirical sciences.
18 By "intra-action" she means the "inseparability of 'objects' and 'agencies of observation,'" a concept that the term "interaction" cannot capture (Barad 1998: 96).
19 Cf. the subtitle of Rouse's book *Knowledge and Power: Toward a Political Philosophy of Science* (Rouse 1987).
20 There is an interesting parallel here at the level of political philosophy. Robert Nozick's (1974) libertarian theory regards all outcomes as equally just that result from free transactions on the basis of an initially just situation. John Rawls (1971), in contrast, argues that even if everybody acts fairly and with good intentions initial justice may still be eroded. The parallel between McCloskey and Nozick is not surprising given McCloskey's endorsement of libertarian political philosophy: "Politically, if you care, I am a libertarian" (McCloskey 1994: 316).
21 Grapard (2001: 280). See also Bergeron's comment on Grapard's essay in Bergeron (2001).
22 J.A. Nelson suggests that feminist economists "break the habits that keep us from seeing all our options. I recommend starting with thinking only one or two impossible things before breakfast" (2001: 302). See also Fricker (2000) and Wylie (2000).

Bibliography

Anderson, Elisabeth (1995) "Feminist Epistemology: An Interpretation and a Defense," *Hypatia* 10: 50–84.
Barad, Karen (1998) "Getting Real: Technoscientific Practices and the Materialization of Reality," *Differences* 10(2): 87–126.

Barker, Drucilla K. (1995) "Economists, Social Reformers, and Prophets: A Feminist Critique of Economic Efficiency," *Feminist Economics* 1(3): 26–39.
Barnes, Barry (1977) *Interests and the Growth of Knowledge*, London: Routledge.
Bergeron, Suzanne (2001) "No More Nice Girls?," in Stephen Cullenberg, Jack Amariglio and David F. Ruccio (eds.) *Postmodernism, Economics, and Knowledge*, London and New York: Routledge.
Bhaskar, Roy (1989) *Reclaiming Reality*, London: Verso.
Biagioli, Mario (ed.) (1999) *The Science Studies Reader*, New York: Routledge.
Butler, Judith (1990) *Gender Trouble*, New York and London: Routledge.
Flax, Jane (1981) "Why Epistemology Matters," *Journal of Politics* 43(4): 1,006–24.
Folbre, Nancy and Heidi Hartmann (1988) "The Rhetoric of Self-interest: Ideology and Gender in Economic Theory," in Arjo Klamer, Robert M. Solow and D. McCloskey (eds.) *The Consequences of Economic Rhetoric*, Cambridge: Cambridge University Press.
Fricker, Miranda (2000) "Feminism in Epistemology: Pluralism without Postmodernism," in Miranda Fricker and Jennifer Hornsby (eds.) *The Cambridge Companion to Feminism in Philosophy*, Cambridge: Cambridge University Press.
Galison, Peter and David J. Stump (eds.) (1996) *The Disunity of Science: Boundaries, Contexts, and Power*, Stanford, CA: Stanford University Press.
Grapard, Ulla (2001) "The Trouble with Women and Economics," in Stephen Cullenberg, Jack Amariglio and David F. Ruccio (eds.) *Postmodernism, Economics, and Knowledge*, London and New York: Routledge.
Harding, Sandra (1991) *Whose Science? Whose Knowledge?*, Ithaca, NY: Cornell University Press.
—— (1995) "Can Feminist Thought Make Economics More Objective?," *Feminist Economic* 1(1): 7–32.
—— (1999) "The Case for Strategic Realism: A Response to Lawson," *Feminist Economics* 5(3): 127–34.
—— (2001) "Comment on Waldy's 'Against Epistemological Chasms: The Science Question in Feminism Revisited': Can Democratic Values and Interests Ever Play a Rationally Justifiable Role in the Evaluation of Scientific Work?," *Signs* 26(2): 511–26.
Hewitson, Gillian (1999) *Feminist Economics*, Cheltenham: Edward Elgar.
Kuhn, Thomas S. (1977) *The Essential Tension*, Chicago, IL: Chicago University Press.
Lawson, Tony (1997) *Economics and Reality,* London: Routledge.
—— (1999) "Feminism, Realism, and Universalism," *Feminist Economics* 5(2): 25–59.
Longino, Helen E. (1990) *Science as Social Knowledge*, Princeton, NJ: Princeton University Press.
—— (2002) *The Fate of Knowledge*, Princeton, NJ: Princeton University Press.
McCloskey, Donald. N. (1985) *The Rhetoric of Economics*, Madison, WI: University of Wisconsin Press.
—— (1993) "Some Consequences of a Conjective Economics," in Marianne A. Ferber and Julie A. Nelson (eds.) *Beyond Economic Man*, Chicago, IL: University of Chicago Press.
—— (1994) *Knowledge and Persuasion in Economics*, Cambridge: University of Cambridge Press.
Mäki, Uskali (1992a) "On the Method of Isolation in Economics," *Poznan Studies in the Philosophy of the Sciences and the Humanities* 25: 319–54.
—— (1992b) "Social Conditioning of Economics," in Neil de Marchi (ed.) *Post-Popperian Methodology of Economics*, Boston, MA: Kluwer.
—— (1993a) "Two Philosophies of the Rhetoric of Economics," in Willie Henderson, Tony Dudley-Evans and Robert Backhouse (eds.) *Economics and Language*, London and New York: Routledge.
—— (1993b) "Social Theories of Science and the Fate of Institutionalism in Economics," in Uskali Mäki, Bo Gustafsson and Christian Knudsen (eds.) *Rationality, Institutions and Economic Methodology*, London and New York: Routledge.
—— (1994) "Reorienting the Assumptions Issue", in R. Backhouse (ed.) *New Directions in Economic Methodology*, London and New York: Routledge.

Mäki, Uskali and Jack Vromen (1996) "How Far is Chicago from Frankfurt?," *Mimeo*, Rotterdam: Erasmus University.

Nelson, Julie. A. (1992) "Gender, Metaphor, and the Definition of Economics," *Economics and Philosophy* 8(1): 103–25.

—— (1996) *Feminism, Objectivity, and Economics*, London: Routledge.

—— (2001) "Feminist Economics: Objective, Activist, and Postmodern?," in Stephen Cullenberg, Jack Amariglio and David F. Ruccio (eds.) *Postmodernism, Economics, and Knowledge*, London and New York: Routledge.

Nelson, Lynn. H. (1995) "The Very Idea of Feminist Epistemology," *Hypatia* 10(3): 31–49.

Nozick, Robert (1974) *Anarchy, State and Utopia*, Oxford: Basil Blackwell.

Peter, Fabienne (2001) "Rhetoric vs. Realism in Economic Methodology: A Critical Assessment of Recent Contributions," *Cambridge Journal of Economics* 25(5): 571–89.

Pickering, Andrew (ed.) (1992) *Science as Practice and Culture*, Chicago, IL: Chicago University Press.

Rawls, John (1971) *A Theory of Justice*, Cambridge, MA: Harvard University Press.

Rorty, Richard (1979) *Philosophy and the Mirror of Nature*, Princeton, NJ: Princeton University Press.

Ross, Andrew (ed.) (1996) *Science Wars*, New York: NYU Press.

Rouse, Joseph (1987) *Knowledge and Power: Toward a Political Philosophy of Science*, Ithaca, NY: Cornell University Press.

—— (1996) *Engaging Science: How to Understand its Practices Philosophically*, Ithaca, NY: Cornell University Press.

Sanders, Lynn M. (1997) "Against Deliberation," *Political Theory* 25(3): 347–76.

Seiz, Janet. A. (1992) "Gender and Economic Research," in Neil de Marchi (ed.) *The Methodology of Economics*, Boston: Kluwer-Neijhoff.

—— (1995) "Epistemology and the Tasks of Feminist Economics," *Feminist Economics* 1(3): 110–18.

Strassman, Diana (1993) "Not a Free Market: The Rhetoric of Disciplinary Authority in Economics," in Marianne A. Ferber and Julie. A. Nelson (eds.) *Beyond Economic Man*, Chicago, IL: University of Chicago Press.

Strober, Myra (1994) "Rethinking Economics Through a Feminist Lens," *American Economic Review* 84(2): 143–7.

Van Fraassen, Bas C. (1980) *The Scientific Image*, Oxford: Clarendon Press.

Wylie, Alison (2000) "Feminism in Philosophy of Science: Making Sense of Contingency and Constraint," in Miranda Fricker and Jennifer Hornsby (eds.) *The Cambridge Companion to Feminism in Philosophy*, Cambridge: Cambridge University Press.

8 After objectivism vs. relativism

Sandra Harding

Scary questions

Widespread puzzlement and fearful anxieties have been voiced in recent decades in response to the threat of relativism that appears to be raised by several kinds of new knowledge projects. These are poststructuralist criticisms of Enlightenment assumptions, post-positivist philosophy and social studies of science, and feminist, multicultural, and postcolonial science studies and social sciences. All of these knowledge projects seem to many observers to abandon or even reject the hope that a single transcultural standard to use in evaluating competing beliefs – ontological or epistemic facts, rules, or principles – can be identified. Without one such standard we have no rationally justifiable standards, no rationally defensible grounds for our knowledge claims, according to this line of thought.

On the one hand we know this cannot be a reasonable position, since in daily life we are perfectly able to produce what most people, including law courts, would regard as rational justifications for our knowledge claims. We do not think that such claims are absolutely, under any conditions, now and forever, true; they are always revisable if additional evidence or a useful new conceptual framework appears. But we do believe that nevertheless we have good evidence and sound argument that justifies holding such beliefs here and now and rejecting other competing beliefs. Whether we are right or wrong to do so in particular cases, we routinely and confidently take such positions with respect to health matters, legal issues, and the everyday choices we must make.[1] The arguments between absolutists and relativists seem to float free of such everyday experiences and the ways we think about them.

Yet there are other contexts in which the absolutist/relativist debates seem troublesome indeed – usually when we are faced with the theoretical frameworks of those recent movements mentioned above. Their criticism of the dominant ontological and epistemological standards for what exists and what we can know about it can seem to imply either that the world does not have a coherent order or that, if it does, counter to the Enlightenment faith, humans are incapable of detecting it or even of demonstrating that we are advancing "the growth of knowledge." These are unsettling thoughts. If there is no such standard, then a damaging judgmental relativism seems the only alternative: if there is not a single, universally valid standard for the best beliefs, then there is no way rationally to decide between competing claims to knowledge, or to know whether (and justify to others that) our own beliefs are right and maximally reasonable ones.

If one agrees that even one's most defensible beliefs about the world around us are shaped by culture (as those new movements claim), has one forfeited any possibility of legitimate rational justification for belief preferences? If one admits that knowledge always is constituted only within particular historical discourses, has one forfeited the possibility of establishing empirical support for one's beliefs by referring to anything beyond discourse? If even one's ontological, epistemic, and methodological standards for sorting beliefs have an "integrity" with their historic era (as Thomas Kuhn [1970] put the point four decades ago, in 1962), is it possible to make objective, reliable, and fair decisions between conflicting theory choices in the natural and social sciences? What does it mean to say that the overtly culturally embedded beliefs that other, non-Western cultures and feminist projects have about nature's order or about social relations can be as universally valid, as objective as – or even more valid and objective than – modern Western scientific beliefs that purportedly are culturally neutral? These are some of the ways such anxieties have been expressed.

Here I focus on the epistemic and methodological issues, though these are always intertwined and co-constituted with ontological issues, as well as with ethical, spiritual, historical, and/or aesthetic and other cultural ones, as we shall see. Each raises distinct issues, yet attention to the epistemic and methodological concerns can, for the moment, be addressed separately.

The epistemic absolutism that produces such anxieties in fact shares two faulty beliefs with the relativist position it so fears. First, recollect that epistemic absolutism holds that there is one and only one rationally justifiable standard for sorting beliefs, now and forevermore, whether or not we have actually yet identified it. Without such a standard, irrationality prevails. Epistemic relativists hold that there are many standards that their cultures take to be rational, but there is no additional, "higher-level," universally valid standard to which to appeal in adjudicating between those different cultural standards. Consequently, there is no truly rational (universally valid) way to justify one's beliefs. "Incommensurability" of belief systems and their standards prevails, and we just have to live with such a situation. In fact, such extreme relativists are scarce, although the absolutist thinks that such a position is held by every poststructuralist, post-positivist, feminist, and multiculturalist – that is, by anyone who challenges the absolutist position.

Nevertheless, the point here is that one faulty assumption shared by such epistemic absolutists and relativists is that words (e.g. expressions of belief) and the world – its things and processes – can and should be completely separable or distinguishable from each other if we are to have rationally justifiable standards for belief. If what we take to be objects and processes in the world cannot be separated from the discursive frameworks through which we learn to identify and continue to think about them, then there can be no rational way to choose between knowledge claims from different such frameworks.[2] Here I ask: Can one sustain the ideal of rational, objective belief choices in a world where words and the things to which they refer have proved in principle not as isolatable, or even as desirable to isolate, as modern philosophies of science presumed? Should one try to do so? My answer to both questions is an unabashed "Yes."

However, I propose that such a goal is achievable only by abandoning a second basic assumption shared by absolutists and relativists, namely that what counts as science or knowledge is fundamentally a set of words or representations of the world, for example sentences or statements about its natural and/or social nature and workings, which must in principle at least perfectly correspond to the way the world is.

This representational notion of science has always been held alongside a quite different one: that science is a distinctive method of inquiry, a set of practices. It is a way of going about figuring out how the natural and social world works. This latter notion finds a home not only in the preoccupation of sciences with designing and conducting research in ways that are "fair" to the way the world is (to the data) and to the severest criticisms of one's inquiry methods, but also in the liberal democratic notion of the importance of fair procedures in the law and in public policy. The notion has been reworked and re-imagined in the last half-century by Thomas Kuhn in his discussion of a research "paradigm" as an exemplar that precedes theorization, in Foucault's discussion of the importance of the founding of the modern prison and clinic as models for methods of observation for the emerging social sciences, in Ian Hacking's (1983) account of the unjustly overlooked importance of intervention to scientific work, and in the development of such insights in Rouse's (1987, 1996) work. Philosophers, sociologists, ethnographers, and historians of science have focused on modern Western scientific practice in their attempt to replace excessively idealized representations of scientific work with ones "naturalized" through more careful empirical study of actual scientific practices. And comparative ethnographies of other cultures' knowledge projects, as well as postcolonial and feminist science and technology studies, have carefully examined inquiry practices in a far broader range of cultures and subcultures than the idealized versions of "real science" usually considered relevant.

Thus the account here brings together insights from diverse sources that form an emerging tendency in philosophies of science to look at how sciences create knowledge through patterns of practice. It is difficult for epistemic relativism to arise if science is thought of as a set of distinctive practices that generate, among other products, representations of nature and social relations such as accurate descriptions and perhaps even causal laws. One can always ask of practices what is their goal, and then judge the adequacy of the practice in terms of the desirability of the goal according to some specified ethical and/or political standard (always only local) and the effectiveness of the practice in reaching it. Conceptualizing science as a set of sentences certainly permits such an understanding, but it tends to encourage the idea that the goal of science is to represent nature's truth, its order, which leads directly toward the damaging fear of relativism. Thus, the proposal here is that we can abandon epistemic absolutism and its goal of articulating the one true story of the natural and social order without giving up rational grounds for our best beliefs. Those grounds are both practical or methodological and also ethical and political.

What is the relevance of this issue to economics? For one thing, neoclassical economics is conceived as a set of practices. Central to the practices of mainstream economics is the notion that economics is defined by its method of analysis, a method that admits only explanations based on contractual exchange between rational economic agents. Formal mathematical models describe economic processes, and outcomes are evaluated solely in terms of economic efficiency, the only criterion considered to be an unambiguous measure of the social good. There are, however, other legitimate goals for economic analyses. As Barker (1995) has argued, rather than being a universally agreed upon criterion, economic efficiency reflects a variety of historically contingent values that privilege autonomy, choice, and market relations. Articulating the goals of social welfare which neoclassical economics has ignored or devalued is a central part of the feminist economics projects. Moreover, feminist economics itself is much more amenable to the sort of analysis I am proposing since it overtly measures the adequacy of its inquiry practices in terms of the desirability of their various social goals.[3] For example, feminist economists have asked if measuring women's labor only through their full-time, year-round work outside the household in the absence of their children is an accurate measurement of their labor and maximally useful for the purposes of improving the working conditions of a society. Or, to put the point another way, they have asked if it is maximally objective and valuable for the purposes of policy intended to improve working conditions to use as the standard for the worker only a full-time, year-round employed male unaccompanied by children. Finding ways to abandon both epistemic absolutist and relativist positions can improve both the rationality of our beliefs and the desirability and effectiveness of economic policy for those committed to advancing social justice.

One final perception here. It is useful to note that the very different social movements whose research projects generated such reactions against epistemic and ontological forms of both absolutism and relativism began to emerge at about the same time – in the late 1950s and 1960s. Moreover, intentionally or not, all of these epistemology/science movements arose alongside significant changes in the global social formation which have brought into existence or made visible a world importantly different from the one imagined in early twentieth-century mainstream philosophies of science.[4] Among such changes have been the end of formal European colonial rule; new economic, political, and social roles for women; rising skepticism about the allegiances of natural and social sciences to militarism, capitalism, white supremacy, and male supremacy; globalization of the economy and the shift from industrial production to the production and management of information; the rise of new identity movements around the world; and the increased dissemination of liberal democracies and rising resistance to them from both conservative and progressive groups around the world (Castells 2000; Gill 1995). Evidently the world changed in the last half-century in ways that unsettled conventional certainties about how knowledge projects are, can be, and should be situated in the world. The epistemic/philosophy of science shifts, however else one might characterize them, have been attempts to update or revise older models of how and for what ends knowledge is produced which are perceived as out of touch with what we now know about the history and present practices of natural and social science inquiry. Philosophies are always engaged with their eras' problematics.[5]

Giving up these two aspects of conventional philosophies of science has other consequences.

Moving past the modernist dream: one post-positivist approach

We can start by remembering the beginnings of post-positivism in the philosophy of science of the 1950s and 1960s. W.V.O. Quine (1953) argued that empirical observations and the theories they are supposed to test can never achieve the independence from each other that either the inductivist or deductivist "logics of scientific inquiry" required. Nor are analytic and synthetic statements as discrete as had been thought. Our scientific and everyday beliefs form a network such that when observations conflict with a favored theory scientists might even find it more reasonable to revise a law of logic rather than to give up any other empirical or theoretical belief. Obviously, this would be an extremely drastic and rare choice.

Then Thomas Kuhn (1970) argued that the new social histories of science emerging in his day pointed to the way moments in the history of the very best scientific research had an "integrity" with their historic era. That is, what Kuhn still referred to as "irrational" cultural factors regularly played crucial roles in distinctive ways of advancing the growth of knowledge. The conventional logical positivist attempt to show that the greatest achievements of Western modern sciences were entirely a result of purely rational practices was a mistake: the "paradigm shifts" that periodically reorganized and energized scientific fields were not explicable in purely rational terms. Kuhn's paradigms were not new theories, he insisted; they were practical exemplars of scientific research – research practices – that subsequent researchers used as a model for their own work. Any re-theorization of nature's regularities could occur only later.

Meanwhile, a similar point was made by Foucault's focus on how the organization and practices of the nineteenth-century clinic and prison modeled social research for the subsequently emerging social science disciplines, as noted above. The practices necessarily preceded the theorizations. His point was that knowledge and power were inextricably linked through particular institutional practices. The bodies of patients and prisoners were forced to release, give up, "confess," the information desired by those who designed the clinic and prison, who would in turn use this information to control additional groups who were already socially disempowered (the diseased, the criminal).

Thus from a number of sources has appeared the argument that it is patterns of practice that make possible distinctive scientific theorizations. The practices produce many phenomena: new kinds of laboratories, techniques of inquiry, networks of researchers and their support staffs, newly visible – perhaps even newly created – things and processes (geologic plates, retroviruses, double helices), demands for new kinds of schooling, new rhetorics of scientific progress, demands for funding, and, yes, sets of sentences that it is hoped represent nature's order.[6]

Such an understanding of the nature of science requires a different philosophy of science. Developing such a philosophy is an important project for feminists. We need to be able to justify the rationality and objectivity of our explicitly politically committed inquiry practices – practices that are intended to reveal how implicitly politically committed (intentionally or not) are androcentric, Eurocentric, and class-exploitative conceptual frameworks of social and natural sciences that are presumed value-neutral. That is, we need to be able to show both that research which might appear to be value-neutral in fact is not, and also that some social values and interests are productive both of knowledge and of social justice – both of which have historically been goals of objective scientific inquiry.

One can summarize central "nodes" of the still-emerging "network" of post-positivist philosophy of science in the following way (these "nodes" are not completely independent of each other, of course):

- *Networks of belief.* The kinds of beliefs or knowledge claims we need to get around in the world cannot in principle be completely isolated from each other. Instead, they form a dense network that links empirical, theoretical, logical, and everyday beliefs.
- *Multiple, discordant, sciences.* Science is not singular, either in practice or in principle, as the strong form of the Unity of Science Thesis held.[7] Scientific elements are not even actually or ideally always "harmonious," as the weaker form of the thesis proposed. This multiplicity and discordance are both

problematic and also fortuitous. It can be useful to link together different kinds of observations and discordant theories as, for example, Darwin did. Discordances between knowledge systems characterize the conceptual shifts ("paradigm changes") through which scientists reorganize most of a field of existing data into illuminating new patterns. Moreover, such discordances mark the distinctive positional, interest, discursive, and organizational resources that different fields, disciplines, and cultures bring to their attempts to understand their allotted or chosen environments.

- *Culture as sometimes productive of the growth of knowledge.* Thus distinctive cultural resources – interests, politics, values – can sometimes advance the growth of knowledge; these can also be destructive of or obstacles to knowledge, but that is not their only possibility. Cultures are "toolboxes," not just "prisonhouses," for the production of knowledge (Harding 1998a: chs. 4, 6). This is another way of saying that words and things cannot be completely separated and distinguished from each other such that "facts" about the "things" can be used to judge the adequacy of our theories (words) about them – one of Quine's and Kuhn's insights. Feminist research has always been engaged, committed to improving the conditions of women's lives – though always also resisting the tendency to turn wishes into purported facts. Feminist politics has been part of scientific method, one could say – no less than have environmental, antiracist, anti-class politics and the politics guiding AIDS research.

- *Mind-independent reality: always out of reach.* Yes, there is a mind-independent reality – or, perhaps, many of them. It was there before humans appeared and will persist when we become extinct. Yet it cannot be that our best knowledge claims are those that uniquely correspond to it. Many theories are consistent with nature's order, but no one could be uniquely congruent with it. Instead, all scientific method ever promised was to identify the best hypothesis, for the moment, of all and only those tested – not the one and only one that could reign eternally unchallengeable. Fortunately, there are always many, many more hypotheses not yet tested, including the quadrillions not yet even formulated, which offer the permanent promise of new and surprising insights into nature's order and social relations. Thus truth in the standard "correspondence" sense of the word in the sciences – a perfect match between words and their referents – is not a useful goal for scientific practices – or at least for the philosophic account of them. Even the positivists understood that only the claims of logic and of religion (or of other forms of dogma) as they put the point – both supposedly immune to empirical tests – could legitimately claim truth. "Temporarily least false of all and only those considered" is the most that scientific method could promise.[8]

- *Sciences as culturally embedded patterns of practice.* Sciences are most usefully conceptualized not as sets of transcultural authoritative statements or representations, such as the laws of nature, but rather as practices embedded in cultural histories, interests, and values. Indeed, cultures store the kinds of information about the world that are most important and useful to them within pre-existing cultural frameworks – beliefs about how the Christian God ordered chaos into a Garden of Eden for his chosen people, about how the Earth is like a spaceship or lifeboat such that its environment must be carefully monitored, and so forth. We learn the world and the pattern of practice (including words) together.[9]

- *Decentered collective subjects of sciences.* Thus the "subject" of science and knowledge – the collective speaker – cannot be the centered, transcultural rational knower of Enlightenment philosophy, but must instead be human cultures in all of their systematic ways of successfully interacting with the worlds around them. Such an understanding can trigger absolutist fears of relativism, yet the argument here has been that such a fear is unnecessary. If one values both Buddhism and the management of chronic pain, it can be rational to seek acupuncture, a practice which is meaningful in the context of Buddhism and also reported to be effective in controlling chronic pain. However, if one values the management of chronic pain and only those belief systems free of religious assumptions, one will have to choose between commitment to a set of apparently effective practices that for many people carry religious assumptions and Western biomedicine, which purportedly distances its accounts from any apparently religious assumptions but has not developed practices effective at managing chronic pain.[10]

Abandoning absolutism and relativism?

Many have commented on how relativism was always the invention, the nightmare, of the absolutist, even if it was often appropriated for either progressive or regressive scientific or political projects (Proctor 1991; Haraway 1991). Here I have been outlining how we can still have a world "out there" beyond our historically local discourses, but we cannot have one that authoritatively chooses for us which knowledge claims to believe. Observations always must be interpreted within socially meaningful frameworks. We can still have justifiable standards for defending our beliefs and practices, but we cannot have ones that do so apart from investments in the perceived strengths of the social values and interests that make conceptual frameworks meaningful. We can still have sciences that illuminate nature's order and social relations for us, but we cannot have ones that uniquely do so for everyone and thus that are reasonably regarded effective and desirable for every culture and its historically local projects. We can have modern Western sciences that can be the very best that we can produce given the cultural and environmental resources available to us and the goals for which we have designed our sciences, but we cannot have ones that are the best we could produce for any goals we might have, or, consequently, that we can confidently depend upon to provide all that we might desire to know in the future.

Indeed, we can be confident that the sciences thought to have advanced the forms of democratic social relations envisioned by the Enlightenment and its heirs today are most likely not the ones that work well to advance the new forms of democratic social relations for which feminisms, multiculturalisms, and postcolonialisms yearn today. Historically distinctive social relations and their favored forms of knowledge-seeking co-constitute each other. The rise of new social values, interests, and the relations these direct requires inquiry practices and principles that can support and in turn be supported by these new forms of hopefully democratic social relations. Our methodological and epistemological choices are always also ethical and political choices.[11]

Notes

1 And we can easily think of recent cases of such collective choices, such as AIDS activists' decision to develop alternative standards for remedy trials different from those of the National Institutes of Health, and environmentalists' development of standards for pesticide use that differed from conventional ones.
2 For one of the most compelling arguments against the separability of words and objects, see Verran (2001). Joe Rouse's work (1987, 1996) is one good place to see the philosophic development of the kind of analysis I use here and in subsequent paragraphs.
3 I am not an economist; I thank one of the reviewers of an earlier draft of this paper for pointing out these examples of the relevance of this issue to economics.
4 It is odd to refer to poststructuralism as an epistemology/science movement, yet it has been preoccupied with denying the philosophic assumptions of Enlightenment science, and it has explicitly been used to illuminating effect by some feminist science theorists – for example by Donna Haraway (1989, 1991).
5 One way to emphasize the urgency of epistemological engagement with the last half-century of shifts in the global political economy is to imagine trying to gain consensus at the United Nations for the claim that there is one and only one empirically and theoretically justifiable standard for deciding between competing knowledge claims, and that standard is the one that elite men in the West support.
6 Some important contributors to or reporters of the post-positivist philosophies of science grounded in this understanding are Barnes (1977), Bloor (1977), Galison and Stump (1996), Hess (1997), Latour (1987, 1988), Latour and Woolgar (1979), Restivo (1992), Rouse (1987, 1996), Schuster and Yeo (1986), Shapin (1994), Shapin and Shaffer (1985), and Traweek (1988). (I count the sociologists, historians, and ethnographers as full-fledged contributors to the new post-positivist philosophies of science.) Feminist and postcolonial contributors and reporters, some of whom fully function in post-positivist Northern circles, include Braidotti *et al.* (1994), Brockway (1979), Crosby (1987), Goonatilake (1984, 1992), Haraway (1989, 1991, 1997), Harding (1986, 1991, 1998a), Harding and Figueroa (2003), Headrick (1981), Hess (1995), Joseph (1991), Keller (1984), Kochhar (1992–3), Kumar (1991), McClellan (1992), Nandy (1991), Needham (1954ff., 1969), Pettijean *et al.* (1992), Sachs (1992), Sardar (1988), Selin (1997), Shiva (1989), Watson-Verran and Turnbull (1995), Weatherford (1988).
7 This still-powerful though discredited thesis holds that there is one world, one "truth" about it, and one and only one science capable in principle of representing that one true story. As political scientists point out, it also assumes that there is one and only one ideal kind of knower capable of producing such an account. This thesis united a social movement from the late nineteenth through mid-twentieth centuries which sought to reveal the singularity (in its reductionist versions) or, in most cases, just the "harmony" of diverse disciplinary investigations

with each other. Thomas Kuhn's influential book (1970) significantly was the last to be published in the University of Chicago Press's Unity of Sciences series. See the essays in the Galison and Stump (1996) collection for histories and analyses of this movement.
8 "Fallibilism" is frequently the term used to refer to this feature of empirical knowledge claims. Yet it is all too often invoked to admit that there is, of course, a rational possibility that the speaker's claims could at some point in the future rationally be regarded as inadequate, but in the meantime such claims deserve to be regarded as robustly adequate or even true, and to be firmly supported by solid empirical evidence and logical reasoning. See Harding (1998b) for further discussions of this and related issues.
9 See Verran (2001) for a fascinating account of how this is the case even for mathematical learning in both the West and elsewhere.
10 Of course, no culture is able to detect all of its cultural assumptions, as historians usefully point out. See Needham (1969) for just one of the many illuminating accounts of the distinctively Western cultural values, including Christian beliefs, that shape the purportedly value-neutral conceptual frameworks of modern Western sciences.
11 My thanks to the reviewers of an earlier draft of this paper for their thoughtful suggestions.

Bibliography

Barker, Drucilla K. (1995) "Economists, Social Reformers, and Prophets: A Feminist Critique of Economic Efficiency," *Feminist Economics* 1(3): 26–39.

Barnes, Barry (1977) *Interests and the Growth of Knowledge*, Boston, MA: Routledge & Kegan Paul.

Bloor, David (1977) *Knowledge and Social Imagery*, London: Routledge & Kegan Paul.

Braidotti, Rosi, Ewa Charkiewicz, Sabine Hausler and Saskia Wieringa (1994) *Women, the Environment, and Sustainable Development*, Atlantic Highlands, NJ: Zed Press.

Brockway, Lucille H. (1979) *Science and Colonial Expansion: The Role of the British Royal Botanical Gardens*, New York: Academic Press.

Castells, Manuel (2000) *The Information Age: Economy, Society and Culture*, vol. 1–3, updated version, Oxford: Blackwell; first published in 1996–8.

Crosby, Alfred (1987) *Ecological Imperialism: The Biological Expansion of Europe*, Cambridge: Cambridge University Press.

Galison, Peter and David J. Stump (eds.) (1996) *The Disunity of Science*, Stanford, CA: Stanford University Press.

Gill, Stephen (1995) "Globalization, Market Civilization, and Disciplinary Neoliberalism," *Millennium: Journal of International Studies* 24(3): 399–423.

Goonatilake, Susantha (1984) *Aborted Discovery: Science and Creativity in the Third World*, London: Zed.

—— (1992) "The Voyages of Discovery and the Loss and Rediscovery of the 'Other's' Knowledge," *Impact of Science on Society* 167: 241–64.

Hacking, Ian (1983) *Representing and Intervening*, Cambridge: Cambridge University Press.

Haraway, Donna (1989) *Primate Visions: Gender, Race, and Nature in the World of Modern Science*, New York: Routledge.

—— (1991) *Simians, Cyborgs, and Women: The Reinvention of Nature*, New York: Routledge.

—— (1997) *Modest_Witness@Second_Millennium.FemaleMan_Meets_Oncomouse*, New York: Routledge.

Harding, Sandra (1986) *The Science Question in Feminism*, Ithaca, NY: Cornell University Press.

—— (1991) *Whose Science? Whose Knowledge? Thinking From Women's Lives*, Ithaca, NY: Cornell University Press.

—— (1994) "Can Feminist Thought Make Economics More Objective?," *Feminist Economics* 1(1): 7–32.

—— (1998a) *Is Science Multicultural? Postcolonialisms, Feminisms, and Epistemologies*, Bloomington, IN: Indiana University Press.

—— (1998b) "Are Truth Claims in Science Dysfunctional?," in Andrea Nye (ed.) *Philosophy of Language: The Big Questions*, New York: Blackwell.

—— (ed.) (2003) *The Standpoint Reader*, New York: Routledge.

Harding, Sandra and Robert M. Figueroa (eds.) (2003) *Science and Other Cultures: Issues in Philosophies of Science and Technology*, New York: Routledge.

Headrick, Daniel R. (ed.) (1981) *The Tools of Empire: Technology and European Imperialism in the Nineteenth Century*, New York: Oxford University Press.

Hess, David J. (1995) *Science and Technology in a Multicultural World: The Cultural Politics of Facts and Artifacts*, New York: Columbia University Press.

—— (1997) *Science Studies: An Advanced Introduction*, New York: New York University Press.

Joseph, George Gheverghese (1991) *The Crest of the Peacock: Non-European Roots of Mathematics*, New York: I.B. Tauris.

Keller, Evelyn Fox (1984) *Reflections on Gender and Science*, New Haven, CT: Yale University Press.

Kochhar, R.K. (1992–3) "Science in British India," parts I and II, *Current Science* (India) 63(11): 689–94; 64: 55–62.

Kuhn, Thomas S. (1970) *The Structure of Scientific Revolutions*, 2nd edn., Chicago, IL: University of Chicago Press; first published in 1962.

Kumar, Deepak (1991) *Science and Empire: Essays in Indian Context (1700–1947)*, Delhi, India: Anamika Prakashan and National Institute of Science, Technology, and Development.

Latour, Bruno (1987) *Science in Action*, Cambridge, MA: Harvard University Press.

—— (1988) *The Pasteurization of France*, Cambridge, MA: Harvard University Press.

Latour, Bruno and Steve Woolgar (1979) *Laboratory Life: The Social Construction of Scientific Facts*, Beverly Hills, CA: Sage.

McClellan, James E. (1992) *Colonialism and Science: Saint Domingue in the Old Regime*, Baltimore, MD: Johns Hopkins University Press.

Nandy, Ashis (ed.) (1991) *Science, Hegemony, and Violence*, Delhi: Oxford.

Needham, Joseph (1954ff.) *Science and Civilization in China*, 7 vols., Cambridge: Cambridge University Press.

—— (1969) *The Grand Titration: Science and Society in East and West*, Toronto: University of Toronto Press.

Petitjean, Patrick and Catherine Jami (eds.) (1992) *Science and Empires: Historical Studies About Scientific Development and European Expansion*, Dordrecht: Kluwer.

Proctor, Robert (1991) *Value-Free Science? Purity and Power in Modern Knowledge*, Cambridge, MA: Harvard University Press.

Quine, W.V.O. (1953) "Two Dogmas of Empiricism," *From a Logical Point of View*, Cambridge, MA: Harvard University Press.

Restivo, Sal (1992) *Mathematics in Society and History: Sociological Inquiries*, Dordrecht: Kluwer.

Rouse, Joseph (1987) *Knowledge and Power: Toward a Political Philosophy of Science*, Ithaca, NY: Cornell University Press.

—— (1996) *Engaging Science*, Ithaca, NY: Cornell University Press.

Sachs, Wolfgang (ed.) (1992) *The Development Dictionary: A Guide to Knowledge as Power*, Atlantic Highlands, NJ: Zed Press.

Sardar, Z. (ed.) (1988) *The Revenge of Athena: Science, Exploitation, and the Third World*, London: Mansell.

Schuster, John A. and Richard R. Yeo (eds.) (1986) *The Politics and Rhetoric of Scientific Method: Historical Studies*, Dordrecht: Reidel.

Selin, Helaine (ed.) (1997) *Encyclopedia of the History of Science, Technology and Medicine in Non-Western Cultures*, Dordrecht: Kluwer.

Shapin, Steven (1994) *A Social History of Truth*, Chicago, IL: University of Chicago Press.

Shapin, Steven and Simon Shaffer (1985) *Leviathan and the Air Pump*, Princeton, NJ: Princeton University Press.
Shiva, Vandana (1989) *Staying Alive: Women, Ecology, and Development*, London: Zed.
Traweek, Sharon (1988) *Beamtimes and Lifetimes*, Cambridge, MA: MIT Press.
Verran, Helen (2001) *Science and an African Logic*, Chicago, IL: University of Chicago Press.
Watson-Verran, Helen and David Turnbull (1995) "Science and Other Indigenous Knowledge Systems," in Sheila Jasanoff, Gerald Markle, James Petersen and Trevor Pinch (eds.) *Handbook of Science and Technology Studies*, Thousand Oaks, CA: Sage.
Weatherford, Jack McIver (1988) *Indian Givers: What the Native Americans Gave to the World*, New York: Crown.

9 How did "the moral" get split from "the economic"?[1]

Julie A. Nelson

Prologue

What do you experience on a typical morning? What do you feel before you put on your social-scientist hat and go to work? Perhaps you wake in the morning and see green leaves blowing in the breeze outside your window. You smell the warm aroma of coffee as you sit in your kitchen. You give a loved one a good-morning kiss. Reading the headlines, you feel pain as you read of new terror on the other side of the globe. You plan your day: some activities you will do out of habit, and others will present choices. What activities will best fulfill your need to earn a living, to be with those you love, to develop your talents, to keep your environment in order and repair, to maintain your human community, to make, you hope, a worthwhile day in a meaningful life? You feel time passing, and rise to move on to the next thing.

But, perhaps, having an educated and "scientific" turn of mind, you also "know" that what you have experienced is just a stream of sensations. Greenness is not in the leaves, nor aroma in the coffee; these are merely the result of waves of a certain length or particles of certain kinds interacting with your nervous system. You have learned that experiences of love and of empathy correspond to stimulation of your own, internal nervous system, perhaps by way of pheromones or other hormonal flows. You have a feeling of purpose, of value, of some things being better to do than others, but you realize that these are "subjective," introspective, and personal. Your ability to earn a living is, you understand, strongly dependent on impersonal market "forces." You feel time passing, but believe that, while it passes for you, the underlying truth and order of the universe are unchanging.

Now you may address the discrepancy between your lived experience and "scientific" intellectual knowledge in any of a number of ways. Leaning towards the objectivist and reductionist side, you may believe that scientific investigation could eventually lead to a full explanation of the precise causal determinants of your morning experience. Or you might take a dualistic approach, drawing a qualitative distinction between the mechanical, deterministic, "physical" aspects of reality and a subjective, conscious, intentional, moral, and social order of reality. Or maybe you become radically subjectivist, considering science to be *totally* a social construct, so that claims to reality outside of the discursive and semiotic hold, for you, no appeal.

The moral and economic split

Are these the only options?

Since the time of Plato, at least, we in the Western dominant cultures have become accustomed to thinking in terms of contrasts between eternal principles and phenomena of change. Since the time of Descartes, Newton, and the Scientific Revolution, we have become further accustomed to thinking along the lines of dualistic distinctions between mind and matter, knower and known, living consciousness and inert materials. These have become elaborated in complex ways, along with further dualisms of value and science, normative and positive, emotion and reason, soft and hard, feminine and masculine. For the most part, "the moral" has been put over on the soft and subjective side – in spite of the best attempts of some analytic philosophers to toughen up its image – while "the economic" goes on the hard and scientific one. Morality is left to the humanists, while mainstream economists pursue "objective" study based on an assumed analogy between economic "laws" (e.g. of supply and demand, or accumulation) and the "laws" of physical science.

This presents a special challenge for feminist economists: in what way do we challenge these dualisms, and how deep are we willing to go? The very term "feminist economics" presents a challenge to standard thinking. Feminism denotes, at a minimum, a commitment to overcoming sexist oppression, which is a distinctly purposive and moral stance. If, first, the dualist notion of the structure of reality is correct, and, second, economics really is like physics, we would need to conclude that "feminist economics" is indeed an oxymoron.

One way to avoid this conclusion is to deny that economics is like physics. Room could be made for less rigid, more socially and morally informed argumentation by taking economics out of the mathematicized and deterministic side of the dualism, and carefully placing it on the side of the changeable, conscious, and purposive. "Socio-economic" or "humanist economic" approaches, for example, often emphasize this strategy, claiming that the nature of economics is different from that of the physical sciences, because the subjects of economic analysis are conscious, social human beings.

The approach in the current essay is quite different. It is not denied that economics is like physics. It denies that *physics* is like "physics" – that is, that the physical world is a value-free clockwork or billiard-ball Newtonian system, as it is often imagined in popular thought. I will argue that moral value is part of physics – that value is part of the very core and immediacy of the world in all its (apparent) parts and times. Therefore it is the foundational dualism itself that I challenge. In order to come up with a practice of economics that is consistent with our lived experience I believe we must explore not just the methodological or epistemological bases of our discipline, but go even deeper, to the ontology (theory of reality) and cosmology (nature of the universe) that ground our analysis.

First, I will give a flavor of what I take to be the key insights of what I will, in shorthand, call a "process" ontology, and then give a very brief genealogy of some of the intellectual streams which have contributed to it and woven around it.[2]

A process worldview

The ontology and cosmology behind the science/value split is one in which mind and matter are considered to be separate "things." There is a given reality "out there," it is assumed, waiting to be known. While values and purposes are something that humans have and sometimes try to impose, external reality is, in itself, gray and colorless, and bereft of intrinsic value, subjectivity, or purpose. Hence religious, moral, and aesthetic thinking are thought of as subjective in their imposition of values, while scientific, technical, and economic thought purport to objectively describe the world as it is.

Taking a very different perspective, in process ontology the real "stuff" of reality is not thought to be matter (objects taking up space), but rather events or *experience*. Time is extremely important here: what we have, at any moment, is new events or happenings that are related to past happenings and that create the basis for events in the next moment. In process thought the world is an organically interconnected whole, as each event subsumes everything that has happened before. Though some previous events are more faintly incorporated than others, none are completely excluded. This is true down to the molecular level (though *experience* does not necessarily imply consciousness), up through each cell that makes up the organism we call our body, and through the social organisms (like families and markets) that we study. Relationships are crucial, as all entities are constituted by their relations to other occasions of experience. Greenness, for example, is not in the leaves, nor in the cones in your eyes, nor merely "all in your mind," but in the "grasped...realized unity" (Whitehead 1997: 69) that constitutes the experience of your observing the leaves. Each event is a concrescence, a growing together, of past events and causes, and an occasion open to spontaneity in the transition to the next. New interactions will happen and new creations – sensations, memories, art, ideas, actions – will come into being. The world "becomes" rather than just "is." The world is unfinished, evolving, open. We are creators in the literal sense.

This ontology leads to the perhaps startling realization that the notion that reality/matter is colorless and purposeless *is an assumption*. Such an assumption seems so tied up in our notions of science that it may be hard to see that this cosmological view is not required by science itself. Science conceived of as methodical inquiry, as openness to new evidence, as experimentalism – such a definition does not rely on a mechanistic worldview. Such a conception of science is quite consistent with a view of experience itself as holistic. Because of the limitations of our senses and our processing abilities, we develop, in everyday life, habits and filters that restrict our perception of our lived moments. Scientific thought, as inquiry, involves extending our perceptions and refining our powers of reflection, and as such is both a part of experience and a purposive seeking to understand and better our lives through (extended) experiences.

In a universe conceived of as open the question of knowledge must be reframed. Our knowledge is not just *about* reality in process thought. Rather, it creatively *adds to* reality. If our knowledge adds to reality – makes a difference – then the question is: does it make the *right* difference? Does the "flux…with our additions, *rise or fall in value?*" (James 1991: 112). Values and morals are of the same fabric as science and economics, not merely incidental.

It may seem to some that this begs the question of morality. "Aha!" one may say. "But what is 'better'? What is 'higher in value'? By what authority are you going to tell me what is valuable?" Such a question, while utterly to be expected if we are used to a modernist and dualistic worldview, is a misplaced one within a process ontology. It assumes that if values exist they must exist as universals, as theoretical invariants, lying out there somewhere waiting to be discovered. Rather, in a process worldview there is no blank slate or impartial "spectator" position. We start with the values and morals we have.[3] These "are" in exactly the same sense as the world we perceive as physical "is." As with our physical resources, we tend to rely in large part on habit in a non-reflective use of them, but we also have the opportunity to try to feel and sense more deeply, and to use our critical faculties more sharply, to increase the wisdom of our conduct. Such a rhythm of experience you already are familiar with from experience. Process thought puts it at the center.

Historical eruptions of process thought

My nutshell description of what I take to be the essence of process thought – the image of the open, alive, continually creating universe – is drawn largely using language from the philosophy of Alfred North Whitehead, with elaborations from the pragmatist philosophy of William James and John Dewey. Such work had a heyday in the Anglo-American world in the earlier part of the twentieth century, and lapped over into the work of institutional economists like John R. Commons and Wesley Mitchell, and into social welfare innovation in the work of Jane Adams. Their challenge of Cartesian ontology, modernist science, classical economic abstraction, and the dualism between science and values was, at the time, well known, widely discussed, and developed to a much larger degree than I can give justice to in this essay.[4] One may also recognize elements of process thought in Marxist thought, though much of Marx's own language also veered towards the mechanistic and scientific. Going back even further, one might note strong parallels in process thought with ancient Buddhist thought, in the images of "becoming," "mindfulness," and "the moment" (see Browning 1965).

Yet, for reasons perhaps yet to be well explained, this intellectual influence lost ground to the more positivist, materialist, anti-metaphysical and abstractly analytical approaches that came to dominate philosophy, economics, and sociology by World War II. Process thought perhaps suffered in philosophical circles from the fact that its major later developer, Charles Hartshorne, concentrated on its religious implications (Griffen 1998). Pragmatist philosophy came to be thought too vague and utopian, relative to analytical standards of precision (Rorty 1998). Institutionalist economics came to be caricatured as an atheoretical school centered on (boring) questions of administrative control or of "unscientific" moralizing.[5] Terms like "life process," "continuity," and "flux" – terms that had been used as groping signs towards what is experienced but not distillable into exact and neutral syllogism – were dismissed as "fuzzy" when the goal turned again to knowledge of precise, impersonal, and transcendental law.[6] The ontological picture of a continually creating, valuable universe came to be dismissed, distorted, and forgotten. What had been a lively and loud intellectual stream shriveled up, and any notion of intrinsic value again became associated with a merely medieval superstitious and magical worldview.

Perhaps it is time for a revival. Elements of process thought have recently been re-emerging across the disciplines and, arguably, in popular life as well, and with some new spins and new justification in the physical sciences.

The contemporary theoretical physics of Ilya Prigogine and Isabelle Stengers, for example, points to *The End of Certainty* and "a science that views us and our creativity as part of a fundamental trend present at all levels of nature" (1996: 7). In feminist theorizing there has been an upsurge in feminist-pragmatist dialog, as in works by philosopher Charlene Seigfried (1993, 1996), a recent adoption of Whiteheadian process ontology by theorist Donna Haraway (1997) and pragmatist ontology by philosopher Linda Alcoff (1996), and feminist-process theological work by Catherine Keller (1986), as well as an ongoing feminist-institutionalist presence within economics. Feminist theorizing, in fact, may lead to the suggestion that part of the historical and psychological resistance to process thought may have a gender-influenced base. Universals, immutability, and precision have long had cultural connotations as masculine and superior, while particulars, change, and vagueness have been associated with lesser-valued images of femininity (e.g. Harding 1986; Bordo 1987; Lloyd 1984).[7] Thus the upsurge in feminist thought and feminist social and political activism may be psychologically and practically crucial if the challenge to the belief system underlying the mechanistic worldview is to be seriously sustained. One can point to other manifestations as well.[8] For example, the holistic health movement, involving mind/body integrative work and meditative techniques, has become increasingly mainstream, and many social and political commentators are pointing to upswings in public interest in body-integrated spirituality.

Conclusion: economics and morality

The interesting question, then, is not about how to bring together the spheres of "the moral" and "the economic," but rather about how and why we seem periodically to fall into a strong belief that they are separate. Most current economists make a strong distinction between "positive" and "normative" judgments, disavowing the latter as out of their area of expertise. Sociologists, political scientists, anthropologists, and even feminist economists buy into this worldview, for example to the extent that we designate commodity exchange as economic and asocial, while gift exchange alone is seen as carrying social ties and ethical values. If we start instead by considering any exchange as a creative event, a world-creating activity that carries ethical meaning as much as it carries any other significance, we are no longer in a split world.

Epilogue

You sit on a chair or couch, reading a book chapter. Do you feel a little bored? A little sleepy? Have you developed a cramp here or a sore spot there as you sit? Besides these black letters on white paper, what else do you see? What sounds are you hearing? Any smells or tastes? Are there any words, concepts, references, images, memories, or questions knocking around in your head? *This* is what you really have, this moment of experience. We can prosthetically extend and deepen our experience with surveys, computers, books, lectures, microscopes, conversations, etc., which allow us to incorporate events in the world imperceptible to our unaided view. We can use logic, categorization, formal analysis, recollection, simulations, models, other mental processes, themselves part of experience, to help us to organize and reflect on our accumulated experience and plan a course of action. What wisdom will we gain, in meeting, enhancing, and reflecting on experience?

Notes

1 Earlier versions of this paper were presented at the panel "The Moral Side of Economics Processes" at the American Sociological Association meetings, Chicago, August 6–10, 1999 and circulated to the ECONSOC discussion list February 2, 2000. I acknowledge the financial support of the Charlotte Perkins Gilman Fellowship for Research on Caring Labor, the Foundation for Child Development, and the Center for the Study of Values in Public Life at Harvard Divinity School. I alone am responsible for any errors and for the views expressed.

2   This is very much my own interpretation of "process thought." I draw on the work of Alfred North Whitehead, and others whom I see as sharing some of the same insights. The reader should be warned, however, that other interpreters of Whitehead come up with very different, and often – unfortunately to my mind – arcane and conservative, interpretations of his often very confusing writings.
3   I explore this issue further in Nelson (2001).
4   I am not attributing what I take to be the kernel of the process view to *all* pragmatists, institutionalists, etc. I find the pragmatism of Dewey and James more centered on it, for example, while that of Charles Saunders Peirce seems at times to reintroduce universals through the back door, with the image of an ultimate end to inquiry. Also, while Whitehead explicitly viewed experience as extending down to the molecular level and below, some of these other thinkers took a mechanistic view of physical processes, when they thought about them, arguing for creativity only at the human level. I treat this as a regrettable lapse in their thought, and one related to the understanding of physical science prevalent at their time.
5   Some suggestions as to why this happened have been advanced. Morgan and Rutherford (1998), for example, trace the loss of pluralism (including institutionalism) in economics to Cold War political pressures that made a retreat into technique and "neutrality" a safer choice for individuals and institutions. Bateman (1998) suggests that disillusionment with Protestant Social Gospel teachings, after their use for nationalistic purposes during World War I, played a role.
6   Whitehead uses the term "process." "Life-process" and "continuity" were chosen by institutional economist Clarence Ayres (1944), along with the rather dated and infelicitous "technological life-process." James uses "flux" (1991).
7   I elaborate on this further in Nelson (2003, forthcoming).
8   One might also want to point to the development of neopragmatism and neo-institutionalist economics in the 1970s and 1980s. However, these schools should be treated with some caution. Neo-institutionalism in economics, for example, tends to concentrate on institutions as systems of formal rules, rather than as also creative, intentional, and evolving elements of lived experience. What I call a process approach takes into account both concrescence *and* transitions, habits *and* change, intelligibility *and* novelty. The neopragmatism of Richard Rorty tends to be more centered on discourse than on the lived experience that gives rise to it, giving in too much, I think, to literary theory. In the intervening years process thought apparently stayed most alive, institutionally and intellectually, in theology, and a process-oriented rethinking of the science/value split arrived a little earlier there (see Griffen 1988). Perhaps even some analytical philosophers are heading in this direction – Jean Hampton's (1998) references to "occult" elements that do not fit into a traditional scientific world view might be taken to point this way.

Bibliography

Alcoff, Linda Martín (1996) *Real Knowing: New Versions of Coherence Theory*, Ithaca, NY: Cornell University Press.

Ayres, Clarence E. (1944) *Theory of Economic Progress*, Chapel Hill, NC: University of North Carolina Press.

Bateman, Bradley W. (1998) "Clearing the Ground: The Demise of the Social Gospel Movement and the Rise of Neoclassicism in American Economics," in Mary S. Morgan and Malcolm Rutherford (eds) *From Interwar Pluralism to Postwar Neoclassicism: History of Political Economy*, Annual Supplement, 30(0), Durham, NC: Duke Univerity Press.

Bordo, Susan (1987) *The Flight to Objectivity: Essays on Cartesianism and Culture*, Albany, NY: State University of New York Press.

Browning, Douglas (ed.) (1965) *Philosophers of Process*, New York: Random House.

Griffen, David Ray (ed.) (1988) *The Reenchantment of Science*, Albany, NY: State University of New York Press.

Hampton, Jean E. (1998) *The Authority of Reason*, New York: Cambridge University Press; published posthumously.

Haraway, Donna (1997) *Modest_Witness@Second_Millennium.FemaleMan_Meets_OncoMouse: Feminism and Technoscience*, New York: Routledge.

Harding, Sandra (1986) *The Science Question in Feminism*, Ithaca, NY: Cornell University Press.

James, William (1991) *Pragmatism*, Amherst, NY: Prometheus Books; first published 1907.

Keller, Catherine (1986) *From a Broken Web: Separation, Sexism, and Self*, Boston, MA: Beacon Press.

Lloyd, Genevieve (1984) *The Man of Reason: "Male" and "Female" in Western Philosophy*, Minneapolis, MN: University of Minnesota Press.

McDermott, John J. (1981) *The Philosophy of John Dewey*, Chicago, IL: University of Chicago Press.

Morgan, Mary S. and Malcolm Rutherford (1998) "American Economics: The Character of the Transformation," in Mary S. Morgan and Malcolm Rutherford (eds) *From Interwar Pluralism to Postwar Neoclassicism: History of Political Economy*, Annual Supplement, 30(0), Durham, NC: Duke University Press.

Nelson, Julie A. (2001) "Value as Relationality: Feminist, Pragmatist and Process Thought Meet Economics," *Journal of Speculative Philosophy* 15(2): 137–51 (Special Issue on "Feminism and Pragmatism," ed. Shannon Sullivan).

—— (2003) "Once More, With Feeling: Process/Feminist Economics and the Ontological Question," *Feminist Economics*. forthcoming.

—— (forthcoming) "Confronting the Science/Value Split: Notes on Feminist Economics, Institutionalism, Pragmatism and Process Thought," *Cambridge Journal of Economics*.

Prigogine, Ilya with Isabelle Stengers (1996) *The End of Certainty: Time, Chaos, and the New Laws of Nature*, New York: Free Press.

Rorty, Richard (1998) "Pragmatism," in Edward Craig (ed.) *Routledge Encyclopedia of Philosophy*, London: Routledge.

Seigfried, Charlene Haddock (ed.) (1993) *Feminism and Pragmatism*, Bloomington, IN: Indiana University Press (*Hypatia* Special issue 8(2)).

—— (1996) *Pragmatism and Feminism: Reweaving the Social Fabric*, Chicago, IL: University of Chicago Press.

Whitehead, Alfred North (1997) *Science and the Modern World*, New York: Free Press; first published 1925.

Part III

Constructing masculine/Western identity in economics

10 The construction of masculine identity in Adam Smith's *Theory of Moral Sentiments*[1]

Edith Kuiper

Introduction

Some feminist economists stress that the *Theory of Moral Sentiments* (*TMS*) (1759) by Adam Smith contains feminist notions of human behavior (see e.g., McCloskey 1996; van Staveren 2001). *TMS* indeed addresses sympathy, passions and feelings, aspects of life and morality that can be conceived as more "feminine" aspects of human nature and that imply a broader view of human behavior than is usually applied by neoclassical economists. Reading the text as a whole, however, and analyzing its argument in detail, the book appears to be more thoroughly masculine in its content than is generally acknowledged.

That Smith's *TMS*[2] and *An Inquiry into the Nature and Causes of the Wealth of Nations* (1776) are gendered is a point that has been made by various authors.[3] Some authors address the absence of women in Smith's moral considerations (see Pujol 1992; Folbre 1992), while others stress Smith's focus on the "masculine" virtues, such as generosity and self-command, in opposition to the "feminine" virtues, such as "humanity," and his focus on the public ("masculine") sphere in opposition of the private ("feminine") sphere or the family (see Rendall 1987; Akkerman 1992). Pocock (1985) identifies the way Smith positions the republican male in opposition to the commercial (feminine) male. Justman (1993) also indicates Smith's perception of commercial man as feminine, and suggests that Smith's plea for the Stoic element of self-command is a way to preserve commercial or prudent man's masculinity in an age of refinement, consumerism, and luxury, all aspects that used to be associated with "the feminine" (Justman 1993: 12–14). In this chapter I take the gender analysis of Smith's *TMS* one step further and address the masculine personality structure that is constructed in *TMS*.

I analyze Smith's arguments on the development of moral behavior as a way to construct a masculine identity, an identity that is considered integral to the mature individual. In this analysis I make use of object-relations theory, a psychoanalytic approach that stresses the importance of the early relation between mother and child for the development of a person's ego and his or her gender identity (Chodorow 1978; Dinnerstein 1976; Klein 1975).

As I am not a psychoanalyst or psychologist by training, it is not my aim here to make claims about Smith's personality structure or the impact of his youth and early relations on his later work. My intension here is, rather, to explore the potentiality of this psychoanalytic approach in the analysis of economic texts and to indicate the importance of implicit psychological presuppositions of an author for his or her theoretical work. I expect this approach to be especially relevant to the analysis of the often implicit use of notions of femininity and masculinity in scientific reasoning, as these are largely grounded in the unconscious perceptions of the author.

Object-relations theory has been applied by feminist theorists in the analysis of work by Plato (Flax 1983; Keller 1985), Bacon (Keller 1985), Descartes (Bordo 1987), Hobbes and Rousseau (Flax 1983).[4] Though the endeavor to apply this twentieth-century theoretical approach to an eighteenth-century text may seem ahistorical, I consider the use of this approach legitimate for a set of reasons.[5] First, the context object-relations theory starts from is the Western nuclear family. This social arrangement, in which the mother is the first and most important caregiver and the father is more at a distance and represents authority, does not differ substantially from the context Smith grew up in: a middle-class household, in which he was brought up by his mother. His father died before he was born. Second, the psychological theories central to *TMS* have been discussed by various commentators who stay close to or within the Freudian line of reasoning (e.g. Lindgren 1973; Campbell 1971; Raphael 1975). I use object-relations theory, which is less phallocentric and allows us to view *TMS* through a feminist lens.

By taking the reader through the text, addressing the structure of the argument, and discussing the development of Smith's impartial spectator through the various editions of *TMS* (there were six editions during Smith's lifetime), I indicate how Smith constructs a masculine identity in his *TMS*. *TMS* is especially interesting because, though meant as a general analysis of men's moral behavior, the story and experience *TMS* feeds on are strongly linked to Smith's own perception of identity and his way of dealing with moral issues.[6] The construction and ongoing process of reconstruction of *TMS* through the various editions can be seen as both a reflection on and a part of the individuation process that took place through Smith's own life. When *TMS* is addressed and analyzed as such, it becomes apparent how establishing a masculine identity, radically separate from women and all the emotionality and passion associated with them, structures Smith's argument. The analysis focuses on Smith's conceptualization of sympathy, the development of the impartial spectator, and the shift made through *TMS* from the importance of a balance between the "soft virtues" and "the great and awful virtues" towards the stress on self-command. Acknowledging and recognizing the masculine character of Smith's description of moral behavior provides a broader perspective on moral behavior and identity, and suggests ways to go beyond what Smith conceived of as masculine virtues and ideals of personhood, a conception that importantly informed later concepts of human identity and rational behavior.

Object-relations theory

What can be and/or has to be considered as "masculine" (and as "feminine") and how to theorize and explain these categories are questions central to women's and gender studies. In this field of study notions of masculinity and femininity are generally understood as highly time and context dependent, and subject to continuous change and power negotiations.

Object-relations theory provides an underpinning and explanation of the specific way notions of masculinity and femininity are given content in Western societies today. It is based on the psychoanalytic tradition and builds on criticisms of Freudian psychology of early childhood development (Chodorow 1978). This approach does not, like Freud's, explain the psychological development of children mainly from the relationship with the father, but theorizes the development of the ego of girls and boys in relation to their mother, the first and most intimate caretaker. Taking late twentieth-century Western middle-class families as the context of reference, the father is assumed to be absent most of the time. According to this theory, there is a substantial difference in the way boys and girls establish their (sexual) identities in relation to their mother and father, which importantly structures the way they deal with social relations through their lives.

Object-relations theory suggests that it is not so much that the body and its primary needs determine the development of the ego, but rather that the ego and its boundaries get established in relation to the environment, especially the mother. Where the child first perceives itself as a unity with the mother, through a process of frustration of its needs and expectations it establishes an increasing awareness of the separateness of the mother and an identity of its own. It is the longing for the reunion with the mother, the re-establishment of this state of intimacy and unity, that importantly causes the longing and anxieties in (sexual) relations later in life. Once a boy becomes aware of being "a boy," in order to attain his masculinity he has to take distance from the mother and shift his orientation and identification towards the father. If the father is predominantly absent the boy may, by lack of a personal relationship with the father, have to more strongly guard his boundaries in relation to his mother and identify with a father who is mostly imagined. When his masculine identity is not well developed and remains vulnerable, the guarding of his ego-boundaries remains an issue throughout his life, and relations to women are perceived as entailing a loss of autonomy. Girls, on the other hand, can achieve their sexual identity while maintaining the relation with their mother; there is no need for them to establish or to guard their ego-boundaries to be feminine. For them, however, lack of ego-boundaries may later in life lead to over-identification with others, and to a less articulated sense of self (Chodorow 1978).

Much more can be said about these early developments and their effects on identity formation and sexual identity. This necessarily rough sketch, due to reasons of space, indicates the main lines along which object-relations theorists such as Chodorow and Dinnerstein explain the association of masculinity with isolation, distance, activity, and control, and femininity with relatedness, fluidness, passivity, and love. Evelyn Fox Keller (1983, 1985) describes the development of the standard perception of science from this perspective and states that this gendered value system has been fundamental to the development of science. To attain insight into the way masculine notions of identity are ingrained in economic texts, we now turn to the analysis of Adam Smith's *TMS*.

The construction of masculine identity

TMS as a treatise on men

Adam Smith's *TMS* (1759) is one of the last in a long line of Enlightenment discourses on the "Nature of Man" articulating Man's character as an independent being.[7] *TMS* was regarded by contemporaries and by Smith himself as his most important work; he worked on revisions his entire life, and he completed the last, sixth, edition two years before his death in 1790. The views articulated in *TMS* were not particularly novel, but together they form an ingenious and coherent perception of the moral agent in which various insights and contemporary discussions come together. They are the concepts of imaginative sympathy and of the impartial spectator, both central to *TMS*, that are considered as Smith's major contributions to the moral philosophy of his time (Raphael 1975: 85).

The way men come to moral judgments is the theme of *TMS* or, as the subtitle to the fourth edition of this work states, it is "An Essay towards an Analysis of the Principles by which Men naturally judge concerning the Conduct and Character, first of their Neighbours, and afterwards of themselves" (Raphael and MacFie 1984: 40). *TMS* focuses on men and their behavior. The opening phrase reads:

> How selfish soever man may be supposed, there are evidently some principles in his nature, which interest him in the fortunes of others, and render their happiness necessary to him, though he derives nothing from it except the pleasure of seeing it.
>
> (*TMS*: I.i.1.1)

As one might expect for a man of his time, Smith distinguishes between women and men in *TMS*, and ascribes to each of them different tasks, behavior, and features. Women were to be treated differently from men (e.g. *TMS*: I.ii.1.2; *TMS*: VII.iii.3.13), and Smith directs himself toward men and to the preservation of (male) virtue (see also Justman 1993: 16).

At the same time he distances himself from women: women are absent as characters in his *TMS*; they are even missing in the discussions on the content and character of all possible relations.[8] In general, when they appear in the text women figure as a foil for the behavior of men, mostly in the negative sense, at a distance or as an extreme case (see, e.g., "the woman in childbed," *TMS*: VII.iii.4). It is man who is at the center of the story in *TMS*, man in the process of establishing a moral and masculine identity.

Imaginative sympathy: the construction and bridging of separateness

After the quote that opens Part I, Chapter 1, Smith continues with a discussion of propriety,[9] more specifically with an explanation of sympathy[10] and the way judgments of conduct are made. Here he establishes the division between the inner and the outer world, referring frequently to "the man-within" and "the man-without." Smith establishes this distinction and subsequently takes the perspective of the man who builds on this distinction.

In Smith's view one cannot have direct knowledge about someone else's feelings. One gets information about other people's feelings and states of mind by imagining how one would feel if one was in the same circumstances (which is not always possible due to the lack of information about the circumstances the other is in), through imaginative sympathy. For Smith, sympathy is similar to a natural force such as gravity, one that is sentimental rather than rational, and makes it possible to know what others experience (Justman 1993: 32). In his definition and account of sympathy, Smith describes his view on inter-human relations:

> Though our brother is upon the rack, *as long as we ourselves are at our ease*, our senses will never inform us of what he suffers. They never did, and never can, carry us beyond our own person, and it is by the imagination only that we can form any conception of what are his sensations.
>
> (*TMS*: I.i.1.2; emphasis mine)

Thus, to acquire information about the emotions and moral considerations of other people, to find out how the brother who is "upon the rack" feels, man has to rely on the imagination. It is the imagination that is used to find out what "this brother" goes through. Notice that no actual communication takes place, no checking the correctness of the imagination of the other's experiences is conducted; there is, so to speak, no *relation* with the other – the contact with the outside world of Smith's isolated Man is predominantly established by means of the imagination.

Though the generally accepted view on Smith's perception of human moral behavior considers Smith's Man as a human being who "feels for others" (see, e.g., Fontaine 1997; Griswold 1999), I want to stress that Smith constructs man as radically isolated from other human beings. The assumption "as long as we ourselves are at ease" in the above quote is important here, because when this is the case – that we can see our brother on the rack and still be at ease – the relation between us and "our brother" is already seriously disturbed, if not cut off. So, Smith starts here with the presumption of a disconnection between himself and the sufferer. This disconnection between the other and the "us" is the basis for further reasoning. Fluidity of emotions and the sharing of feeling are denied; it is made impossible even to discuss this possibility.

For most people however, feeling what the other feels, at least to some extent, is normal practice and the basis of communication. Having access to other people's feelings (people are, for instance, in varying degrees able to pick up when someone is nervous, angry, confused, etc.) and sharing emotions (of grief or joy) have to be distinguished from what Smith states as knowing what the other feels in the same way as the other does himself. Stressing the lack of full accessibility of other people's minds and feelings, Smith subsequently jumps to stating the impossibility of emotional connection and the sharing of feelings. Thus he does not recognize the human connection that precedes language and rational considerations, such as exists, for instance, between lovers and between parents and children (especially in the case of young children who are not yet able to talk). The fact that Smith did not have much experience with this kind of personal connection to other people – he never married, and his mother, his friends, and his books were reported as his three great joys in life (Rae 1977: 327) – might provide something like an explanation for this specific understanding of human relations.[11] The views he presents here however, can also, at a deeper level, be understood as coinciding with his own way of dealing with relations and with other people.

Imaginative sympathy, as Smith understands it, is not the experience of other people's feelings, but of our own as we would live them in a similar situation or as we would imagine ourselves being that other person.[12] Imagining the feelings that go with a specific situation, however, is limited by one's own experiences of similar cases. This implies that the sympathy that can be expected from others is limited by their experiences and approval. The process of sympathy is linked to that of making judgments on the conduct of others. This determination of what is "good" and what is "bad," together with what is "inside" and what "outside," can be considered as a constitutive part in the process of identity formation. Smith takes the feelings and experiences of the agent as a starting point: if the expressions of emotions coincide with our own emotions they are approved of and, if not, they are disapproved of.

> Every faculty in one man is the measure by which he judges of the like faculty in another. I judge of your sight by my sight, of your ear by my ear, of your reason by my reason, of your resentment by my resentment, of your love by my love. I neither have, nor can have, any other way of judging about them.
> (*TMS*: I.i.3.10)

Smith indicates that imaginative sympathy can fail in cases of extreme joy or sorrow. In these cases the moral judgment of one's behavior will be negative, as the others cannot "follow" the emotions shown. In order to make it possible for others to sympathize with them people will tend to adjust their behavior and their passions. This evokes a certain mediocracy of feelings, something Smith considers positive.

On taking distance from women and "the feminine"

In *TMS* the "world-within" is the place of action – the space that is to be explored and the scene where power is established. The "world-without" provides predominantly judgments and threats. Here we see Smith taking distance from women and what he considers "feminine."

In this view, women are the ones who excite men's passions either in the body or in the imagination. In the case in which passions of men for women take their origin mainly from the body, Smith considers it hard to sympathize; these passions are perceived as indecent.[13] The passion of the imaginary kind as "grows up between two persons of different sexes, who have long fixed their thoughts upon one another" (*TMS*: I.ii.2.1) is for Smith much easier to sympathize with, even though

> we may think his passion just as reasonable as any of the kind, yet we never think ourselves bound to conceive a passion of the same kind, and for the same person for whom he has conceived it. The passion appears to every body, but the man who feels it, entirely disproportioned to the value of the object [the woman]; and love, though it is pardoned in a certain age because we know it is natural, is always laughed at, because we cannot enter into it.
> (*TMS*: I.ii.2.1)

These remarks on passions reflect a sexual double standard in which "bad women" are associated with bodily attraction, and "good women" with mind. In both these cases men are no longer seen as autonomous, but as enslaved to their passions. Controlling these passions allows mediocracy to become possible. Women, and what they stand for, are put at a distance and remain inaccessible to Smith. At the same time they represent a threat that has to be overcome in his endeavor of establishing a masculine identity.

After the discussion of various sorts of passions in Part II, Smith deals with ambition, ranks, vanity, the causes of approbation and disapprobation, and the ways to achieve the respect of one's fellow men. As an elaboration of these last aspects, Smith discusses merit and demerit, more specifically the legitimate basis of reward and punishment. In the distinctions and judgments made here, sympathy provides the main foundation. In view of object-relations theory one can say that the ego-boundaries have been set, the terms of good and bad and of reward and punishment have been indicated. Although Smith situates his individual first in relation to his closest personal relations, he is subsequently portrayed as alone in the world, not embedded in family or any social environment, as unsafe, and as dependent on friends and unknown people.

> Though every man may, according to the proverb, be the whole world to himself, to the rest of mankind he is a most insignificant part of it.
>
> (*TMS*: II.ii.2.1)

It is this isolated individual described here who has to attain a moral attitude and/or acquire a masculine identity. This he will do by the identification of what he conceptualizes as the impartial spectator, "the great inmate, the great demi-god within the breast" (*TMS*: VI.iii.18).

The impartial spectator: identification with the father within

According to Smith, men aim for social approval, and therefore moral judgments of fellow men will influence the way they perceive themselves and invoke them to bring their feelings and actions into harmony with those of society. The perceived demands and approval of other people, combined with what the person himself approves of in other men, come together in Smith's "impartial spectator." The impartial spectator is the imagined spectator-within, who judges conduct irrespective of his own situation or passions. Smith states:

> It is not the soft power of humanity, it is not that feeble spark of benevolence which Nature has lighted up in the human heart, that is thus capable of counteracting the strongest impulses of self-love. It is a stronger power, a more forcible motive, which exerts itself upon such occasions. It is reason, principle, conscience, the inhabitant of the breast, the man within, the great judge and arbiter of our conduct.
>
> (*TMS*: III.3.4)

In the process of constructing this image of a fatherly figure and the internalization of a set of masculine values as "the man within," we see here that Smith turns his back on what he considers as associated with the feminine and moves in the direction of what he considers powerful and strong: the man-in-the-breast. Identification with this imagined father will undo the uncertainty about appropriate judgments and behaviors:

> If we place ourselves completely in his [the impartial spectator's] situation, if we really view ourselves with his eyes, and as he views us, and listen with dili-

gent and reverential attention to what he suggests to us, his voice will never deceive us. We shall stand in need of no casuistic rules to direct our conduct.

(*TMS*: VI.ii.1.22)

Smith indicates here the existence and importance of general moral rules or the sense of duty for the guidance of daily behavior, to help men to refrain from despicable behavior and to be trustworthy: to attain a moral identity. Smith declares these general moral rules as "laws of the Deity" or "natural laws" (*TMS*: III.5.6), and the impartial spectator is "the representative of mankind, and substitute of the Deity" (*TMS*: III.2.31n.). As such, the impartial spectator is both universal and culturally and historically contingent.[14] This process of construction, internalization, and subsequent identification with an imagined internal father figure comes more clearly to the fore when we take a closer look at the development of the concept of the impartial spectator over the years.

Raphael (1975) discusses the development of the impartial spectator through the various editions of *TMS*, showing an increase in identification with the impartial spectator and, with that, an increase in the independence of the agent's judgment from the approval of other men, i.e. society.[15] Making use of Raphael's discussion of the various editions of *TMS*, it is possible to indicate two main shifts through these editions. One shift can be characterized as the increasing identification with "the father," or "the demi-god within"; the second as the decreasing importance of the virtue of humanity *vis-à-vis* self-command, which eventually ends in the suppression of feelings of the agent as a condition for acquiring tranquility.

Raphael indicates that in the earliest versions of Smith's lectures (1752), which formed the basis for *TMS*, no theory of the impartial spectator is yet to be found; Smith speaks here of "we," "our heart," and about "any impartial person," which suggests that Smith takes here the perspective of "mankind" that may or may not applaud punishment (Raphael 1975: 88). In the first edition of *TMS* (1759) Smith mentions as a criterion to determine the just degree of resentment or punishment "that degree which had the sympathy of the impartial spectator" (*TMS*: II.i.2.1–2). The impartial spectator here still has the form of a disinterested bystander.

Raphael indicates a shift in emphasis in the second edition. Here the discussion of the imagination of the impartial spectator develops towards the division of one self into two persons. In the second edition (1761) Smith writes:

> When I endeavour to examine my own conduct…it is evident that…I divide myself, as it were, into two persons; and that I, the examiner and judge, represent a different character from that other I, the person whose conduct is examined into and judged of. The first is the spectator…. The second is the agent, the person whom I properly call myself.
>
> (*TMS* III.1.6)

Smith then describes the spectator as "this inmate of the breast, this abstract man, the representative of mankind, and substitute of the Deity" (see also *TMS*: III.2.3.). After he has constructed this imaginary father figure, who constitutes what Freud probably would call a super-ego, Smith comes to conceptualize the image of this impartial spectator as an entity that is increasingly distinct and independent from mankind (Raphael 1975: 91).

Discussing the changes in the various editions and Smith's correspondence on these topics, Raphael indicates the emergence of a gap between mankind's approval, on the one hand, and the independent appraisal by the agent of what it is that constitutes praise-worthiness, on the other. He points out how Smith shifts from stressing social approval (praise) as inducing behavior to focusing on the importance of praise-worthiness, which is perceived increasingly as independent of social approval. In the sixth edition Smith eventually states that "so far is the love of praise worthiness from being derived altogether from that of praise; that the love of praise seems, at least in great measure, to be derived from that of praise-worthiness" (*TMS*: III.2.2–3). With this shift, Smith's initially weak trust in the imagination as a "moral looking glass" is replaced by a full reliance on the imagination of the agent (Raphael 1975: 92). Thus the impartial spectator has become independent and distinct from valuations and judgments of mankind. It is this figure that Smith sets out to identify with.[16]

It is the identification with the abstract man-within that enables man to make judgments on his own accord. As indicated earlier, the requirements, demands, and judgments made by the impartial spectator represent mankind. Identification with the imagined "man-within-the breast" provides man with access to power, and thus with the ability to judge over his fellow men.

> The all-wise Author of Nature has, in this manner, taught man to respect the sentiments and judgments of his brethren; to be more or less pleased when they approve of his conduct, and to be more or less hurt when they disapprove of it. He has made man, if I may say so, the immediate judge of mankind; and has, in this respect, as in many others, created him after his own image, and appointed him his viceregent upon earth, to superintend the behaviour of his brethren.
>
> (*TMS*: III.2.31)

When we perceive Smith's move against the background of his time in which both the Church and the Aristocracy still claimed divine powers and authority, Smith's conceptualization of a judge-within was revolutionary. Applying object-relations theory, however, we see that Smith's conceptualization of moral behavior and identity supplies us with an image of a young man (see also Campbell 1971; Lindgren 1973), of someone who finds himself in the middle of the process of establishing and maintaining his masculine identity.

Object-relations theory pays specific attention to the case of boys to whom the father is not available as a positive identification figure. In this case, it is impossible for the boy to develop his gender identity in a personal relationship with his object of identification. The boy will therefore develop a positional identification with only certain aspects of the masculine role, as the tie between affective processes and role learning is broken. Since the boy's masculine role learning is not to be embedded in a relationship with his father or other men, it rather involves the denial of the affective relationship to the mother (Chodorow 1978: 175–7). This case, which bears many similarities with the process of construction, internalization, and identification of the impartial spectator in Smith's *TMS* described above, is here of special relevance because Adam Smith's father died before he was born. He lived with his mother most of his life. As we will see in the next section, the sense of self, the ego-boundaries, and the manhood of Smith's agent are perceived as being constantly under threat, because of, among other things, personal passions and feelings of the agent. Tranquility is longed for but only attained incidentally, when full identification with the impartial spectator is achieved.

Self-command, the suppression of personal feelings and the importance of love

The second shift I want to discuss here is the increasing stress Smith puts on self-command in the second and sixth edition (see Raphael 1975). Initially Smith distinguishes two kinds of virtues, the "soft and amiable" ones such as humanity,[17] which he placed on a par with the "great and awful" virtues of self-denial and self-government (*TMS*: I.i.5.5). In the second edition, however, self-command and consciousness become perceived as necessary to counter feelings of humanity and love (Raphael 1975: 93). Smith's construction of identity links manhood, self-command, and the establishment of wisdom in opposition to the agent's own feelings. Even in situations in which passions and some self-interest seem almost unavoidable, as in the case of "the man who has lost his leg by a canon shot" (*TMS*: III.3.26), Smith advocates immediate identification with the impartial spectator. This will enable this miserable man, just after he lost his leg, to speak and act "with his usual coolness and tranquility, as he exerts a much higher degree of self-command" (*TMS*: III.3.26). This will bring him, according to Smith, a "much higher degree of self-approbation." Thus:

> The man of real constancy and firmness, the wise and just man who has been thoroughly bred in the great school of self-command...has never dared to forget for one moment the judgment which the impartial spectator would pass upon his sentiments and conduct. He has never dared to suffer the man within the breast to be absent one moment from his attention. ...He does

> not merely affect the sentiments of the impartial spectator. He really adopts them. He almost identifies himself with, he almost becomes himself that impartial spectator, and scarce even feels but as that great arbiter of his conduct directs him to feel.
>
> (*TMS*: III.3.25)

In Part VI, which was strongly revised in the sixth edition, Smith makes a last important shift in the appraisal of the role of humanity relative to self-command (Raphael 1975: 93). He states that propriety is part of the consideration of the sentiments of the impartial spectator and that self-command is basic to the attainment of the virtues of prudence, justice, and beneficence.

Although the identification with the impartial spectator does provide a mechanism to overcome the agent's feelings, the tranquility thus attained remains under constant threat by the continuous flow of feelings, fears, and, in extreme cases, paroxysms. Therefore self-command has to be exercised every moment of the day. If not, "every passion would, upon most occasions, rush headlong…to its own gratification. Anger would follow the suggestions of its own fury; fear those of its own violent agitations" (*TMS*: VI. concl. 2). Feelings thus come to be considered as disturbances of the tranquility attained. Instead of as a source of information about oneself and one's needs, wishes, and desires, personal feelings become considered as a threat, a threat that now comes from within.

This shift towards a one-sided stress on self-command and suppression of feelings goes with a change in the perception of the role and importance of love in *TMS*. Smith states various times in *TMS* that to love and to be loved is very important, if not the most important thing for a person. This insight, however, seems to get lost. His *TMS* ends in Part VI of the sixth edition – written at the end of his life – in a plea for manhood, virtue, and self-command. This revised Part VI varies in tone from earlier ones – it is flatter and less melodic – and, dealing frequently with fear, anger, and anxieties, it leaves the susceptible reader with the image of a sad and lonely old man. Though his natural moral laws may provide men with the approbation of their imaginary father-within and a feeling of control over their lives, in the end this may not be enough as it cannot replace the lack of genuine human connection and relations.

Conclusions

Through its various editions, Adam Smith's *TMS* can be conceived as reflecting an individuation process, one that proceeds and/or backs up the *Wealth of Nations*. The use of object-relations theory helped to indicate the process of construction of a masculine concept of identity through the six editions of *TMS*.

The focus in *TMS* is on men, and individual men are stated to be separate from other human beings in the very beginning of this treatise. Not only does Smith put women at a distance, if not exclude them from the discussions; in various instances he devalues that which he states as or associates with "the female." Sympathy is stated as the way to connect with other people and as the basis for moral behavior. It provides the basis for judgment of others and identification with the impartial spectator. Smith constructs an imaginary father figure, whom he internalizes and with whom he sets out to identify. The impartial spectator, this imagined father-within, provides him with rules for behavior and thus constancy in conduct, as well as access to power and the ability and legitimization to judge his fellow brethren. In the last edition, published two years before his death, Smith included a substantially revised Part VI containing a strong stress on the importance of self-command. In the end it appears to be no longer the balance between humanity and self-command that constitutes the perfect human being; instead, Smith states the full identification with the impartial spectator and the attainment of self-command as the way to attain moral conduct and the desired state of tranquility.

Although I do conclude against characterizing Smith as a feminist – to put it mildly – this is not what is at stake here. My point is to demonstrate the impact of unconscious notions of gender and gender identity on economic theorizing as well as the masculine conceptualization of moral behavior and identity in Adam Smith's *TMS*. The use of object-relations theory has supplied us with a new and surprising story about the content and structure of this important treatise. *TMS* can be conceived as an undertaking which aimed at the construction of a moral and masculine identity that would give the author (his friends, and in the end all mankind with him) the possibility to judge well and, with that, a legitimization for doing so. This concept of identity appears to be self-referring, to posit the individual as an isolated human being whose contact with others takes place mainly through the imagination. In Smith's perception a morally full-grown man achieves a supreme viewpoint and becomes praiseworthy by identification with "the impartial spectator": he has learned how to control his feelings and to attain tranquility. The occurrence of suffering due to external causes provides opportunities to strengthen this control and self-command; anger and fear coming from within invoke even stronger repression of Smith's personal feelings. This concept of identity, which denies the existence and importance of direct emotional connections and conceives emotions as something to be controlled rather than as containing vital information about justified needs and desires, is masculine rather than mature, personal, interested; and culture specific rather than universal.

Notes

1 The Faculty of Economics and Econometrics of the Universiteit van Amsterdam and the European University Institute in Florence provided me with the opportunity of completing this chapter, for which I am grateful. I want to thank Mark Blaug, Annie Cot, Martin Fase, Caroline

Gerschlager, Harro Maas, Michael Perelman, and Margaret Schabas for their comments on earlier versions of this chapter. I want to thank Drucilla Barker in particular for her valuable and constructive suggestions and editorial comments. This final version remains of course entirely my responsibility.

2 I make use here of the 1982 reprint of the Glasgow Edition of the Works and Correspondence of Adam Smith, edited by D.D. Raphael and A.L. MacFie, published by Oxford University Press in 1976 and reprinted with minor corrections in 1979 (Indianapolis: Liberty Fund).

3 See Vivienne Brown (1997) for an overview of the work done in this direction. It should also be noted that the importance of gender for Smith's work has recently been contested in Griswold's extended study on Smith's work (Griswold 1999).

4 On the use of object-relations theory in the philosophy of economics, see Feiner (1995 and reprinted in this volume as Chapter 12) and Hewitson (1999).

5 On the topic of applying object-relations theory in the analysis of philosophical texts, see also Bordo (1987) and Keller (1985).

6 See, for instance, *TMS* (I.i.1.12), which – though implicitly and in generalized wordings – refers to Smith's own experience and life.

7 See, e.g., John Locke (*An Essay Concerning Human Understanding*, 1690), Thomas Hobbes (*Leviathan*, 1651), Jean-Jacques Rousseau (*Discours on Inequality*, 1755), Anthony Shaftesbury (*Characteristics of Men, Manners, Opinions, Times*, 1711), Davis Hartley (*Observations on Man*, 1749), Francis Hutcheson (*A System of Moral Philosophy*, 1755), and Lévesques de Pouilly (*The Theory of Agreeable Sensations*, 1749).

8 In Part VI he refers, for instance, to all those "who usually live in the same house with him" mentioning children, parents, but not a wife (*TMS*: VI.ii.1.2).

9 Propriety (decency) consists in Smith's view of a mediocracy of passions (*TMS*: I.ii.intro.1).

10 Sympathy is very broadly defined by Smith as "our fellow-feeling with any passions whatever" (*TMS*: I.i.1.5).

11 That Smith never married or was involved in any known relationship with a woman invoked Schumpeter to state:

> A fact which I cannot help considering relevant, not for his pure economics of course, but all the more for his understanding of human nature – that no women, excepting his mother, ever played a role in his existence; in this as in other respects the glamours and passions of life were just literature to him.
>
> (Schumpeter 1954: 182)

12 In their discussion on Smith's notion of sympathy, Griswold (1999) and Fontaine (1997) acknowledge the cognitive character of imaginative sympathy as Smith conceptualizes it.

13 Whereas men who give in to such kinds of feelings are held in no high esteem by Smith, he has contempt for the object of their love, who is literally looked upon as dirt:

> When we have dined, we order the covers to be removed; and we should treat in the same manner the objects of the most ardent and passionate desires, if they were the objects of no other passions but those which take their origin from the body.
>
> (*TMS*: I.ii.1.3)

14 For a discussion on the issue of moral relativity, see Lindgren (1973).

15 Although Raphael is here referred to as indicating the shifts in focus and perspective applied in Smith's articulation of the impartial spectator, Raphael himself explicitly claims that Smith's fundamental position remained unchanged; that over his life he may have changed and even reversed his emphasis, but that these have to be considered as "elements in his theory at all stages" (Raphael 1975: 94).

16 Justman (1993) misperceives the role and importance of the impartial spectator in his analysis of *TMS*, as he does not take the psychological role of this construct into consideration, positing that "[t]he man within, that 'demigod',…is too much of a ghostly abstraction to be fully convincing" (Justman 1993: 89).

17 Humanity is the common quality of fellow-feeling: being kind, thoughtful, sympathetic to other people. Smith states about this virtue that it "requires, surely, a sensibility, much beyond what is possessed by the rude vulgar of mankind" (*TMS*: I.i.5.6).

Bibliography

Akkerman, Tjitske (1992) *Women's Vices, Public Benefits: Women and Commerce in the French Enlightenment*, Amsterdam: Het Spinhuis.
Bordo, Susan R. (1987) *The Flight to Objectivity. Essays on Cartesianism & Culture*, Albany, NY: State University of New York Press.
Brown, Vivienne (1994) *Adam Smith's Discourse: Canonicity, Commerce and Conscience*, London: Routledge.
—— (1997) "'Mere Inventions of the Imagination': A Survey of Recent Literature on Adam Smith," *Economics and Philosophy* 13: 281–312.
Campbell, Thomas D. (1971) *Adam Smith's Science of Morals*, London: Allen & Unwin.
Chodorow, Nancy (1978) *The Reproduction of Mothering: Psychoanalysis and the Sociology of Gender*, Berkeley, CA: University of California Press.
Dinnerstein, Dorothy (1976) *The Mermaid and the Minotaur*, New York: Harper & Row.
Feiner, Susan F. (1995) "Reading Neoclassical Economics: Towards an Erotic Economy of Sharing," in E. Kuiper and J. Sap, with S.F. Feiner, N. Ott and Z. Tzannatos (eds.) *Out of the Margin: Feminist Perspectives on Economics*, London and New York: Routledge.
Flax, Jane (1983) "Political Philosophy and the Patriarchal Unconsciousness: A Psychoanalytic Perspective on Epistemology and Metaphysics," in S. Harding and M.M. Hintikka (eds.) *Discovering Reality*, Dordrecht: Reidel.
Folbre, Nancy (1992) "'The Improper Arts': Sex in Classical Political Economy," *Population and Development Review* 18(1), March: 105–21.
Fontaine, P. (1997) "Identification and Economic Behavior Sympathy and Empathy in Historical Perspective," *Economics and Philosophy* 13: 261–80.
Grappard, Ulla (1993) "How to See the Invisible Hand or From the Benevolence of the Butcher's Wife," paper presented at the Out of the Margin Conference June 1993, Amsterdam.
Griswold, Charles L. (1999) *Adam Smith and the Virtues of Enlightenment*, Cambridge: Cambridge University Press.
Hewitson, Gillian (1999) *Feminist Economics: Interrogating the Masculinity of Rational Economic Man*, Cheltenham: Edward Elgar.
Justman, Stewart (1993) *The Autonomous Male of Adam Smith*, Norman and London: University of Oklahoma Press.
Keller, Evelyn Fox (1983) "Gender and Science," in S. Harding and M.M. Hintikka (eds.) *Discovering Reality*, Dordrecht: Reidel.
—— (1985) *Reflections on Gender and Science*, New Haven and London: Yale University Press.
Klein, Melanie (1975) *The Writings of Melanie Klein*, ed. R. Money-Kyrle, London: Hogarth Press.
Lindgren, J. Ralph (1973) *The Social Philosophy of Adam Smith*, The Hague: Martinus Nijhof.
McCloskey, Deirdre N. (1996) "Love and Money," *Feminist Economics* 2(2): 137–41.
Pocock, John G.A. (1985) *Virtue, Commerce, and History: Essays on Political Thought and History, Chiefly in the Eighteenth Century*, Cambridge: Cambridge University Press.
Pujol, Michèle (1992) *Feminism and Anti-Feminism in Early Economic Thought*, Aldershot: Edward Elgar.
Rae, John (1977) *Life of Adam Smith*, New York: August Kelley; first published 1895.
Raphael, D.D. (1975) "The Impartial Spectator," in A.S. Skinner and T. Wilson (eds.) *Essays on Adam Smith*, Oxford: Clarendon Press.
Raphael, D.D. and Alec L. MacFie (1984) "Introduction," in Adam Smith, *The Theory of Moral Sentiments*, Indianapolis: Liberty Fund.

Rendall, Jane (1987) "Virtue and Commerce: Women in the Making of Adam Smith's Political Economy," in E. Kennedy and S. Mendus (eds.) *Women in Western Political Philosophy, Kant to Nietzsche*, Brighton: Wheatsheaf Books.

Ross, Ian (1995) *The Life of Adam Smith*, Oxford: Clarendon Press.

Schumpeter, Joseph A. (1954) *History of Economic Analysis*, London: Routledge.

Smith, Adam (1759) *The Theory of Moral Sentiments*, ed. D.D. Raphael and A.L. MacFie, Indianapolis: Liberty Fund.

—— (1776) *An Inquiry into the Nature and Causes of the Wealth of Nations*, ed. R.H. Campbell and A.S. Skinner, Indianapolis: Liberty Fund.

van Staveren, Irene (2001) *Caring Economy*, London: Routledge.

11 Social classifications, social statistics, and the "facts" of "difference" in economics

Brian P. Cooper[1]

Introduction

Historians have long warned of the perils of accepting various classifications in social statistics as delivering up unproblematic facts. They have examined how census classifications such as "household" and "race" have been subject to ideological manipulation, or have been developed in an environment of bureaucratic infighting or indecision. Many others – philosophers, literary historians, sociologists, anthropologists, political scientists, accountants, and economists – have also examined the contingent nature of various categories of social statistics as measures of difference.[2] This essay offers additional thoughts on how economists might explore questions, epistemological and otherwise, about the "facts" of "difference" in social statistics. By "difference" I mean the outcome of the banal exercise of discrimination that distinguishes an object as something and not something else in social statistics, an exercise vital to those who do theoretical and empirical work in economics. I also mean the perspective that holds social categories as "being revealed by statistics" (Desrosières 1998: 238), which highlights the meanings, moral and aesthetic, one imparts to difference. This essay is about classification, but it is also about facts and interpretations. Taxonomies supply stories about facts. Different groups – social scientists, politicians, bureaucrats, and the public – have struggled to define and value the facts and categories of social life, and their struggles entail social and political consequences.

As with the history of the "classifying imagination" in biology (Ritvo 1997), the existence of folk systems of classification for social phenomena, and their interaction with social scientific systems, muddies distinctions between lay and scientific knowledge. In the first half of the nineteenth century, for example, British political economists puzzled over classifications as they sought to shape the development of the social sciences and to influence public policy. Many of the classifications they fretted over were terms that were already part of the vernacular in Great Britain: "the economy" only came into being in English around 1850, having been derived from "economy," meaning household management.

Other terms, developed by social scientists, became part of everyday language. "Average man," whom everyone claims they are not, was born in the late 1820s, when the Belgian statistician Adolphe Quetelet created him as the statistical embodiment of his proposed new science, social physics. Social physics, Quetelet maintained, would turn political economy, which he identified as Malthus's population principles, into a science (Quetelet 1968: 49).

Taxonomic distinctions also involve politics and the exercise of power. Early nineteenth-century reformers in Great Britain tried to put numbers to old classifications in everyday use, such as "deserving" and "undeserving poor," for example. For the political economist Nassau Senior this effort framed the gathering and arrangement of evidence for the reports of the 1834 Poor Law Commission in Britain, of which he was part. The reports, in turn, led to a rewriting of the meaning of charity in the new poor law.

So, doing histories of social classification can bridge the (apparent) divides between theory and empirical work in economics, between economics as a discipline and common knowledge, and between economic theory and public policy. This essay traces some epistemological and practical consequences that reflect this cross-fertilization between different producers and users of economic facts, social classifications, and social statistics. The first section (pp. 163–6) looks at classifications in the social sciences, of which social statistics are a subset, as technologies – tools to produce knowledge that can be acted on by various parties. Here I also argue that social statistics have developed not just as descriptions, but are prescriptive and aesthetic as well (see also Cooper and Murphy 2000).

When social categories change or are applied to new situations they produce new markers of difference not completely compatible with old meanings. Social classifications reveal as much about the classifiers, their prejudices and anxieties about their own identities, as they do about the classified. This is illustrated in the second and third sections (pp. 166–70 and 170–4), which examine episodes in the nineteenth-century history of British experiences with travel observations, vital statistics, and population censuses. I first examine how observers used two ways of gathering facts and classifying social phenomena in South America in the 1820s. Travelers in South America used both conjectural histories and theories of political economy, employing representative types such as the "gaucho" and statistical aggregates such as "population" in their accounts. The facts observed by travelers in South America stretch to the breaking point conjectural history and political economy frameworks that make England and Englishness the measuring rod and standard of civilization. The evidence gathered by travelers foregrounds the question of whether their facts (and interpretations) could be contained by a systematic framework or whether they were simply idiosyncratic, reduced to a single observer's subjective judgment of difference and sameness. Statistics offered, apparently, a solution: an impartial and universal arbitration and summary of the facts (if not the interpretations).

I say apparently, because population data for South America were either unreliable or missing altogether. If the South Americans lacked basic facts about population size, the British lacked a precise set of classifications about their own population's constituent parts, having only conducted their first decennial count in 1801. The third section (pp. 170–4) examines British census classifications of "occupation" and "family" in the first half of the nineteenth century. Definitions of the two categories changed over this period, as census takers and the public attempted to come to grips both with the changing nature and location of employment and with the rise of ideologies of separate spheres for men and women in Britain. The work to establish stable and useful categories also represents a striking example of how bureaucrats and governments attempt to devise and employ statistical categories derived in specific contexts as universally applicable classifications. Categories developed by William Farr, beginning in 1851, to describe and preserve population in Britain were later applied to conditions in British military camps at home and abroad in order to decrease their horrific morbidity and mortality rates. Tools designed to stabilize the domestic population thus supported the maintenance and extension of empire. This represents one solution to the representational problem, posed by travelers' awkward or missing facts, of how to depict "difference": universal categories can simultaneously obliterate difference and erect hierarchical rankings. But we must not overstate the ability of British authorities to enact this in practice. In India at least, this effort foundered in part due to profound differences between British and Indian concepts of the category "age." This classification difficulty entailed serious consequences for colonial census takers and contemporaries who debated colonial reform. If even so simple and seemingly uncontroversial a category as "age" carries political and moral weight, it also proves the point that we must take social classification seriously.

Social classifications and social statistics: what are they and what do they do?

Doing histories of classifications requires us to ask what social classifications are and what they do. One answer: social classification systems are technologies, the application of knowledge toward practical ends. Classification systems are boxes into which objects can be put; once placed in a box, these objects produce knowledge. Ideal classification systems exhibit consistent and unique principles of ordering, contain categories which are mutually exclusive, and are complete – that is, can contain new objects without doing violence to the first two characteristics of ideal classification (Bowker and Star 1999: 10–11).

How do social classification systems operate? In reality, coding practices, where people attribute a particular case to a particular class, deviate from the ideal: not every object fits neatly into a unique category (Desrosières 1998: 237). In Britain in the eighteenth century, for example, the meaning of the category "gentleman" was in flux, and this engendered a proliferation of descriptions, even whole new categories. While it still implied some idea of birth, manners, and dress, it increasingly became a self-appellation. Boundary cases define classification systems: did an eighteenth-century merchant with money qualify as a "gentleman"? Early in the century Daniel Defoe derided such a hybrid as an "amphibious creature"; by the 1780s others called such strivers "half-gentleman." Better still for revealing categories as moral and epistemological constructs are so-called category "mistakes," objects that end up in places they "should not" be: a laborer could call himself a "gentleman" only at the risk of ridicule. More humorously, a personal servant was sometimes denoted a "gentleman's gentleman." Category mistakes define and enforce epistemological, social, and moral orders. Individuals and groups develop and use social classifications to identify or obscure individual subjects or whole collectivities. Classifications can blind us to certain facts about social life, or they can enable us to imagine new possibilities for description and action, including formulating policies aimed at reforming people, institutions, and spaces.

This is certainly true of classifications in social statistics, which constitute a subcategory of social classifications. Social statistics use quantification, itself a social technology (Porter 1995: ch. 3), to summarize aspects of a designated group and space. Numbers freeze moments of social life, and allow for the communication of facts, in orderly arrangement, at a distance. We should keep in mind that the meaning of "statistics" has itself varied. In the seventeenth century social statistics were an element of "*Statistik*," the description of the state in figurative language and numbers. "*Statistik*" was destined for the eyes of the sovereign, to enhance his or her control of the state.

British political arithmeticians such as William Petty originally supported this vision of the ends of social description, where knowledge flowed to, and overt regulation and order flowed from, the sovereign (Buck 1982). But political arithmeticians deviated from their German counterparts' insistence on exhaustive description. They preferred, instead, summary statistics such as population, births, and deaths as adequate representations of society. Although the German version of statistics lasted into the early part of the nineteenth century, it is the summary, aggregate numerical representation (in tables) that came to be known as social "statistics." Like other social classifications, social statistics are descriptive, and prescriptive. Like other social classifications, their users also interpret them using aesthetic judgment. Not only did Quetelet wish statistics to reveal average man as a source of knowledge for changing the social state, but he designated his "statistical fiction" as "the type of all which is beautiful – of all which is good" (Quetelet 1968: 100). Thus average man is a statistical aggregate, a representative type, and an aesthetic ideal, all rolled into one.

National and international networks help summary statistics do the work of spanning distances. In the eighteenth and early nineteenth centuries Defoe,

Arthur Young, Malthus, and other British men and women traveled, observed, gathered, and arranged the facts themselves. But Malthus did not need to travel to gather all the facts for his work on population: he simply looked most of them up. This act obscures the work of those who translated observations into recognizable categories. It obscures, too, the process by which authors like Malthus read and sifted through travelers' accounts. Readers knew that travelers were notorious for embroidering accounts, traveling the same well-worn paths and repeating the same stories. The split between "mere recorders" and interpreters of facts occurred in statistical agencies as well. The rise of a division of labor in the social sciences between those who gathered data and those who arranged them in meaningful and useful categories accelerated after the creation of bureaucracies to classify the flood of printed numbers in the first third of the nineteenth century in Europe (Hacking 1982: 280, 285, 292–4).

As with other social classifications, we need to concern ourselves with how knowledge is produced by social statistics. How is knowledge made (in)visible by social statistics? For whom is that knowledge destined? What ends does that knowledge serve? Criticisms of the summary nature of social statistics from within and without British classical political economy were common in the first half of the nineteenth century. Critics found statistics inadequate as descriptions and as a basis for reform. James Mill argued that statistics were silent as to causes (Mill 1826: 49–50). And Romantic poets charged that they were too summary, that they missed what is essential in social life, and that they were just plain dull. The commentaries that run alongside statistical tables came in for similar criticism, as imparting either too much or too little meaning to the accompanying numbers (Poovey 1993).

Further, categories such as race, for example, are not timeless and natural, but have names and meanings that are fluid, internally contradictory, and that often change and proliferate. Ideas on Christianity, civility, and rank stood as important influences on British racial thought throughout the eighteenth century; it was only in the last decades of the century that the division between black and white and the markers of skin color, hair texture, and nose shape became predominant in racial thought (Wheeler 2000). Stages of growth theories played critical, if contradictory, roles in this development. On the one hand, contact with commercial civilization was seen as promoting not just economic development but the development of character and conduct. Trade could accentuate similarities rather than "difference": those who came into contact with the British could be transformed into people just like them. On the other hand, commercial society held out the potential to promote and accentuate ideas of "difference," and "to depend on perceived bodily differences economically and commercially" (*ibid.*: 178). Even in the first half of the nineteenth century "race" in Britain could refer to, among other things, a family, an occupational group, people of a region, people of a nation, or, less often, a biological population such as "Negro." Though a statistical category may be contingent and unstable, it, like folk classifications such as "gentleman," becomes increasingly valid or real, with material consequences, once in use as an official classification (Porter 1995: 41–5).

Categories, or Measuring "population" and "civilization" in South America in the 1820s

Categories work well if their users agree upon their designations and meanings. But this was not the case in political economy in the first half of the nineteenth century in Britain. Political economists struggled to establish common definitions for analytical categories such as value (see Malthus 1827, for example). They also sought to classify and quantify populations around the world, using Malthus's population principle as a measuring rod. Travel writing served as an important source of evidence about human similarities and differences for Scottish conjectural historians and British political economists in this period (Dolan 2000a, 2000b: ch. 2; Herbert 1991: ch. 2; Hunt 1993).[3]

Likewise, both conjectural histories and political economy served as important organizing frameworks for travelers' observations. A key question is whether the assumption of human sameness, in terms of psychological propensities, in conjectural history and British political economy erases difference when an observer goes out into the field. In fact, British analysts had to accommodate evidence of differences in behavior that did not neatly fit into their categories. Societies that came into increasing contact with Britain in this period also adapted their systems of knowledge as a result of evidence of "difference" – that is, British practices and beliefs. If we ask how the gaucho, a popular figure in 1820s travel literature, fit into the frameworks of conjectural history and political economy – was he civilized or uncivilized – we should also ask how he and other South Americans regarded the British.[4]

These questions are not idle ones, even for armchair travelers. For instance, the British, keen to invest in Spanish America in the early 1820s, wanted to know the risks and returns of investment in the new republics. British companies sent representatives to South America to check the facts for themselves and assess the prospects for profitable investment in the region. Their accounts and those of fellow travelers settled on a set of general analytical categories under which facts about South America could be arranged. They agreed that a lack of capital, skills, and technology, political instability, the insecurity of property, and bad manners instilled by centuries of ill usage at the hands of the Spanish had all worked to retard the progress of civilization in South America. Their readers, including political economists, joined in this conversation about Spanish America. According to Malthus, political economists needed to examine facts on the moral as well as the material state of society if they were to avoid drawing incorrect inferences about the nature of a civilization from a priori assumptions (Malthus 1989: 381). Such facts would demonstrate, for instance, that fertile soil did not necessarily lead to a large population. For Malthus, the perfect example of this was the observation of the celebrated traveler Alexander von Humboldt that the prodigious fertility of Spanish America produced indolence rather than industry and skill, and that this combination of physical and moral conditions kept the population low (*ibid.*: 380–4).

Yet some British travelers in South America rebutted the oft-repeated charge, echoed by conjectural historians and political economists, that Indians, gauchos, and Creoles were indolent. A visiting mining representative, Francis Bond Head, traveled with the gauchos – 6,000 miles back and forth across the pampas in four months, at an active, not indolent, clip of 13 or 14 hard-riding hours a day – and his extensive conversations with them led him to an empathetic understanding of what he considered the gaucho's view of civilization:

> Vain is the endeavour to explain to him the luxuries and blessings of a more civilized life; his ideas are, that the noblest effort of man is to raise himself off the ground and ride instead of walk – that no rich garments or variety of food can atone for the want of a horse – and that the print of a human foot on the ground is in his mind the symbol of uncivilization.
>
> (Head 1826: 21)

Head concedes that whether a type of people embodied "civilization" was in the eye of the beholder. Its meanings were not just culturally relative, but individually subjective. Head's interpretations of the location and meaning of civilization are of a piece with other contemporary narratives of the region that questioned the assumed link between commercial civilization and virtue.

Despite his moment of cultural relativism, Head did not give the gaucho the final word on the location of civilization. Head's further observations on the gaucho reflect the fact that many of his fellow travelers added another set of categories, from Malthus and the political economists, to order their observations on the degree of civilization in South America. These were facts on population:

> It is true he is of little service to the great cause of civilization, which it is the duty of every rational being to promote; an humble individual, living by himself in a boundless plain, cannot introduce into the vast uninhabited regions which surround him either arts or sciences: he may, therefore, without blame be permitted to leave them as he found them, and as they must remain, until population, which will create wants, devises the means of supplying them.
>
> (Head 1826: 23)

Only the sheer press of numbers would suffice to recruit the gaucho into the "great cause of civilization." Population or the lack of it also determined whether the South American republics were ready to absorb the capital investment necessary to usher in full-scale commercial civilization. European travelers asserted, as had Malthus, that a greater density of population would increase effective demand and multiply desires beyond subsistence needs, setting off a virtuous cycle of economic growth and population growth. Population growth was thus both a marker and an essential determinant of the growth of civilization in South America.

Europeans and South American elites assumed population growth would bring civilization to the continent, but what exactly was the population of the new republics? The statistics were missing or unreliable. John Miers, an English botanist who built and ran the national mint for the government in Buenos Aires, reports three widely varying sets of numbers for cities and provinces of the La Plata Federal Union for the year 1815 (see Figure 11.1). The Spanish had exaggerated the population of their American possessions, in part to inflate their value in the eyes of the world, in part to give pause to any potential invader. The estimates for various towns, cities, and provinces were simply numerical fictions.

The lack of accurate facts hampered British calculations of the risk of investment in Buenos Aires and the rest of Spanish America. A population estimate that was too low/high would under/overstate the "readiness" of the new nations to absorb new capital and new emigrants from Europe. Crucially, the very inaccuracy of the population censuses argued against the presence of the necessary knowledge and infrastructure for foreign investment. The Secretary of State of the United Provinces of Rio de la Plata, Ignacio Nuñez, acknowledged that the principal barrier to capital investment lay in this fact that "Europe knows not my country" (Nuñez 1825: 17). He asserted that "statistical data" on the Americas would indicate "what they are intrinsically worth, and what they actually know," and would thereby secure European investment.

For Miers, the solution to statistical indeterminacy lay in bringing more Englishmen of a certain type to South America:

> The numbers of our intelligent countrymen who are engaged in different parts of this immense continent will afford us the necessary observations and matters of fact, and enable us to give to this country its true value, and to appreciate its actually existent available resources.
>
> (Miers 1826, vol. I: 265)

Both British travelers and American elites envisioned bringing another British type – the hardworking, honest, sober, and prudent artisan – to South America to augment its population and to take advantage of the opportunities that were known. Notwithstanding the risks to the British of "going native," emigration served as a safety valve for surplus population and helped create new markets for British goods. For the South Americans, the immigrants would deploy much needed skills and

...mated census of 1815, according to an official report of the following provinces, is thus stated:—

The Province of	Buenos Ayres	250,000
	Mendoza	38,000
	San Juan	34,000
	San Luis	16,000
	Cordova	100,000
		438,000

A recent traveller has given the following estimate:—

	City.	Province.	Total.
Buenos Ayres	60,000	80,000	140,000
Mendoza	20,000	30,000	50,000
San Juan			20,000
San Luis			20,000
Cordova	14,000	30,000	44,000
			274,000

But from the best information I could obtain, I believe the following is much nearer the truth:—

	City.	Province.	Total.
Buenos Ayres	45,000	40,000	85,000
Mendoza	12,000	8,000	20,000
San Juan	8,000	6,000	14,000
San Luis	2,500	8,000	11,000
Cordova	10,000	12,000	22,000
			152,000

Figure 11.1 Population estimates for La Plata Federal Union for the year 1815
Source: Miers (1826, vol. I: 264).

bring civilization, in the guise of British manners, to the new nations. South Americans did not, however, consider an influx of Europeans, and the British in particular, as an unambiguous good. Many feared that they had shrugged off one colonial power only to risk falling prey to another: they might "go British." These concerns were not entirely unfounded. In 1828 the political economist J.R. McCulloch proposed massive emigration to Spanish America, 50,000 Anglo-Saxon colonists who would "propagate *their* habits and improvements through the whole mass," and who would gradually render "the greater part of South America *essentially*

British" (McCulloch 1828: 209, emphases in original). For South American elites struggling to establish independent identities in the aftermath of revolution, the unwelcome prospect of waves of British arriving on their shores was added to the already visible influence of British manners, capital, and arms.

Travelers of this period took theories of political economy on the road. Their narratives join conjectural history and Malthusian political economy to classify and measure "civilization" in the various regions of South America. Summary statistics potentially allowed writers and readers to transform questions of "difference" observed in South America into questions of numerically measurable degrees of "sameness" within the broad category of commercial civilization. Yet statistics could not settle the issue of degrees of civilization in South America at this time because the numbers either were absent or patently the product of state interest, in the case of the Spanish census figures, or were readily acknowledged by travelers to be personal conjectures. That observed facts were missing, or unreliable, or did not necessarily fit the analytical categories, or even called into question the reliability of these systems of knowledge did not, however, produce any notable effects on social scientists or investors. Soon after Nuñez's account, Quetelet presented a table ranking countries according to their per-capita marriage, birth, and death rates. These summary statistics measured the "scale of population, and we may also add…the scale of civilisation" (Quetelet 1968: 28). That is, Quetelet used Malthusian categories and statistics on family formation and behavior to gauge the degree of civilization. The "two extremities" in his scale were England and Guanaxuato, the chief silver-mining district of Mexico, whose data Quetelet took at face value (Cooper and Murphy 2000: 26). And a cascade of South American defaults on government loans proved decisive in drying up British investment in the late 1820s in a way that disputes over facts and categories – whether about types of people, types of civilization, or statistical aggregates – did not.

What happens when we "classify promiscuously?"

But numbers soon appeared which demonstrated that social statistics could make a difference. Take the category "family," for instance. Some British bureaucrats cast a wide taxonomic net in their census work on "family." This may have been the result of despair at ever gaining any fixed meaning or limited set of meanings for the term. John Rickman, director of British censuses up until 1841, declared in the 1831 census commentary that "the often recurring and unanswerable doubt, as to what is to be deemed a family? – has caused a further alteration in the mode of this inquiry" ([Rickman] 1832: 2). Specifically, difficulty lay in deciding whether to count occupational categories by family or by person. The link between work and family was unclear: was work still centered in the household? And how should the census categorize the (gendered) work roles of men, women, children, and servants? Thus Rickman lamented that "[the 1831 census] had entirely failed, from the impossibility of deciding whether females of the family, children and servants were to be classed as if of no occupation or of the occupation of the adult males of the family" (ibid.).

The principal occupational unit in the British census shifted from persons (1801), to families (1811 and 1821), to families and persons (1831), and, finally, back to persons (1841). William Farr, Rickman's successor, who wrote that "[c]lassification is another name for generalization...the superiority of classification could only be established by the number of facts which it generalized, or the practical results to which it led" (Farr 1837: 93), reveled in the possibilities of classification, taking literally the responsibility, voiced by his friend Quetelet, to measure and classify promiscuously (Quetelet 1963: 75). Farr tinkered with the census categories of both occupations and family in the 1851 census, the first British census widely distributed to the public. Contemporaries were galvanized by one "family fact" revealed by the occupational classifications of the 1851 census: large numbers of single, economically independent women lived among them in England. Shocked commentators termed these creatures "redundant women" and deemed their presence a national disgrace; others, notably Harriet Martineau, called for greater educational and occupational opportunities for women.

The 1851 census revealed the gap between real life, as measured by the census, and an ideal of a domestic sphere where women were defined as mothers or sisters or daughters but did not work for pay. Charles Booth, Farr's successor at the General Register Office (GRO), thought Farr's occupational classifications untidy enough that he refashioned them, in 1881, into classifications by "class" (Szreter 1984). Booth attempted to place the data going back to 1841 on a consistent basis – that is, in accordance with the principles of political economy. In practice, that meant decreasing the number of women the census counted as "occupied" (Folbre 1991: 471–2).[5] Women who worked for wages either were absent from the works of classical political economists or, after Malthus, were relegated to the role of subsistence wage earners (Pujol 1992). The role of political economists in defining women's waged work as of little or no value and their tendency (with the notable exception of John Stuart Mill) to lend theoretical credence to the ideal of separate spheres have been little studied to date (Valenze 1995: ch. 7). Yet it should be seen as an integral part of the histories of the classification of gender differences in the social sciences.

In fact, the 1851 census acknowledged that family could come in many types. One table (see Figure 11.2), "Analysis of the Family in 14 Subdistricts," encompasses 155 "family" types (five principal types, with 31 possible permutations of each). Note that, even though they are "promiscuous" to the point of including empty cells, the classifications hardly exhaust the classificatory possibilities of the table: widow and widower and bachelor and spinster (including "redundant women") are combined categories.

(TABLE XVII.)—ANALYSIS of the FAMILY in 14 SUBDISTRICTS.

			Total.	H. and W.	W' or W".	B. or S.	Head Absent.
				CLASS 1. Husband and Wife.	CLASS 2, 3. Widower or Widow.	CLASS 4, 5. Bachelor or Spinster.	
	Total Families		67,609	41,916	10,854	14,399	440?
	Head of Family sole		24,180	8,610	3,264	12,306	?
C*	Child		26,309	21,413	4,642	226	28
R	Relative		2,435	1,292	477	666	..
V	Visitor		794	494	122	176	2
S	Servant		1,837	808	317	472	240
T	Trade (person engaged in the trade of the head)		107	51	14	33	9
C R*	Child	Relative	3,913	3,132	774	3	4
C V	Child	Visitor	1,695	1,421	269	4	1
C S	Child	Servant	2,735	2,269	425	3	38
C T	Child	Trade (Apprentice, Assistant)	163	149	14	..	..
R V	Relative	Visitor	169	99	33	37	..
R S	Relative	Servant	610	250	105	244	11
R T	Relative	Trade	45	18	16	10	1
V S	Visitor	Servant	306	145	55	72	34
V T	Visitor	Trade	17	10	..	1	6
S T	Servant	Trade	164	58	14	68	24
C R V*	Child	Relative	Visitor	286	245	41	..	..
C R S	Child	Relative	Servant	673	550	120	..	3
C R T	Child	Relative	Trade	36	33	3	..	..
C V S	Child	Visitor	Servant	440	360	66	1	13
C V T	Child	Visitor	Trade	72	65	6	..	1
C S T	Child	Servant	Trade	196	166	18	..	12
R V S	Relative	Visitor	Servant	118	60	20	36	2
R V T	Relative	Visitor	Trade	8	5	2	1	..
R S T	Relative	Servant	Trade	79	35	8	33	3
V S T	Visitor	Servant	Trade	13	9	1	2	1
C R V S*	Child	Relative	Visitor	Servant	89	69	20	..	..
C R V T	Child	Relative	Visitor	Trade	5	5	..	..	..
C R S T	Child	Relative	Servant	Trade	57	50	4	..	3
C V S T	Child	Visitor	Servant	Trade	38	34	..	..	4
R V S T	Relative	Visitor	Servant	Trade	8	3	1	4	..
C R V S T*	Child	Relative	Visitor	Servant	Trade	12	8	3	1	..

Figure 11.2 Family types in the 1851 British census
Source: Census of Great Britain, 1851 (1852), population tables.

Farr eventually substituted "household" for "family" as the preferred classification specifying living arrangements (Cooper, forthcoming). Why? "Household" can denote either people or space. People, families, and whole populations move. If they moved, you could neither count nor reform them. Some, the dregs of society, you did not want to count, anyway. It was far easier to visit households, clean up the spaces, and thereby clean up the people living in those spaces.

That is, Farr based his census classifications, including those of family, not on political economic categories – in fact he expressly opposed Malthusian poor law reforms – but on a medical model of society (Higgs 1991). Farr used the census and more frequently published reports of the GRO's vital statistics to create new measures and to push for sanitary reform. Yet if Farr preferred social medicine to analyze and treat disease and poverty to the laissez-faire bromides of political economists, he shared with them the basic impulse to preserve populations. In the 1851 census he created two new categories relating people to space – population proximity and population density. These new measures were instrumental in Farr's analysis of mortality rates by census registration district. In the 1850s he calculated the crude annual mortality rate of what he considered the national ideal, 17/1000, the average of the top 1/10 of the registration districts, 63 in total. These districts he called "healthy districts," and Farr considered their mortality rate a good estimate of the "natural" mortality rate of the English. It was a good deal below the national average measured by the GRO at the time of the Public Health Act of 1848, 23/1000 (Eyler 1979: 140–1). The act, at the instigation of the GRO, mandated the formation of local health boards to undertake sanitary measures for local districts if the annual mortality rates rose above the national average. The creation of the new category "healthy districts" put even greater pressure on local authorities to undertake sanitary reform. They now had a norm, a "natural" rate, better than the "average" mortality rate, a norm that changed over time, to live up to (Szreter 1991: 438–9).

Farr's categories were descriptive and prescriptive. They were devised to understand how to clean up spaces in order to save lives. And they were successful. Farr's efforts led Florence Nightingale to enlist his aid in the work of the Army Sanitary Commission of 1857. Formed in the wake of the disastrous experience of the Crimean War, the commission was charged with decreasing the horrible morbidity and mortality of British and native soldiers in encampments at home and abroad. Farr's analysis employed the same population proximity and population density grids used in the 1851 census. The camps were horribly overcrowded,[6] and his remedy was simple and persuasive: provide more room for the individual soldiers.

In the report of the Army Sanitary Commission, Farr indicated that measures to preserve the lives of soldiers overseas were necessary for the preservation of the British race and the British Empire:

> The question of military hygiene is rapidly becoming a question of vital importance to the interests of the empire. Upon the British race alone the integrity of that empire at this moment appears to depend. The conquering race must retain possession. Experience has shown that without special information and skillful application of the resources of science in preserving health, the drain on our home population must exhaust our means. The introduction, therefore, of a proper sanitary system into the British army is of essential importance to the public interests.
>
> (*Report*, 1858: 520; quoted in Eyler 1979: 171)

Farr's recommendations made clear that saving British soldiers' lives was as much about eugenics as about military and medical efficiency. The census could be used to manage people and space, preserving and extending the reach of British families and the British race across the globe. The goal of Farr's taxonomic work can also be taken as sanctioning a literal, eugenic erasure of difference.

Yet we should react to Farr's words with caution. There are real limits to government by numbers either of the British or of their overseas subjects. Farr himself, in a July 1857 letter to Nightingale, professed that "human biology imposed limits on sanitary reform" (quoted in Eyler 1979: 188). We can add human agency and the refusal of people to fall into categories designed by bureaucrats and used by policymakers to the factors limiting reform. The history of the census in India, the crown jewel of the British Empire, in the period 1871–1931 is fraught with the consequences of the inability to gather trustworthy data on a category, "age," which census takers in the home country took for granted as reliable and stable (Alborn 1999). Paired with a lack of vital statistics on births and deaths, for example, the faulty age data made judging whether Indian life expectancy was increasing or not a hazardous enterprise. The difficulties spawned technical disputes among actuaries involved in the census. These disputes led to novel technical adjustments of the raw data, and present-day readers of Indian census data ignore these controversies only at the risk of misreading the facts. But the difficulties also generated political debate among supporters and critics of colonialism about the ability of the British to govern a people with traditions – including an indifference to keeping track of one's age – that made information suspect. Thus "census officials [and, I would add, everyone else involved in the debates] came to realize that people, like statistics could be manipulated – but only within limits" (*ibid.*: 89). More generally, for those in the present day who seek to understand demographic history and its relation to political processes, the history of the Indian census reminds us not to limit our inquiries by accepting as fact the categories and numbers printed in official forms.

Conclusion

This paper has sketched a brief history of selected social classifications, a description of the "classifying imagination" in the social sciences. What are some lessons we can glean from this survey of social classification and categorization in social statistics? I suggest we modify Quetelet's position: we must not only classify promiscuously, but understand the limitations of classification, too. Obviously economists need to pay attention to the specific contexts in which people, including social scientists, develop and use apparently universal social classifications. Classifications are fluid and contingent. Some terms, like "age," lack meaning in a given context. In other contexts different groups use the same term to designate similar but different objects. These differences entail specific consequences, some intended, some unintended, for individuals and groups who insist on different social taxonomies than those promulgated in official statistics. Certainly some government agencies have enforced definitions of family narrower than acceptable everyday usages, as is clear to any single person who has inadvertently filed tax returns as a "head of household" in the U.S. and has been caught by the Internal Revenue Service. Colloquial meanings may be more open-ended than social scientific ones, as when Barbara Bush declared at the Republican National convention in 1992 that "family is whatever you say it is." Proliferating definitions may allow a more accurate representation of social life, even for narrow economic purposes. Depending on context, fictive families – unrelated individuals in a family relationship – can constitute more useful categories for understanding flows of assets than the normative construction of the nuclear family. Accepting even a limited expansion of categories can save us from making silly but literally true pronouncements such as a recent one by a researcher that the American family was facing extinction, a statement based on shifts in *household* composition.

Changes in social classifications and statistical categories are not necessarily teleological. Under public pressure, the 2000 U.S. census allowed Americans, for the first time, to fill out multiple racial categories in their responses. Though the census bureau did not make the change promoted by the most insistent pressure groups, which supported the inclusion of a "mixed-race" category, the change has been hailed as an improvement over the 1990 census, since it allows Americans greater choice and voice in identifying themselves. But the new categories come at a cost: researchers ponder how they and policymakers will assimilate the resulting 63 categories into coherent empirical work and policy, given the multiple categories chosen by some respondents. For the moment, the low number who actually chose multiple categories in the 2000 census makes this a problem in theory rather than in fact.[7] A more immediate concern to those, including census enumerators, who like people to fall into (supposedly) well-defined categories is the large and growing number of respondents who refuse to pick a category among even this expanded racial menu and who choose, instead, to identify themselves as "other."[8] But this concern about the "other" ignores the fact that the history of racial and ethnic classification in the U.S. census seems to be defined by its consistent lack of taxonomic consistency: definitions of race and ethnicity in the census have remained unchanged only across the censuses for 1800 and 1810, 1830 and 1840, and 1870 and 1880 (Nobles 2000: 28, 44, Tables 1 and 2).

Classifications do not, however, have to be correct for policy based on them to be effective. Understanding the classification of diseases has important consequences for the debate about the causes of the mortality decline in the second half of the nineteenth century in Great Britain. The decrease came about not due to increases in the standard of living, a view championed by laissez-faire economists who decried the burdens imposed by state expenditures on health; nor did it come about because of new, germ-based, understandings of disease formation and new forms of treatment for disease (especially tuberculosis) formulated by medical specialists. New forms of medical treatment developed after, not before, the drop in mortality. Rather, the lion's share of credit should go to local public health measures (Szreter 1988; Szreter and Mooney 1998). Yet these measures were based on an incorrect understanding of disease formation shared by Farr and other sanitarians.

Even a change in classifications which represents greater accuracy and precision for some users may create logistical nightmares for others. Understanding this fact will allow us to avoid errors such as unquestioningly using Charles Booth's revisions of the census classifications and data on occupations as measures of the number of women who worked for pay in Great Britain in the nineteenth century. This also sanctions the search for alternative, more accurate, measures of women's paid labor-market participation, in this case family-budget studies, whose compilers tried to include all sources of a family's income, not just a male's wage (Humphries and Horrell 1995). Even when we have facts that we can place in a stable and universally accepted category, like "death," understanding the meaning and use of classifications can help us avoid misinterpretation of its causes, as in the case of the aforementioned mortality decline in Great Britain in the late nineteenth century.

The value in understanding the cultural context of classifications and the epistemological consequences goes beyond issues of methodological precision and accuracy. The histories of social classifications and statistics are not just internal histories of economics or the social sciences: they blur the boundaries between lay knowledge, social scientific theories, bureaucratic practices, and public policy. People employ classifications to organize facts about social life, not just in census reports, but in travel literature, letters, speeches, novels, poems, plays, conduct literature, position papers, memos, legislation, and budgets. In the absence of statistics on contraceptive behavior, autobiographies, diaries, and novels – containing facts about individual as opposed to aggregate behavior – help us understand why, for example, fertility declined in Britain starting around 1870 (Kane 1995).

There are moral consequences to categorization, too. If folk taxonomies overlap with classification schemes in the social sciences, they nevertheless often delineate competing visions of (economic) subjectivity and agency, as well as different visions of the means and ends of social analysis. Taking these into account gives us a keener appreciation of what is at stake in measuring "difference" in economics, and the roles social scientific theories play both in making up these classifications and in our ability to act on them. Classifications in social statistics condition our imaginative possibilities for our identities and actions, and our attitudes towards "difference," that is, towards others, as individuals and groups, and towards our environments. Since representative types and statistical aggregates help guide private behavior and public policy, understanding how classifications work allows us better to understand the limits to our ability to describe what "is." This, in turn, allows us better to understand how those descriptions are also prescriptions, visions of "what should be."

Notes

1 I would like to thank Drucilla Barker, Edith Kuiper, Ernest Kilker, and Margueritte Murphy for helpful comments.
2 See, for example, Bell (1996), Poovey (1994), Scott (1988: chs. 2, 5–7), Waring (1999).
3 In conjectural histories, Adam Smith and other writers theorized that societies progressed through four stages of development – hunting, pastoral, agricultural, and commercial. The last stage was characterized by a multiplication of needs and goods, which separated civilized from barbarian societies. Progress through the four stages was unintended, irreversible, and natural. These models of society's "natural progress" served as a model for political economy and its exploration of society's "natural progress of opulence."
4 Examining the role of travel and travel writing in forging and redefining British identities, the identities of those they encountered, and notions of "difference" in the seventeenth through nineteenth centuries has become a burgeoning field in historical and cultural studies (see, for example, Beer 1996: chs. 1–6; Daunton and Halpern 1999).
5 Booth shifted housewives from the "Domestic Class" – which included scholars, paid domestic workers, and those who performed personal services – into the new category "Unoccupied Class."
6 The allotment per soldier in the least crowded camp was only one-twentieth of that per resident in London, and one-half that per resident of East London, the most crowded metropolitan area measured in the 1851 census. If the metropolis were as densely populated as the most crowded camp measured, Farr estimated that it would contain 81 million residents.
7 A little over 6.8 million, or 2.4 per cent of those counted, indicated that they were of two or more races.
8 More than 15 million respondents, some 5.5 per cent of those counted, chose the category "other."

Bibliography

Alborn, Timothy L. (1999) "Age and Empire in the Indian Census, 1871–1931," *Journal of Interdisciplinary History* 30(1): 61–89.
Beer, Gillian (1996) *Open Fields: Science in Cultural Encounter*, Oxford: Oxford University Press.
Bell, Carolyn S. (1996) "Data on Race, Ethnicity and Gender: Caveats for the User," *International Labour Review* 135(5): 535–51.
Bowker, Geoffrey C. and Susan L. Star (1999) *Sorting Things Out: Classification and Its Consequences*, Cambridge, MA: MIT Press.
Buck, Peter (1982) "People Who Counted: Political Arithmetic in the Eighteenth Century," *Isis* 73(266): 28–45.
Census of Great Britain, 1851 (1852) *Population Tables I. Numbers of the Inhabitants. Report, and Summary Tables*, London: W. Clowes & Sons.
Cooper, Brian P. (forthcoming) *Family Fictions and Family Facts: Harriet Martineau, Adolphe Quetelet, and the Population Question in England, 1798–1859*, London: Routledge.
Cooper, Brian P. and Margueritte S. Murphy (2000) "The Death of the Author at the Birth of Social Science: The Cases of Harriet Martineau and Adolphe Quetelet," *Studies in History and Philosophy of Science* 31(1): 1–36.

Daunton, Martin and Rick Halpern (1999) *Empire and Others: British Encounters with Indigenous Peoples, 1600–1850*, Philadelphia, PA: University of Pennsylvania Press.

Desrosières, Alain (1998) *The Politics of Large Numbers: A History of Statistical Reasoning*, trans. C. Naish, Cambridge, MA: Harvard University Press.

Dolan, Brian (2000a) "Malthus's Political Economy of Health: The Critique of Scandinavia in the Essay of Population," in Brian Dolan (ed.) *Malthus, Medicine & Morality: Malthusianism after 1798*, Amsterdam and Atlanta, GA: Editions Rodopi, B.V.

—— (2000b) *Exploring European Frontiers: British Travellers in the Age of Enlightenment*, London: Macmillan Press.

Eyler, John (1979) *Victorian Social Medicine: The Ideas and Influence of William Farr*, Baltimore, MD: Johns Hopkins University Press.

Farr, William (1837) "Letter," *First Annual Report of the Registrar-General*: 92–9 [British Parliamentary Papers, 1839, XVI, 66–71].

Folbre, Nancy (1991) "The Unproductive Housewife: Her Evolution in Nineteenth Century Economic Thought," *Signs* 16(3): 463–84.

Hacking, Ian (1982) "Biopower and the Avalanche of Printed Numbers," *Humanities in Society* 15(3–4): 279–95.

Head, Francis B. (1826) *Rough Notes Taken During Some Rapid Journeys Across the Pampas and Among the Andes*, London: John Murray.

Herbert, Christopher (1991) *Culture and Anomie: Ethnographic Imagination in the Nineteenth Century*, Chicago, IL: University of Chicago Press.

Higgs, Edward (1987) "Women, Occupations and Work in the Nineteenth Century Censuses," *History Workshop* 23: 59–80.

—— (1991) "Diseases, Febrile Poisons and Statistics: The Census as Medical Survey, 1841–1911," *Social History of Medicine* 4(3): 465–78.

—— (1995) "Occupational Censuses and the Agricultural Workforce in Victorian England and Wales," *Economic History Review* 48(4): 700–16.

Humphries, Jane and Sara Horrell (1995) "Women's Labour Force Participation and the Transition to the Male-Breadwinner Family, 1790–1865," *Economic History Review* XLVIII(1): 89–117.

Hunt, Margaret (1993) "Racism, Imperialism and the Traveler's Gaze in Eighteenth-Century England," *Journal of British Studies* 32: 333–57.

Kane, Penny (1995) *Victorian Families in Fact and Fiction*, New York: St. Martin's Press.

McCulloch, John R. (1828) "Emigration," *Edinburgh Review* 47(XCIII): 204–42.

Malthus, Thomas R. (1827) *Definitions in Political Economy*, London: John Murray.

—— (1989) *Principles of Political Economy*, 2 vols., ed. J. Pullen, Cambridge and New York: Cambridge University Press; first published in 1820.

—— (1992) *An Essay on the Principle of Population*, ed. Donald Winch, Cambridge: Cambridge University Press; first published in 1798.

Miers, John (1826) *Travels in Chile and La Plata, including accounts respecting the geography, geology, statistics, government, finances, agriculture, manners and customs, and the mining operations in Chile. Collected during a residence of several years in these countries*, 2 vols., London: Baldwin, Craddock & Joy.

Mill, James (1826) *Elements of Political Economy*, 3rd edn., London: Baldwin, Craddock & Joy.

Nobles, Melissa (2000) *Shades of Citizenship: Race and the Census in Modern Politics*, Stanford, CA: Stanford University Press.

Nuñez, Ignacio (1825) *An Account, Historical, Political, and Statistical, of the United Provinces of Rio De La Plata: with an Appendix Concerning the Usurpation of Monte Video by the Portuguese and Brazilian Governments*, trans., London: R. Ackermann.

Poovey, Mary (1993) " 'Figures of Arithmetic, Figures of Speech': The Discourse of Statistics in the 1830s," *Critical Inquiry* 19(2): 256–76.

—— (1994) "The Social Construction of 'Class': Toward a History of Classificatory Thinking," in Wai Chee Dimock and Michael T. Gilmore (eds.) *Rethinking Class: Literary Studies and Social Formations*, New York: Columbia University Press.

—— (1998) *A History of the Modern Fact: Problems of Knowledge in the Sciences of Wealth and Society*, Chicago, IL: University of Chicago Press.

Porter, Theodore M. (1995) *Trust in Numbers: The Pursuit of Objectivity in Science and Public Life*, Princeton, NJ: Princeton University Press.

Pujol, Michèle A. (1992) *Feminism and Anti-Feminism in Early Economic Thought*, Brookfield, VT: Edward Elgar.

Quetelet, Adolphe (1968) *A Treatise on Man and the Development of His Faculties*, trans. R. Knox, reprint, New York: B. Franklin; first published 1842.

[Rickman, John] (1832) *The Population Returns of 1831*, London: E. Moxon.

Ritvo, Harriet (1997) *The Platypus and the Mermaid and Other Figments of the Classifying Imagination*, Cambridge, MA: Harvard University Press.

Scott, Joan W. (1988) *Gender and the Politics of History*, New York: Columbia University Press.

Szreter, Simon (1984) "The Genesis of the Registrar General's Social Classification of Occupations," *British Journal of Sociology* XXXV(4): 522–46.

—— (1988) "The Importance of Social Intervention in Britain's Mortality Decline c. 1850–1914: A Re-interpretation of the Role of Public Health," *Social History of Medicine* 1(1): 1–37.

—— (1991) "The GRO and the Public Health Movement in Britain, 1837-1914," *Social History Of Medicine* 4(3): 435–63.

Szreter, Simon and Graham Mooney (1998) "Urbanization, Mortality, and the Standard of Living Debate: New Estimates of the Expectation of Life at Birth in Nineteenth-Century British Cities," *Economic History Review*, 2nd series, 51(1): 84–112.

Valenze, Deborah (1995) *The First Industrial Woman*, New York: Oxford University Press.

Waring, Marilyn (1999) *Counting for Nothing: What Men Value and What Women are Worth*, 2nd edn., Toronto and Buffalo, NY: University of Toronto Press.

Wheeler, Roxann (2000) *The Complexion of Race: Categories of Difference in Eighteenth-Century British Culture*, Philadelphia, PA: University of Pennsylvania Press.

12 Reading neoclassical economics
Toward an erotic economy of sharing[1]

Susan F. Feiner

Introduction

> Psychoanalytic theory urges us to examine that which we actively repudiate for the shadow of a loss we mourn.
>
> (Bordo 1987: 105)

For the fully rational actors in the neoclassical drama, all human interactions are an exchange. Every behavior is a giving up in order to receive. A psychoanalytic reading of this view of behavior uncovers some of the unconscious effects of this vision of economic relationships. This, in turn, sets the stage for a new, feminist understanding of economics which has the potential to recast the human activities of production, distribution, and consumption as relations of sharing rather than as relations of exchange. For the ability, capacity, and will to share are a loss long mourned.

Several cautions are in order before we proceed. The reading of neoclassical economics offered here is only one among many; it is not the only accurate reading or even the best reading of mainstream economics.[2] Neither is this paper an analysis of the practitioners of economics. Nor is it an attempt to reduce economics to its essential core. Instead, this work is part of a larger project which seeks to read the history of economic ideas through the psychoanalytic vision of human development formulated by the object relations school (Greenberg and Mitchell 1983). The object relations school considers the mother/child unit to be of primary concern since the qualities of this relationship play a profound role in the genesis of human capacities, including, of course, the capacities to produce, distribute, and consume:[3]

> That we are mothered by women, that in all societies women rather than men have primary parenting responsibilities, is an important social and cultural fact that still bears remarking and analyzing. In those individual and cultural cases where we have some insight into human emotions and psychodynamics, this fact also seems to have significant import for people's

constructions of self and interpersonal relations, for their emotions, their fantasies, and their psychological apprehensions of gender.

(Chodorow 1989: 6)

Taking the mother/child unit as the entry point into psychoanalytic inquiry enables us to conceive of people as fully relational and semi-autonomous, since actions and behaviors are constituted by an individual's "overall orientation to reality, which conditions both the process and content of thought, the perception of reality and the quality of one's relationships" (Godwin 1993: 291). A vision of economic agents emerges in which agents are constituted by their contradictory, ambivalent, and emotionally charged connections to each other. In this way, the psychoanalytic, object relations approach helps us to produce the "third term" needed to deconstruct key economic oppositions like individual and society, rational and irrational, choice and command.[4]

Some have interpreted the radical individualism at the core of *homo economicus* as a denial of social ties. Such a reading goes too far and misses the important point that, even when individuals are seen solely as agents exchanging in markets, such exchanges do constitute relationships. The neoclassical representation of the system of exchange establishes this process as both fully conscious and non-contradictory. That is, each subject confronts every other subject fully aware of what they have and fully aware of what they want. None of the subjects, none of the exchanges, and no aspect of the market process is contradictory: all are fused in a smoothly functioning, frictionless whole.

In contrast, the psychoanalytic reading put forward here interprets the neoclassical vision from the premise that the key ontological concept of exchange, along with the implied concepts of individualism, rationality, and scarcity, convey *both* conscious economic meanings *and* unconscious symbolic contents. At the level of the unconscious these concepts express "wishes," the desire to recreate relationships from the past. Illuminating these meanings opens more and more of the unconscious (repressed) to our scrutiny. On the basis of the insights which emerge we can attempt to conceive new forms of economic relations in which exchange and instrumentality are displaced by sharing and *jouissance* (pleasure) (Dallery 1989).

Many critical observations about neoclassical economics hold that this approach to political economy is an especially important part of bourgeois ideology. That is, neoclassical economics in both its scholarly and popular forms plays an important role in the reproduction of market-driven, male-dominated society. It is not adequate to end with the recognition that neoclassical economics legitimates, justifies, or rationalizes inequalities of class, gender, and race. Instead, we must press beyond this to understand how this system of ideas and symbols constructs and constitutes "a system of hierarchical domination [in which] the regression to the original condition can only be approximated in so far as it is accompanied by a phenomenon of scapegoating, or negative authority," or some other defense mechanism (Hill 1984: 34).

Consider what we would accept as an interpretation of the role of the Catholic Church in medieval Europe. Certainly most of us would acknowledge that the Church was indispensable to the maintenance of authority and the status quo. Yet who among us would settle for an analysis which simply noted that "church ideology was powerful and it was reproduced over time because it benefited the ruling class?" Instead, we would insist that the analysis show how this was achieved, i.e. we would want to understand how Church doctrines and institutions produced these effects.

> In the Catholic Church...decision making [was] a virtual monopoly of the one on top...[a]nd in this situation Freud discovered not only the reward of grandiosity and omnipotence enjoyed by the leader but also the rewards of dependency and relief from responsibility enjoyed by the followers. Both, therefore, enjoy a kind of return to childhood as the child imagines it: a parent with unlimited powers who knows everything and takes care of the child and the child with unlimited freedom to feel safe and provided for. But while this constitutes the unconscious meaning of this structure, its effect on the world is utterly different.
>
> (Hill 1984: 32)

Following Freud's analysis of the Catholic Church as a vehicle for wish-fulfillment (the Church promulgated an ideology which permitted a regression), we can turn our attention to neoclassical economics and its unconscious effects.[5]

This analysis focuses on the symbolic elements of neoclassical economics. The point is not that particular economists have consciously produced the psychological aspects of economic theory which we identify.[6] The point is, rather, that different individuals at different times and places have found various pieces of the theory to be more or less compelling. We are struck by the intensity with which many people, inside and outside the circle of trained academic economists, defend one or more aspects of the neoclassical approach despite the startling incongruities between the economy which neoclassicism describes and the economies of our lives. Appeals to the virtues of exchange side by side with neoclassical notions of human nature often support very regressive social policies. Consequently, it is of some significance to understand the symbolic inner life of the theory.

Economics and psychoanalysis: the undreamed connection

> Our experiences as men and women come from deep within, both within our pasts and, relatedly, within the deepest structures of unconscious meaning and the most emotionally moving relationships that help constitute our daily lives.
>
> (Chodorow 1989: 2)

We are all familiar with the literary search for symbolisms in texts as diverse as Shakespearean sonnets, rock videos, horror movies, and presidential speeches. Only if economics texts are granted a privileged exemption from interpretation can we reject the hypothesis that the texts of neoclassical economics have a symbolic content independent of the conscious intentions of either their authors or consumers. An interpretation of the unconscious wishes and conflicts expressed in these texts goes beyond the rational, conscious surface of economics to reveal an aggressive, narcissistic posturing which functions as a defense against dependence, gratitude, and nurturing.

We note the discursive silence of the paradigm *vis-à-vis* gender/sexuality and community/class. The simultaneity of these repressions refer us to their cartographers, Freud and Marx.[7] Louis Althusser (1991) has written persuasively about the connection between these approaches. According to Althusser, Marx believed that

> bourgeois ideology and its theoretical formulations are designed to dissimulate as they perpetuate the exploitation and domination of the bourgeois class. Marx was convinced that the adversary of the truth that he discovered was not accidental error or ignorance but the organic system of bourgeois ideology, an essential component of the struggle of the bourgeois class.
> (Althusser 1991: 20; emphasis in original)

Consider next Freud's contribution as regards the unconscious "conceived as an 'apparatus' composed of 'different systems' irreducible to a single principle.... This apparatus is not a centred unity but a complex of instances constituted by the play of unconscious repression" (Althusser 1991: 28). What, then, are the unconscious instances at work within the organic science of bourgeois ideology?

Psychoanalysis recognizes that there are no fully conscious (or rational) processes through which individuals come to know themselves as contiguous with some social attributes and not others.[8] One of the remarkable characteristics of neoclassical economics is the intensity with which the discourse insists that race, gender, and class are irrelevant to the understanding of rational behavior – there is just choice, *sui generis*. The denial of these core elements of identity warrants examination.[9]

These social categories (race, gender, class, ethnicity) are alternative (sometimes complementary, sometimes conflictual) ways of organizing difference. Following Winnicott (1988), Chodorow (1989), and others, we insist on the importance of the first experience of difference, i.e. the infant's perception of Mother. Unconscious mental organizations of difference and the social constructions of race, gender, class, and ethnicity are thoroughly impregnated with representations of motherhood, femininity, and sexuality, on the one hand, and the processes of meeting needs, on the other. Original experiences of difference (separateness from Mother) come to be represented by other differences which are commonly, but arbitrarily, associated with it.[10] The intimate connection between the social representation of difference and the individual experience of difference fuels the neoclassical repression of exploitation and oppression and replaces them with symbols (concepts) which are their opposites: freedom and choice. This repression and the anxiety associated with it dominate the symbolic gendered content of the theory.

The symbolic resolution of wants

> As we try to sever want from need, we find that sexual needs, the need for intimacy, and even the need to make meaning of life, take on an unwholesome or frivolous cast. In unavoidable consequence, life begins to make less and less sense. Life is meaningless without wanting, but there is no wanting without needing and therefore no desire without need. As need drains from desire, so does meaning bleed from life. To eliminate need is to kill desire and therefore any appetite for living.
>
> (Dimen 1989: 46)

The Greek root "*ecos*" means home – and our intellectual as well as emotional homes are contradictory sites of physical, affective, and mental production. One of the principal contributions of feminist work in the past two decades has been increased attention to and refinement of the notion that production does occur in the home. To date most of this work has focused on "housework" as either the unpaid surplus labor of house spouses (Matthaei 1991) or the nonmarket work of rational economic actors (Blau and Ferber 1986). In either case there remains a glaring absence: economists have yet adequately to conceptualize the meaning and impact of the emotional activity, conceived as productive work, done in households which so strongly influences psychological life.

This *lacuna* is a consequence of the fact that affective behavior contradicts the implicit quid pro quo which undergirds existing approaches to economics. Conceptualizing nonmarket activity as work, either through the opportunity-cost notion of neoclassical economists or through the surplus-labor notion of Marxist economists does no violence to the "give-and-take" framework. In this sense, both Marxian and neoclassical approaches depend on the quid pro quo of exchange, and in capitalism that exchange is understood as the exchange of equals. But emotional work cannot be made to fit this frame without completely violating its affective, passionate, spontaneous dimensions. Why does economic science defend the boundary between exchange and sharing?

One of the unique features of modern science is that it "consciously and explicitly proclaimed the 'masculinity' of science as inaugurating a new era" (Bordo 1987: 105). Following the work of Bordo (1987), Harding (1986), Merchant (1980) and Noble (1992) on the emergence of the scientific as masculine, we note how this process equated the object of science with that which is external to the scientist. In some prehistoric fantasy world, Man and Nature (Man and who?) were not separate. But the modern perspective erected Nature as the external source of maternal supplies. Man demands the appropriation of Nature to satisfy wants. Nature becomes female and nurturing becomes the province of women. Now, in the economist's version of "the Fall," boundless wanting counterposes a parsimonious Nature in a drama redolent of frustration. Yet salvation is at hand: the site at which wants are met, "the sphere of exchange," that "very Eden wherein alone rule Freedom, Equality, Property and Bentham" (Marx 1967: 176) undoes Man's frustration. The accidental play of language is revealing: as Eden is an anagram for need, the market is a gendered site at which needs are met.

In this material we see economic theory making the market a symbolic representation for the meeting of human needs. Moreover, in this symbolism we also find a very early orientation to the "not-I." For infants, wants and needs are met through the actions of (M)other. In economic theory, wants and needs are met through the actions of markets. The market as a symbol comes to represent motherhood: "patriarchal culture seeks to repress the primordial memory of fusion with and later separation from the maternal body; this fear of the mother is masked in male sexuality" (Dallery 1989: 57). The notion of the free market can be seen as an expression of a wish. In its theoretic and cultural elaboration, the market functions as a substitute for the perfect mother, who is unfailing in her capacity (and willingness) to meet all needs and wants. Thus the idealized market (the home of *homo economicus*) of neoclassical economic theory mirrors the fantasy mother of the unconscious.[11] Mainstream economics means something very specific when it refers to the outcomes for human satisfaction derived from exchange in markets. In a system of perfect markets everyone is as satisfied as they possibly can be precisely because markets work best.[12]

There is a sense, then, that neoclassical economics creates a particular community, the members of which participate in a shared group fantasy – the fantasy that a system of production, distribution, and consumption based on the systematic exploitation of both people and the environment is a "fair" system in which rewards (high incomes) and punishments (low incomes and unemployment) are meted out on an "objective" basis. Insofar as the internal constructs of neoclassical economics contain symbolic images which give life to this fantasy while dissolving contradictions and repressing conflicts, and to the extent that these fantasies resonate with unfulfilled wishes, then part of our struggle against exploitation and oppression must occur at the level of the symbolic.

Every economist learns early on that "economics is the study of the allocation of scarce resources to the infinity of human wants."[13] This initial definition of the object of economic science has many effects, one of which is representational. It is obvious that this definition of economic science depicts the relationship of an infant to its primary caretaker – usually its mother. Newborns exist in a world formed by the immediacy of needs. Pressing infantile needs for food, warmth, and nurturing dominate the first months of experience. The utter dependency of an infant on its caretakers is remarkable. The deep affective, erotic bonds which give meaning to the infant/mother pair are built at least partially by the empathetic resonance between mother and infant: "Our ideal picture of a truly maternal woman is one of an omnipotent, all knowing mother who knows what to do with her infant by sheer intuition" (Kestenberg, quoted in Welldon 1988: 18).

> Infancy (no matter how the social world is organized) is characterized by a state of dependence and powerlessness as well as intense wishes. The infant becomes aware of its dependence on others and its inability to satisfy its own needs. Frustration is projected onto whomever is present for the child, and when the person becomes an internal object, these frustrations, fears, desires, etc., are introjected along with the person. Therefore the mother is internalized along with the child's own powerful feelings about her. The boy, as he represses the mother, must repress all these feelings, too, since they are part of the experience of her. Given how powerful she is in infancy, the son must carefully guard against her power (since it is part of his self). Thus, repression must be as complete as possible so that this internal object can be kept as separate from the conscious self. Otherwise, it would threaten masculine identity and ego boundaries.
>
> (Flax 1983: 246–7)

Mothers, in affirming relationships with their children, try to recognize the child's needs and then set out to meet those needs. Notice the striking similarity between the mother/infant relation and the relation of adults to the market in capitalist society. How can we avoid the anthropological parallel: it is a commonplace of secular analysis to point out that people "create" GOD to help them cope with feelings of powerlessness in the face of a capricious, sometimes hostile NATURE. With the important caveat that the notion of NATURE as external to man is thoroughly modern, it remains the case that "modern man" lives a life in which the vicissitudes of the market are as capricious as NATURE. No single individual can possibly produce all that is desired or all that is needed for survival, and so we – strangers in the night – become inescapably dependent upon each other. Dependence as complete and total as this is frightening. Ambivalence and anxiety rear their heads: "Where there is anxiety, there will almost certainly be found a mechanism of defense against that anxiety" (Bordo 1987: 75).

We can be even more specific about the dependency relations in capitalism. For example, the classes of capitalists and workers can only be understood if some reference is made to markets. Whether one takes the traditional position that markets are the *sine qua non* of capitalism or the position that markets are conditions of existence of capitalism, it must be acknowledged that, absent markets, capitalists will not realize profits or surplus value and workers will not get paid. In short, both capitalists and workers are, in fundamental ways, as dependent upon markets for their survival as are infants upon their mothers. Everyone who lives in a capitalist society is dependent upon the market for their very existence.

The pervasiveness of this dependency is, however, denied by the privileging of exchange. From the point of view of the individual, separation is scarcity. Individuals are seen in neoclassical economics as separated from all others, so there is no way to secure subsistence except through exchange. As an individual, everything is scarce and exchange *is* the only possible solution. The defenses at work here are complex. Representing exchange as ordered by wanting undoes the problem of scarcity while constructing the world as scarcity represses the realities of dependency: "The conversion of a nightmare into a positive vision is characteristic of Descartes" (Bordo 1987: 100). The representation of the market as its opposite reflects this Cartesian solution.

What do markets do? In neoclassical economics markets are the registry of desire backed by purchasing power. The perfectly empathic mother becomes the perfectly competitive market. In such markets, as with fantasy mothers, all wishes are fulfilled. Gratification is total, instant, and infinitely repeating. These markets are sensitive; the intensity of one's desire is represented by the magnitude of purchasing power devoted to the satisfaction of particular wants. As the intensity of desires change, demands shift. In perfect settings, the market responds to these desires just as instantly as we wish our mothers could. Prices rise, signaling a flow of resources.

> The mother-baby unit is at a biological-psychological peak when the mother is ready with her breasts filled with milk just as her baby is being awakened by hunger. Both partners get together and a world of bliss is open to them. Of course, having accepted the reality principal we know that two individuals will never be able to realize these moments in the same way. However, some people have not yet come to accept the reality principle...they are still seeking a promised land of bliss.
>
> (Welldon 1988: 12–13)

Exchange and the denial of sharing

> Although the dream of total union can persist throughout life, another contradictory project may be conceived, psychoanalytic thinkers have suggested, centred around the denial of any longing for the lost maternal union. Instead, the child seeks mastery over the frustrations of separation and lack of gratification through an assertion of self against the mother and all that she represents and rejection of all dependency on her. In this way the pain is assuaged, paradoxically, by an even more definitive separation – but one that is

chosen this time and aggressively pursued. It is therefore experienced as autonomy rather than helplessness in the face of discontinuity between self and mother.

(Bordo 1987: 107)

The significance of the market-as-mother metaphor ramifies through the gendered body of neoclassical economics. We can understand this representation as a "reaction formation, a denial of the separation anxiety…which is facilitated by an aggressive intellectual flight from the female cosmos and 'feminine' orientation toward the world" (Bordo 1987: 100). Indeed, the gendering of economic concepts maintains these defenses.

We begin by noting that, in this theory, exchange is posed as the fundamental economic act and satisfaction occurs as exchanges take place. Exchanges in markets set loose the forces of supply and demand, and, as if by divine providence, all desires are satisfied: there is never too much and there is never too little. Thus, the economists' market (quite unlike the market we all know) symbolizes the wish for the empathetic mother who not only anticipates all needs, but meets them instantly. Marx was quite correct to see this as an Eden: a lost but longed-for world of bliss. And so we can redo his famous circuits of capital in which the infinite sequence Commodities-Money-Commodities (C-M-C) stands alongside the infinite sequence Money-Commodities-Money (M-C-M). Simultaneous with the circulation of commodities in the market is the circulation of meanings: Child-Mother-Child (C-M-C) alongside Mother-Child-Mother (M-C-M).

But the repressed femininity which is the core of the neoclassical fantasy is also a source of anxiety. First, consider Say's Law of Markets, the proposition which in its popular form states that supply creates its own demand, to see yet another of these most curious inversions.[14] One of the primary fears of infancy and early childhood is that demands will not create their own supplies.[15] To the extent that children experience mothers as withholding (after all, a child must first cry to let her needs be known), then food, love, security, and nurturing are not immediately available. Frustration, like other negative emotional states aroused deep within us by those whom we most love, may be internalized and experienced as guilt. The exaltation of market institutions by and within economic theory can be interpreted as a defense against anxieties provoked by the guilty feelings associated with infantile rage at mothers/markets for not being perfect. In this material we clearly see a projection of the wished-for fusion with the perfect mother.

This portrait of the market as a site at which desires are met so perfectly is conjoint with the notion of a general equilibrium: not just one market satisfies desires perfectly, but all markets taken as a whole satisfy desires. This satisfaction emerges simultaneously with the infinity of exchanges. We can see in this another element of the Cartesian response to the shattering of the feminine Cosmos. In medieval worldviews the universe was not only limited, it was also centered, "with a core toward which all movement tended," but the discovery of infinity made the notion of such a core "unintelligible" and the universe now appeared as not only limitless, but "decentered, perplexing and anarchic" (Bordo 1987: 71–2). The general equilibrium model inverts the experience of anxiety in the face of the limitless unknown by ordering the economic cosmos. Equilibrium – that wondrous state in which aggregate demand equals aggregate supply – becomes the new "core" of the universe. That toward which all markets tend returns us to our HOME (*ECOS*) again, resolving anxieties of separation. The rule of the mother/market ensures the return to, or at least the movement toward, home. That which is "not home" is presented as an "imperfection," or "rigidity," and so can (in contrast to the perfection and fluidity of mother markets) be read as a masculine interference in the child's wish to merge with mother.[16]

Note the doubly defensive role of the market fantasy. First, the market as represented precludes frustration. Yet the very mechanisms through which the market accomplishes the meeting of wants are impersonal, cold, and objective. This image is the antithesis of a caring mother and so denies the reality of warmth, emotional contact, and passion as essential to human satisfactions. This "undoing" of infantile dependence on Mother calls into being the auctioneer,[17] whose *tatonnement* or groping ("Touch me, please!") guarantees a return to this womblike home. Reaching the perfect state where all desires are met involves no emotional contact. The meeting of needs and the satisfaction of desire require nothing but exchange. Who says you can't always get what you want? *Homo economicus* always gets what he wants, but he gets it without affective connection. This fantasy eliminates the very possibility of frustrated needs since exchange makes all exchangers better off, all desires are met perfectly, and there is no trading outside equilibrium.

To satisfy desire individuals must go outside themselves and recognize the other, but the specific way that neoclassical economics poses this recognizing is "infantile." That is, the neoclassical vision of subjects as fully autonomous, all knowing, and in possession of true knowledge of the choices available constitutes a regression. The individual autonomy celebrated in neoclassical theory and the omnipotence which accompanies it are reaction formations: in contemporary society people are dependent on each other in ways that they neither choose nor control. Not only are these many dependencies hidden from general view, but the illusion of autonomy is maintained and reproduced through a general celebration of separation.

Separation of the "objective" from the "subjective" and separation of "reason" from "the senses" are an essential part of the play of unconscious repression which animates the neoclassical subject. Yet, as Freud (1989: 387) noted, "[w]hat, in the conscious, is found split into a pair of opposites often occurs in the unconscious, as a unity."[18] In and through the many dimensions of radical separateness, economic subjects come to a unique and privileged knowledge position: not only do economic subjects thoroughly know themselves as repositories of unlimited wants and desires, they also know the infinite array of scarce goods and services which are available to them. Although the representation of omnipotence is a blueprint for self-actualization through choice, this functions psychologically to infantilize subjects, since every action produces only what the subject wants. In the shared group fantasy of economics, the exaltation of exchange reconstitutes the individual as autonomous and grandiose, thereby "undoing" the anxiety associated with the memory of infantile dependence on (M)other. In this way, neoclassical economics constitutes and constructs a psychic defense – a denial in theory – against these anxieties.

Conclusion

The elevation of exchange in modern economics displaces classical concerns for concrete, embodied activities like labor and production. These inescapably physical – some would even say womanly – activities vanish, replaced by autonomous, rational, choosing *minds*. This flight to objectivity is a retreat to pure (men)tation to "undo" the havoc now wreaked by the dynamics of a new mother, the Market (which consequently appears as natural as the Nature which markets constantly seek to subdue). This reading shows us how the intra-personal theory of value, and the idealized vision of market exchange which sustains it, function to relieve separation anxieties. By exalting scarcity and the impossibility of satisfying all wants, neoclassical economics masters separation. What the theory claims as the inevitable state of humanity becomes a solution to itself: the competitive self-interest of rational individuals is the way to satisfaction. The metaphor is doubly revealing and doubly defensive. As human needs are always satisfied in markets, choice is the necessary vehicle to fulfillment, and at the same time the market/choice metaphor guarantees that choices are themselves fulfilling.

We note that grandiosity and omnipotence are associated with the pre-Oedipal, and that in this position there will be a "failure of gratitude," an inability to recognize "just how contingent one's success has been upon the assistance of others. But contingency is incompatible with omnipotence and gratitude is an emotion that is firmly established in the depressive position" (Godwin 1993: 295–6).[19] We understand that one of the appeals of the individualistic, competitive pursuit of desire through market exchange is that these concepts may block a transition to a state in which dependency is not a threat to individuality. The seductive power of neoclassical economics is not simply its formal mathematical elegance; nor is it the reality of its politically regressive policy stance. The seductive power of the paradigm also emanates from a symbolism which gives voice to the unresolved conflicts produced and reproduced in modern society.

The inner fantasies of the neoclassical paradigm are its Teflon™ coating. This paradigm has survived critiques on virtually all fronts. Its assumptions, methodology, rhetoric, internal consistency, and naive dynamics have all been shown to be seriously, even mortally, flawed. And the beat goes on. Economic theory as neoclassical stomp. How is it that this approach, which counterposes an assumed scarcity of Nature (mother) to the insatiability of *homo economicus* (manchild) and then elevates this tension to the guiding principle of economic science, is able to continue to attract adherents while drowning out most voices of dissent? Through what symbolic appeals does this paradigm gather the strength to monopolize our economic vision? It seems safe to say that it is not the market which meets needs, but rather the neoclassical representation of the market which meets needs.

Notes

1 Very sincere thanks are owed to Sandra Morgen and others at the Center for the Study of Women in Society, the University of Oregon, Eugene, Oregon. Many friends and colleagues also provided advice, encouragement and assistance with this project: Jack Amariglio, Susan Bordo, Nancy Chodorow, Harriet Fraad, Rob Garnett, Sandra Harding, David Levine, Lee Levin, and Richard Lichtman read various versions of this paper and offered suggestions for improvement. I hope this version is true to their comments. Edith Kuiper deserves special thanks for the excellent work she has done to bring this whole project to fruition. Any problems remaining with this essay are entirely my responsibility.
2 Such a contention would violate the spirit of psychoanalytic inquiry since work in this tradition takes as a premise that all signs have multiple, overdetermined meanings.
3 While the object relations school derives from the psychoanalytic tradition associated with Freud, this school does not conceive of behavior in terms of the irreducible instincts or drives of classical Freudianism. Another key difference is that the father and Oedipal conflicts are not the central interpretive themes.
4 This approach, through its insistence on the fully relational nature of human perception and action, provides a way out of the dualisms of traditional (neoclassical and Marxian) approaches to economics. For a discussion of the role of dualism in economics, see Nelson (1993).
5 While neoclassical economics and its institutions undoubtedly play a role in maintaining social order, this role is probably not equivalent to that played by the Church in the Middle Ages. The point of this comparison is to suggest that economic ideas, like religious ones, carry unconscious meanings which are probably not part of the conscious awareness of the people who articulate them.
6 The emotional state of the economist is not the subject of this paper.
7 See Fraad (1983) for a discussion of this relationship.
8 The categories of race, gender, ethnicity, and class are of course "social," since these categories could not be "thought" of where there is only one person. A set of readings indispensable to this connection concern the use of *Robinson Crusoe* metaphors within neoclassical economics. See Ulla Grapard (1995), Gillian Hewitson (1994), and Steven Hymer (1980). These essays demonstrate the symbolic contiguity of race and sex in economic exchange metaphors.
9 These traditions are associated with the development of critical social theory (see *The Frankfurt School Reader*, Arato and Gebhardt 1990) and with the development of anti-essentialist, class analytics (see the journal *Rethinking Marxism*).
10 This is an example of metonymy, and the reader will find the set of essays on the use of *Robinson Crusoe* metaphors in economic theory very helpful in illuminating these connections.
11 Consequently any in-the-real shift from homo economicus (to, perhaps, heteroeconomicus) could be likened to weaning. Just as the successfully weaned infant has learned the capacity to trust and through trust is able to deal with loss, communities which give up markets must be able to trust: "[the] infant who is just about ready to be 'weaned', [is] able to deal with loss without quite losing what is [in one sense only] lost" (Winnicott 1988: 35).
12 Of course, there are disagreements about which circumstances are most favorable for markets, with conservatives arguing that markets work best if left alone, and liberals arguing that proper intervention makes markets work better. But within the mainstream the ultimately benevolent nature of the market system is not open to question.

13 Lionel Robbins characterized economics as "the science which studies human behavior as a relationship between ends and scarce means which have alternative uses" (1984: 116). Contemporary textbooks recast this as the relationship between scarce means and infinite wants.
14 This is of course an aggregative concept: no one ever meant that a bumper crop of wheat, for example, gives rise to more demand for wheat. The point is instead that the market system considered as a whole cannot experience a "glut" of commodities, the situation in which there is *general* overproduction.
15 I remember when in my first pregnancy I began to read the La Leche League literature on breastfeeding. Their bulletins and newsletters frequently repeated the dictum that in breastfeeding "demand creates its own supply." I am not making this up! I was completely taken aback by what I thought then was yet another imperialism of economics – now, though, I know that it is Say's Law and not the La Leche League which is expressing a wishful fantasy.
16 As Jane Flax (1983) so brilliantly argues, another element of interference in the world of the perfect mother is "the state."
17 Has anyone in the history of economic thought/practice ever hypothesized that the auctioneer is female?
18 Freud goes on to point out that for some men one of the "pre-conditions" for the choice of love object is that the "object" of affection must not be unattached. The woman becomes desired only if "another man can claim a right of possession" (Freud 1989: 387). The source of this type of object choice is derived from "infantile fixation of tender feelings on the mother," so that all love objects are stamped with maternal characteristics (Freud 1989: 390). How close this is to the role of choice and desire in the fantasy of the omnipotent economic subject.
19 A person in the "depressive position" is not suffering from depression. Rather, this psychoanalytic term distinguishes between narcissism, which blocks gratitude, and an orientation in which gratitude becomes possible.

Bibliography

Althusser, L. (1991) "Marx and Freud," *Rethinking Marxism* 4(1): 17–30.
Arato, Andres and Eike Gebhardt (eds.) (1990) *The Essential Frankfurt School Reader*, New York and London: Continuum International.
Blau, Francine D. and Marianne A. Ferber (1986) *The Economics of Women, Men and Work*, Englewood Cliffs, NJ: Prentice-Hall.
Bordo, S. (1987) *The Flight to Objectivity: Essays on Cartesianism and Culture*, Albany, NY: State University of New York Press.
Chodorow, N. (1989) *Feminism and Psychoanalytic Theory*, New Haven, CT: Yale University Press.
Dallery, A. (1989) "The Politics of Writing the Body: Ecriture Feminine," in A. Jaggar and S. Bordo (eds.) *Gender/Body/Knowledge*, New Brunswick, NJ: Rutgers University Press.
Dimen, Muriel (1989) "Power, Sexuality, and Intimacy," in A. Jaggar and S. Bordo (eds.) *Gender/Body/Knowledge*, New Brunswick, NJ: Rutgers University Press.
England, P. (ed.) (1993) "Theory on Gender," *Feminism on Theory*, Hawthorne, NY: A. de Gruyter.
Ferber, M. and J. Nelson (eds.) (1993) *Beyond Economic Man: Feminist Theory and Economics*, Chicago, IL: University of Chicago Press.
Flax, Jane (1983) "Object Relations, Political Theory and the Patriarchal Unconscious," in S. Harding and M. Hintikka (eds.) *Discovering Reality: Feminist Perspectives on Epistemology, Metaphysics, Methodology and Philosophy of Science*, Dordrecht and Boston, MA: D. Reidel.
Fraad, Harriet (1983) "Marx and Freud: Brothers in Overdetermination," AESA Discussion Paper no. 5, Amherst, MA: Association for Economic and Social Analysis.
Freud, S. (1989) "A Special Type of Choice of Object Made by Men (A Contribution to the Psychology of Love)," in P. Gay (ed.) *The Freud Reader*, New York: W.W. Norton; first published in 1918.

Gallup, J. (1982) *Feminism and Psychoanalysis. The Daughter's Seduction*, Ithaca, NY: Cornell University Press.
Gay, P. (ed.) *The Freud Reader*, New York: W.W. Norton.
Godwin, R. (1993) "On the Deep Structure of Conservative Ideology," *Journal of Psychohistory* 20(3): 289–304.
Goux, J. (1978) *Symbolic Economies: Marx after Freud*, Ithaca, NY: Cornell University Press.
Grapard, U. (1995) "Robinson Crusoe: Quintessential Economic Man," *Feminist Economics* 1(1): 33–52.
Greenberg, J. and S. Mitchell (1983) *Object Relations in Psychoanalytic Theory*, Cambridge, MA: Harvard University Press.
Harding, S. (1986) *The Science Question in Feminism*, Ithaca, NY: Cornell University Press.
Hewitson, J. (1994) "Deconstructing Robinson Crusoe: A Feminist Interrogation of 'Rational Economic Man,'" *Australian Feminist Studies*: 20, summer: 131–49.
Hill, M. (1984) "The Law of the Father: Leadership and Symbolic Authority in Psychoanalysis," in B. Kellerman (ed.) *Leadership: Multidisciplinary Perspectives*, Englewood Cliffs, NJ: Prentice-Hall.
Hunt, L. *The Family Romance of the French Revolution*, Berkeley, CA: University of California Press.
Hymer, S. (1980) "Robinson Crusoe and the Secret of Primitive Accumulation," in Edward J. Nell (ed.) *Growth, Profits, and Property*, Cambridge: Cambridge University Press; first published in 1971.
Jaggar, A. (1989) "Love and Knowledge: Emotion in Feminist Epistemology," in A. Jaggar and S. Bordo (eds.) *Gender/Body/Knowledge*, New Brunswick, NJ: Rutgers University Press.
Jaggar, A. and S. Bordo (eds.) (1989) *Gender, Body, Knowledge*, New Brunswick, NJ: Rutgers University Press.
Kellerman, B. (1984) *Leadership: Multidisciplinary Perspectives*, Englewood Cliffs, NJ: Prentice-Hall.
Langer, M. (1992) *Motherhood and Sexuality*, New York: Guilford Press.
Marx, K. (1967) *Capital*, vol. 1, New York: International Publishers.
Matthaei, J. (1991) "Marxist-Feminist Contributions to Radical Economics," in B. Roberts and S. Feiner (eds.) *Radical Economics*, Norwell, MA: Kluwer Academic Press.
Merchant, C. (1980) *The Death of Nature*, San Francisco, CA: Harper & Row.
Nelson, Julie A. (1993) "Gender and Economic Ideologies," *Review of Social Economy* 51(3), fall: 287–301.
Noble, D. (1992) *A World Without Women: The Christian Clerical Culture of Western Science*, Oxford and New York: Oxford University Press.
Robbins, L. (1952) *An Essay on the Nature and Significance of Economic Science*, 2nd edn., London: Macmillan; first published in 1935.
—— (1984) "The Nature and Significance of Economic Science," in Daniel Housman (ed.) *The Philosophy of Economics: An Anthology*, Cambridge: Cambridge University Press; first published in 1935.
Roberts, B. and S. Feiner (eds.) (1991) *Radical Economics*, Norwell, MA: Kluwer Academic Press.
Rustin, M. (1991) *The Good Society and the Inner World: Psychoanalysis, Politics and Culture*, New York: Verso.
Stern, D. (1977) *The First Relationship*, Cambridge, MA: Harvard University Press.
—— (1985) *The Interpersonal World of the Infant*, New York: Basic Books.
Strassman, D. (1991) "Stories of Power and Objectivity in Economics: The Stake of the Narrator," unpublished paper prepared for and presented to the American Economic Association meetings in New Orleans, LA.
Welldon, E. (1988) *Mother, Madonna, Whore: The Idealization and Denigration of Motherhood*, New York: Guilford Press.
Winnicott, D. (1988) *Human Nature*, New York: Schocken Books.

13 The anxious identities we inhabit

Post'isms and economic understandings

Nitasha Kaul

Introduction

> Nothing much is usually said about the inhabitants of the model.... To borrow Michio Morishima's trope, the people in this model are like the *conventionally invisible men* of the Kabuki theatre, and *only the commodities have speaking parts*.
> (Robinson 1977: 1,320; emphasis mine)

The "discipline" of economics has its discontents. And for good reasons too. The particular form of theorizing most prevalent and most valued is curiously devoid of empirical or conceptual richness. The focus on "modeling" as a method has been critiqued for its various requirements in terms of what the world must be like for such an understanding (via a priori models) to be legitimate. We find that "the world" and "the model" very often do not add up.

Critiques of mainstream economics have a long and diverse history (see Wootton 1938; Ward 1972; Lydall 1998; Mirowski 1989; Ormerod 1994; Keen 2001). In recent times the focus of method-related critiques has been on pointing out the exacting demands of the modeling process – methodological individualism, individual rationality, mathematical formalism, unrealistic assumptions, extremum principles, a particular version of explanation (viz. deductive nomological), etc. (on these, see Schoemaker 1991; Arrow 1994; Walsh 1994; Addleson 1995; Dow 1998; Weintraub 1998; Chick 1998). There is also another related tier of interrogation that has focused on what is conventionally not admitted into the mainstream method as theory. Within this, feminist and ecological critiques play a crucial role. The feminist uncovering of homo economicus as Rational Economic Man (see Grapard 1996; England 1993; Feiner 1999; Hewitson 1999), the literature exposing biases at levels of conceptualization of empirical and theoretical categories (Nelson 1996), work examining the way economic narratives are structured (see McCloskey 1986, 1994; Strassmann 1993a, 1993b, 1994; Strassmann and Polanyi 1995), work tracing the implications of the economic policy for some of the most marginalized sections of society, and work highlighting the pedagogical aspects of feminist economics are only some of the many avenues currently being explored by scholars.

But there is another dimension to this interrogation of economics. This refers to the many post'ist transdisciplinary approaches – poststructuralism; postmodernism; postcolonial theory – which are all, to varying degrees, involved with feminism and deconstruction. It is this conversation that I wish to further here.

One of the central preoccupations of most critical social theory is the question of emancipation and its link to epistemology: knowledge, yes, but will it make things better, and if so, how? Within the context of economics, the questioning of mainstream methods or selection of the "economic" domain is at the same time a questioning of its knowledge claims and the possibility of their justification. Traditional and some reconstructed methodological approaches would turn on demonstrating the relevance or irrelevance of economic theories to the "real world" (see Blaug 1980; on critical realism, see Lawson 1997; Fleetwood 1999). A post'ist stance, on the other hand, would place stress on examining the *mechanisms* which allow such knowledge claims to be uttered as legitimate, laying bare the *expectations* that are associated with the possibility of having made such claims, and unpacking the *historical investment* implicit in such endeavors of knowledge creation and justification.

As I will discuss below, these post'ist interrogations necessarily mean that we need to be skeptical of the easy possibility of emancipation, cautious in the arena of politics carried out under the name of universal signifiers, and aware of the crucial representative dimension of identities. How does this translate in relation to economics, its practitioners and practice? I will argue that an appreciation of the post'ist positions and their emphases (as outlined above) allows us to forego certain problematic notions. Chiefly, it allows us to jettison the conventional one-way relation between "theory" and the "world" where theories can only follow from an external, mind-independent world "out there." Once the focus turns to seeing theories as *productive* enterprises, we can understand theories as producing or naming their own version of what can legitimately be seen as "real." This can help us in linking the *logic of economic theories* with an all-pervasive *economic logic*. The post'ist interrogation allows us to visualize a radically different *role of critique*. And, finally, it can help us to think through the *theory/praxis problematic* which underscores Enlightenment epistemology.

I will address these issues as arising from a proliferation of post'isms and underline their salience for the enterprise of generating economic understandings. The terrain spans epistemology, feminist politics, and economics.

Past which post?

What are the post'isms? The post-modern, the post-structural, the post-colonial – the "post" is an important signifier, but what does it signify? And are all "posts" the same? Lyotard answered this question well with his definition of postmodernism as "an incredulity towards metanarratives" (1984: xxiv). And, as Bauman (1995) has argued, postmodernism signifies modernism coming to terms with its limitations. It is truly tempting to think of "post" merely in terms of the "past" of temporal dimension, as a break, a discontinuity, that which comes after. But the "post" can also be read in other theoretical ways. The "post" is not the simple end/after of what it qualifies; it is, rather, a multifaceted creative *re-*examination of what has been already accepted – to highlight the tensions in the *grounds on which* it *was* accepted. Often the acceptance of a metanarrative about modernity or colonialism relies on thinking in terms of binary structures and unidirectional flows of power and influence. The "post" achieves its purpose of making binary oppositions (e.g. colonizer–colonized, signifier–signified) fuzzy. While recognizing the ubiquitous nature of power relations, it foregrounds the possibilities for resistance and creative negotiation. One noteworthy thing about the various post'ist theories is that they refuse and defy simple neat categorizations,[1] an interesting and useful feature for theoretical forms which seek to deal with the multiplicity of interpretation and existence.

However, this undoing of metanarratives is also fraught with risk. It leaves the arena open for the question of what *follows* from the "post."[2] Depending on how one views the signifier and in what context, there are different answers to what *follows* from the "post." For some, the implications of the gap opened in metanarratives by the "posts" have not been accepted, especially not in economics. For others, it has allowed an analysis of the contemporary mutations of continuing metanarratives (for example for neocolonialism). For some, the promises of the "post" have no hold as they cannot possibly allow meaningful politics (see Ebert 1996). For still others, the "post" has already undermined, by far, the ground of knowledge, and remains an ultimately meaningful proposition.

Post'isms and economic understandings

How do the post'isms relate to the so-called economic understandings? Do they disrupt them fundamentally or just circumscribe their possible terrain? The answer depends on how strong a version of post'ist thought one applies to economics.

For instance, most economic understanding would have us believe in a model of the world where human beings are the center[3] of the universe and nature[4] is at their disposal to produce and consume (though in schizoid states), according to their beliefs (preferences), in order to maximize their utility under conditions of endless want. The post'isms catch it unaware when they bring about the realization that it is not as if we produce and consume in a silent empty docile world with only identical me-selves, but that we – our beliefs, preferences, our very identities – are produced by an external world of the others.

Analyzing events at the level of the individual (methodological individualism) is mistaken because it leaves out the diverse social factors operating at supra-individual levels. It allows individual subjects to be seen as if they pre-exist discourses about subjectivity. Starting from the proposition of the pre-formed, knowing, and discriminating individual who then proceeds voluntarily to transact with others obscures the fact that this is a very *particular* model of individual subjectivity – one that needs to be historically, geographically, and temporally *situated* to be seen as meaningful. But taken as the very *basis* of all other economic understanding it serves to "write out" the myriad methods of knowledge creation that *actually make* humans into such individual "subjects." The post'ist understanding is that we are born into discourses and are shaped by them.

The discourse of economics is a particularly powerful metanarrative (even more so in this late capitalist neocolonial unipolar world saturated with an often unexamined but accepted economic logic). Employing the post'ist themes we can dig into the ways and means by which the foundations of a discipline are laid, and then expose these bases as contingent and particular. This is also an exercise in establishing the difference between an *impossible* universal and general economic knowledge (aesthetically aspired to by most practitioners) *and* an actual process of universal*ization* and general*ization* of a particular form of knowledge based on a particularized model of human subjectivity – and the havoc this causes in terms of dissonance to those who are not adequately imbricated in the belief systems underlying this universalized model of knowledge and subjectivity. This recognition necessarily takes us into the domain of the specificity of contextual and contingent knowledge claims.

Theory and critique

In view of this, we need to question the innocence of method and gesture towards the historicism and values inherent in the choice of method for a social science theory. The substantial discontent over the question of method between mainstream economics and critical approaches paves the way for considering the link between theory and critique.

Of late, it is encouraging to see that the academic "thoughtscape" has also been painted in other, more subversive colors. Different ways of making sense of the "economic" realm have been proposed, some of which may involve a shift away from the positivist frameworks of the mainstream to more fluid, postpositivist, deconstructivist frameworks. Plurality at the level of approaches has been accompanied by similar questioning and plurality at the level of methodology, which has been very significant in encouraging some of the heterodox schools in their questioning of the underlying values of the discipline.[5] There are a wide array of margins (some more frayed than others) including the feminist, Marxist, critical realist, Austrian, neo-Marxist, neo-Ricardian, post-Keynesian, rhetorical, and experimental. Pressure from the margins continues to increase with the advancement of technology and as dissemination of ideas becomes easier, the quest for plurality increases. In this environment several interdisciplinary connexions have been explored (e.g. with literature, philosophy, psychology, physics, computing, psychoanalysis, art).[6]

So in this predominantly center–periphery structuring what observations are forthcoming about the nature of critique? It is important to recall that "theory and critique" are often characterized, both in the mainstream and even in most critical approaches, in a stable way where the purpose of the latter is the advancement of the former, better critique leading to better theory, an "eventually we will get there" view. Within this, critique is seen as largely atheoretical and not an end in itself. This is often used against critical practices, which are accused of not providing an "alternative theory."

However, it is interesting to note that critique can lend itself to several other characterizations. Critique can take the form of disturbing the status quo with a particular end(s) in mind (Butler 2000); it can be the basis for an emancipatory politics achieved by proceeding to theorize differently;[7] or it can *be* theory at any given point in time (Strassmann and Polanyi 1995). I will return to this last point later. Thus, we can untangle critique from its slavish role at the feet of unified theoretical advancement and see it as consisting of multiply-erupting strands of theory.

This might seem strange at first, to consider critique as theory, especially since a lot of potent contemporary critique is in some way or the other a rebellion against "theory." But it should be remembered that "theory," in its grand, unified, solid (neoclassical) sense (against which post'ist critiques rebel), is not the "theoretical" value which critique has traditionally been deemed to lack. So one is arguing both for an unprivileging of the theoretical status and also for the recognition of critique as having theoretical value which is not dependent on better theories being developed.

If anything is common to the many ways in which we can conceive of critique, it is a desire for change, for betterment sometimes (though often admitting a contested notion of "betterment"), for including consideration of the "outside." The above discussion on the nature of critique is relevant because often economists tend to think of critique as mere criticism. I am making the point that there is a difference between the two, that critique is fundamentally an ethical epistemological position. This is because it is the recognition of a plurality of voices, a liberation from the standard narrative, a quest to avoid theoretical foreclosure.

Emancipation and epistemology

Considering the emancipatory possibilities of critique leads one to interrogate the relationship between knowledge and freedom.

Conventionally, emancipation is deemed to be a matter of "the truth shall set you free," a relation where knowledge is redeeming, enabling, enlightening and, seemingly, the more access to a universal store of knowledge one has, the greater one's chances are of freeing oneself from oppression.[8] However, if we look in greater detail at this story of Enlightenment epistemology we can see why it is problematic. Knowledge is not a disinterested factual store of truth which provides ready-made solutions for combating oppression; rather, it is best seen as a successive questioning of previous knowledge claims. Flax (1992) argues that knowledge is not innocent, but a *belief* in the innocence of knowledge serves many purposes. It allows theorists to overcome the conflicts between knowledge and power by inserting the wedge of Reason. It further cements the legitimacy of the theorist in gaining privileged access to some Real. It views the Reason-led exercise of "proper" knowledge (acquired by scientific means) as benevolent and emancipatory. And, finally, it absolves the seekers of such transcendent knowledge (in its many forms of God, Science, Truth) from accepting responsibility for the ways in which such knowledge can be exclusionary, interested, specific, and nonfreeing. Universal emancipation, if only we had enough knowledge, is a false promise of Western Enlightenment modernity. It is also dangerous, for it obscures the processual ways in which discourses actually function in creating legitimacy (*ibid.*).

The temptation to view knowledge as a disinterested factual store of truth which provides ready-made solutions for combating oppressions is revisited throughout the many endeavors of critical social theory. Even some Marxist and feminist metanarratives are not an exception to this. Typically, the ability meaningfully to conceptualize emancipation in such critical social theory requires the anterior presence of a transcendental subject who acts as the marker of knowledge. In order to further utilize such theoretical apparatus this model of subjectivity is then illegitimately universalized. Its illegitimacy is in contrast to a contextualist notion of emancipation as meaningful only within the frame of specific locational questions and particular struggles.

One further point about most conceptualizations of Enlightenment epistemology. This concerns the theory/praxis (gap) problematic – where theory and praxis are understood in a distinct relation that posits theory as promise and praxis as performance, or as knowledge and power in Flax's view. Such (typical) attributions postulate a necessary wedge between the *sophisticated theoretical understanding* of events and the *atheoretical material brute struggles* which can be undertaken following on from such theoretical understanding. It relies upon the notion of theory as providing an unmediated access to an underlying material reality, and the further possibility of theory being harnessed for universal good in practice. This is an artificial divide that is useful to preserve the notion of "innocent knowledge."

The relation between emancipation and epistemology is by no means uncomplicated. What is viewed as an emancipatory project in one context can well be oppressive in another. An example of this is provided by the tortuous relations between the discourses of feminism and anti-colonialism in the colonized world in the late nineteenth and early twentieth centuries (see Gandhi 1998; on the meeting of imperialist and feminist anxieties in fictional work, see Roth 2001). The narratives of emancipatory claims are painfully contingent and contested, even among what would seem to be the most innocuously apparent identity groupings of race, class, and gender.

Collective identities

Recent times have witnessed the rise of new identity politics which recognizes the need for *admitting difference even while claiming solidarity*. Of course, there are problems in recognition and in belonging to these pre-given identity groupings that can be disruptive. Multiple identities can contradict the shared ideals. This has led to calls to abandon identity politics (Hekman 1999) as a divisive strategy that results in a loss of the advantages accruing from possessing a stable identity in the political arena. But a significant problem with any universal emancipatory politics is that it is necessarily based on positing shared ideals, usually some sort of humanist claims, and, because any nontrivial definition of humanism would necessarily be non-neutral, there would always be necessary exclusions. And so it is often the privileged, the powerful, who come to be defined as the norm, and everything/one else becomes the *constitutive outside*. Then, even a laudable narrative of emancipation is carried out on someone's terms and harbors within it the tendency to seek transcendent justifications.

However, these hasty and misjudged calls to undermine the recognition of difference are possibly common to the liberal left and conservative right (see Bramen 2002).[9] The recognition that identities are constructed and fluid needs to be reconciled with the imperative of taking responsibility (on responsible choice of identity, see Sen 1999) for these identities nonetheless. Thus the way forward may lie in affirming the notion of multiple identities while at the same time not being confined to acting *only* on common needs. It is vital to be able to *imagine* such political action.

This question of the *anxious identities that we inhabit* is particularly important for the status of epistemology in emancipatory projects such as feminism.[10] The comforting certainty of the transcendent subject is replaced with the ever more unstable, fleeting subject positions that we come into both as the creators of knowledge about the way we behave and (in a typical circular and cumulative causation case) as ourselves being created in the image of that knowledge. How, then, is there going to be any stable space on which the foundation of knowledge is to be laid?

As it becomes easy to recognize the possibility of being able to see oneself as occupying several different subject positions at the intersection of different discourses and in relation to different issues, this also opens the possibility of comprehending knowledge (and even truth) in less totalitarian and more contextual ways. As Haraway writes, "[p]ositioning implies responsibility for our enabling practices" (1988: 587). Recognizing the inevitability of partial perspective is to admit situated knowledges which are "about communities, not about isolated individuals" (*ibid.*: 590). We no longer have access to the truth of kings and wise male philosophers (or even wise male economists!), but to a pared down, more responsible truth achieved by building collective identities in the face of difference.

The ethics of this re-imagining is often confronted with charges of relativism. Let me address this now. I have said that all knowledge is interested knowledge, all positions are interested positions, that nothing is beyond interrogation. This is not a call for loss of judgment, of all validity, but rather a call to reject the idea of being able universally to pronounce what is valid in every situation.[11]

What I am saying is that every statement is equally intrinsically worthy as every other, but I am not saying that all these statements are of equal value from any particular subject position. This can also be expressed in the following way. There is no universal checklist or hierarchy of worth for different beliefs about the world, but that does not imply, however, that different individuals at the intersection of different discursive knowledges, in accordance with their own positionality, would not have their own hierarchy of worth regarding different beliefs about the world. These are, of course, liable to change in the context of space, time, and issues.

This is not as paralyzing as many have thought.[12] For one thing, it implies that we recognize the *active* role of personal judgment, which is influenced by the available theories (both theories of the self and theories of the world) in the creation of these hierarchies of beliefs. This leads us to a justification of a greater diversity of theories with more explicit interrogation of their metaphysical basis, supporting evidence, and assumptions. Critical self-reflexivity as a criterion both for theories and for their choice is then significant. Judgments are inevitable; however, the contingency and non-universal applicability of the criteria on which they are made need to be explicitly recognized.

Therefore the post'ist destabilization of an essentialist identity does not inaugurate a free-for-all where there are no constraints and no choices; rather, thinking emancipation in terms of collective identities which are based, in the first instance, on an ethical primacy of difference places responsibility at the heart of knowing/being. Finally, the processual nature of achieving something while maintaining identities as *an outcome* (rather than an antecedent) of political practice is an invitation to *continually Other* oneself, thus analyzing power at the site of knowledge.

Poststructuralist feminism and the "text" of economics

Feminist poststructuralism is alive to the discursive constitution of identity and the way power interrupts a narrative. How might we interpellate both mainstream and feminist economics with its insights? A start is to explore the processes by which "economy" is distilled out of "society," to explore the boundaries of the economic and its definitional politics. *This delineation/demarcation of the "economic" itself is an intensely political act, for often privileges accrue to what gets defined as being so.*[13] What gets counted as economic is what is amenable to the neoclassical economic method (see Nelson 1993; Strassmann 1993b), and so the "established order tends to produce…the *naturalisation of its own arbitrariness*" (Bourdieu, in Shapiro and Alker 1996: 208; emphasis mine).

We can deconstruct the conventional ideas of economy/ics (as objective universal knowledge about an externally existing economy/reality) by engaging strands of Continental philosophy[14] which include considerations about the role of the author, the text, intentionality, language, and the effects of power. Such a reading of economic knowledge as textual production enables us to see such knowledge claims as contingent, as exclusionary stories complicit with power.

Let me point out some of the various ways in which arguments relating to texts, stories, and economics have been constructed. Ward characterized economics as storytelling, defined as "an attempt to give an account of an interrelated set of phenomena in which fact, theory and value are all mixed together in the telling" (1972: 179–90). The standard stories of economics convey a picture *not* explicitly stated but conveyed across by the "selection of topics and emphases" (*ibid.*: 183). McCloskey's path-breaking work (especially 1986, 1994) is famous for deconstructing the earlier supposed factual truth-status of economic theories. She rightly points out that we need to pay attention to the workaday practices of economists, to their rhetoric and persuasion, which is the greatest part of economic arguments. Equally important is Strassmann's work (1993a, 1993b), which highlights the ways in which disciplinary authority can mean that the conversation of economics is laden with power imbalances. Her insights regarding the conception of economics as storytelling and economists as storytellers are crucial to feminist enquiry into how and why the mainstream narratives tell the stories they do.

It is against this background that one should evaluate the post'ist claims outlined here. My argument is for reading the economy/ics as a text. A text, not just in terms of a general interpretation of a "text" which can be "read,"[15] but a *textual productive enterprise*. The practitioners and practices are part of the performance of an enterprise of knowledge creation which produces its own Real (the economy) and then claims privileged access to it *as if* it existed already performed – the entity "economy" or the category "economic" as itself the production of the very theories that are supposed to reflect it. And this view of economics as a text (of which economists are themselves a part) helps us to appreciate the very *particular locatedness* of this text. Economics, as a *contingent episteme*, is an ideological product embodying Western Enlightenment imperial colonial modernity (see Kanth 1997).[16]

Thus, in order to examine the ways in which economic knowledge is contingent it becomes essential to move towards thinking of economics (creating knowledge about the economy) *as a text*. Following Shapiro's discussion of a critical political perspective (1989: 13), one could analogously ask: how does reading the economy as a text necessarily involve a questioning of the privileged forms of representation whose dominance has led to the unproblematic acceptance of subjects, objects, acts, and themes through which the economic world is constituted.

When we see knowledge about the economy as the result of textual production, several observations are forthcoming. *In a story about stories, its interesting to ask: what do the stories we tell say about us?* As is increasingly documented, for the most part knowledge formations consist of institutionalized storytelling about this or that aspect of our experience as sentient beings in this world. It is unwise to think of stories as "merely fiction." In fact, fiction itself is less "fictional" than social scientists would like to believe.

For every story that is told there are stories that are not told. So why do we choose to tell some stories rather than others? In the face of an overdetermined reality, the stories that are told are not necessarily the ones that are the most interesting, but the ones that are the most prudent. The outside of the text is not simply the result of omission and/or neglect. It serves a *"constitutive"* function in maintaining the inside.

The story of the economy, as told by the mainstream narratives, is a story that is popular, because institutionalized structures favor it. Thus ultimately storytellers are important too, for stories are complicit with power. History is not a continuous narrative about things as they happened, but a discontinuous and fragmented, albeit consolidated, voice.

Within economics, human beings fit into the picture as objects of knowledge. Economic theories, as stories about this carved-out "economic" realm, usually tell a certain story.[17] It is instructive to note what is the outside of neoclassical stories about the economy: women, nonmarketable ideas/objects, the environment, history, emotions, nonreductive, nonformalizable, nonmeasurable elements of comprehension. The agent (homo economicus) is patterned after an individual with the sorts of privileges in society which traditionally accrue to privileged men (England 1993; Grapard 1995, 1996; Hewitson 1999; Kaul 2001). Similarly, the notion of free choice does not take into account people who do not have free choice: those who are forced, owing to need, or those who do not feel at ease with the neoclassical capitalist ideology. What about people who socially and representationally (for instance through minority stereotyping) find themselves at the sites where choices are not just individual or free but governed by others' perception of them? (See Cudd 1997.)

This story appeals to audiences who see their own image at its interstices. For the minority who see themselves in it, it is a powerful story. For those who do not recognize themselves in the text, there is the role of holding up the institutionalized story as its outside. Indeed, for many the sense of dis-identification can be severe. They are to be the conditions on which closure can be achieved in the text. A necessity for defining, demarcating, and reifying the boundaries of what can legitimately be counted as economic knowledge. This demarcation is useful for the creation of borders, which can then be disciplined and patrolled. It is also useful in dismissing alternative approaches in the name of validity, authority, and legitimacy.

Looking at the study of the economy/ic as a textual production also draws attention to the "word-and-world" links. The poststructuralist argument is that language is not a determinate set of symbols with fixed meanings, a transparent medium of communication. We actuate our existence within language(s). *Theories not only explain, predict, or describe reality, but discursively produce reality/ies.* This performative role of theories enables us to appreciate better the intertwined discursive/material in social theory.[18] The "violence" of economic theories is an "epistemic" one, but also oppression in a material sense. Mainstream theories hinging on self-interest become a paean for an ontology of hedonistic egoism, creating what they name. This actualization takes place within a matrix of power that enables certain voices to be articulated in a meaningful manner. Further, the flows of power ensure that legitimacy is not bound just to utterances, but also to actors.

The other principal point I wish to make relates to critique. In my view, if we see economics as a particular text rather than an objectivist scientific enterprise it allows us to see a different role of critique. Critique functions differently in a textual reading and in an objectivist scientific enterprise. The idea of critical questioning and change in science is strongly tied to the notion of the *accumulation and verification* of knowledge. This notion of critique as subservient to unified theoretical advancement has carried over into economics. There is, however, no determinate fixing of meaning in a textual reading. It is not an attempt to build a solid mass of ever-fixed knowledge but, rather, constant reinterpretations and renegotiations. In reading the economy/ic as a text we recognize *critique as theory* at a situated point in time. The shifting, slipping, sandy meanings of the economy/ic can be recognized as mediated and contextual.

In looking at poststructuralist insights and their focus upon power, language, and perspectivity, especially along with feminist theory, several concerns about the nature of theory and the process of theorization in mainstream economics are addressed. This explicit recognition of power also discredits the "marketplace of ideas" view (Strassmann 1993b), according to which the approach is prevalent because it emerged as the best in the marketplace of ideas. The power of mainstream economics entails possibilities for non-neutral communication and the marginalization of heterodoxy.

Postcolonial sentiment

In developing further this critical engagement, involvement with postcolonial theory is potentially productive, whereas the "postcolonial" is a contested marker and is used sometimes in a solely temporal sense.[19] I am gesturing to an unhyphenated postcolonial (rather than the temporal marker post-of colonial), which crucially procures from the colonial encounter an *agency* for the subjugated Other in this discourse of marginality. This is because it opens up the sutures of modernity and colonialism, questioning all over again their relation to disciplinary knowledge in general and economic knowledge in particular. This questioning, however, is a self-aware exercise of power and memory. It builds upon the idea of acknowledging one's own *political positioning*, of being *critically self-reflexive*[20] regarding one's positionality and interests. An awareness of the power of locations that one speaks and writes from, if made foundational, is also an awareness of the crucial role of the *representation* of the self and the Other. The postcolonial looks at the relations between the text and the wor(l)d, the way imperial worlding has rendered meaningful "Earth to World, East to Orient, Countries to Colonies." Aiming to show knowledge creation as an *"epistemic violence"* rather than simply a disinterested production of facts, Spivak (1988) cautions against even well-meant efforts at simply "including voices": we can only *"point towards the silences,"* we cannot appropriate the subaltern's voice as our own (on issues of the subaltern and historiography, see Guha 1998).

This foregrounds the need to move beyond simple conceptualizations of attainable standpoints of the Other to more complex ideas of a strategic theorization which is combative and particular. In this interrogation of how discourses are harnessed to powerful social forces and, in the name of scientific objectivity, have come to constitute regimes of truth (see Foucault 1980) we realize the urgency of locating all knowledge of economic life in human history, culture, and power relations.

The process of naming is crucial to the further development of thought, so it is this collective strand of ideas that I wish to term the *postcolonial sentiment*.[21] It is a critique, in fact a principled stance in favor of constant critique.

Contextual social political economy

Together with poststructuralist feminist insights, the postcolonial sentiment is a foundational element informing the praxis of contextual social political economy, a non-universalist way of creating specific and interested economic knowledges. As universally valid theoretical frameworks become problematic a recognition of difference is brought about. Often attempts to consider difference see it as a diversion or division from sameness," as variations on the theme, but they do not let difference make a difference! Within a contextual praxis, difference is fundamental otherness and involves considering specific history and context as the starting point of the theoretical lifecycle rather than its culminatory application. Moving consciously in the direction of a multidisciplinary praxis invites the authoring of conceptualized theories in a framework of methodological pluralism. Attention to contexts and praxis of a wider social political economy accommodates diverse insights. What (events, phenomena, behavior) is currently a paradox or anomaly if viewed in economic terms might become more comprehensible when viewed in a theoretical constellation of varied motivations including the social or the political. Equally, new and locationally relevant issues might come into consideration. This will connect the political and the economic; economic knowledge will not be universally valid; and what is considered (defined as) "economic" will be understood differently across different contexts. Racial and cultural elements can be introduced into the analysis, and localized struggles for meaning can arbitrate between competing accounts. Such a praxis will still be capable of admitting a contested notion of emancipation. Recognizing the "contingent foundations"[22] of all knowledge about the economy, the way ahead can be negotiated by admitting "strategic essentialism,"[23] by deploying strategically essentialist categories for explicitly (contested) emancipatory politics.

The aesthetic aspirations of conventional theorizing, especially regarding the need for universally valid, objective knowledge, lead to a "violent" (epistemically) and "oppressive" (materially) exercise where sets of people and ideas get "written out" of the economy. The mapping of human interactions is not akin to postulating the ideal gas law, not least because *power* is the constant twin to knowledge. It continuously mutates and transforms, it censors and creates. A *focus on power as operative in localized settings with a historicized present* is essential to attempting critical theorizing.

Once the legitimacy of theories and theorizing is questioned in this manner, the economy is not a single, simple, universal entity that is omnipresent and lends itself to total comprehension. The economy itself is recognized as a creative metaphor which needs to be filled with particular meanings at particular situations. It need not always be defined as that kind of theorizing which excludes gender, race, class, culture, and ecology. The perforated boundaries of the economy can then be explored with contextual comprehensions. Contextual social political economy is a way of admitting possibilities, and can also be extremely useful in testing the limits of overdetermination (events and processes as the site and result of a multitude of determinations) in theory and its implications for critical practice.

Notes

1 As writers of the postmodern have elaborated, the very word postmodern can signify performances, commodification, fragmentation, shallowness, decenteredness, and much more (see Cullenberg *et al.* 2001).
2 The answer is rather like the lyrics of that John Denver (with Placido Domingo) song "Perhaps Love": "Some say love is holding on, and some say letting go/Some say love is everything and some say…they don't know."

3 Of course there are many ways in which this idea of the central human being plays out, for it is never just a central human being but a central man, and a central white man – his other attributes may be that he is middle class, able bodied, Anglo-Saxon, rational, protestant, heterosexual, and procreatively inclined. The list could go on, but usually very good examples are provided by the candidates for the American Presidency!
4 The ever-present "nurturing feminine" outside, which is to be "controlled." For a discussion of ecological and feminist issues in relation to economics, see *Ecological Economics*, Special Issue, 20/1997.
5 This pluralism can yield enormous advantages in comprehension, but conversation of the center with the periphery is not innocent of the power of censorship.
6 For some examples, see Mirowski (1989); Garnett (1999); Osteen and Woodmansee (1999); Szostak (1999).
7 For instance feminists theorizing a *better* economics, which is informed by gender sensitive concerns.
8 An interesting example of a link between ontology, explanation, and emancipation is provided by the critical realist accounts (see Collier 1994: esp. 169–204).
9 It is no coincidence that people worried about a world of endless difference and fed up with post'isms are usually those with a historical privilege of voice.
10 As people can tell turns in the plot of a movie by a glance at their watch to determine the duration still to go, I am sure you can tell that my argument here is that we can relocate contextual bases of emancipatory politics not merely in spite of but *because* of these anxious identities that we are deemed (not doomed) to inhabit.
11 An idea which has been termed the "egalitarian fallacy." To call for a rejection of the idea of a universally existing and available "valid" (a refusal to uphold the idea of the valid) *does not* mean that all things are equally valid.
12 Haraway perceptively writes: "The alternative to relativism is partial, locatable, critical knowledges sustaining the possibility of webs of connections called solidarity in politics and shared conversations in epistemology" (1988: 584; see also Mouffe 1995).
13 Examples of certain types of work (i.e. housework, carework) and exchange systems (nonmarketed transactions in three-fourths of the world, the gift).
14 Most methodological literature in economics draws solely on the debates in the philosophy of science (including some post-positivist philosophers of science): Popper, Kuhn, Lakatos, and Feyerabend.
15 What is a text? Consider Bennington's remarks: " 'Text' is not quite an extension of a familiar concept, but a displacement or reinscription of it. Text in general is any system of marks, traces, referrals (don't say reference, have a little more sense than that). Perception is a text.... There is no essential difference between language and the world, the one as subject, the other as object. There are traces" (Bennington, in Royle 2000: 7). My argument for reading the economy as a text is different from an alternative one put forward by Brown (1994).
16 Recent attempts to introduce a postmodern interrogation of economics are summarized in Cullenberg *et al.* (2001). However, this is different from a postcolonial critique of economics, which is forthcoming in a volume edited by S. Charusheela and Zein-Elabdin. For my take on the value of a postcolonial memory in economics, see Kaul (forthcoming).
17 Let me summarize: Consumers or firms are like characters in a play acting out the same possible roles in every space and time. Scarce talk of gender or race or place. Consumers demand, producers supply; self-interest being ever present, markets oblige. End of story. Everything else is a complication.
18 For an interesting take on performativity, theory and identity, see Butler (1990, 1993).
19 The recognition of the sites, mechanisms, and representational practices which are active in the construction of specifically interested knowledges is one such theme. I will draw upon Spivak (1988, 1990) and Landry and MacLean (1996).
20 Please note that critical self-reflexivity is entirely different from skepticism.
21 Postcolonial ideas are often interpreted as a position against imperialism and Eurocentrism. *Postcolonial sentiment* is envisaged as a broader idea of criticality and resistance to any universal dominant paradigm – a "sentiment" because it is a normative position of ever-critical self-reflexivity. A

constant questioning awareness of contingent foundations is implied in any theoretical gesture within this framework.
22 Butler (1992: 3–21) advocates avoiding gestures of conceptual mastery. This is not the advent of nihilistic relativism but the very precondition of a politically engaged critique: "The task is to interrogate what the theoretical move that establishes foundations authorises, and what precisely it excludes or forecloses" (*ibid.*: 7) – not to do away with the category of universality, but to "relieve the category of its foundationalist weight in order to render it as a site of permanent political contest" (*ibid.*: 8).
23 Adopting and adapting deconstruction specifically for the postcolonial field, Spivak advocates *strategic essentialism* – "a strategic use of positivist essentialism in a scrupulously visible political interest" (Landry and MacLean 1996: 214). The goal of essentialist critique is not the exposure of error, but the interrogation of the essentialist terms:

> In deconstructive critical practices, you have to be aware that you are going to essentialize anyway. So then strategically you can look at essentialism, not as descriptions of the way things are, but as something that one must adopt to produce a critique of everything.
>
> (Spivak 1990: 51)

Bibliography

Addleson, Mark (1995) *Equilibrium Versus Understanding: Towards the Restoration of Economics as Social Theory*, London: Routledge.

Arrow, Kenneth J. (1994) "Methodological Individualism and Social Knowledge," *American Economic Review* 84(2): 1–9.

Bauman, Zygmunt (1995) *Life in Fragments*, Oxford: Blackwell.

Blaug, Mark (1980) *The Methodology of Economics; Or, How Economists Explain*, Cambridge: Cambridge University Press.

Bramen, Carrie Tirado (2002) "Why the Academic Left Hates Identity Politics," *Textual Practice* 16(1): 1–11.

Brown, Vivienne (1994) "The Economy as Text," in Roger Backhouse (ed.) *New Directions in Economic Methodology*, London: Routledge.

Butler, Judith (1990) *Gender Trouble: Feminism and the Subversion of Identity*, London: Routledge.

—— (1993) *Bodies that Matter: Understanding the Discursive Limits of "Sex"*, London: Routledge.

—— (2000) "The Value of Being Disturbed," *Theory and Event* 4(1); available at http://muse.jhu.edu/journals/theory_&_event/v004/4.1butler.htm (August 2000).

Charusheela, S. and Eiman Zein-Elabdin (eds.) (forthcoming) *Postcolonialism Meets Economics*, London: Routledge.

Chick, Victoria (1998) "On Knowing One's Place: The Role of Formalism in Economics," *Economic Journal* 108(451): 1,859–69.

Collier, Andrew (1994) *Critical Realism: An Introduction to Roy Bhaskar's Philosophy*, London: Verso.

Cudd, Ann E. (1997) "On Social Groups," mimeo.

Cullenberg, Steve, Jack Amariglio and David Ruccio (2001) *Postmodernism, Economics and Knowledge*, London: Routledge.

Dow, Sheila (1998) "Controversy: Formalism in Economics: Editorial Note," *Economic Journal* 108(451): 1,826–8.

Ebert, Teresa L. (1996) *Ludic Feminism and After: Postmodernism, Desire and Labor in Late Capitalism*, Ann Arbor, MI: University of Michigan Press.

England, Paula (1993) "The Separative Self: Androcentric Bias in Neoclassical Assumptions," in Marianne A. Ferber and Julie A. Nelson (eds.) *Beyond Economic Man: Feminist Theory and Economics*, Chicago, IL: University of Chicago Press.

Feiner, Susan (1999) "A Portrait of Homo Economicus as a Young Man," in Martha Woodmansee and Mark Osteen (eds.) *The New Economic Criticism: Studies at the Intersection of Literature and Economics*, London: Routledge.

Flax, Jane (1992) "The End of Innocence," in Judith Butler and Joan W. Scott (eds.) *Feminists Theorize the Political*, London: Routledge.

Fleetwood, Steve (ed.) (1999) *Critical Realism in Economics: Development in Debate*, London: Routledge.

Foucault, Michel (1980) *Power/Knowledge: Selected Interviews and Other Writings 1972–1977*, ed. Colin Gordon, London: Harvester Wheatsheaf.

Gandhi, Leela (1998) *Postcolonial Theory: A Critical Introduction*, Edinburgh: Edinburgh University Press.

Garnett, Rob F. (1999) *What Do Economists Know?: New Economics of Knowledge*, London: Routledge.

Grapard, Ulla (1995) "Robinson Crusoe: The Quintessential Rational Economic Man?," *Feminist Economics* 1(1): 33–52.

—— (1996) "How to See the Invisible Hand; Or, From the Benevolence of the Butcher's Wife," paper presented at the first IAFFE conference, Washington DC, July 1992, revised version.

Guha, Ranajit (ed.) (1998) *A Subaltern Studies Reader: 1986–1995*, Minneapolis, MN: University of Minnesota Press.

Haraway, Donna (1988) "Situated Knowledges: The Science Question in Feminism and the Privilege of Partial Perspective," *Feminist Studies* 14(3): 575–99.

Hekman, Susan (1999) *Feminism, Identity and Difference*, London: Frank Cass Publishers.

Hewitson, Gillian J. (1999) *Feminist Economics: Interrogating the Masculinity of Rational Economic Man*, Cheltenham: Edward Elgar.

Kanth, Rajani Kannepalli (1997) *Breaking with the Enlightenment: The Twilight of History and the Rediscovery of Utopia*, Atlantic Highlands, NJ: Humanities Press.

Kaul, Nitasha (2001) "Feminism in Economics: Theoria and Aporia," in Carolyn Brina, Carolyn Britton and Alison Assiter (eds.) *Millennial Visions: Feminisms into the 21st Century*, Cardiff: Cardiff University Press.

—— (2002) "A Critical *Post* to Critical Realism," *Cambridge Journal of Economics* 26(6): 709–26.

—— (forthcoming) "Writing Economic Theory (An)Other Way," in S. Charusheela and Eiman Zein-Elabdin (eds.) *Postcolonialism Meets Economics*, London: Routledge.

Keen, S. (2001) *Debunking Economics: The Naked Emperor of the Social Sciences*, London: Zed Books.

Klein, E. (1998) *Economic Theories and their Relational Structures: A Model-Theoretic Characterisation*, London: Macmillan Press.

Landry, Donna and Gerald MacLean (eds.) (1996) *The Spivak Reader: Selected Works of Gayatri Chakravorty Spivak*, London: Routledge.

Lawson, Tony (1997) *Economics and Reality*, London: Routledge.

Lydall, Harold (1998) *A Critique of Orthodox Economics: An Alternative Model*, Basingstoke: Macmillan Press.

Lyotard, Jean-François (1984) *The Postmodern Condition: A Report on Knowledge*, Minneapolis, MN: University of Minnesota Press.

McCloskey, Donald N. (1986) *The Rhetoric of Economics*, Sussex: Harvester Press.

—— (1994) *Knowledge and Persuasion in Economics*, Cambridge: Cambridge University Press.

Mirowski, Philip (1989) *More Heat Than Light: Economics as Social Physics, Physics as Nature's Economics*, Cambridge: Cambridge University Press.

Mouffe, Chantal (1995) "Feminism, Citizenship and Radical Democratic Politics," in Linda Nicholson and Steven Seidman (eds.) *Social Postmodernism: Beyond Identity Politics*, Cambridge: Cambridge University Press.

Nelson, Julie A. (1993) "The Study of Choice or the Study of Provisioning? Gender and the Definition of Economics," in Marianne A. Ferber and Julie A. Nelson (eds.) *Beyond Economic Man: Feminist Theory and Economics*, Chicago, IL: University of Chicago Press.

—— (1996) *Feminism, Objectivity and Economics*, London: Routledge.

O'Brien, Eugene (1998) " *What Ish My Nation??*: Towards a Negative Definition of Identity," *Minerva: An Internet Journal of Philosophy* 2; available at http://www.ul.ie/philos/vol2/negation.html (August 2000).

Ormerod, Paul (1994) *The Death of Economics*, London: Faber.

Osteen, Mark and Martha Woodmansee (1999) *The New Economic Criticism: Studies at the Interface of Literature and Economics*, London: Routledge.

Poovey, Mary (1998) *A History of the Modern Fact: Problems of Knowledge in the Sciences of Wealth and Society*, Chicago, IL: University of Chicago Press.

Robinson, Joan (1977) "What are the Questions?," *Journal of Economic Literature* 15(4): 1318–39.

Roth, Marty (2001) "Gilman's Arabesque Wallpaper," *Mosaic* 34(4): 145–62.

Royle, Nicholas (2000) "What Is Deconstruction?," in Nicholas Royle (ed.) *Deconstructions: A User's Guide*, Basingstoke: Palgrave.

Schoemaker, Paul J.H. (1991) "The Quest for Optimality: a Positive Heuristic of Science?," *Behavioural and Brain Sciences* 14: 205–45.

Sen, Amartya Kumar (1999) *Reason Before Identity*, Oxford: Oxford University Press.

Shapiro, Michael J. (1989) "Textualizing Global Politics," in James Der Derian and Michael J. Shapiro (eds.) *International/Intertextual Relations: Postmodern Readings of World Politics*, Lexington, DC: Heath.

Shapiro, Michael J. and Hayward R. Alker (eds.) (1996) *Challenging Boundaries: Global Flows, Territorial Identities*, London: University of Minnesota Press.

Special Section (1998) "Controversy: Formalism In Economics," *Economic Journal* 108: 1,826–69.

Spivak, Gayatri Chakravorty (1988) "Can the Subaltern Speak?: Speculation on Widow Sacrifice," in Cary Nelson and Lawrence Grossberg (eds.) *Marxism and the Interpretation of Culture*, Chicago, IL: University of Illinois Press.

—— (1990) *The Post-Colonial Critic: Interviews, Strategies, Dialogues*, ed. Sarah Harasym, London: Routledge.

Strassmann, Diana L. (1993a) "The Stories of Economics and the Power of the Storyteller," *History of Political Economy* 25(1): 147–65.

—— (1993b) "Not a Free market: The Rhetoric of Disciplinary Authority in Economics," in Marianne A. Ferber and Julie A. Nelson (eds.) *Beyond Economic Man: Feminist Theory and Economics*, Chicago, IL: University of Chicago Press.

—— (1994) "Feminist Thought and Economics; Or, What Do the Visigoths Know?," *American Economic Review* 84(2): 153–8.

Strassmann, Diana L. and Livia Polanyi (1995) "Shifting the Paradigm: Value in Feminist Critiques of Economics," *Forum for Social Economics* 25(1): 3–19.

Szostak, Rick (1999) *Econ-Art: Divorcing Art From Science in Modern Economics*, London: Pluto Press.

Walsh, Vivian C. (1994) "Rationality as Self-Interest Versus Rationality as Present Aims," *American Economic Review* 84(2): 401–5.

Ward, Benjamin N. (1972) "Storytelling," *What's Wrong with Economics?*, London: Macmillan.

Weintraub, E. Roy (1998) "Axiomatisches Mißverständnis," *Economic Journal* 108(451): 1,837–47.

Wootton, Barbara (1938) *Lament for Economics*, London: George Allen & Unwin.

Part IV
Beyond social contract
Theorizing agency and relatedness

14 "Holding Hands at Midnight"

The paradox of caring labor[1]

Nancy Folbre

> The man who only lives for making money,
> Lives a life that isn't necessarily sunny.
> Likewise the man who works for fame.
> There's no guarantee that time won't erase his name.
> The fact is, the only work that really brings enjoyment
> Is the kind that comes from girl-and boy-ment.
> Fall in love, you won't regret it.
> That's the best work of all if you can get it.
> Holding hands at midnight, 'neath the starry sky,
> Nice work if you can get it,
> And you can get it if you try.
> ("Nice Work If You Can Get It," by George and
> Ira Gershwin, © 1937 Chappell and Co.
> (Renewed); all rights reserved by permission)

Despite its name, this famous jazz standard is not really about work at all, at least not as economists define it. It never refers to dishwashing or diaper changing, the kinds of tasks that most of us would happily pay others to do for us. Rather, it suggests that a particular motive for work – love – is intrinsically superior to the desire for money or fame. Like many songs Ira and George Gershwin wrote during the Great Depression, it defends personal values against the dictates of the marketplace.[2]

Holding hands at midnight is nice work because it is caring work. But it seldom pays well, depending on whose hands one is holding. This poses something of a paradox for economists. If caring is its own reward, it need not command an economic return. But if caring labor receives no economic return at all, will it persist? If the economic costs of caring go up, will the supply of it decline? These are questions that economists have historically been reluctant to address. They are, however, quite relevant to three public policy issues with which feminist economists, in particular, are concerned: pay equity, the valuation of nonmarket work, and greater public support for parents.

In this paper I define "caring labor," discuss several different reasons why it may be undervalued, and explore the possibility that the expansion of competitive markets will eventually reduce its supply. The first section (pp. 213–17) develops a definition and a taxonomy that stresses the importance of the motives underlying the supply of labor. The second section (pp. 217–24) shows that both neoclassical and institutionalist economic theories help explain why caring is economically disadvantageous. It also questions whether the appropriate response is simply to stop caring. The third section (pp. 224–7) discusses some of the more important implications for feminist public policy.

The concept of caring labor

Feminist theorists are increasingly fond of the term "care," but have yet systematically to explore its economic implications.[3] Joan Tronto writes: "Caring seems to involve taking the concerns and needs of the other as a basis for action."[4] The very concept threatens the underpinnings of neoclassical economic theory: rational economic man maximizes a utility function that does not include any consideration of other people's welfare, especially those outside his immediate family.[5] But caring implies reciprocity, altruism, and responsibility.

A definition

"Caring labor" is a colloquial term that carries many different connotations. It is sometimes used to refer to specific activities (such as childcare or eldercare), or end-results (such as feeling cared for). Virtually any form of labor can be described as "caring" in the sense that it results in activities that help meet the needs of others. It could be defined quite broadly, since virtually all economic activities are rooted in the provisioning of human existence.[6] Also, people "care" about many things other than people: animals, vegetables, their environment, their principles, and so on.

But the real challenge of the phrase lies in its emotional connotations, as a type of labor distinct from that which most economists analyze in terms of measurable output per hour. Because I want to pursue the feminist emphasis on caring as concern for others and want to ask what determines its supply, I will focus on motivations and use the term caring labor to denote a caring motive: *labor undertaken out of affection or a sense of responsibility for other people, with no expectation of immediate pecuniary reward.*[7]

The caring motive is particularly crucial to meeting the needs of children, the elderly, the sick, and other dependants but is by no means restricted to these tasks. Also, there is a distinction between motives and effects: a person may undertake a certain task out of love or caring for another person. That does not necessarily mean that the other person feels "cared for." In fact, the attentions may actually be unwelcome. Alternatively, a person may feel no real affection or emotion yet still succeed in providing care. For instance, a well-trained but ill-humored nurse may provide better medical care than a loving parent; a dispassionate but skillful psychiatrist may assuage feelings of despair better than a loving spouse.

But even if caring labor does not always provide the best care, we expect a general correlation between the two, especially when part of the task is to make someone feel cared for rather than simply to change the bedpan or apply a theory. Within the general category of emotional needs there is at least one that cannot adequately be met by labor supplied only for money. Love cannot be bought.

Sometimes, the motive for engaging in a certain activity affects the quality of the service being provided. Consider Richard Titmuss's classic research on the blood donations for transfusions.[8] In an era when the quality of blood was difficult to monitor, he found that countries that relied on voluntary donations of blood, like Great Britain, fared much better than those, like the United States, which paid donors. People who gave blood for money were more likely to lie about their medical history and less likely to offer uninfected blood.

Defining caring labor as "undertaken out of affection or a sense of responsibility for others, with no expectation of immediate pecuniary reward" excludes labor that is offered *only* in response to wages. However, it does not exclude all labor in wage employment, because some people do not work for money alone. Nor does the definition exclude any particular category of tasks, because one could engage in an activity that does not involve any direct care of people (like cleaning up toxic waste) that is nevertheless motivated by a desire to help others.

Comparison to related concepts

Caring labor is associated with tasks that women often specialize in, such as mothering. But the concept diverges from many related terms in the feminist economist's vocabulary, such as "family labor," "unpaid labor," "reproductive labor," "sex-affective production," or "social reproduction," which emphasize the location or type of work in a "separate sphere." Precisely because it focuses on motives, caring labor can apply to both men and women, the market and the family, production and reproduction.

Often concepts of caring have been embedded in the treatment of related concepts. Karl Marx, like the other classical political economists, stressed the distinction between production for use and production for exchange. Production for use implies circumstances in which the producer has control over his or her own means of production, and it is motivated by direct need for the product. This does not necessarily involve caring labor. For instance, raising food for one's own consumption or providing the services necessary to reproduce one's own labor power are requirements of subsistence. No love or affection or sense of responsibility whatsoever need be involved. Still, Marxists have often assumed that production for use is more likely than production for exchange to be motivated by caring.

The neoclassical tradition, which takes utility maximization as its starting point, can flexibly accommodate an infinite number of distinct motives for labor. But it does not offer an adequate conceptualization of caring labor, because it takes utility functions as exogenously given and ignores the issue of how they are socially constructed. Neoclassical economists tend to lump all non-pecuniary preferences together and interpret all motivations in terms of preferences. Most would interpret caring as a manifestation of exogenously given, probably biologically determined, altruism.[9]

A typology of caring motives

But altruism is only one of three possible motives for caring labor, which also include long-run reciprocity and the fulfillment of obligation or responsibility. The phrase "no expectation of immediate pecuniary reward" does not imply absence of self-interest. Caring labor may be elicited by long-run expectations of reciprocity of either tangible or emotional services.

Reciprocity is a much looser form of exchange than that which normally takes place in markets, and tends to be based on implicit rather than explicit contracts, enforced by norms of cooperation. Sometimes these are quite specific in nature: You scratch my back, I will scratch yours. Often, though, they are quite general: You care for me, and I will care for you. Both affection and a sense of responsibility foster reciprocity, though it may tend to break down if the probability of payback declines.

Such reliability can be interpreted in terms of a prisoner's dilemma, a situation where two parties are better off if they cooperate (or care) but both fear the other will fail to cooperate (or care). Social norms can help prevent a coordination (or caring) failure. The perceived probability of success will affect the supply of cooperation and/or caring. It is embarrassing and painful to care for someone if they do not care for you.

A second type of caring labor is entirely unrelated to coordination problems, based on interdependent preferences that take an altruistic form. That is, one gets pleasure from other people's wellbeing; making other people happy makes one happy. This is caring in the most emotional sense of the word, the type of caring that often characterizes couples and kin, but is by no means restricted to families. Altruism does not imply selflessness: the degree of altruism may vary considerably depending on the relative weights assigned to other people's preferences relative to one's own.[10] And altruism may be partially endogenous; the preference itself may be extinguished by punishment.[11]

Virginia Held offers an example of this motivation in her description of the intention and goal of mothering: "to give of one's care without obtaining a return of a self-interested kind. The emotional satisfaction of a mothering person is a satisfaction in the well-being and happiness of another human being."[12] Genevieve Vaughan generalizes this motivation with her writings on the "gift economy."[13]

A third type of caring labor is based, not on preferences per se, but on a moral category of obligation or responsibility. A mother does not always get up in the middle of the night to tend to a crying child out of altruism or affection; sometimes she gets up simply because she takes it to be her responsibility.[14] One could, of course, describe fulfillment of an obligation as a preference, or a metapreference, but doing so trivializes the importance of obligation as a moral category.[15] Economists are fond of an old Latin saying: *de gustibus non est disputandum*, "there's no arguing about tastes." There is plenty of arguing about obligations, because they are often enforced by political and legal means.

Which comes first, the preference or the principle? It is difficult to say, and all three caring motives described here are not only interrelated but also difficult to distinguish empirically. Reciprocity rests to some degree on moral categories of obligation. Preferences are shaped by a socialization process that features both norms and obligations. One could certainly construe a degree of altruistic behavior as an obligation, as Tronto and others do when they describe the need for "an ethic of care."[16] Still, norms, preferences, and values are distinct. Norms are patterns of behavior characteristic of a certain culture; preferences are the desires of a particular individual; values are grounded in claims of universality that transcend any particular culture or individual.

Reciprocity is an anthropological concept with a calculating but social orientation. The books do not necessarily balance for every individual, as in voluntary market exchange. Altruistic preferences are a psychological concept, especially when treated as partially endogenous. Obligation is a philosophical concept that turns on right and wrong. It is based on values, rather than norms or preferences. The triad offers three related escape routes from the individualistic, selfish, and essentially amoral reasoning of rational economic man.

This categorization of distinct but related motives for caring labor diverges from both Marxian and neoclassical economic theory in its interdisciplinary emphasis on norms, preferences, and values. As the following discussion will show, the social construction and contestation of these has important implications for the supply of caring labor.

The value of caring labor

Many feminist scholars suggest that women are penalized by specialization in work that involves the care of other people.[17] Although she couches her analysis of care in moral and philosophical terms, Joan Tronto cites women's concentration in low-paying jobs that require the care of other people as evidence that "care is devalued and the people who do caring work are devalued."[18] Perhaps she means that people should care more about care.

Economists are less interested in the ethical than in the counterfactual dimension – to argue that a type of labor is devalued or undervalued means that it is valued less than it would be under a better set of institutional arrangements. Both neoclassical and institutionalist economic theory offer some arguments along these lines, and the argument one accepts has important implications for the remedy one proposes.

Undervaluation in a neoclassical framework

Within an orthodox neoclassical framework that takes utility functions as exogenously given and assumes perfect markets, the notion of "undervaluation" of labor does not make much sense. It is helpful to review some of the specific ways this framework has been used to counter feminist arguments. But it is also important to recognize that a less orthodox application of neoclassical reasoning – one that does not assume perfect markets – offers some very plausible insights into undervaluation.

A utility-maximizing individual who decides to forgo some possible income by engaging in labor that offers no pecuniary return must, by definition, enjoy compensation in the form of greater utility. Their actions reveal their preferences; they cannot, by definition, be any worse off in utility terms than an individual earning higher pay. Jacob Mincer and Solomon Polachek implicitly use this reasoning when they suggest that women choose to specialize in less well-paying jobs because this is more consistent with their family responsibilities.[19] Similarly, Gary Becker suggests that women earn less than men because they devote more effort to housework.[20]

By stressing the impact of supply-side factors on the sexual wage differential, neoclassical economists downplay the role of demand-side factors, such as direct discrimination against women in the labor market. They also imply that observed differences in income are entirely voluntary. Victor Fuchs argues that women derive more utility from children than men do and are therefore more likely to assume responsibility for them. Although we cannot make interpersonal utility comparisons, we are left with the comforting thought that mothers must, after all, be just as happy as the fathers who fail to contribute to their children's support or care, even if they are living in poverty.[21]

The conviction that the sexual division of labor has no unfortunate consequences for women is a common feature of orthodox neoclassical theory, characteristic even of some feminist practitioners like Shoshana Grossbard-Schechtman.[22] However, this welfare-neutrality is challenged when the assumptions of orthodox theory are not met in the real world. Interference with markets and/or market imperfections, phenomena perfectly consistent with neoclassical theory, can lead to the undervaluation of certain types of work.

A good example is the "crowding" hypothesis formalized by Barbara Bergmann.[23] By this account, the collusive behavior of men leads to the exclusion of women from well-paid, highly skilled occupations. This crowds them into less well-paying jobs, and, by increasing the supply of their labor to these jobs, lowers the wage below that which would exist in competitive equilibrium. Women's work in general is undervalued.[24]

In this scenario, a demand-side problem (collective action leading to discrimination) creates a supply-side problem (crowding) that has nothing to do with a caring penalty per se. What may appear to be a case of caring labor (women explaining that they like low-paying jobs even though they pay less) is actually a post-hoc rationalization, because women actually have little choice. If this is the case, forms of caring labor performed by men are not penalized, and the remedy for undervaluation is simple: eliminate the male collusion that leads to overcrowding. As the supply of labor to predominantly women's jobs shifts back to the left, wages in those jobs should rise. We are left, however, without any explanation of why women are so often crowded into forms of work, such as childcare, teaching, and nursing, that we often associate with caring labor.

Another approach to undervaluation consistent with the neoclassical framework builds on the theory of externalities. Consider, first, the possibility that workers who provide caring labor enjoy positive externalities or receive "psychic income" from providing it. This would be consistent with both the altruistic and the obligation motives described above, and would increase the supply of labor to certain jobs, thus lowering their market wage. It leads to the same result as occupational crowding, but in this case caring workers lower the wage for non-caring workers.

Lester Thurow develops a useful analysis of psychic income, although he does not apply it to caring labor, or to gender differences in wages.[25] He argues quite persuasively that such externalities lead to market failure and inefficient allocation of resources (contrary to the traditional compensating differentials argument). Higher psychic income does not necessarily compensate for lower money wages, because of the lack of tradability between the two. But Thurow's conclusion offers only weak support for the notion that caring labor is undervalued, since psychic income is likely to make up at least part of the difference.

Another kind of externality-based argument focuses on third-party effects. For instance, I have argued that children are public goods and that caring labor devoted to their nurturance benefits taxpayers as a whole.[26] Sociologist James Coleman makes a similar point, though he arrives at very different policy conclusions (see later discussion, p. 226).[27] Similar reasoning could be applied to situations in which services that entail the care of other people are purchased by a third party. Children in daycare centers or schools do not hire their own teachers.[28] Patients in hospitals or nursing homes do not hire their own nurses. Workers are hired for their ability to meet the needs of clients, not for their feelings toward them. Workers with a predisposition for caring labor may provide important positive externalities, especially for dependants who appreciate, but cannot necessarily assess, the value of the emotional caring they receive.

Why would not employers, competing with one another to attract clients, try to internalize these externalities? They are beset by information problems. Apart from the fact that clients themselves may not know what is good for them, no one may be sure. Many parents who utilize daycare centers worry about the high turnover rate of daycare workers, which is likely to interfere with emotional bonding and truly caring labor. But it is difficult to say exactly how important such caring labor actually is to children's long-run development.

In his important work on the dependence of quality on price, Joseph Stiglitz argues that work that is difficult to monitor generally commands a higher-than-normal wage.[29] The difficulty of monitoring would seem particularly great in service jobs that involve looking after dependants such as children, the sick, and the elderly, jobs for which we would like to hire caring workers. Yet these jobs are generally considered poorly paid. At first glance, this circumstance might seem to exemplify a reversal of Stiglitz's logic, a case where employers actually hope to get higher-quality work by paying less.

Upon closer consideration, however, it simply calls for more careful specification of Stiglitz's argument, which applies only to situations in which work effort has a discernible impact on product or service quality, even though the work itself is difficult to monitor. In many personal-service jobs, both work effort and product/service quality are difficult to monitor, especially when they are being paid for by a third party. If consumers cannot discern the benefits of genuinely caring labor, they cannot pressure employers to hire genuinely caring workers.

Neoclassical approaches to the value of caring run the gamut: caring may be an innate predisposition that penalizes caring labor only in pecuniary terms. From a more feminist perspective, caring may be devalued simply because women perform it. Or caring may be underpaid because of externality and information problems. All these arguments are interesting, and they invite empirical research. An alternative non-neoclassical approach, however, focuses on what might be termed a "pre-market" problem.

Institutionalist approaches to undervaluation

Institutionalist economics treats norms, preferences, and values as partially endogenous and asks how they evolve. It also takes collective action seriously, asking how people may come to identify with, and pursue common interests within, social groups.[30] This approach, which encompasses the work of many non-economists as well as economists, offers an alternative to the neoclassical emphasis on self-interested individualism and contractual exchange. It also provides a distinctive explanation for the undervaluation of caring labor: Norms, preferences, and values have been socially constructed in ways that work against the interests of women as caretakers.

Barbara Bergmann applies an institutionalist approach to gender inequality when she describes the development of a sexual caste system based on the enforcement of gendered norms of behavior.[31] She emphasizes that social norms imposed on women interfere with what might otherwise be rational decisions. In "The Economic Risks of Being of Housewife," for instance, she offers a multitude of reasons why specialization in nonmarket work is economically risky. Bergmann challenges the anachronistic norm that assigns women this task.[32]

Some feminists working outside the discipline of economics focus on what economists term preferences, without necessarily calling them that. Consider Nancy Chodorow's formulation of object relations theory: women's specialization in parenting means that young girls, unlike young boys, are constantly in contact with an adult of the same gender. They may develop a less bounded, less oppositional sense of self, and be more concerned with other people's welfare.[33]

Even if such preferences are not inscribed in childrearing practices, they may be forged by the sexual division of labor itself. The performance of certain kinds of work may weaken the operation of self-interest. So Ann Ferguson implies in her discussion of sex/affective labor, the process of meeting other people's needs:

> The sex/affective labour that women do for wages and in the family has a distinctive character. By and large it involves mediating and nurturance skills that encourage women to identify with the interests of children, husbands or lovers, clients, patients, and customers, thus making it difficult for women to take an oppositional stance of the sort necessary to acknowledge one's involvement in an exploitative exchange of labour.[34]

Note that Ferguson does not argue that women are completely altruistic, or that they "naturally" have more interdependent preferences. Rather, she suggests that engaging in the tasks of caring for others elicits caring labor; with sufficient practice, men might develop such preferences.

Sociologists Paula England and Barbara Kilbourne also emphasize the possibility that women may have a less "separative" self, though they are less interested in the causes than the consequences. In their critique of neoclassical bargaining models, they suggest that women's greater commitments to children and family relationships weaken their individual bargaining power.[35] Similarly, both Torunn Bragstad and Kristen Dale argue that women internalize a norm of caring that results in a very inequitable division of household labor.[36]

The implications of such norms and preferences are by no means limited to the household sphere, as Paula England shows in her empirical analysis of compensable factors in job-evaluation for pay equity. Predominantly female jobs are underpaid partly because many of the skills required for these jobs are poorly valued. In her analysis of the relationship between the pay rates and types of skill required by detailed occupations, England finds a net negative return to nurturance. By contrast, the exercise of authority has a very positive impact on occupational pay.[37]

An orthodox neoclassical economist would, of course, retort that workers may enjoy nurturing more than they enjoy exerting authority, and the relative pay represents a compensating differential.[38] One might immediately note that men seem to love exerting authority. But, apart from this objection, why are women so much more likely than men to manifest the costly nurturing preference? While Becker and other neoclassicists resort to socio-biological arguments, the institutionalist argument is that nurturing preferences are essentially imposed on women.

An emphasis on the unfortunate outcome of a particular set of preferences presumes, of course, some criteria other than utility (or happiness) by which the outcome can be judged. Amartya Sen explicitly provides such a framework with his argument that utility maximization is not an appropriate goal for social welfare. He emphasizes values, rather than norms or preferences; individuals should have equal opportunities to develop their human capacities.[39] He argues that women have not only been denied such opportunities, but, in many cases, even denied awareness of their own oppression.[40]

Joan Tronto pushes the connection between caring and oppression even further in an observation that she makes almost in passing: A propensity to care may actually be created by conditions of subordination. Robbing individuals of opportunities to effectively pursue their own self-interest may encourage them to live "through others," using caring as a substitute for more selfish gratification. Tronto cites evidence that members of minority groups, as well as women, put more value on caring and sharing than on the pursuit of individual self-interest.[41]

In sum, institutionalist explanations share a common emphasis on a social construction of caring that penalizes women. But they offer many different and conflicting accounts of the underlying process. A feminine norm of care may be a kind of trick imposed by men who use it to extract extra care for themselves. Or norms of care may be socially necessary, but imposed primarily on women as a means of lowering costs to men. Caring preferences may be an almost incidental result of the social organization of childrearing or the larger sexual division of labor. Or they may actually be a by-product of subordination, in which case an end to subordination would bring an end to caring labor.

Obviously, these contending explanations have very different implications. The feminist project has always recognized the importance of consciousness-raising – challenging sexist norms, preferences, and values. But what exactly should take their place? The answer depends, in part, on what feminists decide about the value of care.

Equality or difference?

Neither economics nor any other social theory provides any basis for choosing among norms, preferences, or values on the basis of which ones are right, or proper, or optimal. The disorienting lack of any scientific compass probably helps explain why economists have avoided the territory. But feminists have necessarily faced this dilemma from the very outset. Should we recreate ourselves in a more masculine image? Or should we seek, instead, to eliminate the economic penalty imposed on distinctively feminine norms, values, and preferences?

An econometric metaphor may be useful. Imagine a multiple regression model in which the dependent variable is economic welfare, and the independent variables include, in addition to every standard set of structural and human capital variables, three vectors that measure the extent of femininity in norms, preferences, and values. Some of the variables are structural, some are individual, and all are unobservable. The hypothesis developed above is that there is a negative rate of return to femininity, and the dilemma, restated, is: should those who want to increase their economic welfare try to decrease their femininity or try to modify the rate of return?

In feminist vocabulary, these questions have been packaged as the "equality vs. difference" debate, shorthand for the issue of prioritizing equality with men vs. revaluing the ways that women are different from men. In this debate, most feminist economists have favored equality. "Caring" has traditionally been seen as a feminine quality that handicaps women in economic competition, especially by economists, like Barbara Bergmann, who are basically optimistic about the impact of capitalist development on women.[42]

The reasoning is straightforward: as long as women accept caring labor as their God-given responsibility or think that it is "unfeminine" to demand higher pay, they will be economically penalized. Therefore women must be willing to enter traditionally male occupations and compete more aggressively with men in order to improve their position. As Myra Strober puts it, women should not romanticize their "difference" from men, because this "glorifies existing stereotypes of female behavior."[43]

It follows that women should be suspicious of caring. Romance can be a misleading, an ideological construction that is used to trap women into unrewarding commitments. As Barbara Bergmann pointed out in a comment on a previous version of this paper, the Gershwin lyrics quoted above represent the dangers of sexual infatuation that can trick women into commitments as wives and mothers. They do indeed represent a risky form of sentimentalism. But why is the risk so high?

Partly because of the structure of an economy that rewards individuals far more generously and reliably for the pursuit of their own self-interest than for the genuine care of others. The connection between anti-caring and pro-market views is not incidental. It is suggested by the econometric metaphor: changing the rate of return on masculinity implies tampering with a market process. It also requires a collective effort likely to suffer from considerable free-rider problems and very high transaction costs. What that means, in ordinary language, is that it would be a very big hassle. Changing one's individual level of femininity or caring might be a bit easier (depending partly on one's personal propensities) because it does not require collective action (though it may be facilitated by the support that collective consciousness-raising can provide).

The moral legitimacy of markets derives from the claim that the individual pursuit of self-interest benefits everyone. Therefore there is no need to worry about the supply of caring labor. By contrast, an emphasis on rewarding caring has somewhat anti-market implications, simply because the market does not elicit caring. Ulrike Knobloch and Maren Jochimsen explain that "A whole economy organized according to the principles of housekeeping would be a caring economy. In such a caring economy the satisfaction of the existing material and nonmaterial basic needs would take priority over the production of new material goods."[44] This is not a market economy.

However difficult such a socialist feminist economy might be to achieve, some feminists would see it as preferable to capitulation to the masculinist principles of self-seeking competition.[45] Indeed, some argue that a market economy cannot exist without the support of a caring economy that coordinates the process of social reproduction.[46] The issue cannot be reduced to the simplistic terms of capitalism vs. socialism, or markets vs. central planning, because it impinges directly on a more practical issue: the relative roles of the market, the family, and the state in modern economies.

The strategy that feminists choose depends largely on the approach taken to the undervaluation of care. Interestingly, the most important differences do not coincide with the boundary between neoclassical and institutionalist thought. Those who adopt either (a) the conventional neoclassical presumption that undervaluation is not a problem or (b) the institutionalist view that caring norms and preferences are simply a means of subordinating women or a result of their subordination (that is, they fulfill no real function) will favor a reduction in women's caring behavior. These feminists will have little reason to worry about the need to regulate or limit markets.

On the other hand, feminists who adopt either (c) the neoclassical view that caring provides important externalities or (d) the institutionalist view that caring labor is a necessary task that has been unfairly and disproportionately assigned to women will fear a reduction in women's caring behavior. Such a reduction will have adverse consequences for the economy as a whole unless it is counterbalanced by an increase in men's caring labor. These feminists will worry about the inadequacies of markets, and will propose both limits and alternatives to them.

Public policies and caring labor

If you do not literally "value" caring labor, its supply may decline. But if you start running out, you cannot buy more at the corner store. Public policy could play an important role in addressing this paradoxical problem, but is constrained by the nature of caring labor itself. Passing a law stipulating that everyone must engage in a certain amount of unpaid work or childcare would not necessarily increase the supply of genuinely caring labor.

On the other hand, providing positive rewards, such as public remuneration for caring labor, could have the effect of reinforcing the existing sexual division of labor.

Feminist economists, all too familiar with trade-offs, should explore the costs and risks of such policies in more detail. But we should also recognize that debates over public policy often hinge on underlying values that, in the long run, influence both norms and preferences. How do we, ourselves, value caring labor? How important do we think it is to the full realization of human capacities?

The debate over pay equity is often described as a debate over the appropriate role of markets vs. administrative methods of setting wages. But those who are most enthusiastic about markets are those who believe that the supply and the value of female skills like nurturance are either exogenously given or relatively unimportant. If women are paid less for nurturing jobs they should simply look for jobs that pay more. Most advocates of pay equity quarrel less with the direct effects of the market than with the social and cultural devalorization of skills like nurturance.

A more complicated dynamic has emerged in discussions of the measurement of unpaid household work, long an issue among feminists.[47] A recent bill introduced in Congress, the Unremunerated Work Act of 1993, would require the Bureau of Labor Statistics to conduct time-use surveys to measure the unwaged labor of women and men, both in their homes and in their communities, and to include these measures in U.S. national statistics, including the gross national product (GNP). Many, but not all, feminist economists support the bill. Some critics, like Barbara Bergmann, argue that "anything that romanticizes housework and childcare is bad for women"; these are forms of work that should be "industrialized" because they can be performed more efficiently outside the home.[48]

Ironically, other critics of the Unremunerated Work Act put forward exactly the opposite argument, that analyzing "labors of love" in quantitative terms is demeaning. As Ellen O'Brien puts its, "[i]mputing a value to housework and adding it to the GNP necessarily privileges a particular conception of the relation between paid and unpaid work (or market and non-market consumption); namely, that which describes them as perfectly substitutable."[49] The reduction of caring labor to some common denominator with market labor threatens to impose a masculine perspective that privileges efficiency over affection, quantity over quality.

The same Catch-22 has discouraged feminists from demanding more public support for parental labor. Those who want to encourage women to be more ambitious in the marketplace fear that more support for working parents, such as paid parental leave or family allowances, would encourage women to stay home with the kids and lose seniority. The only pro-family policy that they enthusiastically support is the expansion of paid childcare.

On the other hand, many feminists who believe that nonmarket caring labor has intrinsic value fear that this value would actually be undermined by putting a price on it. As Julie Nelson puts it, "if support for parenting is considered 'payment' for children it implies that children are commodities; if it is considered 'compensation' for children it implies that children are burdens."[50] In other words, the only way to preserve the true value of this work is not to pay for it – another example of the paradox of caring labor.

Pro-market feminism looks with disfavor on comparable worth, counting housework, and public support for parental labor. This disfavor reflects not only the masculine tradition of liberal individualism, but also a certain confidence that women will not and cannot become too individualistic, or too "selfish" for their own good. Whatever the penalty, they will continue to express those aspects of their human nature that we associate with caring. Reading Bergmann, one gets the impression that women may be so prone to caring that they need to be prodded to be a bit more selfish.[51]

The opposite of pro-market feminism, with roots in the socialist as well as liberal traditions, is not necessarily anti-market, but defends the importance of nonmarket institutions that regulate and constrain market behavior. Hence a greater tendency to support comparable worth, counting housework, and support for parental labor. This support emerges less from concern about the short-run efficiency of markets than from worry about their long-run impact on norms, preferences, and values.

This approach requires more systematic discussion of the ways that caring labor *should* be valued. Many possibilities lie between the two stark alternatives of letting the market value it and refusing to put any monetary value on it at all. In pressing for more support for parental labor, for instance, feminists could reject the notion that it should be paid for on the basis of the "value" of its product.[52] Nor should parents be paid more for children who are more "difficult" than others. But they should be entitled to some minimum level of decent support for a form of nonmarket caring labor that benefits society as a whole.[53]

Similarly, in estimating the value of nonmarket work in the home, economists could carefully stipulate that any estimate of its market value can provide only a "lower bound" of its real value. Studies of comparable worth could challenge both workers and employers to reconsider the value of certain kinds of skills and better appreciate their positive impact on the quality of goods and services. And the reminder that markets do not automatically value care should serve as an impetus to find other ways to encourage and reward it.

Feminism has played an important role in challenging the patriarchal family, helping establish new rights for women and children, and demanding a new definition of family commitments that goes beyond traditional, hierarchical, and necessarily heterosexual models. How ironic it would be if progress on this front were neutralized by an individualism so extreme that it renders the best of family values obsolete. An economy based purely on the pursuit of self-interest does not leave much room for love, baby.

Notes

1. None of the inadequacies of this paper can be attributed to any lack of caring labor. Tom Weisskopf made many substantial contributions to the arguments presented here. Drucilla Barker, Barbara Bergmann, Samuel Bowles, Kristin Dale, Paula England, Shoshana Grossbard-Schechtman, Janet Seiz, Marianne Hill, Julie Nelson, Ron Stanfield, Diana Strassmann, and two anonymous reviewers offered important comments and criticisms.
2. The economics of Gershwin's "Who Cares?" is even more explicit: "Let a million firms go under, I am not concerned with stocks and bonds that I've been burned with," and "Who cares what banks fail in Yonkers?/Long as you've got a kiss that conquers."
3. See, among others, Ruddick (1980); Gilligan (1982); Waerness (1984); Noddings (1984); Tronto (1987, 1993); DeVault (1991).
4. Tronto (1993: 105).
5. For a sophisticated theoretical treatment of this issue, see Becker (1981b); for a textbook summary, see Frank (1991).
6. Nelson (1993).
7. In technical terms, I mean to say that in the short run the supply of caring labor is fixed and insensitive to price. Graphically, it can be represented by a vertical supply curve.
8. Titmuss (1970).
9. Although Becker has recently written a great deal on endogenous preferences, these are analyzed in an individualistic framework that largely ignores both the social construction of preferences and forms of collective action to enforce these. On this subject, see Folbre (1993).
10. For a relatively non-technical discussion of altruism, see Frank (1991: ch. 7).
11. For an interesting treatment of endogenous preferences, see Elster (1983).
12. Held (1990: 298).
13. Vaughan (1990).
14. Nelson (1992a).
15. Sen (1987).
16. Noddings (1984) actually argues the opposite, that "natural" feelings of care are the basis for the development of ethical principles.
17. See, for instance, Ferguson (1989) and Folbre (1994a).
18. Tronto (1993: 114).
19. Mincer and Polachek (1974); Polachek (1981). See also the telling critique by England (1984).
20. Becker (1981a: 56). Becker tends to emphasize the greater productivity of women in household and nonmarket work, rather than their greater preferences for performing it.
21. Fuchs (1988).
22. Grossbard-Schechtman (1993).
23. Bergmann (1986); Michèle Pujol (1992) argues that Barbara Bodichon sketched the "crowding" argument in the late nineteenth century.
24. Though Bergmann formally applied this only to the analysis of market wages, it can easily be extended to an analysis of women's nonmarket work in the home.
25. Thurow (1978, 1980–1).
26. Folbre (1994a, 1994b).
27. Coleman (1993).
28. Diana Strassman (1993) develops a more detailed critique of the limits of a choice-theoretic approach to the welfare of children.
29. Stiglitz (1987).
30. For a more complete discussion, see Folbre (1994a: ch. 1; 1994b).
31. Bergmann (1986).
32. Bergmann (1981).
33. Chodorow (1978).

34 Ferguson (1989: 97).
35 England and Kilbourne (1990).
36 Bragstad (1989); Dale (1994).
37 England (1992: 164).
38 England herself rebuts the compensating differential argument (1992: 69–72).
39 Sen (1984).
40 Sen (1990).
41 Tronto (1987: 647, 650).
42 See Chapter 1, "The Break-Up of the Sex-Role Caste System," in Barbara Bergmann's classic *The Economic Emergence of Women* (1986).
43 Strober, cited in Noble (1993: 35).
44 Knobloch and Jochimsen (1993).
45 Matthaei (1994).
46 Folbre (1994a); see also Beer (1993).
47 See Waring (1988) and Folbre (1991).
48 Cited in Noble (1993: 35).
49 O'Brien (1993: 16).
50 Julie Nelson, personal communication.
51 In her response to an early draft of this paper that included this statement, Bergmann replied, "You have got me right: I do believe there can be too much unpaid caring labor."
52 This has actually been proposed by sociologist James Coleman (1993).
53 See my "Children as Public Goods" (Folbre 1994b).

Bibliography

Akerlof, George (1982) "Labor Contracts as Partial Gift Exchange," *Quarterly Journal of Economics* 97(4): 543–70.

Becker, Gary (1981a) *A Treatise on the Family*, Cambridge, MA: Harvard University Press.

—— (1981b) "Altruism in the Family and Selfishness in the Market Place," *Economica* 48(1): 1–15.

Beer, Ursula (1993) "The Transformation of Gender Relations in the Transition from Socialism to Capitalism," paper presented at the workshop in "The Political Economy of Family Policy and Gender Relations," Johns Hopkins University, Washington, DC, August.

Bergmann, Barbara (1981) "The Economic Risks of Being a Housewife," *American Economic Review* 7(2) (May): 8–86.

—— (1986) *The Economic Emergence of Women*, New York: Basic Books.

Bloom, Alan (1987) *The Closing of the American Mind*, New York: Simon & Schuster.

Bowles, Samuel (1989) "Mandeville's Mistake: The Moral Autonomy of the Self-Regulating Market Reconsidered," unpublished paper, Department of Economics, University of Massachusetts.

Bragstad, Torunn (1989) "On the Significance of Standards for the Division of Work in the Household," unpublished paper, Department of Economics, University of Oslo, Norway.

Carr, Lois (1993) "Social Norms, Social Beings, and Individual Preferences," paper presented at the conference "Out of the Margin: Feminist Perspectives on Economic Theory," Amsterdam, The Netherlands, June 2–5.

Chodorow, Nancy (1978) *The Reproduction of Mothering*, Berkeley, CA: University of California Press.

Coleman, James (1993) "The Rational Reconstruction of Society," *American Sociological Review* 58 (February): 1–15.

Collard, David (1978) *Altruism and Economy*, New York: Oxford University Press.

Dale, Kristin, 1994) "What Has Love Got to Do With It?" paper presented at the meetings of the International Association for Feminist Economics, Milwaukee, July 29–31.

DeVault, Marjorie L. (1991) *Feeding the Family: The Social Organization of Caring as Gendered Work*, Chicago, IL: University of Chicago Press.

Elshtain, Jean (1981) *Public Man, Private Woman*, Princeton, NJ: Princeton University Press.
Elster, Jon (1983) *Sour Grapes*, London: Cambridge University Press.
England, Paula (1982) "The Failure of Human Capital Theory to Explain Occupational Sex Segregation," *Journal of Human Resources* 17(3) (summer): 358–70.
—— (1992) *"Comparable Worth": Theories and Evidence*, New York: Aldine deGruyter.
England, Paula and Barbara Kilbourne (1990) "Feminist Critiques of the Separative Model of the Self: Implications for Rational Choice Theory," *Rationality and Society* 2(2) (April): 156–72.
Ferber, Marianne A. and Julie A. Nelson (eds.) (1993) *Beyond Economic Man: Feminist Theory and Economics*, Chicago, IL: University of Chicago Press.
Ferguson, Ann (1989) *Blood at the Root: Motherhood, Sexuality, and Male Dominance*, London: Pandora Press.
—— (1991) *Sexual Democracy: Women, Oppression, and Revolution*, Boulder, CO: Westview Press.
Folbre, Nancy (1982) "Exploitation Comes Home: A Critique of the Marxian Theory of Family Labour," *Cambridge Journal of Economics* 6: 317–29.
—— (1991) "The Unproductive Housewife: Her Evolution in Nineteenth Century Economic Thought," *Signs: Journal of Women in Culture and Society* 16(3): 463–84.
—— (1993) "Guys Don't Do That: Gender Coalitions and Social Norms," paper presented at the meetings of the American Economics Association, Anaheim.
—— (1994a) *Who Pays for the Kids? Gender and the Structures of Constraint*, New York: Routledge.
—— (1994b) "Children as Public Goods," paper presented at the meetings of the American Economics Association, January 3–5, Boston, *American Economic Review* 84(2) (May): 86–90.
Folbre, Nancy and Heidi Hartmann (1988) "The Rhetoric of Self Interest and the Ideology of Gender," in Arjo Klamer, Donald McCloskey and Robert Solow (eds.) *The Consequences of Economic Rhetoric*, Cambridge: Cambridge University Press.
Fox-Genovese, Elizabeth (1991) *Feminism Without Illusions: A Critique of Individualism*, Chapel Hill, NC: University of North Carolina Press.
Frank, Robert H. (1991) *Microeconomics and Behavior*, New York: McGraw-Hill.
Frank, Robert, Thomas Gilovich and Dennis T. Regan (1993) "Does Studying Economics Inhibit Cooperation?," *Journal of Economic Perspectives* 7(2) (spring): 159–72.
Fuchs, Victor (1988) *Women's Quest for Economic Equality*, Cambridge, MA: Harvard University Press.
Gilder, George (1981) *Wealth and Poverty*, New York: Basic Books.
Gilligan, Carol (1982) *In a Different Voice: Psychological Theory and Women's Development*, Cambridge, MA: Harvard University Press.
Grossbard-Shechtman, Shoshana (1993) *On the Economics of Marriage*, Boulder, CO: Westview Press.
Held, Virginia (1990) "Mothering vs. Contract," in Jane Mansbridge (ed.) *Beyond Self-Interest*, Chicago, IL: University of Chicago Press.
Knobloch, Ulrike and Maren Jochimsen (1993) "Towards a Caring Economy: Ideas on the Ethical Enlargement of the Economic Method," paper presented at the conference "Out of the Margin: Feminist Perspectives on Economic Theory," Amsterdam, The Netherlands, June 2–5.
McCloskey, Donald (1994) "Bourgeois Virtue," *American Scholar* (spring): 177–91.
Matthaei, Julie (1994) "Why Marxist and Anti-Racist Economists Should be Marxist–Feminist–Anti-Racist Economists," paper presented at the meetings of the American Economics Association, Boston.
Mincer, Jacob and Solomon Polachek (1974) "Family Investments in Human Capital: Earnings of Women," *Journal of Political Economy* 82 (March–April), pt. II: 576–608.
Nelson, Julie (1992a) "Towards a Feminist Theory of the Family," paper presented at the meetings of the American Economics Association, New Orleans.
—— (1992b) "Gender, Metaphor, and the Definition of Economics," *Economics and Philosophy* 8: 103–25.

—— (1993) "The Study of Choice or the Study of Provisioning? Gender and the Definition of Economics," in Marianne A. Ferber and Julie A. Nelson (eds.) *Beyond Economic Man: Feminist Theory and Economics*, Chicago, IL: University of Chicago Press.

Noble, Barbara Presley (1993) "Male, Female Leadership Styles Hot Subject of Controversy," *Springfield Union*, August 18: 35.

Noddings, Nel (1984) *Caring: A Feminine Approach to Ethics and Moral Education*, Berkeley, CA: University of California Press.

O'Brien, Ellen S. (1993) "Putting Housework in the GNP: Toward a Feminist Accounting?," paper presented at the conference "Out of the Margin: Feminist Perspectives on Economic Theory," Amsterdam, The Netherlands, June 2–5.

Polachek, Solomon (1981) "Occupational Self-Selection: A Human Capital Approach to Sex Differences in Occupational Structure," *Review of Economics and Statistics* 63(1) (February): 60–9.

Polanji, Karl (1957) *The Great Transformation*, Boston, MA: Beacon Press.

Pujol, Michèle (1992) *Feminism and Anti-Feminism in Early Economic Thought*, Aldershot, UK: Elgar.

Ruddick, Sara (1980) "Maternal Thinking," *Feminist Studies* 6(2) (summer): 342–67.

Schumpeter, Joseph (1950) *Capitalism, Socialism, and Democracy*, 3rd edn., New York: Harper Torchbooks.

Sen, Amartya (1984) *Commodities and Capabilities*, Amsterdam: North-Holland.

—— (1987) *On Ethics and Economics*, New York: Blackwell.

—— (1990) "Gender and Cooperative Conflicts," in Irene Tinker (ed.) *Persistent Inequalities: Women and World Development*, New York: Oxford University Press.

Stanfield, J. Ronald (1986) *The Economic Thought of Karl Polanyi*, London: Macmillan.

Stanfield, J. Ronald and Jacqueline Stanfield (1994) "Where Has Love Gone?: Reciprocity and the Nurturance Gap," unpublished paper, Department of Economics, Colorado State University.

Stiglitz, Joseph (1987) "The Causes and Consequences of the Dependence of Quality on Price," *Journal of Economic Literature* 25(1) (March): 1–48.

Strassmann, Diana (1993) "Not a Free Market: The Rhetoric of Disciplinary Authority in Economics," in Marianne A. Ferber and Julie A. Nelson (eds.) *Beyond Economic Man: Feminist Theory and Economics*, Chicago, IL: University of Chicago Press.

Thurow, Lester (1978) "Psychic Income: Useful or Useless?," *American Economic Review* 68(2) (May): 142–8.

—— (1980–1) "Psychic Income: A Market Failure," *Journal of Post Keynesian Economics* (winter): 183–93.

Titmuss, Richard (1970) *The Gift Relationship: From Human Blood to Social Policy*, London: Allen & Unwin.

Tronto, Joan (1987) "Beyond Gender Difference to a Theory of Care," *Signs: Journal of Women in Culture and Society* 12(4) (summer): 644–63.

—— (1993) *Moral Boundaries: A Political Argument for an Ethic of Care*, New York: Routledge.

Vaughan, Genevieve (1990) "From Exchange to Gift Economy," paper presented at "The Other Economic Summit," Houston.

Waerness, Kari (1984) "The Rationality of Caring," *Economic and Industrial Democracy* 5: 185–211.

Waring, Marilyn (1988) *If Women Counted: A New Feminist Economics*, New York: Harper & Row.

15 Integrating vulnerability
On the impact of caring on economic theorizing

Maren A. Jochimsen

The provisioning of caring services is a social as well as an economic issue and it is increasingly difficult even for conventional economists to continue to consider caring activities *pre*-economic just because they have traditionally been performed in the informal realms of the economy and without pay. Caring services have long left the original realm of their provisioning and are performed in all realms of the economy – in the individually private sector of personal living structures (family), in the civil society, in the public sector and an increasing fraction in the market. Caring relations not only constitute a very fundamental, crucially important part of social and economic relations; they constitute the basis of any human activity – including economic activities (Jochimsen and Knobloch 1997). It is imperative, therefore, that economic theory should have an adequate theoretical concept of caring activities.

The story which conventional economic theory unfolds, however, is a story about the autonomous and the independent. No wonder that the science should have problems dealing with those whose autonomy is temporarily or permanently limited or entirely lacking. For "if [economists] persist in characterizing people as people only insomuch as they can be seen as autonomous agents – requiring that the world be fitted into [economists'] norms of methodological individualism – [economists'] modeling stops here" (J.A. Nelson 1996: 65).

Under such methodological circumstances, telling the story of young children, the frail elderly, the sick, and the disabled, who are dependent on steadily caring assistance, is difficult. The integration of caring situations into economic thinking poses the task and the challenge of conceptualizing a situation of human interaction quite different from the typical exchange situation. In studying caring situations, concepts such as limited autonomy, asymmetry, and dependency come into focus. Perspectives in economic theorizing are changed. New light is shed on the importance and role of gift and reciprocal relationships. Theoretical reasoning which emerges from these relationships sketches its own paths of analysis, taking its own directions and leading to its own theoretical (and political) implications.

This contribution takes exceptions to the supposed rule of autonomy and independence in economics as a starting point and explores in somewhat more detail the concepts needed to conceptualize caring relations. The article starts with a discussion of existing basic conceptual approaches to caring in economic literature (pp. 232–6). In a second step, the concept of an effective caring situation is proposed to integrate these approaches within a common frame of reference (pp. 236–8). In a third step, the impact of caring on economic theorizing is addressed (pp. 238–43).

Basic conceptual approaches to caring in economics

In general economics, both practical understanding and systematic use of a theoretical basis for the evaluation of caring activities are still widely dispersed. Caring activities are usually studied in the context of their often dominant institutional realm of provisioning (e.g. household work), following what are perceived as some of their eminent characteristics (e.g. unpaid work), or within theoretical approaches which deal with issues outside organized pecuniary formal (taxed) market coordination (e.g. all forms of subsistence work or informal work). Only a few authors have taken on the systematic conceptualization of caring activities in economics. Four basic conceptual approaches may be distinguished and these will be briefly sketched below. They find themselves in a curious and interesting field of tension characterized by the attempt to understand the provision of caring within the traditional analytical framework of economic science, on the one hand, and the recognition of the need to develop new and additional analytical tools in the conceptualization of caring, on the other.

Caring as the result of preferential choices

The study and interpretation of caring behavior through the lens of utility-maximizing, consistent, forward-looking behavior has been undertaken most explicitly by new home economics (e.g. Becker 1976, 1981, 1996; Gustafsson 1993, 1994). The conceptualization of caring as the result of preferential choices leads to two different concepts of caring based on two different sets of assumptions:

- a concept of caring between equally capable adults characterized by interdependent utility functions (economic altruism) of caregiver and care receiver;[1]
- a concept of parental care for children which assumes that the (dependent) care receiver figures as a durable consumption or production good within the set of commodities which render utility to the caregiver.[2]

Different from caring among equally capable adults, caring for children is not conceptualized as a relationship between two persons with interdependent utility functions; rather, the care receiver is conceived as a non-person, a family commodity rendering psychic (or other) income to the caregiver.[3]

The focus is on fully capable autonomous agents. Yet modeling caring with the tools of a theoretical approach based on assumptions of symmetry and autonomy has important implications in two respects. In both cases, potentially underlying asymmetries and dependencies do not come into the theoretical picture and are neither discussed nor analyzed – a circumstance which is especially unsatisfactory with regard to the conceptualization of caring situations for dependents. In the absence of a concept of asymmetry, autonomy and equality of caregiver and care receiver are presupposed. In the absence of a concept of dependency, autonomy and the possibility of voluntary entry into and exit from caring situations are assumed.

The absence of asymmetry and dependency in a concept shaping social interaction leaves this approach void of a concept of a dependent person. The exclusive conceptualization of caring as an intimately private household commodity confines this concept of caring to the informal, unpaid, private sphere of the economy. The product of caring is considered non-transactable. The motivational background remains ultimately unclear since moral and utility considerations are mixed. Self-interest, though in its altruistic version (attached self-interest), prevails.

Caring as the result of other-regarding choices

A concept which is able to counter the insufficiencies of altruism with regard to caring and still incorporate utility arguments is the concept of commitment as advanced by Amartya Sen in 1977 (Sen 1997b). Although not proposed as an explicit conceptualization of caring services, the concept focuses on other-regarding, not on self-interested behavior and may be applied to the analysis and understanding of caring – especially of caring for dependents (see also J.A. Nelson 1998).

Sen's concept of commitment operates on welfare and utility calculations, yet focuses on other-regarding rather than self-regarding behavior. Sen conceptualizes commitment as a *counter*preferential choice in terms of "a person choosing an act that he [or she] believes will yield a lower level of personal welfare to him [or her] than an alternative that is also available to him [or her]" (Sen 1997b: 92). By explicitly linking acts of commitment to a conscious *decrease* in the welfare of the actor, Sen is ruling out the possibility that the actor might be tempted by any self-interested welfare calculation. The point is that there is no *intended* maximization of one's own utility or welfare in actions motivated by commitment. With the concept of commitment, accordingly, Sen introduces a concept of activities which are primarily motivated by the desire to increase the welfare of persons *other* than the economic actor her- or himself (*ibid.*: 92).[4] There is, therefore, an important distinction between altruism and commitment.[5] It becomes possible to recognize "the indisputable fact that [a person's activities] can well be geared to considerations not covered — or at least not *fully* covered — by his or her own well-being" (Sen 1987: 41). Commitment operates on welfare and utility calculations, yet takes these to an other-interested rather than a self-interested perspective. As such, it is a challenge to economics since it keeps one perspective that is familiar to economists but changes the other.

If applied to caring behavior, the concept of commitment successfully captures the *other*-interested perspective so important for the provision of caring for dependents. Committed caring behavior provides security for the care receiver since care receivers (as well as society) can assume that committed caring takes place even if no psychic income is to be expected in either the short, medium or long term. Nor have long-term expectations of reciprocity to be assumed.

The preference theoretical point of view which constitutes the basis of Sen's concept of commitment, however, — although commitment entails a moral perspective (Sen 1997b: 93) — is unable to incorporate moral motives since moral categories are distinct from welfare considerations (Sen 1987: 41). There is, accordingly, an important difference between the preference-based concept of committed caring and caring services motivated by moral obligations or feelings of duty — yet these motives play an important role in the provision of caring.

Caring as the result of a caring motivation

Another group of concepts of caring activities in economics stress the crucial role of a caring motivation in bringing a caring situation about. I call these concepts *two-fold* concepts of caring because they distinguish two dimensions of caring and assume that two ingredients are needed for the effective provision of a caring service: the provision of an instrumental caring service (*instrumental* dimension) and a caring motivation (*communicative* dimension) (e.g. Tronto 1993: 104; Folbre 1995; J.A. Nelson 1998; Folbre and Weisskopf 1998). Motivations from which caring activities may spring include welfare as well as moral considerations such as affection, a sense of responsibility or obligation, intrinsic enjoyment, expectations of long-term reciprocity, a well-defined and contracted-for reward, fear of punishment stemming from coercion — ranged on a continuum from the most caring to the least caring (Folbre and Weisskopf 1998: 178, Table 1). A caring motivation is considered important because it ensures the production of the "joint product" (*ibid.*: 180), namely the "confirmation...that someone cares about them" (*ibid.*: 180) on the care receivers' side and the "warm glow" (*ibid.*: 181) on the caregivers' side, thereby capturing the non-commodifiable part of caring.

Two-fold concepts of caring take the concept of caring beyond the household and the family, beyond the neighborhood and the working place to which the Beckerian production of household commodities was conceptually confined. By declaring that motives crucially matter in the provisioning of real caring, they emphasize that "[p]recisely because it focuses on motives, caring [work] can apply to both men and women, the market and the family, production and reproduction" (Folbre 1995: 76). The *integrative* product of caring, as the joint product may be called more precisely, may be produced independently of the family context; it may be produced for strangers. The integrative product of caring is individually and personally generated, but the structures it enhances benefit the whole society. Through its inherently ethical dimension the integrative product refers to the societal and public dimension of caring situations (e.g. Folbre 1994: 254; Plantenga 1998). With the help of the two-fold concept of caring, demand and supply of care services might be specified into demand for communicative and instrumental caring services and the policy tasks reformulated (Folbre and Weisskopf 1998: 174).

However, focusing on the importance and role of the caring motivation or making it the defining characteristic of caring activities may run the risk of individualizing and privatizing caring as well as of sentimentalizing it. To think of caring primarily in motivational terms may lead to the reasoning that caring is entirely individual and no sensible statements are admitted in general on the effectiveness of a given caring situation or the failure to achieve a satisfactory level of caring activities.[6]

Caring as a constitutive act

Susan Himmelweit (1996) has argued that the dualistic treatment of motivation versus activity might presuppose too much of the neoclassical economists' emphasis on choice behavior. According to Julie Nelson, "the motivation/activity dualism is one angle from which to analyze phenomena, and not a problem in itself. The danger is in forgetting that there is another angle as well" (J.A. Nelson 1998: 16). For caring – especially the performance of caring services for dependents – is not always purposive activity, in the sense that people may have the choice of performing this activity or not. Not caring is not conceived as an option, since caring itself structures people's lives and the lives of many care receivers hinge on their caregivers. Especially in caring situations in which the care receiver is existentially dependent on the caregiver, "not caring is not usually an operational alternative" (Himmelweit 1996: 9).

The role of moral motivations in the provisioning of caring situations is widely discussed, prominently in the work of political philosophers (e.g. Noddings 1984: 5; Tronto 1993: 125–55; Sevenhuijsen 1998: 36–68; Kittay 1999: 50). Caring behavior is ultimately to be considered a social matter as well, and may reflect a sense of identity involving the recognition of other people's goals and the mutual interdependencies involved. The performance of caring, and especially of caring services for dependent care receivers, is inspired by values central to a person's character and identity as well as other intrinsic motivations and is not so much the result of choice behavior. It is rather a *constitutive act*, connected to the identity of the caregiver. The performance of the caring activity is not separated from life and self, but constitutive of the caregiver and not separate from his or her relations with other people.[7] As Julie Nelson puts it, one diapers the baby "because one is in a relationship of responsibility for the baby" and not primarily because of a motivation which "may strike one now but not tonight or tomorrow" (J.A. Nelson 1998: 15). To avoid the creation of yet another dualism between choice behavior and constitutive acts, Nelson proposes a "conceptual middle ground of[...]'influenced choices' or 'roles with some freedom,' in which [would be reflected] *both* the agent's constitution in connection with his or her social and natural environment and his or her individual agency" (*ibid.*: 15; cf. also 1996: 31–3).

The concept of an effective caring situation

Considering the above, a framework is needed for the analysis of the enormous range of caring situations, bringing the existing theoretical approaches together and integrating them in a common frame of reference. I propose to do so by working with the analytical construct of a component concept of a *caring situation*. The concept assumes the effective performance of a caring activity.[8] A caring situation is characterized by the presence of a specific unilocational *caring relationship* between a *caregiver* and a *care receiver*. The direct caring relationship between caregiver and care receiver has to be sustained by resources coming from the *provider* of the relationship (see Figure 15.1). The resources may come from within the caring relationship if they are provided by the caregiver or the care receiver themselves. They may also come from a provider or providing institution outside the caring relationship.[9]

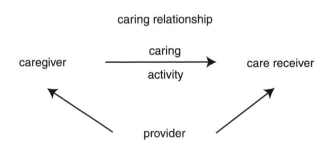

Figure 15.1 The caring situation

Like any other situation in which human action takes place, a caring situation may be conceived as being composed of three analytically separate components: the *motivation component* due to which a caring situation is initiated and continued, the *work component* due to which a caring relationship is established and maintained, and the *resource component* due to which a caring relationship is provided for and sustained in terms of material support and time.[10]

The main hypothesis behind the component concept is that the achievement of caring activities, in terms of satisfaction and fulfillment of caring needs, depends on the combination of all three components. The working together of all three components determines the quality, extent, and kind of the caring activity performed. Consequently, all three components have to be present and retain their function if an effective caring situation is to come about and to continue.

The work component and the motivation component without the resource component cannot sustain a caring relationship and secure a caring situation over time. The resource component will be useless in the absence of a motivated and capable caregiver. And, as important as the motivation component may be for any initiative to the performance of a caring activity, the caring motivation alone will neither perform the work nor sustain a caring relationship. For even a person with a strong caring motivation, the self-sacrificing caregiver, has to be capable of performing the caring service as well as securing the resources to sustain the person cared for and her- or himself. An (over)emphasis on one of the components, for example the motivation component, to the neglect of the others may lead to a distorted analysis of caring situations. The component concept of an effective caring situation takes account of this fact by conceptualizing and analyzing caring situations along the importance of all three components, respectively.

The concept of a caring situation is suitable to incorporate the study of all economic actors involved in the provisioning of a caring activity. The perspectives of the care receiver, the caregiver, the material and/or financial provider, and the institutions outside the caring relationship may be integrated in the study within a common frame of reference – a characteristic of the concept which is of special relevance when studying questions of economic justice (e.g. Fraser 1997b). The conceptual introduction of the provider in addition to the caregiver and care receiver renders the concept of a caring situation more complex. By widening the focus of the analysis in such a way, the concept can allow for bilateral as well as multilateral caring situations. Different caring situations in different realms of the economy may be taken into account.

The component concept itself is pre-institutional. Yet it provides a helpful framework to understand and evaluate the social organization of caring situations in general and the specific forms of institutionalization in the provision of caring in particular. With the help of the component concept three different basic structures underlying caring situations may be identified and analyzed:

1 The organization of the resource component *within* the caring relationship. In this case either caregiver or care receiver controls the resources sustaining

the caring relationship — as is the case, for example, if a single parent cares for a child or an elderly parent sustains his or her caregiving children.
2   The organization of the resource component *outside* the caring relationship. In this case an outside provider controls the resources needed to sustain the relationship. This is the case if, for example, the state pays a caregiver to care for a sick care receiver.
3   The organization of the resource component *partly inside and outside* the caring relationship. This is the case if, for example, the care receiver has to pay part of the wage of the caregiver or gets subsidies from the state or some other person or institution.

The respective structure of a caring situation has an influence on the asymmetries and dependencies involved. Different institutional arrangements may be evaluated as to the effect which their structure has on asymmetries and dependencies. If the material resources to sustain the caring relationship come from an outside provider, such as the state, a material asymmetry is induced between the caregiver and the care receiver with regard to the provider. The asymmetry in material resource control between the partners in a caring relationship and an outside provider enhances the possibility of material dependency of caregiver and receiver. It weakens their bargaining power and limits their options of voice and exit. One may say, therefore, that if caring situations are organized in such a way that the resource component is personally separate from the caring relationship, if work and resource component are personally split — as was the case, for example, in the typical bourgeois family with a gender division of labor — the material dependency of caregiver and care receiver on the provider may be enhanced. In this case, the direct influence of the caregiver — as that of the care receiver — on the quality and extent as well as the shaping of the work component diminishes, as the caring relationship itself is dependent on other persons or institutions for support.

The institutional arrangements which provide caring situations — whether in the informal or in the formal realm of the economy, whether the provider is a family member, friend, neighbor, government agency or government worker, or a worker hired on the market — may be studied with regard to their effectiveness and their sustainability, whether they take these asymmetries and dependencies into account, alleviate or aggravate them. The component concept therefore elaborates and enables the study of caring activities *across* the different realms of the economy in which they are provided within a common frame of reference.

The impact of caring on economic theorizing

The component concept helps to structure the analysis of caring situations within a common frame of reference. The integration of caring activities and caring situations into the theoretical body of economics, however, has far-reaching implications for economic theory. Its conceptual and analytical contributions constitute a complement, on the one hand, and an extension of the analytical tools of economic theory, on the other. It goes beyond the mere addition of a field of research to which the existing analytical tools and assumptions may be applied, but implies changed perspectives in economic theorizing. It equips economics with basic conceptual assumptions and concepts to analyze the human interactions fundamental to human provisioning and the economy and society as a whole.

Relatedness

In the systematic conceptualization of caring for dependents one has to go beyond the common assumption of independent autonomous economic agents in full command of their physical and mental capabilities and free to choose their entry into or exit from market exchange situations. The absence of asymmetry and dependency in a concept shaping social interaction leaves this approach void of a concept of a dependent person.

According to Joan Tronto, "definitive [about caring activities affecting others] is a perspective of taking the other's needs as the starting point for what must be done" (1993: 105). It is the needs of the care receiver which make the caregiver act.[11] The decisive influence of the needs and capabilities of the *other* to determine the kind of caring activity to be performed is especially apparent in crucial and undisputed caring situations for young children, the frail elderly, the sick, and the disabled. In these situations self-care is impossible, failing, or rather limited in relevance, and the neediness of the care receiver is extreme. Caring for dependents[12] calls for a shift in the perspective of analysis from the person performing the activity to the person affected by it.

From the point of view of dependents and people involved in their care the world looks different: independence, symmetric exchange, free choice, and the possibility of exiting appear as exceptional circumstances. Asymmetry, dependency, relatedness and interconnection, power and responsibility, and gift-giving are concepts central to the analysis of caring situations. In the analysis of existential caring situations as they are to be found in child- and eldercare, care for the sick and the disabled, the conceptual focus is shifted – from autonomy and independence to limited autonomy and dependence, from symmetrical starting positions to asymmetric starting positions, from voluntary choice to forced entry and barriers to exit, from unattached self-interest to commitment and moral responsibilities.

Furthermore, caring for dependents poses specific conceptual tasks to economic theorizing which are inherently due to the permanently or temporarily limited or entirely lacking autonomy of the dependent care receiver.[13] The dependent care receiver does not have that characteristic central to the concept of economic man in economics – namely autonomy in decisions, and choices which are based on the individual's preferences not on somebody else's. Limits to this principal capability to identify and outwardly manifest one's own preferences are, according to conventional economic theory, imposed only as regards the information available, not by age, or physical or mental health of the individual.

A conceptualization of caring involves a *connective* model of the individual. It presupposes that human beings are not separative (independent and disinterested) individuals concerned with their own self-interest in one way or another, but persons-in-relation, embedded in social relationships and institutional settings and capable of emphatic connections with others (England 1993; J.A. Nelson 1996: 68–71). Otherwise no behavior committed to the need of the other would be possible.

Asymmetry

The analysis of caring situations further assumes that caring situations encompass qualitatively and quantitatively asymmetric relationships as far as differences in the starting positions of the partners involved are concerned.[14] It also has to include the general assumption of the possible dependencies of the actors involved. From the point of view of the asymmetric dependency relation, the symmetric relationship appears as one possibility, as the special case of a caring situation where two equally capable partners meet.[15]

Three different kinds of asymmetries are to be distinguished:

- asymmetry in capabilities which refer to the respective capability of the caregiver and the care receiver to perform the caring service;
- asymmetry in the control of resources which refer to their respective power to control the resources needed, or to the incapability of the care receiver to provide any or equivalent returns;
- asymmetry with regard to the caring motivations which refer to the motivational background of the persons involved in a caring situation.

Dependency

Dependency, in this article, is understood as limited options to entry into and exit from caring situations – in analogy with the common understanding of independence in economics. The concept of independence in economics is closely connected to the concept of freedom of choice. The independent economic agent is an agent who is free to enter or exit an (exchange) situation. Dependency, in contrast, is to be understood as a force to entry and as a barrier to exit. Dependency therefore also reflects the – not necessarily voluntary – relatedness of the actors involved. The concept of dependency serves to capture limited options to entry into and exit from caring situations, which specifically include the care receiver's or caregiver's limited control over the extent and kind of the caring service to be provided.

In Western societies "dependency" is a highly ideological term. In a world ruled by assumptions and values of personal autonomy and individual independence, the term faces a difficult standing. Yet dependency has not always been negatively viewed. The term has undergone significant changes since the nineteenth century and its positive connotations have almost disappeared (Fraser and Gordon 1997). Research on issues of care, however, reclaims the power of the concept of dependency to capture essential human relations which exist alongside moments of autonomy (e.g. Kittay 1999; Sevenhuijsen 1998: chs. 1, 2).

Asymmetries in caring situations may possibly and actually lead to different forms of dependency. They may lead to existential dependency, material dependency, and motivational dependency, respectively, and – under specific circumstances – to their exploitable forms. The asymmetries and dependencies involved in caring situations may vary in degrees. They may be especially striking in the provision of caring for dependents, whereas they may be virtually absent in caring for kin or caring among equals. The degree of asymmetry involved, as well as the grade of dependency, is shaped by the following:

- the capabilities of the care receiver with regard to self-care;
- the existentiality of the needs to be cared for;
- the institutional organization of the access to and control over the resources needed to sustain a caring relationship;
- the ideological context in which the caring activity is provided.

The respective asymmetries and dependencies in a caring situation may be situated with the help of the component concept. They do not concern only the care receiver. They may involve the caregiver as well. Moral responsibility, for example, and the tendency towards sacrifice create what can be called *derived vulnerability* for the caregiver. The asymmetry which is at stake here is a motivational asymmetry between caring persons and non-caring persons within the caring situation itself or between the persons in the caring situation and those outside, society. Thus, the neediness of another can exert very strong social or individual power – particularly when it confronts the caregiver with a strong caring disposition. (This situation may be one of the main reasons why there has, for example, never been an encompassing, long-term strike of housewives or nurses.)

Due to their moral dimension (Sevenhuijsen 1998; Kittay 1999; Tronto 1993; Bowden 1996), caring situations witness a strong *producer loyalty*.[16] When caring motivations are present, spontaneous exit abruptly changes character: the applauded rational behavior of the alert participants in market transactions shifting to a better exchange situation becomes disgraceful desertion (cf. also Hirschman 1970: 98). Exit becomes uncaring behavior (e.g. M.K. Nelson 1990: 220), and moral considerations such as a sense of responsibility, duty, or personal affection result in sacrifice – i.e. in a prolonged one-way transfer of caring services at the expense of the caregiver's possibilities to self-care – or induce caregivers to stay in exploitative caring situations (Ferguson 1989: 97; see also Hochschild 1983: 150).[17]

Underlying power structures

Different from the concept of independence, where issues and questions of power and control only figure by their negation, the concept of dependency, on a very general level, is intrinsically connected with questions of power. Caring situations for dependents are inherently connected with, shaped and influenced by the power structures underlying them. Power here may be the physical capability and skill to perform a caring service. There is power with regard to control over and access to the resources needed for caring, as well as social and moral power as to who feels responsible for actually performing the caring work. The different kinds of power can be enhanced by societal structures (Radin 1996: ch. 11; Himmelweit 1997; Folbre 1994: chs. 1–3).

Split functions and one-way transfers

Caring situations are characterized by split functions and exhibit a typical nonmarket structure. Infants, mentally handicapped, or mentally confused elderly are not able to manifest market demand either in terms of material resource control or with regard to their capability to enter market contracts – other people have to do it for them. If the dependency service is bought with the help of a provider, the functions of demanding, buying, and consuming the service are split. This is the case, for example, when children buy a dependency service for their parents with the help of state money. The care receiver has no influence on the amount or the price of the caring services provided. Caring situations are multilateral situations of one-way transfers rather than the bilateral two-way transfer characteristic of exchange situations. Split functions, here, are the result of the care receiver's existential dependency as well as of the material asymmetry among the persons involved in a caring situation. They are not limited to the informal realm; the nonmarket structure of classical caring situations is also to be found in caring situations which are coordinated via the market.

The conceptual differentiation of caring situations from economic exchange situations and the step beyond assumptions of autonomy, symmetry, independence, and the absence of power open possibilities and options for the analysis of caring situations beyond their interpretation as exchange situations. Within such an analytical framework the grades and shades of existential, material, and motivational asymmetries which characterize most caring situations, and the resulting questions of the power structures among the persons involved as well as their existential, material dependency and social-psychological dependency can be made subjects of study and discussion. Also, coordination mechanisms such as gift-giving and reciprocity come to the fore (Jochimsen 2001).

Conclusion

Relatedness, asymmetry, dependency, power structures, split functions, and one-way transfers are concepts central to the analysis of caring situations. They are indispensable complements to the conventional box of analytical tools for economic analysis, since independence, autonomy and symmetry, and exchange would remain self-referential without their respective counterparts. Once studied more closely, however, the latter develop a theoretical impact well beyond being mere negations of concepts central to conventional analysis.[18] Asymmetry and dependency render the analysis sensitive to the power structures underlying caring situations and to the relatedness and vulnerability of the partners involved in them. With the help of these concepts, non-exchange elements so important in human interaction become detectable and visible. The use of sensitive tools in the analysis of caring situations is an important step in the direction of adequate longer-term political solutions – it is their precondition.

By the same token, the argument for the integration and incorporation of caring situations is not an argument for pre-(social) contract times[19] and the integration of caring into economic theorizing is no step backward – on the contrary. It is a step providing analytical tools to render economic science sensitive, attentive and responsive to situations different from exchange situations and a step closer to the integration of the full range of human interaction into economic theory. In this sense, it also renders analytical tools for a social contract theory which is able to integrate non-autonomous, dependent persons and allow caring situations to come about and prosper. After all, limits to autonomy in human life seem to be more the rule, and independent autonomy more the exception.

Notes

1 Caring between equally capable adults is mainly conceptualized in Becker's theory of marriage (Becker 1976: 205–50), but is also carried further in his writings on social interaction and altruism (*ibid.*: 253–94; 1996: 139–61).
2 These children presumably will be able-bodied, healthy children as "[c]hildren of many qualities are usually available, and the quality selected by any family is determined by tastes, income, and price" (Becker 1976: 175) and apparently not by genes, accidents, fate, inevitable dependencies, and the like.

3 The concept has been widely criticized, for example by Blau *et al.* 1998; Bergmann 1995; J.A. Nelson 1998.
4 Note that the comparison is between anticipated welfare levels, and therefore this definition of commitment excludes acts that go against self-interest resulting purely from a failure to foresee consequences.
5 It should be noted here that economists are not always clear about their understanding of economic altruism. Some understand altruism, not in the Beckerian sense, but as similar to Sen's notion of commitment.
6 To avoid such a one-sided emphasis, caring has been conceptualized by political scientists in terms of a practice (e.g. Ruddick 1989: 132–3; Tronto 1993: 104, 118; Kittay 1999: 32–3).
7 Cf. also Radin 1996: 105.
8 Accordingly, it presupposes the integral completion of all four phases of the caring process: "caring about," "taking care of," "care-giving," and "care-receiving" as discussed by Tronto (Tronto 1993: 105–8).
9 Conceptualizing a caring situation in such a way includes, of course, an analytical simplification, in the sense that in reality a single caregiver might have to attend to more than one care receiver (as is the case, for example, in families and nursing homes) and/or one care receiver might have more than one caregiver to look after him or her. Also, there can be different providers sustaining a single caring relationship (as is the case, for example, if family income and state subsidies go together in the provision of childcare).
10 The component concept is developed in more detail in Jochimsen (1999).
11 Although it is acknowledged that caring for others may also include the need of the caregiver to care, and in this special case may even be motivated by this need exclusively.
12 Kittay uses the term "dependency work" (1999: 30) for this kind of caring services, which I have referred to as "core or primary caring activities" in previous papers (Jochimsen 1998a, 1998b).
13 The point is not to refuse the care receiver his or her autonomy. The aim is to make sure one includes those care receivers who do not have any.
14 Cf. also Biesecker 1996: 11–13.
15 The concept of asymmetry – in allowing for shades and grades of asymmetry – may also allow for the symmetric case, whereas the concept of symmetry – as there are no shades or grades of symmetry – is not able to encompass asymmetric relations.
16 The argument of motivations preventing exit is also found in Albert Hirschman's deliberations on loyalty, which – though primarily addressed towards *consumer* behavior *vis-à-vis* firms and organizations, in contrast to the *producer* behavior which is in question here when studying the behavior of the caregiver – help to shed further light on the relationship between caring motivations and the possibilities of exit (Hirschman 1970: 82–3, 92).
17 Sacrifice may be understood as a form of motivational dependency, since caring behavior "does not require, and in fact forbids, that one go from the one extreme of neglect to the opposite extreme of self-sacrifice" (J. A. Nelson 1996: 71, fn.8). Julie Nelson argues that the self-sacrificing caregiver "who simply reacts to any and all demands, regardless of cost, is guilty of being irresponsible to at least one human being in her (or his) care: herself (or himself)" (J.A. Nelson 1996: 71, fn. 8; on the lack of self-respect and self-love, see also J.A. Nelson 1999: 50). The case of motivational dependency shows that, in fact, care for others and care for the self are strongly interlinked and any failure to pay attention to this circumstance may, over a shorter or longer period of time, create conflict and a moral dilemma. Own-account caring services and non-service caring activities serve an important function with regard to the comprehensive understanding of the provision of caring activities in general.
18 Cf., for example, Nancy Hartsock, who argues that a quite different kind of economic analysis results if the mother–child relationship is made the point of reference (Hartsock 1985).
19 Social contract theory conventionally assumes that society and economy are run by autonomous and independent economic and social agents in full command of their physical and mental capabilities and equally free to choose to enter or exit a social contract (Buchanan 1975).

Bibliography

Abel, Emily K. and Margaret K. Nelson (eds.) (1990) *Circles of Care: Work and Identity in Women's Lives*, Albany, NY: State University of New York Press.
Becker, Gary S. (1976) *The Economic Approach to Human Behavior*, Chicago, IL, and London: University of Chicago Press (paperback 1978).
—— (1981) *A Treatise on the Family*, Cambridge, MA: Harvard University Press.
—— (1996) *Accounting for Tastes*, Cambridge, MA, and London: Harvard University Press.
Ben-Ner, Avner and Louis Putterman (eds.) *Economics, Values, and Organization*, Cambridge: Cambridge University Press.
Bergmann, Barbara R. (1995) "Becker's Theory of the Family: Preposterous Conclusions," *Feminist Economics* 1(1): 141–50.
Biesecker, Adelheid (1996) "Kooperation, Netzwerk, Selbstorganisation: Prinzipien für eine faire und vorsorgende Ökonomie," in Adelheid Biesecker and Klaus Grenzdörffer (eds.) *Kooperation, Netzwerk, Selbstorganisation: Elemente demokratischen Wirtschaftens*, Pfaffenweiler: Centaurus.
Biesecker, Adelheid and Klaus Grenzdörffer (eds.) (1996) *Kooperation, Netzwerk, Selbstorganisation: Elemente demokratischen Wirtschaftens*, Pfaffenweiler: Centaurus.
Blau, Francine D., Marianne A. Ferber and Anne E. Winkler (1998) *The Economics of Women, Men, and Work*, 3rd edn., Upper Saddle River, NJ: Prentice-Hall; first published in 1986, 2nd edn. 1992.
Bowden, Peta (1996) *Caring: Gender-Sensitive Ethics*, London and New York: Routledge.
Buchanan, James M. (1975) *The Limits of Liberty: Between Anarchy and Leviathan*, Chicago, IL, and London: University of Chicago Press.
England, Paula (1993) "The Separative Self: Androcentric Bias in Neoclassical Assumptions," in Marianne A. Ferber and Julie A. Nelson (eds.) *Beyond Economic Man: Feminist Theory and Economics*, Chicago, IL, and London: University of Chicago Press.
Ferber, Marianne A. and Julie A. Nelson (eds.) (1993) *Beyond Economic Man: Feminist Theory and Economics*, Chicago, IL, and London: University of Chicago Press.
Ferguson, A. (1989) *Blood at the Root: Motherhood, Sexuality and Male Domination*, London: Unwin Hyman/Pandora Press.
Folbre, Nancy (1994) *Who Pays for the Kids? Gender and the Structures of Constraint*, London and New York: Routledge.
—— (1995) "'Holding Hands at Midnight': The Paradox of Caring Labor," *Feminist Economics* 1(1): 73–92.
Folbre, Nancy and Thomas Weisskopf (1998) "Did Father Know Best? Families, Markets, and the Supply of Caring Labor," in Avner Ben-Ner and Louis Putterman (eds.) *Economics, Values, and Organization*, Cambridge: Cambridge University Press.
Fraser, Nancy (1997a) *Justice Interruptus: Critical Reflections on the "Postsocialist" Condition*, New York and London: Routledge.
—— (1997b) "After the Family Wage: A Postindustrial Thought Experiment," in Nancy Fraser, *Justice Interruptus: Critical Reflections on the "Postsocialist" Condition*, New York and London: Routledge.
Fraser, Nancy and Linda Gordon (1997) "A Genealogy of 'Dependency': Tracing a Keyword of the U.S. Welfare State," in Nancy Fraser, *Justice Interruptus: Critical Reflections on the "Postsocialist" Condition*, New York and London: Routledge.
Gustafsson, Siv S. (1993) *Feminist Neoclassical Economics*, Paper 93–255, Tinbergen Institute: Amsterdam.
—— (1994) "Childcare and Types of Welfare States," in Diane Sainsbury (ed.) *Gendering Welfare States*, London: Sage Publications.
Hartsock, Nancy C.M. (1985) *Money, Sex, and Power: Toward a Feminist Historical Materialism*, Boston, MA: Northeastern University Press; first published 1983 (New York: Longman).

Himmelweit, Susan (1996) "Conceptualizing Caring," paper presented at the International Associaton for Feminist Economics Conference, Washington, DC, July.
—— (1997) "Why Do We Care about Caring?," paper presented at the ASSA meetings, New Orleans, January 4–6.
Hirschman, Albert O. (1970) *Exit, Voice, and Loyalty: Responses to Decline in Firms, Organizations, and State*, Cambridge, MA, and London: Harvard University Press.
Hochschild, Arlie Russell (1983) *The Managed Heart: Commercialization of Human Feeling*, Berkeley, Los Angeles, CA, London: University of California Press.
Jochimsen, Maren (1998a) "Towards a Concept of Caring Activities (1)," paper presented at the Political Economy Seminar at Harvard University, March 31.
—— (1998b) "Towards a Concept of Caring Activities (2)," paper presented at the Belle van Zuylen Institute, University of Amsterdam, December 4.
—— (1999) "Conceptualizing Caring Activities in Economics," paper presented at the EAEPE (European Association for Evolutionary Political Economy) Conference, Charles University, Prague, November 4–7.
—— (2001) "Kooperation im Umgang mit Verletzlichkeit: Eckpunkte der Organisation von Sorgesituationen in der Ökonomie," paper presented at the annual conference of the Institute for Institutional and Socio-Economics, University of Bremen, February 23.
Jochimsen, Maren and Ulrike Knobloch (1997) "Making the Hidden Visible: The Importance of Caring Activities and their Principles for any Economy," *Ecological Economics* 20, Special Issue: Women, Ecology, and Economics 2/1997: 107–12.
Kittay, Eva F. (1999) *Love's Labor: Essays on Women, Equality, and Dependency*, New York and London: Routledge.
Nelson, Julie A. (1996) *Feminism, Objectivity, and Economics*, London and New York: Routledge.
—— (1998) "For Love or Money – or Both?," paper presented at the International Association for Feminist Economics/Out of the Margin 2 Conference, Amsterdam, June; revised July.
—— (1999) "Of Markets and Martyrs: Is It OK to Pay Well for Care?," *Feminist Economics* 5(3): 43–59.
Nelson, Margaret K. (1990) "Mothering Others' Children: The Experiences of Family Day Care Providers," in Emily K. Abel and Margaret K. Nelson (eds.) *Circles of Care: Work and Identity in Women's Lives*, Albany, NY: State University of New York Press.
Noddings, Nel (1984) *Caring: A Feminine Approach to Ethics and Moral Education*, Berkeley, Los Angeles, CA, and London: University of California Press.
Plantenga, Janneke (1998) "The Economics of a Female Friendly Welfare State: The Case of Child Care Services in Sweden and the Netherlands," paper prepared for the Out of the Margin 2/IAFFE Conference in Amsterdam, June 2–6.
Radin, Margaret Jane (1996) *Contested Commodities*, Cambridge, MA: Harvard University Press.
Ruddick, Sarah (1989) *Maternal Thinking: Towards a Politics of Peace*, Boston, MA: Beacon Press.
Sen, Amartya (1987) *On Ethics and Economics*, The Royer Lectures, Oxford: Basil Blackwell.
—— (1997a) *Choice, Welfare and Measurement*, Cambridge, MA: Harvard University Press; originally published in 1982, Oxford: Blackwell.
—— (1997b) "Rational Fools: A Critique of the Behavioural Foundations of Economic Theory," in Amartya K. Sen, *Choice, Welfare and Measurement*, Cambridge, MA: Harvard University Press; first published in 1977, *Philosophy and Public Affairs* 6 (summer): 317–44.
Sevenhuijsen, Selma (1998) *Citizenship and the Ethics of Care: Feminist Considerations on Justice, Morality and Politics*, London and New York: Routledge.
Tronto, Joan C. (1993) *Moral Boundaries: A Political Argument for an Ethic of Care*, New York and London: Routledge.

16 An evolutionary approach to feminist economics
Two different models of caring

Susan Himmelweit

For an approach to economic behavior to be able to claim to be feminist, it must satisfy certain conditions. First, it must be able to explore differences between people's behavior, including that of men and women, and make the existence of such differences in behavior fundamental to its approach. Second, feminism is based on the notion that gender difference is structural, not incidental, to society. So in order to be able to analyze the position of women and men in society a feminist economic approach must be able to see differences between individuals and their behavior as structural – that is, dependent on relationships and interactions *between* people in systematically different positions in society. Third, the approach must be able to explain change, for the feminist project assumes that society and people's behavior within it can change: empirically, too, it is clear that we are living in an age of rapidly changing gender differences. Finally, it must be able to conceive the domain of economics and economic change sufficiently widely to be able to take account of all factors that have a significant impact on gendered behaviors within the economy.

The mainstream neoclassical approach to economic behavior fails on all four counts. It does not fulfill the first condition because it does not *require* the existence of different types of behavior or individuals in an economy. Neoclassical economics has a long history, stretching back to Marshall and beyond, of discussing economic processes in terms of the behavior of a representative agent. Differences in behavior across society are reduced to differences in the inherent preferences or initial endowments of individual agents, and these are incidental to the analysis; without affecting the basic structure of the model, all agents could conceivably have the same preferences and initial endowments (Kirman 1992).

Second, where agents differ it is only in these individual characteristics; there is no room for the existence of any structured relationships, such as those of gender, *between* agents giving rise to differences in behavior. Third, change figures in neoclassical theory mainly by its absence. There is a highly developed analysis of equilibrium conditions, under which change does not take place, but no standard technique for analyzing economic processes out of equilibrium. If one is trying to understand a world in which differences between individuals, including gender, appear to be both structural and continually reproduced in changing forms, not to be able to explain the connection between difference and change is a serious problem.

Finally, neoclassical economics was developed as a tool for analyzing market relations of mutually beneficial exchange and is based on the assumption that individual traders act in pursuit of their self-interest. While neoclassical analysis has been extended into other domains, the approach has great difficulty explaining why anybody takes part in perhaps the most significantly gendered behavior of all, that of caring for others. Caring is not usefully analyzed as the result of a choice based on self-interested utility maximization alone (Himmelweit 2002a). Indeed, to care for another, by definition, implies some motivation other than self-interest. People make choices about *how* they carry out caring responsibilities, but the process by which such responsibilities are assigned is one of family and community negotiation within societal norms and obligations (Finch 1989; Finch and Mason 1993). That does not sit easily with a model of actions chosen on the basis of given self-interested preferences; by definition, social norms are influenced by feelings about other people and responsive to the actions of others (Elster 1989).

Formally, the neoclassical approach can be adapted to incorporate feelings of social obligation and behavioral norms. These can be modeled either as constraints, reducing the set of available choices, or as preferences, weighting certain outcomes with the satisfaction of having fulfilled social obligations, detracting from others where the transgression of social norms produces a disutility. But, either way, if norms respond to the actions of others, so do constraints or preferences. This vitiates one of the main results of the neoclassical model of the economy, that all the effects of people's behavior on each other are mediated through markets (Himmelweit 2001).

Further, preferences could be altruistic and depend on the utility of others. However, to introduce such consumption externalities undermines the welfare theorems of general equilibrium theory, particularly in the more plausible case where an individual's utility depends only on observable aspects of another's life and does not require that one individual has inherent knowledge of another's utility function (Collard 1978). A theory based on showing how the pursuit of self-interest allows a market economy to work is, not surprisingly, thrown into disarray if it is asked to incorporate behavior that can only be interpreted within this framework as saying that behavior is not entirely selfish.

Further, none of these modifications of the neoclassical approach capture the fact that doing something because one feels one should is different from doing something because one likes its outcome. When people behave out of a sense of moral obligation, their assessment of different outcomes is not generally the determining factor in motivating their actions. The consequentialist approach of neoclassical economics, which assumes that people decide what to do by assessing the consequences of their actions, cannot leave room for the possibility that factors other than how their behavior will work out affect what people do. This, Elster claims, is the essential difference between rational action and behavior driven by norms; the former is concerned with outcomes, with consequences, the latter with the actions themselves: "Rationality is essentially conditional and future-oriented. Its imperatives are hypothetical, that is, conditional on future outcomes one wants to realize. The imperatives expressed in social norms either are unconditional, or if conditional, are not future-oriented" (Elster 1989: 98).[1]

An evolutionary approach

A more feminist economic approach would not set itself the task of fitting caring into the same motivational structure as market-oriented behavior, as though all behaviors were of the same type. Rather, it would consider a variety of different types of behaviors, with different motivational structures. It would be desirable to see the range of different types of behavior as open, so as to consider how new forms of behavior come about and outdated forms of behavior drop out, as cause and consequence of changing social norms. By analyzing the interaction between different types of behaviors, and the ways in which they are modified or replaced by new forms of behavior, one might hope to be able to analyze a wider range of behaviors and the processes by which they change.

This suggests that an evolutionary approach might be a better one for feminist economics to adopt. An evolutionary approach considers a population and the conditions under which some members of the population survive to reproduce themselves while others fail to do so and so drop out of the population. Such populations do not have to consist of people. Instead, such an approach could be applied to the population of all *behaviors*. Such a population would encompass a broader range of behaviors than those that can be modeled within the solely consequentialist approach of neoclassical economics. In particular, it would allow us to model behavior, including caring, in which individuals engage for reasons that do not entirely depend on their behavior's consequences, as norm-driven behavior was characterized above.

To call such an approach "evolutionary" draws on an analogy of the biological process of evolution by natural selection whereby organisms adapt and species evolve not by any conscious plan. Rather, a population changes because only the "fitter" members of it survive to produce offspring. This may be a useful analogy for analyzing behavior, such as caring, where people behave in a particular way because it accords with their sense of what it is right to do. Nevertheless, their behavior will be acted out in a social world and have material and other effects, for example on family income or their sense of self-worth, which may be crucial in determining whether that form of behavior continues.

In the biological model, change happens through natural selection. Individual members of a population do not change. Rather, the characteristics of the population change because individuals who are "fitter" in the current environment survive and reproduce themselves more frequently than those who are less fit. The characteristics of the less fit individuals who do not survive to reproduce are thus selected out and become less frequent in the population. Characteristics passed on by the survivors to their offspring become more frequent and, in a slow process of natural selection over many generations, will come to dominate the population. Further, this process is augmented by random mutation, so that new attributes continually enter the population too.

However, human behavior does not change by natural selection and random mutation alone. People can choose to modify behavior, to copy others or adapt their behavior for various reasons. In analyzing human behavior it makes sense to allow for mechanisms of change less blind, more consciously directed at the individual level, and therefore faster than natural selection alone. I shall call these sorts of evolutionary models "adaptive." Such models are still evolutionary, because the process of adaptation depends on "fitter" types of behavior becoming more numerous as less fit types of behavior are dropped or modified. However, in adaptive models people may accelerate this process by consciously choosing to modify their behavior, rather than just being passive recipients of randomly assigned new behaviors. For all evolutionary models, most of the interesting content is in the criteria of "fitness" by which behaviors survive and, for adaptive models alone, in the process by which behaviors that do not survive are modified.

So how such a model works out depends on the specific criteria of fitness used. More than purely material criteria will be needed to model the spread of behavior, such as caring, that is informed by social norms. In particular, within this framework if social norms affect behavior it must be that one criterion of fitness for a form of behavior is the extent to which it is endorsed by current social norms. If it is also true that the strength of social norms depends on the extent to which behavior supports them, then whether any particular type of behavior becomes more prevalent depends, at least in part, on the extent to which other people's behavior appears to endorse the same social norms. An adaptive model of behavior based on social norms is therefore likely to incorporate some degree of density dependence, in which the more prevalent a behavior is, the more likely it is to spread, because the norms that support it are strengthened by others behaving in accordance with those norms.[2] This produces a form of positive feedback, which could be the cause of the widespread cultural differences to be found in caring and other norm-dependent behavior.

This illustrates one of the major advantages of using evolutionary models to understand behavior that varies across cultures. All evolutionary models posit two-way causation between effects at the population level and individual behavior. In particular, for economists they provide an alternative to the methodological individualism of neoclassical economics, in which an analysis of micro-level behavior is supposed to be both necessary and sufficient to explain macro-level phenomena. In such models macro-level phenomena such as culture can only be the result of exogenous individual differences. This means that cultural change cannot be understood as an endogenous process and has to be seen as the result of exogenous changes in individual preferences. Evolutionary models, by contrast, explore processes of selection and modification that link the individual and societal levels, and can explain how individual behavior is both shaped by and shapes population-level phenomena, such as cultural difference.

Evolutionary models have successfully been applied to the analysis of technological change, where a similar concern with processes of diffusion of ideas and how new forms of behavior arise is relevant. There is something to be learned from these models in analyzing social change. Evolutionary models of technological change concentrate on how new forms of behavior (both new techniques of production and search routines for developing them) come to be adopted and how their adoption changes the environment in which subsequent behavior takes place (Nelson 1995). In these models the identities of economic agents are constituted by the rules that govern whether and how their behavior changes (Vromen 1997).

Rather than seeing technological change as exogenous to the system, as traditional neoclassical models do, in these models cumulative change can arise endogenously from a similar positive feedback process to that described above for cultural change (except that it is profitability that determines fitness rather than whether behavior is supported by current social norms). New ideas are continuously created, but only those that are profitable survive to be adopted as new technologies. Which these are will depend on the environment, which includes the behavior of others. Thus the behavior of agents adapts to the environment, which is in itself an effect of the behavior of other agents (Metcalfe 1988, 1994). For example, if the benefits of adopting a particular technology increase with the number of other adopters, positive feedback generates path-dependence and may "lock in" a whole industry to a technology that is not in any objective sense superior to its competitors (Arthur 1989, 1994; David 1985). For example, VHS is now the standard video-recording format not because of any inherent technical superiority, but because it established an early lead in the market over its rivals. In these situations either a single type of behavior (use of a technology) becomes dominant throughout the market, as in the production of video recorders, or distinct clusters develop whose members adopt a similar type of behavior to each other but behave differently from members of other clusters.

This seems a fruitful analogy for modeling caring behavior, where people are engaged in a process of both working out what to do in particular circumstances and constructing their own moral identities (Jordan *et al.* 1994; Duncan and Edwards 1997). In these processes they are influenced not only by their own personal and familial experiences, but also by social or group norms, understandings of gendered individual and familial responsibilities that are shared by a group of mutually influential people. These norms can be seen as providing guidelines by which people work out what to do and assess their own behavior (Finch 1989; Finch and Mason 1993). But such group norms are themselves shaped by the behavior of others in the group in similar circumstances.

The following two sections of this paper give examples to illustrate how an adaptive approach might be used to model behavior that is influenced by norms. The first is a model of how behavior and norms influence each other in a situation where there are just two potential courses of action and two competing social norms (pp. 252–7). The second is a model of how two competing motivations or *types of behavior* interact with each other and thus have mutually dependent growth paths (pp. 257–63). In terms of the second model, the two "courses of action" in the first model are both examples of the same "type of behavior" – that is, they are both examples of behavior motivated by mothers' care for their children. Thus the first model is a partial model, looking at how particular courses of action are chosen in a particular situation, while the second is a general model, in that it looks at competition between aggregate types of behavior covering all situations. I shall call them my "micro" and "macro" models, respectively, although the distinction between the two bears little relation to that traditionally drawn in economics.

A "micro" model

This model considers a situation in which there are two competing social norms, each of which supports a particular course of action. We can take as examples of such competing social norms two different ideas of a mother's responsibility to her children. These are:

- *Norm 1*: that a mother should be on hand whenever needed to deliver personal care to her children.
- *Norm 2*: that a mother should provide as high a material standard of living for her children as she can.

These are competing norms to which mothers are subject. Mothers in general will be subject to both norms, but we shall assume that at any point in time an individual mother will feel one more strongly than the other.

In practice, there are a variety of different ways of fulfilling each of these norms and some courses of action may allow both norms to be at least partially fulfilled. But, to illustrate the model, let us assume that the norms are incompatible and that there is only one course of action a mother can take to fulfill each norm, i.e.:

- *Course of action 1*: not take employment, in order to be on hand for her children whenever needed.

- *Course of action 2*: take employment, to give her children the highest feasible standard of living.

So course of action 1, not taking employment, is in accordance with norm 1, believing that mothers should be on hand for their children whenever needed; and course of action 2, taking employment, is in accordance with norm 2, believing that mothers should provide their children with the highest feasible standard of living. This does not mean that no mother who feels norm 1 more strongly than norm 2 will take employment; nor does it mean that every mother who takes employment necessarily feels more subject to norm 2. There are factors other than these norms which affect people's actions. However, it does mean that each course of action is in accordance with a particular norm, and that people taking a particular course of action are giving support to the corresponding norm at a societal level. Those mothers who do not take employment are in their behavior conforming to, and thus strengthening, norm 1, whereas those who take employment are behaving in accordance with, and thus strengthening, norm 2.

Because there are only two courses of action and two norms to be considered, the situation can be represented in two dimensions. In Figure 16.1 average behavior is represented along the horizontal axis, with the proportion of mothers taking course of action 1 – that is, not taking employment – measured from left to right. This means that, symmetrically, the proportion adopting the other course of action, course of action 2, taking employment, is measured from right to left.

The vertical axis can be used to measure the relative strength of the norms – that is, the proportion of mothers who think mothers in general should behave according to each norm (whether or not they themselves actually do so). Along this axis, the proportion of mothers believing that it is more important for mothers to be on hand whenever needed to deliver personal care to their children, norm 1, is measured upwards; and the proportion believing that it is more important for mothers to provide the highest possible material standard of living for children, norm 2, is measured down the vertical axis.

To make this a dynamic model, two assumptions need to be made about the relationship between norms and behavior:

- *Assumption 1*: the strength of a norm depends positively on the proportion of people who conform to it. As a greater proportion of people behave in accordance with a norm, more people feel they should do so.
- *Assumption 2*: behavior tends towards the strength of the norm – that is, when the proportion of people who believe in a particular norm exceeds the proportion whose behavior conforms to it, more people will be induced to behave in accordance with that norm. Where norms are weaker than actual behavior, conformity to the norm will fall.

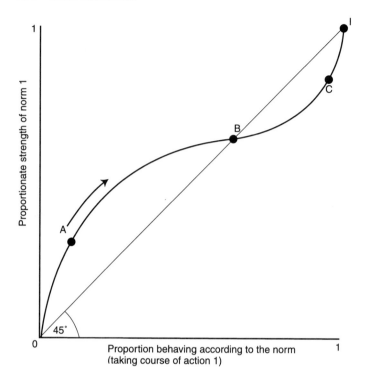

Figure 16.1 Norms and behavior with sluggish norms

Source: adapted from Hargreaves-Heap (1992) and Himmelweit (2001).

The curve in Figure 16.1 traces the relative strength of the two norms as a function of the proportion of the population behaving in conformity to each. The "response" curve slopes upward by assumption 1, that the strength of a norm depends positively on the proportion of people conforming to it. Where the curve crosses the 45° line, at B, the proportion of people behaving according to each norm equals the proportion believing most strongly in that norm. This makes B an equilibrium, by assumption 2.

In Figure 16.1, norms are sluggish around B; this means that the relative strength of the two norms does not change much in response to changes in behavior. Because the response curve is flatter than the 45° line around B, any change in the proportion behaving in accordance with the two norms results in a smaller proportionate change in the relative strength of the two norms. This makes B a stable equilibrium, and from A or C norms drive behavior towards B, by assumption 2, that behavior tends towards the strength of the norm. At A a greater proportion of people believe more strongly in norm 1 than the proportion who behave according to it, while at C a greater proportion believe more strongly in norm 2 than behave according to it. In both cases, then, the process by which behavior adjusts towards the norm results in convergence on B.

But this only happens if norms are sluggish at the equilibrium. In Figure 16.2 norms are volatile and a change in behavior around D has a larger than proportionate effect on the strength of the norm. D is an unstable equilibrium because the norm curve at D is steeper than the 45° line. This means that to the left of D, at E say, where a smaller than equilibrium proportion of mothers behave according to norm 1, the relative strength of norm 1 is nevertheless less than the proportion of mothers behaving according to it. So the numbers doing so will fall, weakening further support for norm 1. Similarly, to the right of D, at F say, where a larger than equilibrium proportion of mothers behave according to norm 1, the relative strength of the norm is greater than the proportion of mothers behaving according to it, and so the numbers doing so will rise, strengthening norm 1 further. (This story could have been told equally well in terms of the effects on norm 2.) In Figure 16.2 there are only two stable equilibria, in each of which the whole population conforms to one norm or the other. Starting from D, a bandwagon effect can be set off in either direction, through changing norms changing behavior changing norms, etc.

The eventual outcome is path-dependent. From an initial equilibrium at D, the eventual outcome depends on the direction in which the first move from D happened. Was there an initial jolt to the previous equilibrium that made mothers more likely to take employment, such as a sudden increase in male unemployment? Or was the initial jolt provided by an event that made people more likely to approve of mothers as financial providers, perhaps the publication of a new survey showing how important family income was to children's future success? In either case, from D such events will move behavior towards a greater proportion of mothers in employment and norms towards greater support for norm 2, with which such behavior accords, until eventually equilibrium is achieved again. In Figure 16.2 this can only happen when all mothers are in employment and everyone believes norm 2 more strongly than norm 1, but a different response curve might cross the 45° line again above the origin, giving a less uniform equilibrium.

Conversely, the initial jolt from equilibrium at D may decrease the proportion of mothers in employment or increase the strength of norm 1. The former could happen if there was a cutback in public services, throwing women out of work and making their presence at home more needed; the latter perhaps if a spate of media attention to childcare scandals resulted in a moral panic about parents entrusting children to childcare. In either case, norms and behavior will subsequently change together to intensify the effect of the initial change until eventually equilibrium is achieved again. In Figure 16.2 this happens only when

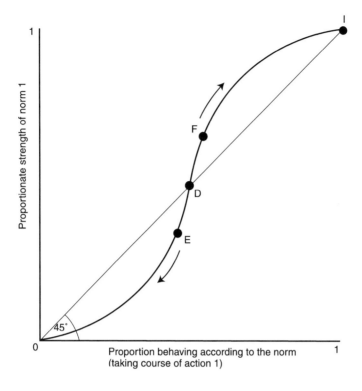

Figure 16.2 Norms and behavior with volatile norms
Source: adapted from Hargreaves-Heap (1992) and Himmelweit (2001).

no mothers are in employment and everyone believes norm 1 more strongly than norm 2, but again a different response curve might cross the 45° line again lower down, giving a less uniform equilibrium.

Such processes of positive feedback can potentially generate multiple equilibria in a model like this. The eventual outcome is then path-dependent; it depends on historical events. A similar endogenous process involving positive feedback and path-dependence can arise whenever there are alternative courses of action and, as we saw with technology, may generate "lock-in" to particular solutions, as choices made by others change the availability and desirability of different courses of action. This need not depend on social norms alone. For example, if out of a range of childcare solutions more people begin to use workplace nurseries where they are available, this may lead other employers to create more nursery places, reducing their cost and providing parents with experience to assess whether their children might benefit from nursery care. Such positive feedback may lock in that caring solution at the expense of others, say child-minding or community nurseries, which then become relatively more costly and have less chance to demonstrate their benefits to parents.

Such path-dependence can explain why caring behavior varies across localities and cultures. It also provides a reason why policymakers cannot see their role as purely providing what people want, because what people choose to do will depend on what others have chosen to do and there is no inherent reason to assume that what becomes the most popular choice is in any a priori sense superior (Sunstein 1997). Policymakers will need to make some judgment about the relative merits of different forms of care to ensure that "less desirable" forms of care do not lock out preferable ones. Moreover, the possibility of such processes reducing the choices available to parents needs to be taken into account in assessing future directions of change. Another implication is that behavior requiring cultural change, for example change in the gender division of caring within households, may be difficult to initiate but may take off rapidly after a certain threshold has been reached.

A "macro" model

As well as looking at the particular courses of action adopted in particular situations, evolutionary theory can also be used to look at types of behavior and social motivations at a more general level. These form another concern of policymakers and social commentators, often expressed in terms of a growing "parenting deficit" or "caring deficit," loosely defined notions that play a key role in a particular story told about the decline of community values in modern times (Elshtain et al. 1992; Folbre 1994). The story runs along the following lines: because of the growing penetration of the market into family life, behavior by parents, and by mothers in particular, is less likely to be motivated by an ethic of care and more likely to be motivated by self-interest. On the assumption that a caring motivation is necessary to the delivery of effective care, this means that children, and by extension others needing care, are being less well looked after than they used to be. Similar stories are told about other groups in society, for whom nonmarket based norms are being eroded by the growing pull of market-oriented behavior, such as state employees losing their commitment to public service or artisans failing to take pride in their work. In these stories, what are being contrasted are not just individual courses of actions in particular circumstances. Rather a whole type, or population, of behaviors based on a common type of motivation, such as behavior motivated by an ethic of care, is being contrasted with another population of actions based on a different type of motivation, such as behavior motivated by self-interest.

So far I have only considered using evolutionary models to model competing forms of behavior within a particular limited context. In the "micro" model considered earlier, two options, to stay at home or to take a job and earn money, were direct competitors as possible *courses of action* to solve a particular dilemma: how a mother should best fulfill her responsibilities to her child.

However, we can also consider the issue of competing *modes of behavior*, where modes of behavior are types of behavior grouped together by certain characteristics, such as their motivating force, and exemplified by particular courses of action. In the example given earlier, both courses of action could be seen as motivated by a sense of doing what is right as a mother and thus examples of the same mode of behavior.

In this light, consider two modes of behavior: one that we can call "caring" behavior, broadly behavior motivated by an ethic of care for others. Compare this with another mode of behavior, "self-interested" behavior, based on the rational calculation of the consequences of actions to the individual unit to which the decisionmaker belongs. These two modes of behavior can be seen as examples of alternative motivating forces for behavior, which may or may not in practice be in competition with each other.

Some modes of behavior may be specific to particular sorts of people. For example, the ethic of care may not appeal to certain people at all and therefore none of their behavior may be motivated by it. More plausibly, people may adopt multiple, possibly conflicting, identities, and it is to these that different modes of behavior appeal. Identities held by the same person could include "good worker," "careful shopper," or "dutiful daughter." Which modes of behavior thrive will then vary according to the range and timing of these portfolios of identities. Thus, a woman in her working identity may be more inclined to adopt courses of action that exemplify a mode of behavior based on a norm of good service, while in her shopping identity she may choose courses of action by the rational calculation of consequences for her family, and as a dutiful daughter may be more concerned with the demonstrative effect of different courses of action.

Whether modes of behavior are in competition with each other will then depend on the extent to which they appeal to similar identities and the extent to which such identities overlap, i.e. are held by the same person. If only women are supposed to be caring and only men to adopt identities on which market-based norms thrive, then there is no direct competition between these two modes of behavior. Indeed, in the traditional model of a male-breadwinner/female-carer household gendered identities do not overlap. The behavior of the wife, based on an ethic of care for her husband and children, complements the husband's pursuit of the family's self-interest in the market, so these two modes of behavior are mutually reinforcing. In a less gendered society, where both masculine and feminine identities may be open to both modes of behavior, there will be more competition between them as they compete for the hearts and minds of the *same* people.

Modes of behavior encompassing many different courses of action can be seen as analogous to biological species consisting of many individual organisms. Within biology, it is ecological theory that considers interactions between different species.[3] Whether two species are in competition depends on whether they need to exploit the same resources. Niche separation occurs when species specialize in their use of resources. Species that have (or have made) different ecological niches are not in competition with each other (Silvertown 1996).

For modes of behavior, a significant limiting resource is people's time. Nearly all courses of action take time, and there are limits to the extent to which they can be carried out simultaneously. There is therefore competition for the resource of time between courses of action. However, if modes of behavior specialize in the identities to which they appeal, then this competition is reduced, as happens when men's and women's time are not interchangeable resources. The traditional separation of gender identities functions, therefore, like a niche separation, with caring behavior having female identity as its specialist niche, and male identity providing such a niche for self-interested market-oriented behavior.

Time may not be the only limiting resource for courses of action; there may also be other resource limitations, such as those of space or money. As well as competing directly to exploit scarce resources, modes of behavior may also compete by interfering with each other. So, for example, by characterizing caring behavior as misguided, the denigration of "do-gooders" may be effective in increasing the population of courses of action based on self-interest at the expense of those based on an ethic of care.[4]

Interactions between two species or modes of behavior can be classified according to the effect each has on the other. Table 16.1 summarizes four possible interactions (leaving out borderline cases in which just one species/mode of behavior has no effect on the other). The terms used in the table imply nothing in themselves about how these interactive effects occur; as we have seen, competitive effects may occur for a variety of different reasons. One species "gains" from the presence of another species if its numbers increase more in the presence than in the absence of that second species. Which type of interaction holds between any two particular species will depend on the environment; for example, prey can become a competitor if both predator and prey depend on the same water supply and water becomes a scarce resource. So the nature of the interaction between two species may change according to circumstances and will be influenced by factors external to that interaction.

We can use this biological analogy to consider the interaction between the two modes of behavior considered above: "caring" behavior, motivated by an ethic of care for others, and "self-interested" behavior, based on the rational calculation of the interests of the individual unit to which the decisionmaker belongs. It was suggested above that in a society characterized by the traditional male-breadwinner/female-carer household, where gendered identities do not overlap, these two modes of behavior are mutually reinforcing, an interaction

Table 16.1 Interactions between species (or modes of behavior) classified by advantage or disadvantage to each species

Symbol	Type of interaction	Who gains or loses
0/0	"independence"	neither species affects the other
+/+	"mutualism"	both species gain
+/−	"predation / parasitism"	one species gains, the other loses
−/−	"competition"	both species lose

Source: adapted from Silvertown (1996: 18).

characterized as mutualism (+/+) in Table 16.1. This is a stronger claim than that they do not compete, which would be characterized as independence, a (0/0) interaction. Rather, the modes of behavior are mutually reinforcing because market-oriented behavior by men is both supported by and enables caring behavior by women. There is little competition between the two types of behavior because there is an absolute gender division of tasks, so that the modes of behavior do not compete for the resource of time. Time is a gendered resource and each mode of behavior has its own niche. In a society characterized by male-breadwinner/female-carer households, men's and women's time are specialized resources; market-oriented actions require the former, caring actions the latter. The two modes of behavior are therefore not in competition.

However, if women can earn money for their families as well as provide care, these two modes of behavior start competing with each other for the resource of women's time. Market-oriented and caring behavior may continue to depend upon each other, but they are now also in competition for some resources. Whether the dependence of the caring mode of behavior on the market-oriented mode is any less than it used to be is a moot point. Time-use surveys indicate that the amount of time spent on market-oriented behavior has increased at the expense of domestic activities. However, the content of these domestic activities seems to have changed, so that an increasing amount of that time is spent on directly caring activities as opposed to the more physical types of domestic work, such as cooking and cleaning (Himmelweit 1995). How these different effects balance out will determine where in Table 16.1 the interaction between the two species is located.

The relationship between the two modes of behavior does not have to be symmetrical. Assuming that competition for women's time has made the net effect of market behavior on caring behavior negative, there are two possible interactions depending on the net effect in the other direction:

- *Interaction 1*: market-oriented behavior might still benefit from caring behavior. This is the (+/−) interaction, characterized as predation or parasitism.
- *Interaction 2*: the two might be in net competition with each other (−/−).

We can consider predation/parasitism as the more likely first step in a movement from mutualism, since it would be unlikely that the interactive effects had switched simultaneously from + to − in both directions at the same time. The language of predation or parasitism is frequently used in economics. For example, the public sector is sometimes talked about as "predatory" or "parasitic" on private enterprise, meaning that the former is both sustained by and a drain on the private sector. Feminists concerned about the non-recognition of women's unpaid contribution to the economy have been keen to point out a similar relationship between the market economy as a whole (public and private sectors together) and a caring economy centered on unpaid work in the household and voluntary work in the community (Himmelweit 2002b). This argument appeals to the "predation" of market-oriented behavior on caring behavior.

It can be shown that predator/prey interactions result in convergence to either a single equilibrium or a limit cycle (May 1981). Figure 16.3 shows the form such a cycle might take, with the numbers of the prey population (solid line) peaking before those of the predator population (dashed line).[5] This is what one would expect; when prey are at their peak, predators are doing exceptionally well and will therefore still be growing in numbers.

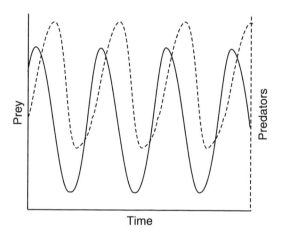

Figure 16.3 Populations numbers over time of prey (solid line) and predator (dashed line)
Source: May (1981: 82).

If instead of mutualism a predator–prey relationship does now characterize the relationship between caring and market-oriented behavior, we would expect to see such cycles in the relative frequency of each mode of behavior. Recent history, in which market-oriented behavior (the predator) has won out over caring behavior (the prey), could be interpreted as the phase in such a cycle when predator numbers are still increasing but, because of the effects of their predation, prey numbers are falling. If so, we can expect the predator population (market-oriented behavior) to start falling shortly too, as its supply of resources becomes reduced through falling numbers of prey. As the number of predators falls, conditions improve for the prey (caring forms of behavior) and eventually their numbers will start to increase again. Certainly, much comment in the popular media during the 1990s shared this expectation by suggesting that the self-seeking "greed" of the 1980s had overreached itself and would soon be replaced by more appreciation of "people" skills.[6]

An alternative interpretation would expect the fundamental relationship between the two modes of behavior to continue to shift in the same direction. By this interpretation, the $(+/-)$ of the predator–prey relationship should be seen as only a stage in the movement towards the $(-/-)$ relationship of competition, in which market-oriented behavior frees itself from its dependence on caring behavior. The increasing range of caring services that can be purchased on the market could be given as evidence of this. When two species are in direct competition with each other for the same ecological niche it is the "fitter" one that survives, and the only equilibrium is the complete annihilation of the less fit. Once gender no longer determines whether individuals are open to market-oriented or caring modes of behavior, then there will be no distinction in their ecological niches. In that case the "fitter" mode of behavior will drive out the less fit. Currently it appears that market-oriented behavior tends to win when it is in direct competition with caring behavior. If this continues to be the trend, then the population of caring behaviors will continue to fall until it either becomes extinct or, more likely, is reduced to such a low level that the dependence of market-oriented behavior on it is re-established. North American vignettes spring to mind, whether the mythical Wild West as a society destroyed by its own lawlessness, or a popular view of contemporary crime in U.S. cities as both a consequence of inadequate parenting and a likely cause of economic decline.

A more optimistic view of present trends would point out that "less fit" species sometimes adapt and find new more specialized niches of their own. To put this into the language of the parenting deficit, so far it appears that the opening up of competition for women's time between market-oriented and caring modes of behavior has produced a shift towards the former at the expense of some domestic activities. However, it appears from time-use studies that the more marketable, work-like aspects of women's traditional role are declining faster than the more specifically personal, nurturing aspects. Further, there are some indications that such nurturing behavior is also invading men's time. Time-use studies show, for example, that men are taking more of a role in childcare, even if they are not increasing their participation in other forms of domestic labor (Himmelweit 1995). If that is the case, it may be that the caring mode of behavior is adapting to changed circumstances. The market-oriented mode of behavior may indeed be winning out over those activities that formerly were seen as part and parcel of a woman's role in caring for her family but could just as well be carried out impersonally and purchased as services through the market. However, the caring mode of behavior may be surviving by specializing in core personal caring activities that cannot really be encompassed within a market orientation. Whether that means that the surviving courses of action within the caring mode of behavior will prove fitter and better able to withstand competition from market-oriented modes of behavior remains to be seen.

Conclusion

This paper, by looking at two examples, has used an evolutionary approach to model aspects of economic behavior with which neoclassical economics has difficulty but which are key to feminist concerns. The aim was to demonstrate that this approach might be a useful one for feminist economics to adopt. The two examples in this paper showed that one advantage to feminists of evolutionary models is that they can explore different types of behavior without reducing them all to aspects of outcome-oriented maximization. A second advantage is that an evolutionary approach models a process that depends on relationships between members of a population. Be they people or behaviors, whether members of a population survive depends on how they relate to others in that population. In the first example in this paper, the survival of particular courses of action depended on the extent to which others behaved in similar ways. A third advantage of evolutionary models is that they are designed to be able to explain the process of change; both models in this paper mapped possible trajectories of change. Finally, by using evolutionary models the domain of economics and economic change can be expanded to take account of norms, values, and identities, all of which, feminists claim, have a significant impact on gendered behaviors within the economy.

These were the four conditions that this paper set for an approach to economic behavior to be considered feminist. It remains to be seen whether evolutionary models can deliver further useful insights. I hope in this paper to have made an argument for continuing to explore whether that might be the case.

Notes

1 Max Weber's distinction between substantive and formal rationality captures the same idea without implying that behavior motivated by morality is thereby "irrational." In Weber's distinction utility maximization would be seen as "formal rationality," while "substantive rationality" is that governed by moral purposes that override the calculation of the best means to meet given ends (Weber 1968).
2 Hannan and Freeman's ecological model of organizational populations uses a similar notion of density dependence to explain how certain forms of organizations become more or less numerous. In their model, density serves as a surrogate for "difficult-to-observe features of the material and social environment" (Hannan and Freeman 1989: 131).

3   Competitive and other types of interaction between modes of behavior are then analogous to inter-specific interactions, whereas competition between two different courses of action belonging to the same mode of behavior, which was considered in the earlier example, is analogous to intra-specific competition between individual organisms of the same species.
4   In biology, there are also two types of competitive mechanism. *Interference competition* occurs where one species interferes with another's access to resources, while *exploitation competition* occurs where they affect each other only through the depletion of a limiting resource. For example, leaves on many plants have two functions: one to allow the plant to photosynthesize the nutrients it needs from sunlight, and the other to shade the ground around it to make it harder for other plants to survive and compete for nutrients from the ground. Insofar as leaves are broader than they need to be just for the plants' own needs for photosynthesis, it is interference rather than exploitation competition that has produced this adaptation.
5   In the case considered in Figure 16.3 there is a stable limit cycle rather than a single equilibrium. Which limit occurs depends on the intrinsic growth rates of predator and prey and the capacity of the environment to support members of the prey species on their own. The predator species cannot survive on its own (May 1981: 79–82).
6   However, this does not necessarily mean that the growth in caring behavior is taking place in the home. Indeed, it has been suggested that as work for the market takes over more and more of people's lives, domestic time has had to become more productive and work-like. Conversely, people are finding that their more satisfying and less strained relationships are those that they develop in the course of their employment (Hochschild 1997).

Bibliography

Arthur, Brian W. (1989) "Competing Technologies, Increasing Returns and Lock-in by Historical Events," *Economic Journal* IC: 116–31.

—— (1994) *Increasing Returns and Path Dependence in the Economy*, Ann Arbor, MI: University of Michigan Press.

Collard, David (1978) *Altruism and Economy*, Oxford: Martin Robertson.

David, Paul (1985) "Clio and the Economics of QWERTY," *American Economic Review Proceedings* 75: 332–7.

Duncan, Simon and Ros Edwards (1997) "Lone Mothers and Paid Work: Rational Economic Man or Gendered Moral Rationalities?," *Feminist Economics* 3(2): 29–62.

Elshtain, Jean, Enola Aird, Amitai Etzioni, William Galston, Mary Ann Glendon, Martha Minow and Alice Rossi (1992) *A Communitarian Position Paper on the Family*, Washington, DC: Communitarian Network.

Elster, Jon (1989) *The Cement of Society*, Cambridge: Cambridge University Press.

Finch, Janet (1989) *Family Obligations and Social Change*, Cambridge: Polity Press.

Finch, Janet and Jennifer Mason (1993) *Negotiating Family Responsibilities*, London: Routledge.

Folbre, Nancy (1994) *Who Pays for the Kids? Gender and the Structures of Constraint*, London: Routledge.

Hannan, Michael T. and John Freeman (1989) *Organizational Ecology*, Cambridge, MA: Harvard University Press.

Hargreaves-Heap, Shaun (1992) "Bandwagon Effects," in Shaun Hargreaves-Heap, Martin Hollis, Bruce Lyons, Robert Sugden and Albert Weale, *The Theory of Choice: A Critical Guide*, Oxford: Blackwell.

Himmelweit, Susan (1995) "The Discovery of 'Unpaid Work': The Social Consequences of the Expansion of 'Work,'" *Feminist Economics* 1(2): 1–19.

—— (2001) "Caring for Children," in Susan Himmelweit, Roberto Simonetti and Andrew Trigg (eds.) *Microeconomics: Neoclassical and Institutionalist Perspectives on Economic Behavior*, London: Thomson Learning.

—— (2002a) "Economic Theory, Norms and the Care Gap, or: Why Do Economists Become Parents?," in Alan Carling, Simon Duncan and Rosalind Edwards (eds.) *Analysing Families: Morality and Rationality in Policy and Practice*, London: Routledge.

—— (2002b) "Making Visible the Hidden Economy: The Case for Gender Impact Analysis of Economic Policy," *Feminist Economics* 8(1): 49–70.

Hochschild, Arlie Russell (1997) *The Time Bind*, New York: Henry Holt & Company.

Jordan, Bill, Marcus Redley and Simon James (1994) *Putting the Family First*, London: UCL Press.

Kirman, Alan P. (1992) "Whom or What Does the Representative Individual Represent?," *Journal of Economic Perspectives* 6(2): 117–36.

May, Robert M. (1981) "Models for Two Interacting Populations," in Robert M. May (ed.) *Theoretical Ecology*, 2nd edn., Oxford: Blackwell Scientific Publishers.

Metcalfe, J. Stanley (1988) "The Diffusion of Innovations: An Interpretative Survey," in Giovanni Dosi, Luc Soete and Christopher Freeman (eds.) *Technical Change and Economic Theory*, London: Pinter Publishers.

—— (1994) "Competition, Fisher's Principle and Increasing Returns in the Selection Process," *Journal of Evolutionary Economics* 4: 327–46.

Nelson, Richard (1995) "Recent Evolutionary Theorizing about Economic Change," *Journal of Economic Literature* 33(1): 48–90.

Sen, Amartya (1977) "Rational Fools," *Philosophy and Public Affairs* 6: 317–44.

Silvertown, Jonathan (1996) "Ecology: The Study of Interactions," in Open University, *S 328 Ecology, Book One: Interactions*, Milton Keynes: Open University.

Sunstein, Cass (1997) *Free Markets and Social Justice*, New York: Oxford University Press.

Vromen, Jack J. (1997) "Evolutionary Economics: Precursors, Paradigmatic Propositions, Puzzles and Prospects," in Jan Reijinders (ed.) *Economics and Evolution*, Cheltenham: Edward Elgar.

Weber, Max (1968) *Economy and Society*, New York: Bedminster Press; first English translation published in 1922.

17 Domestic labor and gender identity

Are all women carers?

Gillian J. Hewitson[1]

Introduction

Unpaid labor in the home – caring labor – is of major significance to the economy. It underpins the ability of people to provide labor to the paid economy and is an essential component of the development of future citizens, workers, and taxpayers. The sexual division of this labor is a major issue for feminists across the social sciences.

Although the past thirty to forty years have seen dramatic rises in women's labor-market participation in Western countries such as the United States and Australia, there has also been virtual constancy in the sexual division of unpaid labor over this period. Specifically, despite massive increases in their labor-force participation, women who live with men continue to undertake, on average, twice the amount of unpaid work in the home as their partners. When the couple has children the ratio of women's to men's unpaid labor rises dramatically, and this occurs independently of the paid work hours of the women. Unpaid domestic tasks are also strikingly sex segregated, with women undertaking most food preparation and clean-up, laundry, general cleaning, and physical care of children, and men undertaking most car care, pet care and some other outside tasks. Furthermore, women typically bear the responsibility for organizing and planning domestic tasks and, sometimes, allocating some of them to others, ensuring their completion and training others in their performance. That is, domestic labor is an occupation for most women, whether or not they have paid occupations, but typically simply a series of tasks for most men (Dempsey 1988; Bittman and Lovejoy 1993). These differences in men's and women's roles in the physical and emotional maintenance of families are frequently not even a topic of discussion of any kind within households: it "just happens…sort of automatically," in the words of one survey respondent (Bittman and Pixley 1997: 167; ellipsis in original).

Economists and feminist economists have sought to explain these facts, and the aim of this paper is to problematize the "naturalness" of the subjectivities produced in these accounts of the relationship between sexual difference and the sexual division of caring labor. In the next section I argue that unpaid domestic labor falls within the definitions of caring labor developed by feminist economists (pp. 267–8). Seen in this way, domestic labor becomes a site at which the relationships between caring, sex, gender, heterosexuality, and feminist and non-feminist economic theorizing can be examined. In the subsequent section I outline some examples of economists' explanations of the sexual division of labor, examining models which privilege sex (or biology) and those which privilege gender (or social construction) (pp. 268–72). In the fourth section I argue that, implicitly or explicitly, these explanations draw upon a concept of caring which equates it with femininity or femaleness (pp. 272–80). This concept of caring, in turn, is precisely the one theorized as a defining characteristic of gender identities within feminist object relations theory, which underlies an important area of feminist economic theorizing on the masculinity of the economic individual. Briefly, in object relations theory, given the dominant parenting arrangements of modern Western societies, the normal feminine identity is one with both the capacity and the desire to care and undertake caring labor, and the normal masculine identity is one which does not have this capacity or desire.

In that section I also undertake a critique of object relations theory to show that theorizing gender identities in this way commits theorists to an essentialist understanding of sexual difference as determined by a heterosexual and biologically defined complementarity of the sexes. Although many non-feminist economists, and perhaps some feminist economists, would agree with this view of sexual difference, most feminist economists maintain that it is socially defined gender rather than biologically defined sex which explains the social roles of men and women, and hence the sexual division of caring labor. Indeed, this is precisely the appeal of object relations theory, since it appears to be a theory of mothering as a social rather than a biological category. I show that this reading remains problematic, and that it is the sex/gender distinction which is at the root of the problem. I discuss some of the implications of the "compulsory heterosexuality" which the sex/gender distinction inevitably implies. I give a brief overview of how poststructuralist, or deconstructive, feminist theory is one way out of this impasse, since in deconstructive feminism the biological body, which underpins both sex and gender in the sex/gender distinction, is theorized. In deconstructive feminism, sexual difference is understood as emerging from non-essentialized, but nevertheless embodied, subjectivities which are dependent upon discourses for their lived experience. Deconstructive feminists are not, therefore, compelled to answer the question "Are all women carers?" with a "Yes."

Unpaid domestic labor is caring labor

Caring labor has been defined in two ways within the feminist economic literature (Folbre 1995; Folbre and Weisskopf 1998; Badgett and Folbre 1999;

Himmelweit 1999). On the one hand, caring labor is produced by a motivation to care *about* others, and hence is about the identity of the carer. Caring labor which is motivated by a desire to care is "labor undertaken out of affection or a sense of responsibility for other people, with no expectation of immediate pecuniary reward" (Folbre 1995: 75). Related motives for undertaking caring labor under this definition also include obligation, altruism, and reciprocity (*ibid.*: 76–7). In such situations a relationship between carer and "caree" is created, and the caring is dependent upon the identity of the individuals in that relationship.

On the other hand, caring labor can be an activity which does not derive from an attribute of the carer themselves, but rather from the nature of the work – it is work involving caring *for* others. Thus this second definition guides us to examine the activity, rather than the carer, to identify whether or not the labor is caring. Since a plethora of activities which directly or indirectly meet the needs of others could thereby be construed as caring, caring labor under this definition is restricted to activities involving non-incidental face-to-face contact between the carer and the recipient. Here the carer's activity is a response to the needs or desires of the recipients rather than a response to their own intrinsic motivations.

Unpaid domestic work can be defined as caring labor using both of these definitions: it consists in work which is caring about and/or for others. It is an activity which is not monetarily compensated, and it may or may not be motivated by a caring identity. These definitions overlap when unpaid carers undertake domestic labor, not out of their own sense of affection or responsibility for those they are looking after, but rather for non-altruistic or selfish reasons. To define domestic labor as caring labor means that all aspects of such work – including the multitudinous ways in which effort is expended in emotional or nurturing activities, behaviors, or thoughts – are included. Beasley (1994: 101–3), Himmelweit (1995) and Donath (2000) discuss the problematic issue of measuring the "emotional" or "other" economy and, in particular, the way in which conventional measurements of unpaid labor exclude the personal, emotional, and nurturing – caring about – components which are primarily the responsibility of women, and therefore lead to the underestimation of the ratio of women's to men's domestic labor in the survey data now routinely collected by Western governments. In this paper I discuss domestic labor in terms of this broader perspective of caring labor in order to make clear the underlying importance of the concept of caring in feminist and non-feminist economic constructions of sexed economic subjectivity.

Sex, gender and caring labor in economic models of the sexual division of labor

Both these definitions of caring labor are implicitly used by new home economists to explain women's specialization in unpaid domestic work. First, women's role as the unpaid workers within households is a function of their biology, and hence is an aspect of their identity – they are biologically motivated to care about others. Second, unpaid labor is an activity which women undertake for their own self-interest. Once married, a woman's utility is maximized when the utility of her altruistic wage-earning husband's utility is maximized. Women are assumed to undertake childrearing for biological (motivational or identity) reasons, and, since there are economies of scale for women but not for men in childrearing, women will also perform caring labor in the home in their own self-interest even before any children are present. A brief outline of Becker's (1991) classic analysis clarifies these points.[2]

The essence of Becker's new home economics model of the domestic production of nonmarket goods and services using inputs of labor time and market-purchased goods is that the selfish members of families maximize the utility function of the altruistic head, who is employed in the paid labor market. Family members specialize in the paid labor market or in domestic labor in accordance with their relative productivities in those sectors. In households of identical individuals no more than one person will contribute time to both the paid labor market and household work, the dual contributor being equally productive in the two sectors. To maximize household output those who are more productive than the dual contributor in the market sector will specialize there, while those who are more productive in the home will become specialized domestic workers. Thus, in a household of two identical adults, if one specializes completely in the market, the other may either specialize in housework, or undertake both housework and paid labor. Constant or increasing returns to scale in the production of household commodities raise the payoff to specialization and each member will specialize in one sector only. In the model outlined so far, the identity of the altruistic head is simply a function of comparative advantage.

To identify who will specialize in the paid labor market, and hence who will be the altruistic head of the household, biological sex must be introduced. Women are defined as having a comparative advantage in household work because of their role in the reproductive process. Upon giving birth, instead of making a decision at the margin, a woman's nine-month investment in the fetus predisposes her to commit at least several more years to dedicated care of the child (*ibid.*: 37). Not only does a woman, but not a man, have innate biological commitments to caring for children, but a woman experiences childbearing and childcare economies of scale if she has specialized in domestic labor. That is, a woman can reduce the cost of additional children by undertaking childcare of older children at the same time as she produces additional children. This means that "an hour of household or market time of women is not a perfect substitute for an hour of the time of men when they make the same investments in human capital" (*ibid.*: 38). The implication is that the sexual division of labor is efficient.

Women's comparative advantage in domestic labor, then, is so deeply embedded in the biology of reproduction that even the time of childless married women with the same market and nonmarket human capital as their husbands will specialize in domestic work. That parents anticipate grandchildren and train boys and girls appropriately, giving them greater productivity in paid and unpaid labor, respectively, simply amplifies, but is not the source of, women's comparative advantage in domestic labor, and hence such sex-specific, male-breadwinner/female-carer investments are indeed efficient. These investments are inefficient, however, if the child grows into a "deviant" adult – homosexual, or "biologically oriented" to the market if a woman, or to household activities if a man. Households containing such individuals are less efficient than those of "biologically normal" people because they cannot take advantage of biological complementarity in child production (*ibid.*: 38–41).[3]

In short, in the new home economics, biologically "normal" women expect to have children and to live in a male-breadwinner/female-carer household. "Normal" women rely "on men for provision of food, shelter, and protection," and "normal" men rely "on women for the bearing and rearing of children and the maintenance of the home [and the men themselves]" (*ibid.*: 43). Thus, in the new home economics male bodies are productive and cared about and for by wives, enabling them to "hunt," "soldier," "farm," and "engage in other 'market' activities" (*ibid.*: 30). Female bodies, on the other hand, are reproductive and maternal – they give birth and are therefore specially equipped, indeed programmed, to care for husbands and children, whether or not they are married or have children. "Normal" women specialize in domestic labor well before these events in order to take advantage of the future economies of scale available from that use of their time. Both nature and economic efficiency are served by the social arrangements which reflect these capacities and desires of sexed bodies. As noted, women or men who do not choose these paths are economically inefficient biological deviants.

Economists have also examined the sexual division of labor within bargaining frameworks, although usually indirectly in discussions of issues such as household expenditure patterns. Seemingly unlike Becker's use of an explicitly biological basis for the sexual division of labor, these bargaining models use the concept of gender, where biologically female women are feminine and biologically male men are masculine. In Lundberg and Pollack's (1993) model the bargaining power of each spouse is determined by their wellbeing in their "separate spheres," which is the non-cooperative equilibrium to which the spouses revert should they fail to agree on a distribution of marital resources. This equilibrium is characterized by spouses undertaking the activities assigned to their socially sanctioned and exogenously determined genders – husbands specialize in earning income and wives specialize in domestic labor. This "voluntary contribution equilibrium is maintained by social enforcement of the obligations corresponding to generally recognized and accepted gender roles" (*ibid.*: 994). That is, it is social norms rather than biological differences between men and women which close the model. Socialization, including institutional factors such as the possibility of making binding and enforceable agreements prior to marriage, is the mechanism by which the social norms of gender are maintained (Lundberg and Pollack 1996). An implication of the significance of social norms in the model is that when the spouses do negotiate a mutually acceptable bargain or cooperative equilibrium the distribution of domestic labor and its responsibilities may not even have been included in the set of resources over which they bargained (see also Seiz 1991). Furthermore, if the distribution of domestic labor is a bargaining issue, husbands may prefer the non-cooperative equilibrium to an outcome in which their gender identity, or membership of the gender category of "man"/"masculine," is threatened by their relative contribution to domestic labor required by any bargain to which their wives will agree. Indeed, the data seems to tell us that a version of the separate-spheres outcome dominates in Western economies: specifically, in many households both men and women work for pay, but women also undertake most of the caring labor sanctioned as "women's work" by the social norms of gender.

The importance of membership in social categories of gender in determining the relative contributions of husbands and wives to domestic labor is a key insight of Akerlof and Kranton (2000), who incorporate socially sanctioned gender roles into the bargaining framework by inserting "gender identity" into the utility functions of the bargaining spouses. The categories of "man" and "woman," to which a person has been assigned on the basis of biology, constrain the gender-identity choice such that men have a masculine gender identity and women have a feminine gender identity (*ibid.*: 716).[4] The spouses maximize utility subject to the dictates of their gender identity. The relative hours spent by husbands and wives in the performance of paid and unpaid labor is the result of their utility-maximizing strategies to maintain membership of their gender categories. Specifically, both partners suffer a loss of utility when the wife works more than half the couple's total labor market hours ("men's work") or when the husband contributes more than half the unpaid domestic labor ("women's work") since these situations cause a loss of coherence with the content of their respective gender identities. Thus when wives increase their relative hours in the labor market, causing both partners a utility loss due to the incompatibility of this change with their gender identities, husbands reduce their relative domestic labor contribution, creating an offsetting utility gain for each spouse.

One implication of this model is that a husband is unlikely to choose anything but a traditional masculine identity given the economic benefit of doing so. Indeed, his utility-maximizing strategy seems to be to assert his commitment to the most traditional of masculine gender prescriptions and simultaneously encourage his wife to work! This may explain the coexistence of, on the one hand, Akerlof and Kranton's (2000: 735) claim, in an application of their identity model to occupational segregation, that the women's movement has been successful in changing gender prescriptions such that women have moved into the labor market and into "men's jobs" and, on the other hand, the fact that the forces which led to these changes in paid labor-market outcomes seem to have failed miserably in changing the gender prescriptions relevant to the distribution of domestic tasks and responsibilities, a distribution which shows little variation from that characterizing the 1950s and 1960s. Indeed, researchers in the area of unpaid labor contend that women continue to have the responsibility for managing household labor, while husbands deliberately resist and avoid "helping" their wives by actively pursuing a series of strategies which maintain the status quo. Examples of such strategies include ignoring wives' requests or pleas for help; telling their wives that they will complete tasks they have been asked to do, and then simply failing to do so; feigning incompetence; and avoiding tasks through intimidation, threats, and violence (Bittman and Lovejoy 1993; Bittman and Pixley 1997: ch. 6).[5]

The constraints deriving from gendered identities in the marriage market may help to explain wives' continued commitment to a domestically defined and hence caring gender identity while simultaneously working part or full time in the paid labor market. Men's gains from marrying a high-earning wife may be more than offset by the fact that the high-earning wife will have greater bargaining power and may therefore be able to pressure them into domestic labor, reducing their sense of masculinity (Badgett and Folbre 1999). Indeed, it has been found that men whose wives are decisionmakers on the job are more likely to share household labor than are men whose wives do not have such authority on the job (Shelton and John 1996). Thus in this model, high-earning women, who do not conform to traditional femininity – Beckerian "biological deviants" – are penalized in the marriage market, motivating many women to stay within stereotypically female occupations and to maintain their control of domestic labor so as to attract a high-earning husband. Alternatively, high-earning women may employ other women – rather than men – to fulfill their domestic labor responsibilities. So women and men both have a stake in maintaining the connection between femininity and caring. The question which feminist economists have sought to answer is why it is that gender identities signify these particular behaviors.

Gender and feminist economics: a critique

Feminists of several different theoretical persuasions have argued that women's "biological disadvantage" can be found, not within nature, but within the social interpretation of nature. The conceptual distinction between sex and gender has been a cornerstone of much feminist theory since the 1960s – indeed, it has been the "foundational motif of feminism" (Chanter 1995: 13). It allows feminists to discount the importance of biology as an explanation of the sexual division of labor and to argue instead that this division of labor is due to the socialization of individuals into persons gendered as masculine or feminine. In other words, women are the carers in the home because of a socially defined feminine gender identity and not because female biology dictates that it be so. That this caring and connected feminine selfhood is an outcome of women's socially defined role in mothering is central to the conceptual frameworks of many feminist economists. The paradigmatic feminist work on caring is that of the object relations theorist Chodorow (1978; see also Dinnerstein 1976; Flax 1983), and her work has left an immeasurable legacy to second-wave feminist theory and to feminist economics.[6] At this point, it is important to delineate the key characteristics of object relations theory and its links to feminist economics.

Object relations theory is an explanation of how and why the social relations between the sexes, and associated institutional structures, are reproduced. It theorizes masculine and feminine genders as the psychic identities of men and women, which are produced as a function of childrearing arrangements characterized by women's mothering and men's breadwinning. During the formation of a separate self during childhood, masculine and feminine identities are created differently because of the fact that it is the mother, rather than the absent father, from whom children must learn to separate. The masculine identity is one formed in opposition to the ever-present female carer, and hence is characterized by detachment, while the feminine identity is characterized by the connection to others and the desire to care about and for them, since girls identify with, rather than against, the femininity of their mothers:

> The establishment of a boy's identity and his individuality is a psychic process in which the boy struggles to renounce identification with mother and the nurturing she represents...manhood is defined as a flight from femininity and its attendant emotional elements, particularly compassion, nurturance, affection and dependence.
> (Kimmel and Kaufman; quoted in McMahon 1999: 180)

Men's identification with the absent figure of the father/breadwinner therefore entails significant anxiety about maintaining their gender, unlike girls, who have a secure sense of identity because they have a concrete model – the mother – with whom to identify (Young 1990: 36–9).

Two feminist economic analyses of the ways in which social gender – as understood through object relations theory and related feminist literature – rather than biological sex functions to identify femininity as caring and connected and masculinity as separate and autonomous are the influential works of England (1993) on the "separative self" and Nelson (1996) on the "gender compass." England (1993) is critical of the use within neoclassical economics of the "separative-self" model of the individual, a model which she argues primarily describes men. The existence of the masculine sense of separativeness and the feminine sense of connection means that the separative-self model is gendered, since it leaves out the experience of those who feel connected to others and who exist within relational networks by assuming that "humans are autonomous, impervious to social influences, and lack sufficient emotional connection to each other to make empathy possible" (*ibid.*: 37). Like England, Nelson argues that separation and connection are socially, rather than biologically, linked to masculinity and femininity (Nelson 1996: 15), and that the model of "economic man" reflects these gender associations: he is "radically separate from other humans and from nature; the emphasis is on separation, distance, demarcation, autonomy, independence of self" (*ibid.*: 30). These traits of masculinity can also be seen in the definition and accepted methodology of the discipline (Nelson 1993; 1996: chs. 1–3).

Men experience a "stunted" emotional life, then, as a result of the masculine personality formed in the early years of childhood when they must repulse feminine traits in order to become separate persons. The implication of this theory is that the responsibility for the actions of men which are driven by "normal masculinity" can hardly be slated to individual men, who were not responsible for the sexual division of labor which produced their masculine identities. Indeed, it follows from their psychology that "most men are afraid of behaviour or attitudes that even hint at the feminine" (Kimmel and Kaufman; quoted in McMahon 1999: 180). In particular, men's resistance to the caring work of domestic labor, and even (as reported in note 5) their violence which such labor may precipitate, is understandable in this context as a necessary strategy to maintain their masculinity and psychological wellbeing. By contrast, women's passage into femininity produces their capacity for caring about and for others, complementing men's incapacity for caring.

This implication of object relations theory appears regularly in the area of masculinity studies which McMahon (1999: 198–202) has called the "wounded man narrative," but, to my knowledge, it has not been spelled out in this way in the feminist economics literature. Indeed, the point that men can be understood as lacking agency with respect to their action or non-action around caring does not seem to have been fully appreciated by those feminist economists who use this model of gender. It is important to understand that this model of masculinity and femininity involves a particular construction of sexual difference at the same time as it purports to offer an explanation of men's and women's lived experience, particularly that of men's devaluation of women. What it does not offer is a way of changing these socially determined genders. Furthermore, the construction of gender in this model replicates the biological model of the sexes, which implicitly or explicitly underpins the analyses of the sexual division in caring labor of the models outlined the previous section (pp. 268–72). These points are elaborated in the paragraphs which follow.

Object relations theory does not, in fact, provide a helpful explanation of the sexual division of labor because its explanation of this phenomenon is circular, and therefore it offers no means by which the situation may change to allow other forms of gender personalities to develop. Men do not undertake caring labor because they are fundamentally incapable of it, lacking as they do the necessary capacities for nurturing, empathy, or using the needs of others as the basis of action, and, hence, the emotional capacity to care for or about others. Such behavior would conflict with their early identification with the absent breadwinning father. The benefit to men of their nonperformance of caring labor is that they are able to maintain their sense of autonomous, unconnected, and most especially non-feminine selves, which is essential for their psychological health as individuated humans. Thus the division of labor itself is used to explain the division of labor: men do not undertake caring labor in the home because men do not undertake caring labor in the home (McMahon 1999: 190–3).[7] The only way for the division of labor to change is for men to undertake caring labor (particularly mothering), but men's personality structures prevent them from doing so.

Moreover, the essence of masculinity is its need and desire to repulse the feminine, and this desire finds social expression in men's ability to create the social institutions which express and satisfy this desire. In Chodorow's words, "men have the means to institutionalize their unconscious defences against repressed yet strongly experienced developmental conflicts" (Chodorow; quoted in Hewitson 1999: 82). Thus men have needs and interests which involve dominating women and keeping them well away from the public sphere, where they would generate anxiety in men and reduce their psychological wellbeing, and, furthermore, this psychological drive enables men actually to structure society independently of the interests or actions of women. The circularity of the model means that men have the ability to structure the world according to their own needs, when those needs were themselves a product of the structure of society. Thus, gender differentiation coincides with men's domination of women (Young 1990: ch. 2). This is precisely the reasoning of a biological account of society: men's biology means that they have certain interests, and these interests are reflected in society's institutions, including gendered identities. Both accounts of gendered identities assume or construct a natural complementarity between men and women. This applies also to the explanation of gender, rather than sex, which is provided by object relations theory, since the psychic structures of men and women are reflected in the institutions of the sexual division of labor, and since these institutions continue to reproduce these psychic structures, change is not possible (Cornell 1991: 50–1). Thus, object relations theory may claim to explain men's and women's gendered (and hence malleable) experiences, but because it identifies psychic personality structures with social institutions and neither of these can change without the other changing first, it does not offer a plausible solution to the problem of the sexual division of labor, and should be viewed as socially essentialist.[8]

Of course, it is not the case that men are never observed undertaking caring labor. Not only do many men undertake caring-for tasks, although most frequently in the role of their wives' "helpers," but many have also revealed a capacity to nurture their children, and hence the capacity to care about others. Indeed, men's childcare is dominated by the more "connected," caring-about activities such as playing with their children, rather than by the more instrumental, caring-for activities of cleaning and cooking for children.[9] Moreover, "some apparently quite unexceptional men, products of conventional mothering, routinely perform primary care of others," though usually when there is an absence of women to perform these tasks (McMahon 1999: 197). This nurturing capacity of men does not sit easily with object relations theory. Specifically, there are in existence men who were mothered by women who are capable of and willing to nurture others, and who therefore deviate from the heterosexual complementarity of the genders which is explained by object relations theory. Again, this mirrors the existence, in Becker's (1991) model, of the "biological deviants" who fail to conform to the norm of heterosexual complementarity.

However, the masculine personality of object relations theory, particularly its traits of independence and autonomy, can be reinterpreted as a gender fantasy or, using McNay's (1991: 129) Foucauldian phrase, an "imaginary signification," rather than a reality which constrains men's ability to care about and for others. The independence of those men who allow women to care about and for them as if they were children is thereby premised upon their dependence upon women. This dependent relationship is precisely what is envisaged in object relations theory. As both sexes are parented by women, both sexes experience an exclusive mother–child relationship and develop a primary union with a woman. Each longs to return to this state of pre-Oedipal oneness with the maternal body. Heterosexual women recreate the primary union by entering relationships and becoming mothers themselves. Heterosexual men, on the other hand, are able to directly reproduce the exclusive mother–child bond through sexual relationships with women, and these replicate for men the relationship of the child to its mother (Fuss 1989: 48).[10]

The social essentialism of object relations theory is to give the fantasy of male independence and autonomy, and to give female nurturing and dependence, the appearance of an unchangeable reality. As McNay argues: "Once the female [or male] sex has come to connote specific feminine [masculine] characteristics, this 'imaginary signification' produces concrete effects throughout diverse social practices. These concrete effects are not the expression of an immutable feminine [masculine] essence" (McNay 1991: 128). But biologically as well as socially essentialist accounts of the sexual division of labor imply that the concrete effects of the imaginary significations of bodies *are* expressions of immutable feminine and masculine essences.

Notice that, like the economic models outlined in the previous section (pp. 268–72), accounts of gendered identities must assume a natural complementarity between men and women. This is because when the "sex" of the sex/gender distinction is untheorized and appears to be excluded from the analysis, it reappears to ground the notion of gender, since it is ultimately biological complementarity which explains the gender roles. Thus the complementarity of the traditional, biologically defined, heterosexual breadwinner/carer model maps onto object relations accounts which view this model as a reflection of masculine and feminine personality formations. Using either sex or gender normalizes breadwinner/caregiver models. As will be shown below, an alternative for feminist economists is to draw on feminist theory which theorizes sex, and hence eliminates the essentialism of accounts of gender by rejecting the distinction between natural sex and social gender.

To summarize the argument so far: the economic theories of the sexual division of labor outlined in the previous section derive from an essentialized biology of the two sexes, and that of object relations theory from essential genders which reflect the two sexes. And they posit precisely the same heterosexual complementarity. Furthermore, since neither biology nor psychic structures are changeable in these models, neither offers a way of altering the situation. The implicit endorsement of essentialist understandings of biological difference is a general feature of models which, in trying to escape such biological renderings, draw upon the seemingly nonbiological concept of gender. One solution to this dilemma is to drop the sex/gender distinction and theorize identity (subjectivity, in poststructuralist terms) as embodied such that sexed bodies, rather than being causal, are themselves a creation. These points need some elaboration.

Feminist economists have overwhelmingly rejected the idea that sex or the biologically defined body is the basis of the identities of men and women. As has been pointed out, many have used object relations theory to develop an account of identities as gendered rather than sexed. However, these accounts retain the body as the untheorized referent of gender, and sex and sex categories invariably precede and create gender categories. In short, behind femininity there is femaleness – it is women rather than feminine persons who have caring personalities, and men rather than masculine persons who do not. As Tina Chanter has pointed out:

> If sex is always already gendered, it is equally true that gender is always already sexed. In other words, it is not by accident that we habitually distinguish two genders from one another; the duality of gender, as feminine and masculine, is integrally bound with our similarly habitual distinction of the female sex...from the male sex.
>
> (Chanter 1995: 44)

Accounts of gender using a distinction between sex and gender in order to avoid biologism therefore suffer from significant limitations in this quest, haunted as they are by two genders, and hence two sexes.[11]

If the biological complementarity of the sexes is the basis of models of gender, we find that not all people will fit into the models. Excluded from these analyses are, to use Becker's revealing terminology, the "biological deviants." Such deviants include homosexuals; women who have a commitment to the market rather than the home ("career women"); women and men who both work and share the domestic labor equally; women who remain childless – predicted to be around 25 per cent of the present population of Australian women (Australian Bureau of Statistics 2002); "new fathers," or those who participate "fully in the emotional joys of parenthood" (McMahon 1999: 124, ch. 5); "househusbands" – in fact, anyone but heterosexuals who are acting, or will act, as biological complements to the opposite sex. Becker (1991), Lundberg and Pollack (1993), Akerlof and Kranton (2000), and object relations theory do not offer an explanation of these biological anomalies or identificatory failures and forms of resistance to "normal" gender psychologies. But, just as many feminists were lambasted in the 1980s for their implicit assumption that the feminist subject is white, so some gender feminisms should be lambasted by the "deviants" for their essentialism and universalism with respect to women's (and men's) experiences of, and responses to, mothering.[12]

A useful phrase to describe the complementarity which appears in accounts of caring labor using either sex or gender as its basis is the "heterosexual matrix." Butler uses this term to characterize

> a hegemonic discursive/epistemic model of gender intelligibility that assumes that for bodies to cohere and make sense there must be a stable sex expressed through a stable gender (masculine expresses male, feminine expresses female) that is oppositionally and hierarchically defined through the compulsory practice of heterosexuality.
>
> (Butler 1990: 151n.)[13]

We can use this notion of compulsory heterosexuality, which constructs legitimate, sexually differentiated subjectivities as either reproductive (mother/domestic worker) or productive (breadwinner), to interpret the "deviants" produced within the models discussed in this paper as a series of marginalized subjectivities or excluded "others" who reveal very clearly the limitations of the sex/gender distinction.[14]

This discussion of deviants brings us to the point that there are a multiplicity of bodies: not all female bodies are reproductive and not all male bodies are productive. Not all women seek to "reproduce mothering," and when they do, not all want to reproduce the sexual division of labor of their parents; not all are able, for a variety of reasons, to have their own children, even when they want to; not all have relationships with men – some have them with women and some not at all. And this is only the very beginning of the ways in which women can be differentiated in relation to the normative heterosexuality of biologically and socially essentialist accounts, let alone other normative discourses of sexual difference. The same kind of reasoning applies to men. Thus, not only is there no such thing as "*the* (read unsexed) body," but there is also no such thing as "two bodies," or indeed, "two sexes" or "two genders" (see Gatens 1996), as compulsory heterosexuality requires. It is clear, then, that the economic models discussed in the previous section, as well as the feminist economic analyses which are premised upon object relations theory, privilege and hence produce as normative the reproductive and productive embodiment of women and men, respectively.

Compulsory heterosexuality also reveals the importance of distinguishing between domestic labor as a series of tasks and domestic labor as an occupation. We know that men can and do carry out domestic tasks, both caring about and caring for others, albeit for much less time than women, and we also know that what it is that men do not do is undertake domestic labor as an occupation. Men's embodiment as productive both excludes this possibility and installs heterosexual masculine subjectivity as normative. It is not men who cannot fit into the domestic sphere, where they function as the nurtured breadwinners, but women who fit only very problematically into the sphere of paid employment, where their bodies signify reproductivity rather than productivity, so that single women, married women, women who do not have children, women who do not want children, women who do have children, indeed all women, face an impossible struggle at one level or another to replicate the embodied subjectivity of the productive breadwinner.

Thus, a different way to see the complementarity between the gender roles is to see that men and women do not have unified subjectivities organized around coherent gender identities which motivate certain appropriate behaviors, but, rather, are embodied in particular ways which, in a world in which one must be either a man or a woman, are utterly dependent on the discourses of sexual difference and hence on the normalized subjectivity of the "opposite sex." One of these discourses is precisely that of the "naturalness" of sex and/or gender complementarity. I have argued that although these discourses provide us with explanations of the sexual division of caring labor they do not offer us guidance for change because of the lack of agency which inheres within the theorized identities.

However, feminist poststructuralists who draw on such theorists of the body as Irigaray, Derrida, and Foucault are often misunderstood to be biologically essentialist. This misunderstanding may in part arise due to the nomenclature of "difference feminism," taken to mean the opposite of "equality feminism" and hence understood as arguing for essential differences as opposed to the socially constructed gender differences which form the basis of feminist demands for equality. Poststructuralist-informed difference feminism, or, as Gatens has described it, "deconstructive feminism," on the other hand, is not concerned with privileging an essentially biological difference between the sexes. Rather, it is concerned with the mechanisms by which bodies are recognized as different only in so far as they are constructed as possessing or lacking some socially privileged quality or qualities.

(Gatens 1996: 61)

It must be understood that rejecting compulsory heterosexuality does not mean rejecting the idea that the body has a materiality. But it is a rejection of the way in which compulsory heterosexuality requires that certain materialities of sexed bodies come to stand for the whole of the body, and indeed subjectivity. So, for example, Butler has asked:

> [U]nder what discursive and institutional conditions, do certain biological differences...become the salient characteristics of sex. ...When people ask the question "Aren't *these* biological differences?", they're not really asking a question about the materiality of the body. They're actually asking whether or not the social institution of reproduction is the most salient one for thinking about gender.
>
> (Butler 1994: 34)

Deconstructive feminists therefore refuse the dualisms of sex and gender, and the related dualisms of nature and culture, and body and mind (Gatens 1996: 130), and hence avoid the essentialism of those accounts which, wittingly or unwittingly, install compulsory heterosexuality as the norm.[15]

Conclusion

In this paper I have argued that whenever the sexual division of caring labor is explained using the sex/gender distinction – either sex, ignoring gender; or gender, ignoring sex – the two types of explanation problematically dissolve into one. Object relations theory is particularly open to this criticism because of its social essentialism. This is significant because of the influence which object relations theory and related literatures have had in feminist economics. In place of the sex/gender distinction, which ends up normalizing biologically defined heterosexual complementarity, I have offered, albeit briefly, an alternative approach within which the sexed materiality of the body is itself the object of theorizing.

Notes

1 I would like to thank Harry Clarke, Neil Perry, Andrea Waschik, Robert Waschik, and participants in a seminar at the Department of Economics at Franklin and Marshall College for their discussion and helpful comments on this paper. I am especially grateful to Drucilla Barker and Edith Kuiper for their very insightful and constructive editorial input, and no blame for any shortcomings of the paper should be attributed to them.

2 See also Siow (1998) and the discussion in Hewitson (2001) for a more recent example of this reasoning.
3 Note that Becker is not deliberately using the term "deviant" in a pejorative sense, but rather in the sense of deviations from biological normality.
4 Note that this is a common usage of the term "gender," i.e. gender is the social understanding of the biological categories of man and woman. Many feminist economists also use the term in this way. For example, in her discussion of gender in economic theory Blau maintains that gender refers to "the distinctions which society has erected on [the] biological base [of sex]" (Blau 1987: 492; see also Ferber and Nelson 1993: 9–10). This point is taken up in more detail below (pp. 276–80).
5 In fact, the relationship between domestic labor and domestic violence is frightening. McMahon reports a study in which 78 per cent of male perpetrators of domestic violence who were asked why they had beaten their wives gave answers in terms of their wives' failures to meet their expectations and standards around the performance of housework (McMahon 1999: 30; see also Shelton and John 1996).
6 Object relations theory has influenced vast areas of feminist theorizing. For example, on science and the scientific method, see Keller (1989), Harding (1981, 1986), and Bordo (1987); on feminist standpoint theory, see Hartsock (1983); on feminist ethics, see Gilligan (1982); and on feminist mothering theory, see Ruddick (1982). Note that my criticisms of object relations theory which follow apply also to the feminist literature which has built on this theory to explore these other issues, especially insofar as it is used by feminist economists (see Hewitson 1999: 78–87).
7 Furthermore, if current arrangements signify "male domination" of women (or, indeed, of the discipline of economics and economic theorizing), then that too is explained within a circular structure where male domination presupposes the existence of male domination (Young 1990).
8 On essentialism, see Grosz (1990).
9 In 1994 all Australian women's measured share of the physical care of children was 84 per cent and full-time employed women's share was 76 per cent. The share of full-time working women and others in playing with children, however, was only 60 per cent (Bittman and Pixley 1997: 113).
10 Chodorow argued that most women are heterosexual because they develop an erotic attachment to their fathers to escape the merging between them and their mothers. Being attached to both parents means that a woman will develop adult relationships with men but recreate her early identification with her mother by having a baby (Young 1990: 39). Should a woman fail to attach to her father, and become a homosexual, she, like men, will directly reproduce the exclusive mother–child bond through sexual relationships with women. (Why she may then also want children, as many lesbians do, is unclear.) Homosexual men, however, have no means of recreating the primary union, and hence have no means of being represented in object relations theory (Fuss 1989: 48).
11 For reasons of space, these limitations cannot be fully explored here. The reader is referred to McNay (1991), Gatens (1996), Hewitson (1999: 109–28), Prokhovnik (1999: ch. 3), Butler (1990: ch. 1) and Chanter (1995: ch. 1).
12 For a critical analysis of object relations theory and its universalization of women's mothering experience by ignoring issues of race and class, see Spelman (1988: ch. 4). See McMahon (1999: 182–98) for an excellent critical overview of object relations theory. For other critics, see the references cited in McMahon and in Hewitson (1999: 81, 132).
13 Butler changed the term "heterosexual matrix," used in her *Gender Trouble* (1990), to "heterosexual hegemony" in *Bodies that Matter* (1993) because this "opens up the possibility that this is a matrix which is open to rearticulation, which has a kind of malleability" (Butler 1994: 36).
14 Richardson (1998) is an example of an analysis using the notion of compulsory heterosexuality. She has shown how compulsory heterosexuality is an indispensable element of discourses around the formation of "the nation" and national identity. Homosexuals, for example, lack certain of the rights of citizenship of heterosexual people, such as being able to defend their country, being able to marry, and being free of victimization because of their sexual orientation.

15 There are important differences in the theorizing of the materiality of the body in works such as those of Butler (1993) and of feminist philosophers such as Gatens (1996) which have necessarily been glossed over here. An excellent discussion is given in Colebrook (2000). Note also that the aims of this paper could not, for reasons of space, include a more developed analysis of caring labor using these kinds of understandings of the body. However, a paper which at least introduces the reader to a Foucauldian analysis of the sexual division of labor is that of Cameron (1998).

Bibliography

Akerlof, G.A. and R.E. Kranton (2000) "Economics and Identity," *Quarterly Journal of Economics* 115(3): 715–53.

Australian Bureau of Statistics (2002) "Mothers Day 2002: ABS Facts for Features," May Media Release; available at http//www.abs.gov.au/ausstats.

Badgett, M.V.L. and N. Folbre (1999) "Assigning Care: Gender Norms and Economic Outcomes," *International Labour Review* 138(3): 311–26; available at http//infotrac.galegroup.com.

Beasley, C. (1994) *Sexual Economyths*, St. Leonards, NSW: Allen & Unwin.

Becker, G.S. (1991) *A Treatise on the Family*, 2nd enlarged edn., Cambridge, MA: Harvard University Press.

Bittman, M. and F. Lovejoy (1993) "Domestic Power: Negotiating an Unequal Division of Power Within a Framework of Equality," *Australian and New Zealand Journal of Sociology* 29(3): 302–21.

Bittman, M. and J. Pixley (1997) *The Double Life of the Family*, St. Leonards, NSW: Allen & Unwin.

Blau, F. (1987) "Gender," in J. Eatwell, M. Milgate and P. Newman (eds.) *The New Palgrave*, vol. 2, New York: Stockton.

Bordo, S. (1987) "The Cartesian Masculinization of Thought," in S. Harding and J.F. O'Barr (eds.) *Sex and Scientific Inquiry*, Chicago, IL: Chicago University Press.

Butler, J. (1990) *Gender Trouble*, New York and London: Routledge.

—— (1993) *Bodies that Matter*, New York and London: Routledge.

—— (1994) "Gender as Performance: An Interview with Judith Butler," *Radical Philosophy* 67: 32–9.

Cameron, J. (1998) "The Practice of Politics: Transforming Subjectivities in the Domestic Domain and the Public Sphere," *Australian Geographer* 29(3): 293–307.

Chanter, T. (1995) *Ethics of Eros*, New York and London: Routledge.

Chodorow, N. (1978) *The Reproduction of Mothering*, Berkeley, CA: University of California Press.

Colebrook, C. (2000) "From Radical Representations to Corporeal Becomings: The Feminist Philosophy of Lloyd, Grosz, and Gatens," *Hypatia* 15(2): 76–93.

Cornell, D. (1991) *Beyond Accommodation*, New York and London: Routledge.

Dempsey, K. (1988) "Exploitation in the Domestic Division of Labour: An Australian Case Study," *Australian and New Zealand Journal of Sociology* 24(3): 421–36.

Donath, S. (2000) "The Other Economy: A Suggestion for a Distinctively Feminist Economics," *Feminist Economics* 6(1): 115–23.

Dinnerstein, D. (1976) *The Mermaid and the Minotaur*, New York: Harper & Row.

England, P. (1993) "The Separative Self: Androcentric Bias in Neoclassical Assumptions," in M.A. Ferber and J.A. Nelson (eds.) *Beyond Economic Man*, Chicago, IL, and London: University of Chicago Press.

Ferber, M.A. and J.A. Nelson (1993) "Introduction: The Social Construction of Economics and the Social Construction of Gender," in M.A. Ferber and J.A. Nelson (eds.) *Beyond Economic Man*, Chicago, IL, and London: University of Chicago Press.

Flax, J. (1983) "Political Philosophy and the Patriarchal Unconscious: A Psychoanalytic Perspective on Epistemology and Metaphysics," in S.G. Harding and M.B. Hintikka (eds.) *Discovering Reality*, Dordrecht: D. Reidel Publishing.

Folbre, N. (1995) "'Holding Hands at Midnight': The Paradox of Caring Labor," *Feminist Economics* 1(1): 73–92.

Folbre, N. and T.E. Weisskopf (1998) "Did Father Know Best? Families, Markets, and the Supply of Caring Labour," in A. Ben-Ner and L. Putterman (eds.) *Economics, Values, and Organization*, Cambridge: Cambridge University Press.

Fuss, D. (1989) *Essentially Speaking*, New York: Routledge.

Gatens, M. (1996) *Imaginary Bodies*, London and New York: Routledge.

Gilligan, C. (1982) *In a Different Voice*, Cambridge, MA: Harvard University Press.

Grosz, E. (1990) "A Note on Essentialism and Difference," in S. Gunew (ed.) *Feminist Knowledge*, London: Routledge.

Harding, S. (1981) "What is the Real Material Base of Patriarchy and Capital?," in L. Sargent (ed.) *Women and Revolution*, Boston, MA: South End Press.

—— (1986) *The Science Question in Feminism*, Ithaca, NY: Cornell University Press.

Hartsock, N.C.M. (1983) "The Feminist Standpoint: Developing the Ground for a Specifically Feminist Historical Materialism," in S.G. Harding and M.B. Hintikka (eds.) *Discovering Reality*, Dordrecht: D. Reidel Publishing.

Hewitson, G.J. (1999) *Feminist Economics*, Cheltenham and Northampton, MA: Edward Elgar.

—— (2001) "A Survey of Feminist Economics," *La Trobe University School of Business Discussion Papers*, Series A 01.01.

Himmelweit, S. (1995) "The Discovery of 'Unpaid Work': The Social Consequences of the Expansion of 'Work,'" *Feminist Economics* 1(2): 1–20.

—— (1999) "Caring Labor," in R.J. Steinberg and D.M. Figart (eds.) *The Annals of the American Academy of Political and Social Science* 561 (Special Issue on Emotional Labor): 27–38.

Keller, E.F. (1989) "Feminism and Science," in A. Garry and M. Pearsall (eds.) *Women, Knowledge and Reality*, Boston, MA: Unwin Hyman.

Lundberg, S. and R.A. Pollack (1993) "Separate Spheres Bargaining and the Marriage Market," *Journal of Political Economy* 101(6): 988–1,010.

—— (1996) "Bargaining and Distribution in Marriage," *Journal of Economic Perspectives* 10(4): 139–58.

McMahon, A. (1999) *Taking Care of Men*, Cambridge: Cambridge University Press.

McNay, L. (1991) "The Foucauldian Body and the Exclusion of Experience," *Hypatia* 6(3): 125–39.

Nelson, J.A. (1993) "The Study of Choice or the Study of Provisioning? Gender and the Definition of Economics," in M.A. Ferber and J.A. Nelson (eds.) *Beyond Economic Man*, Chicago, IL, and London: University of Chicago Press.

—— (1996) *Feminism, Objectivity and Economics*, London and New York: Routledge.

Prokhovnik, R. (1999) *Rational Woman*, London and New York: Routledge.

Richardson, D. (1998) "Sexuality and Citizenship," *Sociology* 32(1): 83–100.

Ruddick, D. (1982) "Maternal Thinking," in B. Thorne and M. Yalom (eds.) *Rethinking the Family*, White Plains, NY: Longman.

Seiz, J.A. (1991) "The Bargaining Approach and Feminist Methodology," *Review of Radical Political Economy* 23(1/2): 22–9.

Shelton, B.A. and D. John (1996) "The Division of Household Labor," *Annual Review of Sociology* 22: 299–322.

Siow, A. (1998) "Differential Fecundity, Markets, and Gender Roles," *Journal of Political Economy* 106(2): 334–54.

Spelman, E.V. (1988) *Inessential Woman*, London: Women's Press.

Young, I.M. (1990) *Throwing Like a Girl*, Bloomington, IL, and Indianapolis, IN: Indiana University Press.

Part V
Rethinking categories

18 Empowering work?

Bargaining models reconsidered[1]

S. Charusheela

[I]n the critical thought of blacks in the West, social self-creation through labor is not the centre-piece of emancipatory hopes. For the descendents of slaves, work signifies only servitude, misery, and subordination.

(Gilroy 1993: 40)

Introduction

Feminist scholars have made divergent assessments of the effects of the feminization of labor under capitalist economic reorganization on women's empowerment.[2] This essay critiques the widespread assumption that paid labor empowers women, an argument that has been made most forcefully within feminist economics with the help of neoclassical game-theoretic bargaining models of intrahousehold decisionmaking. I argue that the attractive concept of bargaining in this literature conceals powerful assumptions about the social organization and subjective experience of paid work.

The next section traces the logic by which neoclassical game-theoretic models link women's employment to empowerment (pp. 287–90). The subsequent section draws on social-historical studies of working-class, ethnic-minority, and non-Western women's labor-market experience to give us an alternative picture of women's employment (pp. 290–5). The fourth section concludes the essay by examining the theoretical issues that are raised by these different experiences (pp. 295–8).

The location of employment in bargaining models

In the past two decades, scholars from a variety of perspectives – ranging from micro-rational neoclassicism to Marxist-institutionalist feminism – have deployed the concept of bargaining to analyze women's economic inequality and/or subordination.[3] The strongest impact of this concept in the field of economics has come through the development of neoclassical game-theoretic models of intrahousehold bargaining.

The application of game theory to household interaction is conventionally dated to Manser and Brown (1979, 1980). Subsequent literature has developed this framework in a variety of directions.[4] Game-theoretic models vary depending on what variables are seen as subject to bargaining and negotiation in the game, what variables are seen as setting the relative bargaining power of the negotiating parties, and how the game itself is specified.[5]

Intrahousehold bargaining seeks to describe the process by which household members decide how labor is allocated and outputs are distributed. The household is usually seen as consisting of two people who engage in a "game" in which each individual seeks to maximize his/her "returns" (defined as utility, or some other similarly single-valued quantum such as income or output).

In the typical model of this genre, an individual chooses between remaining/cooperating in a marriage/household or leaving.[6] Their choice depends on which option provides higher returns. The returns available to individuals upon divorce, separation, or non-cooperation constitute an individual's fallback position (or, more ominously, threat point). Income from a job contributes to this fallback position. When household members decide to cooperate they negotiate over shares of household work and consumption. The core intuition of these models is that the better the alternatives to staying in the marriage or household (i.e. the better the fallback), the stronger the bargaining position of the individual, making it more likely that the bargain works in his/her favor. Thus, anything that improves a person's relative fallback position improves his/her bargaining position within the household.

In general, the implication of bargaining models is that increases in women's independent incomes increase their relative fallback position and thus their bargaining power in the home (and, presumably, their status and wellbeing in society at large). The implicit conclusion is that any process that intensifies women's incorporation into wage-labor is empowering. Women's incorporation into wage-labor holds such a strong place in the vision of intrahousehold empowerment that many models use women's wage-income as the sole factor explaining intrahousehold bargaining power. Indeed, wage-income is often used both to *explain* women's subordination and to *measure* their emancipation, with labor-force participation rates made a key index in historical and cross-cultural comparative studies of women's progress.

This vision of empowering work is the perspective we associate with liberal feminism from the second wave. Here, the main cause of women's subordination lies in their exclusion from employment and consequent entrapment and isolation in the home. Thus the key to women's emancipation lies in their entry into the workplace. Employment provides women with the financial independence needed for autonomy and freedom, and with the sense of self-worth and self-confidence that partaking in the public sphere and escaping the bonds of entrapment in the home is seen as bringing. Further, by entering the world of work women gain public recognition and status for their achievements, thus increasing the overall status of women within the home and in the broader society. Among U.S. feminists, Betty Friedan (1963) provides a good example of this perspective. Based on this vision, liberal feminist organizations like the National Organization of Women in the U.S. made efforts to increase women's employment and employability a key agenda for the second wave of feminist activism in the West.[7]

Within contemporary economics this liberal feminist approach informs the mainstream development literature on intrahousehold bargaining. One of the strongest explications and extensions of this perspective can be found in Sen (1990).[8] Here, beyond the fallback effect of the wage, Sen adds the concept of *perceived contribution* to the factors that affect bargaining power. He suggests that bargaining power is influenced by societal perceptions about different individuals' contributions to the family. These perceptions are held by both men and women, and reflect conventional presumptions about who is contributing more, or more substantively, to the household.

If women's contributions are in the form of household activities and men's contributions take the form of wages, even though both contributions are equally important for the maintenance of the household, the *perception* may be that men contribute more, and men will have a stronger bargaining position. Given such perceptions, since employment creates a visible, monetary contribution to the household's income, women's employment increases the *visibility* of contributions made by women to the household, thus increasing their bargaining power.

Here, Sen links the bargaining literature to the literature on the invisibility of women's work and opens the door to a broader feminist discussion of the public–private split that generates this invisibility. However, his solution is simply to draw women into the (pre-given, masculinized) public sphere. Thus his reading of the issue is close to Friedan's (1963) discussion of women's entrapment in the home, and his conclusions take us in liberal feminist directions.

In addition, Sen (1990) notes that women may be socialized to lack a strong concept of their own (individual) interests. Thus women's *perceived interests* may cause them not to use their bargaining power to further their own interests, further exacerbating intrahousehold inequalities.[9] To the extent that employment brings social validation and recognition, women's self-esteem and self-confidence increases. Furthermore, as employment allows women to interact with a world beyond their home they begin to think differently about their own interests. Though this additional psychological effect is by no means assured, entry into the workplace thus increases the possibilities of women gaining such new, liberated identities, which in turn increases their bargaining capacity in the home (Chen 1995). Perceived interest opens the door to critical feminist insights about the social construction of consciousness and identity. But the mainstream discussion of perceived interest (e.g. Nussbaum 2000), especially in the ways that it is applied to non-Western cultural contexts, returns us to a liberal-modernist imagination of what the liberated female self looks like (Charusheela, forthcoming).[10]

Thus, despite the diversity of contexts discussed or differences in model specification, we find that within this liberal-modernist framework employment empowers: it increases autonomy, self-worth, bargaining capacity. Thus, to the extent that processes such as globalization or development foster women's participation in waged labor, they empower women. If they are detrimental to women it is because they fail to incorporate women *adequately* into the labor force (and other relevant markets) or because (non-modernist) culture constrains this empowerment potential from *expressing* itself in the bargaining process.

This assessment is made explicit in the World Bank's 2001 report, *Engendering Development*, which draws heavily on the intrahousehold bargaining literature.[11] The report understands the gender impacts of policies mainly in terms of how "failures to recognize...gender-differentiated constraints when designing policies can compromise the effectiveness of those policies, from both equity and efficiency perspectives" (World Bank 2001: 14). Thus the problem does not lie in the policies' general agenda. Rather, it is that gendered factors require some additional ameliorative effort to more directly target women and incorporate them into this (pre-given) agenda.[12]

Counter-histories of women's incorporation into wage-labor

Within feminist thought, women of color from both the First and Third worlds (hooks 1981, 1984; Collins 1990; Anzaldúa and Moraga 1981; Mohanty 1984; Spivak 1985; Trinh 1989; Ong 1988) have noted that this liberal-modernist feminist vision, far from reflecting the universality of women's oppression, reflects the experience and perspective of very specific groups of women – mainly white, upper-class women in Western societies. This section demonstrates the locatedness of the mainstream bargaining models' vision by asking, what is the experience of labor-market entry that informs these liberal visions of empowering work?

I take up three interlinked presumptions about:

- the determinants of women's labor-supply decisions;
- the determinants of women's employment options;
- the relationship between development and reduced burdens of housework for women.

I show that these reflect an upper-class, white, European and U.S. experience by contrasting them with experiences of working-class, ethnic-minority, immigrant and non-Western women. This gives us a counter-history of paid labor, linking it not to empowerment, but to dispossession, exploitation, and structural disempowerment.

The determinants of women's labor-supply decisions

The standard neoclassical literature argues that women's labor-supply decisions are determined by the relative returns of market and nonmarket work. When the relative returns for engaging in paid labor outweigh the returns for engaging in nonmarket labor women move into the labor market. The volume of labor they supply is determined at the margin, as they supply labor up to the point where the marginal returns on both activities equalize. Thus, within these standard models we see an image of choice, where women *choose* between paid and unpaid labor. Here, women start to enter the labor market as the returns to their for-market activities increase and/or the returns to their nonmarket activities decrease. This happens as women's wages in the labor market rise and/or as mechanization, marketization, and reduced fertility[13] decrease the returns to women's nonmarket activities.

In this analysis, women's labor-market entry increases proportionate to class. This is because as income level goes up that increases the ability to access mechanization and to reduce burdens of household work through purchases of goods (e.g. going to a restaurant instead of preparing a meal). Higher income (or higher levels of development) also correlates to lower fertility, and thus lower burdens of childcare.[14] Thus, as income increases, not only are wages higher, but returns to reproductive activities start to drop as well. If this is right, then upper-class women should have entered the arena of wage-labor first (as their marginal returns would tip in favor of paid labor before it would tip for poorer women). But the literature on working-class and minority women's labor shows us that, in general, poorer women have been the first entrants into the labor market. In the Third world, where the majority of the worlds' population resides, poor women still "outrank" their upper-class sisters in terms of their labor-market entry.[15]

How do we account for this disparity? We note that the neoclassical models present the labor-supply decision as a choice, where women "choose" on the margin about whether to enter the labor market or not, and, if so, how much time to spend in the labor market. But for working-class women, immigrant women, ethnic-minority women in the First and Third worlds, work was and is necessary simply to put food on the table.

Some game-theorists explain the "oversupply" (i.e. beyond the point where it makes "marginal" sense) of labor for lower-income women by showing that women may also choose labor as a strategic aspect of intrahousehold bargaining, to ensure their partners do not get too great a bargaining advantage over them – this effect of "oversupplying labor" is especially marked where the woman's wage disadvantage is large due to higher levels of wage inequality (see Ott 1995).[16] Here, women scramble to balance work and family and keep multiple jobs in order to maintain their bargaining position *vis-à-vis* their *partners*. But the literature indicates that overworked women are rarely undertaking extra burdens of work as part of a strategy to increase their power in the home – often such situations reflect limits to power in *both* productive and reproductive spheres and women's difficulties obtaining leisure (Nash and Fernández-Kelly 1983; Benería and Roldán 1987; Benería and Feldman 1992; Safa 1995).

What is missing in these analyses of the labor-supply decision is a basic fact: Except for the fast-shrinking population of self-sufficient peasant families on family farms, reproductive labor cannot "produce" nonmarket outputs *without* market-purchased inputs. Thus the models fail to capture the extent to which *absolute income levels* determine labor-market entry, often in ways that swamp the effects of "marginal returns" to work in and out of the home. This is mainly because these models fail to see income as an *input* – and often a non-substitutable one – into women's nonmarket production function, and tend to depict the choice as between nonmarket and market-purchased *outputs*.[17] Thus, in these models we can do a "partial equilibrium" analysis of the effects of work on women without paying attention to the contexts that *push* – rather than pull – women into the labor force. But once we recognize that increased dependence on marketized products and/or lower wages may expel workers out of the household and into the marketplace in order to ensure that minimum levels of survival are met, we begin to get a very different image of the experience of work and of labor-market entry for women from different class backgrounds.

The determinants of women's employment options

Beyond the economically and structurally constructed differences in the decision-making process around labor supply, women from different backgrounds enter very different worlds of work. Neoclassical approaches explain the differences between these two worlds as the result of *supply-side* differences in the economic capabilities of differentially located women. In particular, neoclassical models assume that the key problem is human capital. When they examine working-class, ethnic-minority, non-Western women, neoclassicals argue that these women's "specialization" in nonmarket activities leaves them unable adequately to accumulate the "human capital" needed to engage in for-market activity. Furthermore, poor women have lower levels of educational attainment, which compounds the problem.[18] But for these factors, they too could enter well-paying and secure careers.

But positing "human capital development" as a general explanation, and hence as a strategy for handling the differential workplace experiences of members of different ethnic communities, fails to consider whether there is much *mobility* in the labor market. It also ignores the larger structural parameters that track workers into different jobs in the process of incorporating new members into the workplace. *How* do minority women get to enter the labor market? What are the jobs being created *for* them? Can they simply enter any occupation?

Historically, ethnic-minority women in the West did not get to enter the labor market based on "for-market" skills. They entered as nannies, housemaids, domestics – or, if less lucky, as prostitutes and sex workers (Dill 1988; Glenn 1981; Amott and Matthaei 1996). All these are job categories where the key skills are extensions of nonmarket activities. Minority women did not end up here mainly because of their "lower" market skills compared with their white sisters, but because they were barred from competing for other jobs within a structure that *tracked* women from minority groups into categories of necessary – and necessarily cheap – labor. This process was crucially linked to a racialized structure, where minority women were brought to do the work that nobody else – including white women – wanted to do (Glenn 1991). More than reproductive services, they produced leisure for upper-class women, a point we return to below.

Though civil rights activists have managed to reduce the racialized tracking of women and men into jobs, the care with which immigration and other laws are designed and redesigned to *control* labor-market flows indicates that this remains a key force in the types of jobs that are available for immigrant women from non-Western countries. Immigrant women from the non-West remain the single largest source for nannies, maids, and domestics in the U.S. (Romero 1992). This seems to have little to do with "education." For example, the Philippines, which has one of the best gender-ratios for education in Asia, is also the largest exporter of labor in the world. The majority of the labor it exports in the form of "overseas contract workers" (OCWs) is female. These workers do not get to enter race- or gender-integrated careers that draw on their education. The preponderance of OCWs are tracked into jobs as nurses (at the upper end), maids, nannies, domestics, or as "hostesses/dancers" (Lim and Oishi 1996; Wong 1996). The world these workers enter is very different from the world that young European women who work as au pairs enter. Human capital seems to be fairly irrelevant here; national origin appears much more relevant in explaining these labor-market differentials.

We see a similar pattern in the job categories for non-Western women created within their own national borders. For working-class women in the Third world, a key occupation remains that of maidservant (Chaney and Castro 1989). The same pattern emerges even in arenas where the jobs created are not direct extensions of reproductive services: The export zones (not just the garment, but also the electronics assembly work) hardly value high educational attainment in their employment practices. Race, ethnicity, and nationality (working in conjunction with gender) seem to be much more important.[19]

By raising questions about the link between human capital acquisition – whether around the "reproductive" qualities of women's nonmarket activities or the acquisition of educational qualifications – and job placement, these historical patterns raise a deeper issue. The underlying question is whether the image of education translating into better jobs is *structurally* unrealistic – today we see that, though education translates into better jobs for the educated compared to the less educated, the formal education needed to *get* good jobs has been increasing. This indicates that educational attainment may correlate to income mainly because it reflects class privilege, with education acting as an entry hurdle. If so, education is acting as a "class marker" in this process that tracks workers into raced and classed job categories. Skills or education do not *explain* the differential outcomes.

The relationship between development and reduced burdens of housework for women

As noted above, neoclassical models posit that women find paid labor more rewarding as returns to unpaid labor fall. A key link here is that development processes result in such a reduction. But evidence hardly suggests that working-class women have entered the labor force as they found free time on their hands as the returns to unpaid labor diminished with development. Instead, their experience is of a double, or even triple, burden. How have *upper-class* women gained freedom from household chores? Part of the story is, no doubt, the role of mechanization in reducing women's reproductive burdens. Another part is decreased household duties due to fewer children. One more part – a much smaller part – is men's increased willingness to share household duties.

But an important part – one that has not received adequate attention in the mainstream economics literature – is hidden under the "marketization" rubric: the ability of upper-class women to use a portion of their income to purchase reproductive goods from the market. Who produces these marketized goods? Who acts as the nanny, maid, food-service-sector worker, garment producer? Usually it is other women, women from minority, working-class, Third-world, immigrant backgrounds. And what ensures that the *cost* of purchasing these goods from the market is low enough to *make* it "rational" for upper-class women to purchase them while entering the labor market? It is the racial–class structuration of wages and job categories noted in the previous subsection (pp. 292–4).

The story of development empowering women has another side to it – that of *some* women's empowerment becoming enabled by the cheap labor supplied by their less fortunate sisters (and some less fortunate brothers). Ethnic-minority, working-class women provide the cheap services of nannies, maids, and domestics within the home that allow other women to leave the home and enter the empowering world of work. Working-class women, ethnic-minority and non-elite Third-world women also provide the cheap labor that ensures that key goods purchased outside the home – ranging from computers and clothes to "take-out" food – remain cheap enough to *make* the marginal return for (upper-class) incomes outweigh the returns to undertaking production within the home.[20] Thus we need to consider the extent to which some women's *choice* to enter the labor market rests on other women's *necessity* to do so based on structurally generated divergences of the types noted in the subsection on women's labor-supply decisions (pp. 290–2).

If this is the case, we should reconsider how far "development" can be seen as a *general* solution to the problem of women's reproductive burdens. The macro-structural logic of this process rests at least in part on *shifting* the burden of that work down the line to other shoulders. Left unanswered in such shifts is whether the women whose low wage *enables* the reduction of work burdens for upper-class women earn enough to then become freed from reproductive burdens themselves. Who cares for the nannies' kids?

Intersubjective difference in economic analysis: bargaining models reconsidered

The above discussion shows us the locatedness of the bargaining models' liberal-modernist vision of empowering labor. This vision reflects the experiences of women who enter the labor force from locations that *allow* work to be empowering – educated, upper- and middle-class women, usually white, who face not a job but a career. In such a context, of course, work is felt and known as a choice, and a liberating one. But for women who do not come from such locations the experience of work is often far from empowering. The above discussion suggests that such differences in the experience of work emerge from within the broader race–class structure of the economy.

This raises theoretical issues about the types of analytical frameworks we use for feminist economic analysis. As Agarwal (1997) points out, while bargaining models are attractive for feminist economists as an alternative to unitary models of the household, the mainstream bargaining literature has tended to ignore a variety of issues. She notes:

> [T]hese formulations, consisting mostly of formal models, are restricted in their ability to incorporate the full complexity of gender interactions within the household, and the simultaneity of various forms of decision-making. In addition, most say little about gender relations beyond the household.
> (Agarwal 1997: 2)

Here, I contribute to the growing literature on critical limits to neoclassical bargaining (Seiz 1991; Nelson 1995; Agarwal 1997) by showing the limits of efforts to address difference within the neoclassical game-theoretic framework.

I begin with the question of sameness and difference. As we move past purely universalist approaches which posit sameness and homogeneity everywhere, we find three distinct ways of theorizing difference: difference as *deviance*, difference as *diversity*, and difference as something *intersubjectively constituted within social structures of power and control*.

When difference is treated as *deviance* the individual subject of liberal-modernity is posited as the norm and/or the ideal, and differences from it are treated as deviances from the ideal. When difference is conceptualized as *diversity*, differences between groups are recognized but groups are not ranked.

However, differences are understood as reflecting *localized* variations in context, with no underlying link between the experiences of the different and separable groups. A third way to think of difference is to see it as reflecting and emerging out of structural differences in *location*. The distinction between the *localized* and the *located* here centers on the issue of power within a structure of interaction that makes differentially constituted experiences for differently located groups of people. This understanding of difference moves us to an *intersubjective* comprehension of experience and meaning, where the differences *themselves* emerge out of the power dynamics embedded in the processes of economic interaction *between* the different groups.

Here, I use the terms deviance, diversity, and intersubjective difference to denote these three ways of theorizing the experiences of different women within our analyses. I argue that neoclassical theory – including its game-theoretic variants – is founded on a social ontology that requires it to theorize difference as either deviance or diversity. Intersubjective difference is unthinkable in neoclassical economics for foundational reasons. No amount of respecifying models or fine-tuning parameters will alter the fact that insights about intersubjective phenomena cannot be captured by this theory.

Below, I consider several efforts to fix up bargaining models and discuss their limitations. I draw on the list of critical limits to bargaining models raised by Agarwal (1997). One issue raised in the previous sections and also identified by Agarwal is whether employment is the only factor determining fallback positions.[21] While McElroy's (1990) addition of extra-household environmental parameters (EEPs) to bargaining models avoids making the wage the sole determinant of bargaining success, EEPs remain exogenous to the model. This procedure treats the resetting of different aspects of the fallback positions generated by marketization as exogenous, and cannot take up the link between the loss of alternate means of supporting oneself, low wages, and labor-market entry created by marketization raised above (pp. 290–2).

More broadly, how do we model the questions of social perception and meaning raised by Sen and others? Katz (1997) has proposed attaching a parameter or weight to functions of the basic cooperative bargaining model. Thus, one could incorporate Sen's (non-neoclassical) insight about perceived contributions and interests by attaching weights to indicate differences in men's and women's ability to translate their fallback position into gains. However, this procedure treats intersubjective questions of perception and meaning as exogenous. This seems unsatisfactory, as it presumes that issues of perception and meaning are separable from the socialization that a process of intrahousehold bargaining would *itself* create.

Katz (1997) also proposes that we use non-cooperative games as an alternative way of getting at issues of power and control in intrahousehold bargaining. But, while this procedure can help ensure that our models reflect asymmetric power relations within the household, it still treats key asymmetries (such as asymmetries in perception of contributions or asymmetries in ability to convert fallbacks into actual gains through bargaining) as exogenous, rather than as intersubjectively generated. Furthermore, in all these models we lack guidelines on how to choose among the various models on offer (Katz 1997: 36). This is because each household emerges as an essentially separate and separable unit. Thus this procedure cannot handle the challenge to feminist theorizing that the counter-histories of work discussed above raise.[22]

All these procedures approach difference as diversity – that is, as a variety of local contexts. Not only are we not told where these exogenous parameters and rules come from, but the possibility that they might come in part from within the model is excluded. With EEPs (McElroy 1990) and parametrization (Katz 1997), the thinking subject is approached by dividing her into an ideal modernist individual, on the one hand, and various external parameters, on the other, which together add up to the experience of the working-class, ethnic-minority, or Third-world woman. Here, issues of culture and subject-formation are added on as essentially *separable* modifiers of a pre-given structure. The unchanged bargaining subject at the core of the model remains an ideal upper-class white woman, reflecting an underlying difference-as-deviance approach beneath the more visible difference-as-diversity one.

Even where questions of structure–agent interaction are partially endogenized through particularities of rules in non-cooperative games (Katz 1997), all we have is adaptations of models to describe *localized* differences, still leaving us within the confines of diversity.[23] Thus, to the extent that the issues raised in the previous section are addressed, they are taken up as additional factors that may *modify* economic interaction, but do not *emerge* out of the structure of economic interaction itself.

Why do game-theoretical models fail in their efforts to take up difference? This is because these models contain a very *thin* comprehension of the broader economic structure that *positions* individuals differently. Because their analytical framework conceptualizes society as a field of interaction between *individual* agents, such models do not, and cannot, address questions concerning the relationship between broader processes of economic structuring and restructuring and the *constitution* of differentially located subjectivities in their analysis. Aspects of intersubjective interaction that construct experience and meaning very differently for differentially located subjects remain hidden by the neoclassical game-theoretic models.

Thus, to the extent that such models recognize differences between women, they do so through the lens of diversity in local particularities. The very thin concept of economic structure allows the analysis to proceed as if the particularities of one woman's context are quite unrelated to the very different context her less privileged sister may face. Class is simply differences in income; race and ethnicity differences in culture; and so on. If there are some (potential) links around race and/or class location, these are orthogonal, in that race, class, nationality, and ethnicity are essentially separable from gender. Thus, one can use "ceteris paribus" and "comparative static" exercises that distil the essential, universal (read particular) "female" experience and treat race, class, and ethnicity as essentially additive. These models are unable to recognize that differences reflect structured differences in locatedness or positionality, and so differences between women reflect differences in subjectivity that are created and recreated in intersubjective interaction. Intersubjective approaches see differences as emerging *from* interaction within unequally structured relationships. This is very different from simply noting that differences exist, but not seeing the differences themselves as the product of interaction *between* the two differing parties.

This absence of attention to intersubjective dimensions of economic interaction reflects a modernist understanding of subjecthood, and can be seen in the implicit *meanings* attached to the experience of paid labor. In these models, paid work acts as the sphere of autonomy, of alternatives and choices, even of increased visibility and increased senses of contribution and self-worth, for people trapped by home, by tradition, by culture, and so on. But paid work has a very different historical memory and meaning for descendants of slaves, for displaced peasants, for racialized migrants, and immigrants brought in to be the cheap labor at the bottom of the labor market. The actual experience of work, far from being a liberation from the bonds of home, was and is often demeaning, undignified, and oppressive.

Notes

1 Thanks to Edith Kuiper, Drucilla Barker, and Colin Danby for comments and suggestions.
2 See, for example, the conversation on postmodernism and postcolonialism between McCloskey (2000) and Spivak (2000).
3 Mainstream neoclassical bargaining is discussed below. For examples of non-neoclassical scholars who draw on frameworks inspired by interdisciplinary Marxist-institutionalist-feminist thought, see Folbre (1986, 1988, 1994); Agarwal (1990, 1994, 1997).
4 See McElroy and Horney (1981), Ott (1992, 1995), Bourguignon and Chiappori (1992), Lundberg and Pollack (1993), and Kanbur and Haddad (1994). For surveys and critical reviews of this scholarship, see Haddad *et al.* (1994, 1997), Hart (1995), Doss (1996), and Katz (1997).
5 Games can be cooperative or non-cooperative (see Katz 1997 for a critical discussion of the pros and cons of these two ways of modeling intrahousehold bargaining from a feminist perspective). They can also be "static" (single-period) or "dynamic" (multi-period or repeated games). In repeated games the results of the game from one period may influence outcomes in the next, and agents may factor in the consequences of their decisions for their bargaining position in the next period when undertaking their maximization decisions in the previous period (see Ott 1995, and Kanbur and Haddad 1994 for examples of multi-period games). One can include further twists around possible differences in levels of contract enforceability over the period the game is played (Ott 1995) – similar issues of enforceability are raised in critiques of Becker's "Rotten Kid" theorem (Doss 1996: 1,598).
6 In the model of Lundberg and Pollack (1993) the alternative to cooperative marriage is not divorce, but the establishment of separate spheres.
7 Reflecting on this vision after almost two decades, Friedan describes the first stage of the second wave of the U.S. feminist movement as follows:

> Once we broke through the feminine mystique and said that women were people, we merely applied the abstract values of all previous liberal movements and radical revolutions, as defined by men, to protest our oppression, exploitation and exclusion from man's world, and to demand an equal share of its powers and rewards as previously wielded and enjoyed by men.
>
> (Friedan 1981: 239)

Thus, she notes, the "first stage focused on equal opportunity and equal pay for women doing the work that men did before" (ibid.: 241). She concludes that this mode of thinking was a problem (because it maintained a public–private split in our comprehension of work and simply sought to integrate women into a male-defined sphere of the public), and calls for a brand new way of thinking for the second stage of feminism. This move is positive, although she does not acknowledge or credit feminist scholars from ethnic-minority and radical traditions who have raised this point.

8 As we will see in the concluding section (pp. 295–8), Sen's insights begin to take us in very non-neoclassical directions. Thus, his use of game-theoretic bargaining models to frame his discussions of intrahousehold dynamics is best seen as a heuristic link, rather than a formal one.

9 Papanek (1990) seeks to capture a similar idea through her concept of compulsory emotions. Other scholars raise this in terms of socialization of consciousness (Nussbaum 2000: 114).

10 The role of modernism in this framework becomes even clearer when we examine the literature on gender-divergent responses to development projects by agricultural households (Jones 1983, 1986; Guyer and Peters 1987; Carter and Katz 1997). A closer look at the literature on agrarian production shows that, in general, what these models examine is how and why women may, in an effort to maintain intra-familial bargaining position, refuse to supply labor to production activities that generate income for their *husbands*. *Extra-familial* employment (or, more accurately, independent, "separate-spheres" production), in fact, sets the fallback position, and hence any increase in that sphere is positive for women. The policy conclusion thus follows: The key to successful agrarian policy is designing projects that increase women's participation in extra-familial paid labor or for-market production. Indeed, it is quite unclear whether it makes a difference for empowerment whether women supply labor or outputs, as long as the income goes to them and not to their husband/family.

   The same general result can be extended from the specifically agrarian, mainly (non-North) African, contexts addressed by the literature taken up above, to producer-households more generally. Hence, development planners propose to empower women through policies that increase their direct incorporation into the market for a host of cultures and contexts. A classic example of this is the widespread influence of the Grameen Bank model of providing credit for women's income-generating activities, a model that has become part of the project for attaining women's emancipation by promoting women's micro-enterprise development worldwide.

11 Bergeron (2001) provides a deconstruction of the language of gender-inclusion and gender-empowerment within the World Bank discourse promoting globalization and development.

12 This positive assessment of globalization and economic restructuring is not generally shared by feminist economists addressing the issue from alternate perspectives and frameworks (see Benería et al. 2000).

13 In this literature, fertility reduces as children move from being a productive asset to a consumption item due to development, and as the costs of children rise. Additional factors (risks associated with child mortality) may also strategically redo the general numbers – but not the overall direction – of these results.

14 Fertility can increase at very high income levels. But this applies to a very small fraction of women even in rich countries, as it refers primarily to situations where families are so well off that the cost of children becomes irrelevant in making fertility decisions.

15 Making this point entails counting "undercounted" sectors of paid work (work in the informal sector, women's for-market agricultural activities, and so on). See Benería (1992) for a discussion.

16 This result is in contrast to models where the same strategic process leads men to *curtail* women's for-market activities as a way of maintaining bargaining advantage.
17 The closest one comes to understanding the importance of marketization for setting the context in which commodities are not merely final outputs but inputs into nonmarket production – especially the production of humans and "human capital" – outside the Marxist literature on enclosures and the processes by which labor becomes "freed" to erupt into the labor market, is in the literature on endowments (see Sen 1981). But I have not seen any of the neoclassical discussions of the household take this point into account in their models of the labor-supply decision.
18 This lower educational attainment could in turn be attributed to their gender – but it is rarely attributed to race/class in the same way, in the sense that we see no bargaining models that show us how a dominant community may use their advantage to ensure that their countries "underinvest" in minorities in order to maintain bargaining advantage.
19 The structural conscription of non-Western women into sexualized and/or servile labor within the transnational organization of labor is particularly linked to neocolonial projects expressed through militarization and neoliberalism. This is most visible when we examine the social processes that draw women into the ambit of work around military bases and in the tourism industry, and when we interrogate the social relations that emerge around work in these job categories (Enloe 1990).
20 This point does not even address the issue of "mechanization" as a means of reducing reproductive burdens. The link between non-Western women's economic subordination and Western upper-class women's freedom from reproductive burdens under processes of development becomes much clearer once we ask, how do we get the resource control needed to ensure our technology *enables* us to reduce reproductive burdens? After all, mechanization becomes part of the story only if you can afford the electricity to run the machines in addition to being able to pay for the appliances – which raises issues about energy consumption and resource control across classes both locally and globally.
21 Additional factors affecting the fallback can include ownership of property; and nonmarket resources such as access to commons resources, social safety nets provided by the state, support from nongovernmental organizations, or access to traditional support systems from kin, community, and friends (Agarwal 1990, 1994).
22 If the neoclassical models face difficulties in handling the intersubjective issues raised by social perceptions, they have even more difficulty with intersubjective issues of identity and motivation, such as those raised by perceived interest. To the extent that perceived interest could be taken up by the neoclassical framework, it would have to be handled as a question of economic altruism by women who prioritize the interests of others above themselves. See Agarwal (1997: 22–8) for a careful discussion of the issues of perceived interest and altruism.

In the neoclassical framework, one would model this by incorporating the utility function for household members into women's utility functions. In general, game-theoretic bargaining models do not model altruistic behavior. This is because the game-theoretic framework ontologically requires separated and separable selves to work – Mirowski (2002) notes that game theory's conception of the self goes well beyond the Walrasian neoclassical conception of a self in an asocial world (which is more amenable to this type of modification), becoming a self that views others as antagonistic (and thus not amenable to such modifications). While one can modify utility functions to take up bargaining on behalf of third parties (so one can incorporate effects on children into women's utility functions, for example), it is quite unclear what it would mean for the set-up of bargaining models if one were to bargain on behalf of the *opposing* party. Thus, one could not handle the issue of perceived interests raised by Sen and others within the structure of bargaining models.
23 As noted above, the underlying subject of game theory is even more restrictive than the standard neoclassical subject. If non-cooperative games do not treat difference as deviance, it is because difference is erased by theorizing essentially homogenous subjects. Subjects may face a diversity of contexts (rules), but are themselves essentially unchanged.

Bibliography

Agarwal, Bina (1990) "Social Security and the Family: Coping with Seasonality and Calamity in Rural India," *Journal of Peasant Studies* 17(3): 341–412.

—— (1994) *A Field of One's Own: Gender and Land Rights in South Asia*, Cambridge: Cambridge University Press

—— (1997) " 'Bargaining' and Gender Relations: Within and Beyond the Household," *Feminist Economics* 3(1): 1–51.

Amott, Teresa and Julie Matthaei (1996) *Race, Gender and Work: A Multicultural Economic History of Women in the United States*, rev. edn., Boston, MA: South End Press.

Anzaldúa, Gloria and Cherríe Moraga (eds.) (1981) *This Bridge Called My Back: Writings by Radical Women of Color*, Watertown, MA: Persephone Press.

Benería, Lourdes (1992) "Accounting for Women's Work: The Progress of Two Decades," *World Development* 30(11): 1,547–60.

Benería, Lourdes and Shelley Feldman (eds.) (1992) *Unequal Burden: Economic Crises, Persistent Poverty, and Women's Work*, Boulder, CO: Westview Press.

Benería, Lourdes and Martha Roldán (1987) *The Crossroads of Class and Gender: Industrial Homework, Subcontracting, and Household Dynamics in Mexico City*, Chicago, IL: University of Chicago Press.

Benería, Lourdes, Maria Floro, Caren Grown and Martha MacDonald (eds.) (2000) *Globalization*, Special Issue of *Feminist Economics* 6(3).

Bergeron, Suzanne (2001) "Challenging the World Bank's Narrative of Inclusion," paper presented at the Allied Social Science Associations meetings, New Orleans.

Bourguignon, François and Pierre-André Chiappori (1992) "Collective Models of Household Behavior: An Introduction," *European Economic Review* 36(2–3): 355–64.

Carter, Michael and Elizabeth Katz (1997) "Separate Spheres and the Conjugal Contract: Understanding the Impact of Gender-Biased Development," in Lawrence Haddad, John Hoddinott and Harold Alderman (eds.) *Intrahousehold Resource Allocation in Developing Countries: Methods, Models and Policies*, Baltimore, MD: Johns Hopkins.

Chaney, Elsa and Mary Garcia Castro (eds.) (1989) *Muchachas No More: Household Workers in Latin America and the Caribbean*, Philadelphia, PA: Temple University Press.

Charusheela, S. (forthcoming) "The Promise and Limits of Martha Nussbaum's Universalist Ethics," *Feminist Economics*.

Chen, Martha (1995) "A Matter of Survival: Women's Right to Employment in India and Bangladesh," in Martha Nussbaum and Jonathan Glover (eds.) *Women, Culture, and Development: A Study of Human Capabilities*, New York: Oxford University Press.

Collins, Patricia Hill (1990) *Black Feminist Thought: Knowledge, Consciousness and the Politics of Empowerment*, Boston, MA: Unwin Hyman.

Dill, Bonnie Thornton (1988) "Our Mothers' Grief: Racial Ethnic Women and the Maintenance of Families," *Journal of Family History* 13(4): 415–31.

Doss, Cheryl (1996) "Testing Among Models of Intrahousehold Resource Allocation," *World Development* 24(10): 1,597–609.

Enloe, Cynthia (1990) *Bananas, Beaches, and Bases: Making Feminist Sense of International Politics*, Berkeley, CA: University of California Press.

Folbre, Nancy (1986) "Hearts and Spades: Paradigms of Household Economics," *World Development* 14(2): 245–55.

—— (1988) "The Black Four of Hearts: Towards a New Paradigm of Household Economics," in Daisy Dwyer and Judith Bruce (eds.) *A Home Divided: Women and Income in the Third World*, Stanford, CA: Stanford University Press.

—— (1994) *Who Pays for the Kids? Gender and Structures of Constraint*, New York: Routledge.

Friedan, Betty (1963) *The Feminine Mystique*, New York: Norton.

—— (1981) *The Second Stage*, New York: Summit Books.
Gilroy, Paul (1993) *The Black Atlantic: Modernity and Double Consciousness*, Cambridge, MA: Harvard University Press.
Glenn, Evelyn Nakano (1981) "Occupational Ghettoization: Japanese American Women and Domestic Service, 1905–1970," *Ethnicity* 7(4): 352–86.
—— (1991) "Racial Ethnic Women's Labor: The Intersection of Race, Gender, and Class Oppression," in Rae L. Blumberg (ed.) *Gender, Family and Economy: The Triple Overlap*, Newbury Park, CA: Sage Publications.
Guyer, Jane and Pauline Peters (eds.) (1987) *Conceptualizing the Household: Issues of Theory and Policy in Africa*, Special Issue of *Development and Change* 18(2).
Haddad, Lawrence, John Hoddinott and Harold Alderman (1994) "Intrahousehold Resource Allocation: An Overview," Policy Research Working Paper no. 1255 (February), Washington, DC: World Bank.
—— (eds.) (1997) *Intrahousehold Resource Allocation in Developing Countries: Methods, Models and Policies*, Baltimore, MD: Johns Hopkins.
Hart, Gillian (1995) "Gender and Household Dynamics: Recent Theories and Their Implications," in M.G. Quibria (ed.) *Critical Issues in Asian Development: Theories, Experiences and Policies*, New York: Oxford University Press (for the Asian Development Bank).
hooks, bell (1981) *Ain't I a Woman: Black Women and Feminism*, Boston, MA: South End Press.
—— (1984) *Feminist Theory From Margin to Center*, Boston, MA: South End Press.
Jones, Christine (1983) "The Mobilization of Women's Labor for Cash Crop Production: A Game-Theoretic Approach," *American Journal of Agricultural Economics* 65(5): 1,049–54.
—— (1986) "Intra-household Bargaining in Response to the Introduction of New Crops: A Case Study from Northern Cameroon," in Joyce L. Moock (ed.) *Understanding Africa's Rural Households and Farming Systems*, Boulder, CO: Westview.
Kanbur, Ravi and Lawrence Haddad (1994) "Are Better Off Households More Unequal or Less Unequal?," *Oxford Economic Papers* 46: 445–58.
Katz, Elizabeth (1997) "The Intra-Household Economics of Voice and Exit," *Feminist Economics* 3(3): 25–46.
Lim, Lin Lean and Nana Oishi (1996) "International Labor Migration of Asian Women: Distinctive Characteristics and Policy Concerns," *Asian and Pacific Migration Journal* 5(1): 85–116.
Lundberg, Shelly and Robert Pollack (1993) "Separate Spheres Bargaining and the Marriage Market," *Journal of Political Economy* 101(6): 988–1,010.
Manser, Marilyn and Murray Brown (1979) "Bargaining Analysis of Household Decisions," in Cynthia Lloyd, Emily Andrews and Curtis Gilroy (eds.) *Women in the Labor Market*, New York: Columbia Press.
—— (1980) "Marriage and Household Decision-Making: A Bargaining Analysis," *International Economic Review* 21(1): 31–44.
McCloskey, Deirdre (2000) "Postmodern Market Feminism: Half of a Conversation with Gayatri Chakravorty Spivak," *Rethinking Marxism* 12(4): 27–36.
McElroy, Marjorie (1990) "The Empirical Content of Nash-Bargained Household Behavior," *Journal of Human Resources* 25(4): 559–83.
McElroy, Marjorie and Mary Jean Horney (1981) "Nash-Bargained Household Decisions: Toward a Generalization of the Theory of Demand," *International Economic Review* 22(2): 333–50.
Mirowski, Phillip (2002) *Machine Dreams: Economics Becomes a Cyborg Science*, New York: Cambridge University Press.
Mohanty, Chandra Talpade (1984) "Under Western Eyes: Feminist Scholarship and Colonial Discourses," *Boundary 2* 12(3)–13(1): 333–58.
Nash, June and María Patricia Fernández-Kelly (eds.) (1983) *Women, Men, and the International Division of Labor*, Albany, NY: SUNY Press.

Nelson, Julie (1995) "Economic Theory and Feminist Theory: Comments on Chapters by Polachek, Ott, and Levin," in Edith Kuiper and Jolande Sap (eds.) *Out of the Margin: Feminist Perspectives on Economics*, New York: Routledge.

Nussbaum, Martha (2000) *Women and Human Development*, New York: Cambridge University Press.

Ong, Aihwa (1988) "Colonialism and Modernity: Feminist Re-presentations of Women in Non-Western Societies," *Inscriptions* 3(4): 79–93.

Ott, Notburga (1992) *Intrafamily Bargaining and Household Decisions*, Berlin: Springer-Verlag.

—— (1995) "Fertility and Division of Work in the Family: A Game Theoretic Model of Household Decisions," in Edith Kuiper and Jolande Sap (eds.) *Out of the Margin: Feminist Perspectives on Economics*, New York: Routledge

Papanek, Hanna (1990) "To Each Less Than She Needs, From Each More Than She Can Do: Allocations, Entitlements, and Value," in Irene Tinker (ed.) *Persistent Inequalities: Women and World Development*, New York: Oxford University Press.

Romero, Mary (1992) *Maid in the U.S.A*, New York: Routledge.

Safa, Helen (1995) *The Myth of the Male Breadwinner: Women and Industrialization in the Caribbean*, Boulder, CO: Westview Press.

Seiz, Janet (1991) "The Bargaining Approach and Feminist Methodology," *Review of Radical Political Economics* 23(1–2): 22–9.

Sen, Amartya K. (1981) *Poverty and Famines: An Essay on Entitlements and Deprivation*, New York: Oxford University Press.

—— (1990) "Gender and Cooperative Conflicts," in Irene Tinker (ed.) *Persistent Inequalities: Women and World Development*, New York: Oxford University Press.

Spivak, Gayatri C. (1985) "Three Women's Texts and a Critique of Imperialism," *Critical Inquiry* 12(1): 243–61.

—— (2000) "Other Things are Never Equal: A Speech," *Rethinking Marxism*, 12(4): 37–44.

Trinh, T. Minh-ha (1989) *Woman, Native, Other: Writing Postcoloniality and Feminism*, Bloomington, IN: Indiana University Press.

Wong, Diana (1996) "Foreign Domestic Workers in Singapore," *Asian and Pacific Migration Journal* 5(1): 117–38.

World Bank (IBRD) (2001) *Engendering Development Through Gender Equality in Rights, Resources, and Voice*, New York: Oxford University Press (for the World Bank).

19 Economic marginalia

Postcolonial readings of unpaid domestic labor and development

Cynthia A. Wood

In this essay, I explore the implications of postcolonial feminist thought for analyses of mainstream economics' marginalization of unpaid domestic labor, or housework. Through close readings of theories of economic development, I consider the following questions: Do "third-world" contexts force development economists to recognize the existence of women's work which is ignored in economic analyses of the North?[1] If so, does this imply the incorporation of unpaid domestic labor? Are there differences in the unpaid domestic labor of women in the South and those in "developed" countries which are relevant to this discussion? How do "first-world" experiences shape definitions of economic activity? What are the implications of all of this for the material lives of women currently subjected to "development"?

I argue that the existence of different forms of nonmarket work in "less developed" countries complicates mechanisms of marginalizing unpaid domestic labor in development economics. This analysis deconstructs foundational assumptions of economics to show how they reproduce and reinforce postcolonial systems of power, to the particular detriment of many women in the South. It is premised on the belief that what appears on the margins is often most revealing of a discourse and most productive of new directions. Slips of the tongue, things seen peripherally, unexpected metaphors or absences can guide us to the rifts or seams of a discourse and be used to pry it apart. These marginalia are the traces of the obscuring and obscured in economics, good reasons to look at unpaid domestic labor and the "third world" together.

Such an approach is vital to understanding the material effects of development on women in Asia, Africa, and Latin America. The huge development industry which has emerged over the last fifty years applies policy in these regions based on hegemonic theories of economic development. Such theories marginalize the experiences of women generally and those of Southern women in particular. People being "developed" have little input into development policy, and often no choice in whether or not it is applied, despite extraordinary as well as everyday forms of resistance which constantly challenge mainstream development in the field(s).[2] Women often lose even more than men in this scenario.

While feminist economists have devoted considerable and sophisticated attention to the theoretical exclusion of unpaid domestic and caring labor from mainstream economics, they have generally done so without taking into account differences between women in the North and South (e.g. see Folbre 1995; Himmelweit 1995, 1999; Woolley 1999; Nelson 1999; Jefferson and King 2001). Even those who discuss third-world women's unpaid work do not necessarily recognize the implications of these differences for conceptualizations of domesticity, care, and labor, or for policies deriving from these conceptualizations when applied to the South (e.g. see Folbre 1986, 1994; Akram-Lodhi 1996; Floro 1999).[3]

Not looking at differences results in unintended "first-world" bias in feminist economic analysis of unpaid domestic labor.[4] For example, stating that time-use trade-offs for work are between wage-labor and unpaid domestic labor ignores other possibilities that might be relevant in some areas of the South, such as unpaid subsistence farming or care for small animals (see Himmelweit 1995). Similarly, saying that unpaid domestic labor consists of activities such as "cleaning, cooking, and childcare" does not appear to define these activities in terms of first-world experience. However, it elides important differences in conditions of work which will not be considered by Northern audiences unless their attention is drawn to them explicitly; cleaning a house with open windows and a dirt floor in southern India is very different (both qualitatively and quantitatively) from doing so in an urban apartment in the U.S.[5]

Related to the problem of first-world bias in conceptualizations of unpaid domestic labor is that of homogenizing the experiences of women in places other than the North. This is particularly an issue in the context of development, which gives little attention to differences in the regions subjected to it. This essay concentrates on first-world bias and highlights differences in the unpaid domestic labor of "North" and "South," which poses the danger of homogenizing women across each of these problematic categories. In part, this problem emerges from material conditions; some women are at the receiving end of development, others are not, and this is something that unifies them despite their diversity. But I am also working with conceptualizations within economics which depend upon opposing categories of North and South. I use these categories only in hopes of disrupting them. There is also a dearth of empirical data on differences in women's unpaid work across the South, largely due to the conceptual biases I discuss. Where possible, I attempt to call attention to these differences and suggest the implications of varieties of unpaid domestic labor for economic theory.

If feminist economics is not to contribute to the marginalization and homogenization of Southern women's experiences it must incorporate the insights of postcolonial theory and pay attention to these economic marginalia. My discussion of the treatment of unpaid domestic labor and other nonmarket production in development economics serves in part to reinforce feminist analysis of the marginalization of such labor in mainstream theory generally. But it also illuminates the postcolonial face of that marginalization, as assumptions about economic progress and definitions of economic activity are revealed in the hinterlands to be gendered constructions constituted through first-world experiences and interests, which do special harm to women in the South.

Reading development and the market

Much feminist work has shown that the market is privileged in mainstream economic theory and that this results in the marginalization of unpaid domestic labor (Himmelweit 1995; Waring 1988; Wood 1997). Development economics is no exception to this generalization.[6] Economists of the early postwar period, such as P.N. Rosenstein-Rodan, Ragnar Nurkse, Walt Rostow, and W. Arthur Lewis, focused on how to bring about market growth in less developed countries through government-directed investments in physical capital (Bruton 1958: 219; Arndt 1981: 465; Myrdal 1981: 507; Meier 1984: 6). Most of these economists did not discuss nonmarket economic activity at all; a few discussed it in terms which marginalized it. This absence of attention is striking given the importance of subsistence agriculture in economies defined as "underdeveloped" largely due to small and inadequate markets (see Rosenstein-Rodan 1958: 245; Nurkse 1958: 257).

It is so striking that it alerts us to look more closely and to ask some questions at/from/of the margins. What is the function of inattention to nonmarket economic activity in postwar contexts of globalizing corporate capitalism? Whose interests are served by its marginalization, when "development" is constituted by gendered processes and institutions, as it must be? Postcolonial feminist theory suggests that this marginalization is neither coincidental nor inconsequential to understanding development economics. Since noncommodity production is most important in economies of the South, and is dominated by poor folk of all genders and by women from various classes, its marginalization serves to (re)enforce "first-world" as well as male bias in development economics.

It is perhaps obvious to say at this point that the North is the model for economic progress in development economics, which assumes that the third world "develops" to the degree that it becomes like the "first world." Yet the connotations of this are subtle and inextricably implicated in postcolonial systems of domination. It is not just that economies of the South must come to have markets, for example, but that they must have the same or similar markets as those in the North. In some cases they must come to have them in the same way that the North did or does. None of this is gender-neutral, though it may appear to be so. As Catherine Scott points out, the view of modernization which underlies such a conception of development is situated "in opposition to a feminized and traditional household" (Scott 1995: 5).

In the early postwar period this is most evident in W. Arthur Lewis's dual economy model, which recognized the "traditional" nonmarket sector as economic, but only to better understand how and why to eliminate it. Lewis argued that many workers in underdeveloped economies have a marginal productivity of labor equal to zero: farmers, casual workers, petty traders in the informal economy, "retainers" such as domestic servants, and women in the household. The movement of surplus labor from this "subsistence sector" to the "capitalist" sector of the formal market would automatically bring about an increase in productivity and therefore growth (Lewis 1958: 402–6). Acknowledging the subsistence sector as economic, he simultaneously defines it as "less" economic than the formal market sector: "what one gets are very heavily developed patches of the economy, surrounded by economic darkness" (ibid.: 409).

Lewis's understanding of the subsistence economy includes women's unpaid domestic work such as "grinding grain, fetching water from the river, making clothes, cooking the midday meal, teaching children, nursing the sick, etc." (ibid.: 404; see also Elson 1999: 96–7). But, like all economic activities, this work could be performed better in the market sector. According to Lewis, "the transfer of women's work from the household to commercial employment is one of the most notable features of economic development" (Lewis 1958: 404). Women's economic activity, both paid and unpaid, is relegated to the margins by Lewis's analysis. In the "economic darkness" which surrounds the capitalist sector is an economy dominated by women, working in subsistence farming, in the informal economy, in domestic service, and in the household.[7]

The marginalization of noncommodity production in development economics carries with it that of unpaid domestic labor. The primary mechanism of marginalization is the privileging of the market, which confirms an important aspect of feminist analysis of the exclusion of unpaid domestic labor in mainstream economics. However, the postcolonial context is not dispensable to this analysis. Incorporating the various experiences of women of the South requires more than adding third-world examples; the conceptual apparatus must begin with awareness of difference among and between women of different regions, cultures, and classes. Analyzing definitions of economic activity in the context of development provides further insight on this point. What is meant (and not meant) by work, production, and economic activity is shaped by gender, but always in a postcolonial frame.

Defining economic activity

While the commoditized aspects of Lewis's subsistence economy can be readily identified as economic within development economics, the noncommodity sector is more difficult. Some nonmonetary definition of economic activity must be constructed to distinguish the large (if inferior) nonmarket economy from those activities considered noneconomic. As in models of household production, a "third-party criterion" is generally used to make this distinction in development models which acknowledge the existence of nonmarket economic activity. According to this criterion, if an activity or its product could be performed by a third party and sold on the market, then that activity is economic. This definition is not neutral. Considering the third-party criterion in the light of postcolonial feminist theory reveals "first-world" as well as masculinist biases which have serious consequences for women in the South.

I have argued elsewhere that there are two problems with the third-party criterion from a feminist perspective, one theoretical and one practical (Wood 1997). The theoretical problem is that by setting the market as the defining standard for economic activity, this criterion affirms its privileged position in economic analysis and thereby marginalizes all forms of noncommodity production. The means of inclusion thus serves to reinforce the marginality of unpaid domestic labor. The practical difficulty is that the third-party criterion is applied inconsistently, so that much unpaid domestic labor is excluded from definitions of economic activity even when it is marketable. Childcare, cooking, and cleaning house, regardless of the conditions under which they are performed, are officially excluded from the UN System of National Accounts (Wood 1997: 57–8; see also Waring 1988; Benería 1992).

How does postcolonial theory complicate this analysis? A closer look at the Lewis model reveals an implicit first-world bias that is reproduced in development theory and policy generally. As examples of women's household work, Lewis lists activities which in the North are generally or often performed on or for the market ("grinding grain, fetching water from the river, making clothes, cooking the midday meal, teaching children, nursing the sick, etc.") (Lewis 1958: 404). Household activities which make up the majority of unpaid domestic labor in the North, such as cleaning house, basic childcare, and cooking the evening meal, are not listed.

This is a subtle distinction, but one which reveals how Northern experience shapes the apparently neutral third-party criterion. Aspects of women's unpaid domestic labor in the South which resemble household work performed by women in the North are excluded from Lewis's and other development practitioners' implicit definition of economic activity, occupying the deepest shadows beyond even the economic darkness which Lewis suggests will be eliminated with development.[8] But those aspects of Southern women's unpaid domestic labor which would be handled on the market in the North should, at least in theory, be counted and addressed in development economics. There is thus not only a third-party but also a "first-world" criterion underlying this definition (Wood 1997: 59–63).

This "first-world/third-party" criterion is implicit in much development economics after Lewis, and is endemic to development policy focusing on women. Such policy generally includes education, family planning, and the enhancement of women's earning capabilities as major objectives. But the provision of wells and alternative sources of fuel to end the need to carry water long distances or collect firewood are among the most common project goals supported by development agencies (see Leonard 1989; Tinker 1990: 35–44). Unpaid domestic labor such as childcare or cleaning house is rarely included in policy design or evaluation.

What is the problem with the first-world/third-party criterion for women in the South? At first glance it seems to be the same as that which other feminist economists have criticized (e.g. Folbre 1994; Himmelweit 1995). The exclusion of unpaid domestic labor affects what development economics defines as the legitimate terrain of analysis. Childcare or cleaning house, even when performed under very poor conditions, are not signs of an economy's underdevelopment. Consequently, this work will not be addressed in development theory or policy, except possibly as instrumental to some other (market) goal. This is so despite extensive feminist analysis which shows that understanding unpaid domestic labor is fundamental to improving women's lives (see Benería and Sen 1981; Elson 1989; Leonard 1989; UNDP 1995; UNIFEM 2000). The important point that poor conditions make such labor more difficult for many women in the South does not alter this basic feminist critique, except as a matter of degree.

However, a postcolonial perspective demands attention to difference. Even within the context of feminist critiques of the marginalization of unpaid domestic labor and the negative consequences of this marginalization for women it is likely that differences in such labor across the world matter enough to require re-evaluation of a theory built from first-world women's experience. Are what we lump together as childcare or housework really the same activities when performed under radically different conditions of work, in diverse social and economic contexts? Do not the daily realities of high infant and child mortality in Northeastern Brazil and Sub-Saharan Africa or common traditions of child fostering in the Andes require us to re-evaluate conceptualizations of "childcare" (Scheper-Hughes 1992; Weismantel 2001)? What do chickens in a home with an open door do to our understanding of "cleaning house," which implicitly derives from first-world experiences? These questions should lead to a reassessment of feminist economic analysis of unpaid domestic labor.

Remember also that the first-world/third-party criterion only marginalizes those aspects of Southern women's unpaid domestic labor which look like such labor as performed in the North. Consequently, not only does it define economic activity in market terms, and thereby exclude a certain type of unpaid domestic labor from economic analysis, but it also sets the first world as the norm or standard for defining such activity. By doing so it reinscribes models of development which drive all the various regions and cultures of the South to become as much like the North as possible without interfering with postcolonial systems of domination. For women across the South, this means that the same development policies which disregard various important and time-consuming aspects of their unpaid childcare, housecleaning, and cooking also look at other components of their unpaid domestic labor ("grinding grain, fetching water from the river, making clothes, cooking the midday meal, teaching children, nursing the sick, etc.") as something to be eliminated or transformed so that their lives mirror those of women in the North.

The effect of this bias on women in the South is difficult to evaluate. On the one hand, hauling water and collecting wood is onerous work, and women who have to do it are happy to get rid of it. On the other hand, in the context of development as currently theorized and practiced this work can only be gotten rid of in particular ways, and the process is necessarily accompanied by other first-world baggage. Women who would like to have running water might not be so happy to find themselves in isolated households, without the shared labor, companionship, and support of extended family, for example, but if the purpose of development is to produce a homogeneous South that looks like a (subordinate) North they get the whole package, willy-nilly. The implications of this for women will depend on the differing social, economic, and cultural contexts in which they live.

Social development and basic needs

Development economists in the late 1960s and 1970s concentrated on "social" objectives such as the redistribution of income, the eradication of absolute poverty, and the provision of basic needs (see Arndt 1987: 89–113). Arguing for the dethronement of gross national product (GNP) as the primary focus of development, these economists also called attention to the importance of nonmarket activity (e.g. Chenery *et al.* 1974: xv, 4, 245, 247). However, achieving social goals was not identical to economic development, which continued to be understood in market terms (*ibid.*: 47, 245). "Social development" thus contributed to the marginalization of unpaid domestic labor just as in other theories of economic development, by reinforcing the centrality of the market. An implicit first-world/third-party criterion also operated in most definitions of the "traditional" economy, which excluded certain aspects of women's unpaid work from economic analysis and reinforced the North as the model for development (*ibid.*: xv, 190). Only the basic-needs approach explicitly asserted the importance of unpaid domestic labor in addition to women's other nonmarket work. While it also privileged the market, its treatment of economic activity requires a somewhat different reading from those discussed above.

Economists focusing on basic needs argued that development must concentrate on the provision of minimum levels of health, education, nutrition, housing, water supply, and sanitation if world poverty was to be eradicated (Streeten *et al.* 1981: vii, 25). The importance of poor women's unpaid domestic labor to this process was recognized from the outset (*ibid.*: 5). According to the International Labour Organization (ILO),

> [Women's] contribution to the satisfaction of the basic needs of the household is as great as, if not greater than, that of men. Rural women in particular share with men, and often (especially in some African countries) take the major responsibility for, the task of growing food crops for the family. …Their household activities are completely ignored in the statistics of national product. Yet they prepare food, fetch and carry water and wood…make, or at least wash and mend, the family's clothes, look after and educate children, and maintain minimum standards of health and cleanliness in the home.
>
> (ILO 1977: 60)

This presentation of women's work is not founded upon an underlying first-world/third-party criterion. Unpaid domestic labor resembling that performed in the first world, such as washing clothes, looking after children, and cleaning house, is treated as central to the basic-needs approach, as is other nonmarket work which is generally particular to women in some areas of the South, such as growing crops, carrying water and fuel, and making clothes. However, despite its promise in promoting the inclusion of all aspects of Southern women's unpaid labor, the basic-needs approach does not ultimately challenge the market focus in development economics which contributes to the marginalization of such labor. The potential for improving market indicators is a recurrent theme in *First Things First*: "better performance in meeting basic needs tends to lead to higher growth rates in the future" (Streeten *et al.* 1981: 101).

A postcolonial feminist reading of basic needs must begin with the importance of nonmarket work to development. Lourdes Benería and Gita Sen have pointed out that the basic needs literature presents unpaid domestic labor as instrumental to the goal of basic needs (and, by extension, market growth). The potential benefits of a basic-needs strategy for women are therefore limited because their subordinate position is not challenged and may be reinforced by policy (Benería and Sen 1982: 169). Streeten suggests that

> Women and the roles they are permitted to play are important for meeting basic needs. …Strategies that improve the education, income, and access to basic needs of women may be more productive than other approaches because of the role of women in child care, food preparation, and education in the home.
>
> (Streeten *et al.*: 157)

Streeten's remarks imply that the basic-needs strategy (and consequent increases in market growth) depends on the exploitation of "women and the roles they are permitted to play," especially their unpaid domestic labor. This is key to understanding the function of basic-needs strategies for development in global systems of domination. While a look at the theory tempts us to accept the gift horse of explicit policy devoted to women, postcolonial feminist analysis prompts us to look it in the mouth. Whose interests are served by directing policy towards basic needs? The answer is that it is contested terrain. The managers of Malaysian rubber plantations provide free plots of land to women for subsistence agriculture knowing that they can thereby pay lower wages (Momsen 1991: 63). The women and their families may eat better nonetheless, depending on how low the wage goes. Similarly, if basic needs policy functions to direct Southern women's nonmarket labor so that it is ever more efficiently exploited in the interest of global capitalism, that does not mean that women cannot benefit from the policy. But it does not mean they necessarily benefit, either, since anything they gain is incidental to the policy's aim.

This shows itself most clearly in mainstream development's assimilation of basic needs. The current interest in gender at mainstream development institutions derives in part from basic needs' recognition of women's work. But the vision of women as the means to an end is commonplace in gender analyses at these institutions. "Investing in women," one such institution argues, "has a particularly high rate of return" (USAID 1990: 2; see also World Bank 2001). This instrumentalism suggests that only insofar as there is a coincidence between women's needs and market growth along lines defined by and for the North will those needs be considered; investments in the household or in women's economic activity unique to specific areas or cultures of the South are not justified in economic terms unless they contribute to this end, and policy interventions which conflict with this goal will not take place.

Neoliberal development

Since the late 1970s neoliberalism has dominated development economics, especially at international financial institutions such as the International Monetary Fund (IMF) and the World Bank. Neoliberal economists argue that "getting prices right" through an unfettered market is the best motor of development, which is defined as growth in the commodity sector (see Bauer 1984: 158; Lal 1985: 5; Meier 2001: 17–19). As we have seen, this definition marginalizes unpaid domestic labor by setting market growth as the only appropriate goal of development. But the emphasis on price as the means of achieving this goal virtually eliminates the possibility of its inclusion. More than any other theoretical approach to development, neoliberal economics depends on the identity of value with price. From this perspective, the absence of price suggests the absence of economic value, so unpaid domestic labor cannot be treated as an economic activity.[9]

Feminist economists have shown that women bear a disproportionate share of the costs of policies for structural adjustment, the cornerstone of neoliberal approaches to development, and that this is due largely to theoretical biases which exclude unpaid domestic labor (see Elson 1989; Benería 1999). As Diane Elson points out, theoretical marginalization does not preclude (though it may be a prerequisite for) the policies' dependence on such labor (Elson 1989: 57–8). Nevertheless, the World Bank has almost completely ignored feminist critiques of structural adjustment, in part because such critiques rely upon the assertion of unpaid domestic labor as an economic activity (see Wood 2002a).

Again, a postcolonial feminist approach must consider difference and power in analyzing neoliberal development. Structural adjustment policies are only applied in "third-world" or "transition" economies, and they are imposed by international financial institutions without the consent of the population of those economies, often over protests. The unacknowledged dependence of adjustment policies on unpaid domestic labor is specific, therefore, to the women of countries being "adjusted." The failure of the Bank and others involved in the construction and implementation of such policies to see this dependence (an amazing feat, given the vast feminist literature on the topic as well as the aforementioned protests) is equally specific. Its function is to enable the expanded exploitation of Southern women in the interests of global capitalism, via policies to which only they are subjected.[10]

Gender and development

As a result of the dramatic rise in the field of gender and development, many, if not most, development economists now believe that gender is an important analytic category for understanding and promoting development.[11] However, their interest is limited to market-based discussions of women's employment and credit, with attention to education and health sometimes justified as "social" prerequisites for economic development (see Meier and Rauch 2000: 263–88). In this context, women's unpaid domestic labor is important only insofar as it affects formal labor-force participation or is instrumental to the basic needs of families (and consequently market growth).

The gender and development literature itself sometimes reproduces theoretical constructions which marginalize unpaid domestic labor. Ester Boserup's classic *Woman's Role in Economic Development* makes almost no mention of such labor and defines development in market terms (see Boserup 1970: 29–30). The first-world/third-party criterion is also evident in Boserup's analysis: collecting food and wood, making clothes and baskets, and grinding grain are mentioned as part of subsistence production, but childcare and cleaning house are not (*ibid.*:

162–3; see also Benería 1992: 1,549). Her book thus helped marginalize unpaid domestic labor in development economics even as it brought much-needed attention to gender.

Other feminist economists highlighted early on the importance of unpaid domestic labor in their analyses of development (see Benería and Sen 1981, 1982; Sen and Grown 1987). Nevertheless, contemporary discussions of women's work in the literature often exclude such labor (Wood 1997: 64). No generalization can be made about the role of the gender and development literature in the marginalization of women's unpaid domestic labor, except that a feminist perspective is no guarantee of its inclusion.

Ultimately, the literature on gender and development is not generally derived from mainstream economics, and often is in conflict with such an approach. It could be argued that the closer an analysis of women and development comes to representing a mainstream economic perspective, the more likely it is to marginalize unpaid domestic labor (e.g. see World Bank 2001). Given the current power of international institutions such as the World Bank to affect the lives of women on a daily basis, it is tempting to frame the analysis of gender and development in terms likely to appeal to such institutions, many of which are dominated by mainstream economics. The danger of turning too far in that direction is demonstrated by the fate of unpaid domestic labor in mainstream development policy, which can exploit such labor in practice in part because it is excluded from theory.

Many alternatives to mainstream development economics have emerged from feminist critiques which attempt to articulate the perspective of third-world women. But feminist analysis of development must also be postcolonial if it is to avoid essentializing women of the South and recreating a new homogeneous model of development based on first-world interests and experience. This is much more difficult than it appears, as postcolonial feminist theory suggests.

Marginalia, power, and representation

Postcolonial feminist theory highlights the operation of power and history in the process of privileging and making marginal. From this perspective, it is not accidental that the unpaid domestic labor of poor Southern women, and the women themselves, are made invisible in mainstream economics. Their invisibility, so violently maintained, is a sign of their significance (see Spivak 1999: 200). The trick is to discover what interests are served by marginalizing this labor and these women in the way that they are marginalized in mainstream economics generally and development economics in particular.

Consider again Lewis's remark on development: "what one gets are very heavily developed patches of the economy, surrounded by economic darkness" (1958: 409). An important resident of this economic darkness is the poor third-world woman working in the traditional, noncapitalist, nonmarket sector of the economy. Development is the process of eliminating this sector, thereby bringing women into the light of capitalist markets and a feminized/feminizing global labor force. This story functions to justify policy designed to transform Southern economies into something radically different. If these changes serve the interests of the people and institutions promoting development, it is a story which bears scrutiny. If women are particularly privileged characters in the story, it is important to know why.

Chandra Mohanty (1991) points out that much development theory is premised on the assumption of a homogeneous "third-world woman" who has certain essential characteristics: she is traditional, passive, uneducated, a victim. Any development theory based on this characterization implicitly situates development and its practitioners as the third-world woman's savior. The third-world-woman-as-victim not only justifies but mandates development as it is currently constituted, and in a development industry dominated by international financial institutions such as the World Bank this mandate is perhaps most necessary for development economics. Furthermore, development is mandated whether or not the woman appears to want it (because her backwardness makes her a poor judge). Finally, because third-world women are imagined as all the same and unchanging in this scenario, agents of development do not need to learn anything about or adapt to the situations of particular women or regions (see Wood 2001).[12] From this perspective, any concern with addressing or allowing for differences between people/women is misplaced. The coincidence of these results with the core assumptions of mainstream economics and the needs of a globalizing capitalist economy for a feminized labor force are close enough to raise suspicion. The implications for women of the South are grave enough to demand action.

However, action must emerge from the understanding that we are all entangled in postcolonial systems of power and that these entanglements are not nullified by our goodwill. There are no clean and easy answers to questions of development in a postcolonial world (Barker 1998; Spivak 1999; Wood 2001). Speaking with third-world women may serve both to achieve participation and to justify traditional or alternative forms of development controlled by the North. The desire for this speech may be motivated as much by the developer's need to feel appreciated as it is by solidarity. That many Southern women resist development in part by demanding that their voices be heard does not make this problem go away; nor does the good faith or hard work of feminist development practitioners. None of this implies that positive change in the material conditions of women in the South or in postcolonial structures of domination is impossible. It does mean that those who work to achieve such change must learn to live with difference, uncertainty, and the constant need to interrogate what is done in the name of development.

Implications and conclusions

I argue in this essay that aspects of the unpaid domestic labor of women in the South continue to be marginalized in theories of economic development which establish other nonmarket activities as economic. At the same time, first-world experiences shape these theories' conceptualizations of economic activity and development in subtle but important ways. This argument has relevance for feminist analysis of unpaid domestic and caring labor in mainstream economics, but I would like to focus on implications for women in the South.

First, conceptualizations of economic activity based only on the experience of people in the North have material effects. As only one example of this, the first-world/third-party criterion establishes distinctions which dictate specific policy directions with respect to women's unpaid labor; women's work in areas targeted by development policy is driven to look like that of women in the North, with no consideration of differences in that work or the conditions surrounding it. Women may benefit in some ways from such policy, but there will also be losses, which will vary depending on the history and culture of different regions, as well as the skills, personalities, and desires of individual women. These losses are unlikely to be considered in evaluations of development.

Second, while the focus on the market in development economics over time has marginalized unpaid domestic labor in theory, this should not disguise the fact that in practice development policy has relied and continues to rely upon it, whether through the provision of basic needs or the cushioning of economic "shocks" of structural adjustment policies. The rigidly maintained invisibility of such labor in development economics, even in the context of the inclusion of other nonmarket forms of labor and production, is only symptomatic of this dependence.

Finally, questions of representation and power so central to postcolonial feminist theory must become a topic of conversation in feminist economics, because they have material implications. Implicit assumptions about "women in the South" often manifest themselves in the development literature. Photographs and documentaries depict appealing poor women – often smiling, almost always working, usually young, with children, certainly not hostile. Reports discuss the beneficial effects of development on women who apparently have no characters but are always enthusiastic about the project in question. These are representations which disfigure and disguise women and differences between them, and they make their way into policy in pernicious ways. Not all assumptions and representations are obvious, as Mohanty and others have shown, but, obvious or not, they have become so normalized that they can be difficult to see (e.g. Hale 1995). Feminist economics must work not only to see, but to transform representations which enable the (post)colonial domination of women in the South. The extent to which feminist economics itself reinforces or disrupts economic discourse harmful to women of the South is an open question, but it is one which must be explored if it is not to contribute to this domination.

There are alternatives to mainstream development economics which offer great promise of fully incorporating the various unpaid domestic labors of women in Africa, Latin America, and Asia. While the human development approach promulgated by the United Nations Development Programme (UNDP) has been criticized for an emphasis on education and health which might lead it to an instrumental perspective on gender, it is much more likely to be responsive to such criticisms than mainstream development economics (see UNDP 1995; Elson 1999: 104–5; UNIFEM 2000: 18–21). The recent UNIFEM report *Progress of the World's Women 2000* works to "engender" human development theory and policy analysis more fully, and does so through an emphasis on unpaid domestic labor. But these alternatives must avoid reproducing subtle mechanisms of marginalization and domination which work to the detriment of women in the South.

Notes

1 Using problematic language in reference to what is now often called the "South" and the "North" is unavoidable, largely because this language reflects problematics of power in the world. This is particularly so in development economics, which is founded on the assumption that economies in need of "development" ("poorer" countries) lack something that "developed" economies ("richer" countries) have. I still sometimes use the terms "third world" and "first world," because I believe they encapsulate specific representations of "them" and "us" that continue to enable postcolonial systems of domination.
2 Recent interest in "participatory" development at international development institutions is misleading, since such institutions are not accountable to the "beneficiaries" of their policies and decide for themselves what will count in evaluating development (see Cooke and Kothari 2001).
3 This is true even of the excellent literature on gender and structural adjustment, which has probably done the most to call attention to the relationship between economic policy and unpaid domestic labor in the South, because it analyzes the consequences rather than the causes of the marginalization of such labor in mainstream economics (see Benería 1999; Elson 1989; UNIFEM 2000: 27–9).
4 Such bias has been noted in other contexts (see Hale 1995).
5 This can occur even when examples are primarily from the South (see Floro 1999 for one example).
6 For comprehensive overviews of development economics, see Todaro and Smith (2003), Arndt (1987), and Elson (1999).
7 Bernard Walters argues that the lingering classical tradition in development economics, as exemplified by Lewis, offers interesting possibilities for a new feminist economics which fully incorporates unpaid domestic labor, because it never "attempted a complete divorce of productive and reproductive activities" or "subscribed to the fetish that all value arises from exchange" (Walters 1999: 421). I agree that this is a promising approach. However, the often subtle mechanisms by which unpaid domestic labor is marginalized even in classical models should not be underestimated and require further exploration.
8 This suggests the need to qualify Diane Elson's point that Lewis "envisaged what feminists subsequently called 'reproductive work' (that is, the unpaid work in households and communities that is necessary to reproduce the labour force and the social fabric) being transferred to the capitalist sector" (Elson 1999: 97).

9 This argument is central to feminist economic analysis of the marginalization of unpaid domestic labor (e.g. see Jefferson and King 2001: 73–4). The existence of mainstream theories of household production does not negate the point, largely because both the market and price remain privileged. For example, Gary Becker suggests that his work applies economic arguments to noneconomic decisions, and indicates his unwillingness to define unpaid domestic labor as economic by referring to it as "non-work" activity and "'productive' consumption" (Becker 1965: 494). While other household production models are more inclusive, none has succeeded in bringing about the incorporation of such labor in mainstream economics as an economic activity on a par with the market (see Wood 1994).

10 Since it would be difficult to think of a more efficient use of resources (in neoliberal terms) than to pay nothing for something necessary for market growth, any future incorporation of unpaid domestic labor into neoliberal analysis is likely to be as instrumental as that of the basic-needs approach.

11 The institutionalization of this belief in the discourse of development economics is less clear, however. Some important texts have only cursory references to women or none at all (see Meier and Stiglitz 2001). Others devote considerable attention to gender analysis (Meier and Rauch 2000: 263–88; Todaro and Smith 2003).

12 The teaching of development, as well as its practice, shares responsibility for this. For example, "case studies" are commonly used in classes on gender and development to demonstrate the variety of women's experiences, but they may also perpetuate the character of a homogeneous third-world woman who adapts to varying circumstances (Wood 2002b).

Bibliography

Akram-Lodhi, A. Haroon (1996) "'You Are Not Excused from Cooking': Peasants and the Gender Division of Labor in Pakistan," *Feminist Economics* 2(2): 87–105.

Arndt, H. W. (1981) "Economic Development: A Semantic History," *Economic History and Cultural Change* 29(3), April: 457–66.

—— (1987) *Economic Development: The History of an Idea*, Chicago, IL: University of Chicago Press.

Barker, Drucilla K. (1998) "Dualisms, Discourse, and Development," *Hypatia* 13(3): 83–94.

Bauer, P.T. (1984) *Reality and Rhetoric: Studies in the Economics of Development*, London: Weidenfield & Nicolson.

Becker, Gary S. (1965) "A Theory of the Allocation of Time," *The Economic Journal* 75 (September): 493–517.

Benería, Lourdes (1992) "Accounting for Women's Work: The Progress of Two Decades," *World Development* 20(11): 1,547–60.

—— (1999) "Structural Adjustment Policies," in Janice Peterson and Margaret Lewis (eds.) *The Elgar Companion to Feminist Economics*, Northampton, MA: Edward Elgar.

Benería, Lourdes and Gita Sen (1981) "Accumulation, Reproduction, and Women's Role in Economic Development: Boserup Revisited," *Signs* 7(2): 279–98.

—— (1982) "Class and Gender Inequalities and Women's Role in Economic Development: Theoretical and Practical Implications," *Feminist Studies* 8(1): 157–76.

Boserup, Ester (1970) *Woman's Role in Economic Development*, New York: St. Martin's Press.

Bruton, Henry J. (1958) "Growth Models and Underdeveloped Economies," in A.N. Agarwala and S.P. Singh (eds.) *The Economics of Underdevelopment*, New York: Oxford University Press.

Chenery, Hollis, Montek S. Ahluwalia, C.L.G. Bell, John H. Duloy and Richard Jolly (1974) *Redistribution With Growth*, London: Oxford University Press.

Cooke, Bill and Uma Kothari (eds.) (2001) *Participation: The New Tyranny?*, New York: Zed Books.

Elson, Diane (1989) "The Impact of Structural Adjustment on Women: Concepts and Issues," in Bade Onimode (ed.) *The IMF, The World Bank and African Debt*, vol. 2, Atlantic Highlands, NJ: Zed Books.

—— (1999) "Development, Theories of," in Janice Peterson and Margaret Lewis (eds.) *The Elgar Companion to Feminist Economics*, Northampton, MA: Edward Elgar.

Floro, Maria Sagrario (1999) "Double Day/Second Shift," in Janice Peterson and Margaret Lewis (eds.) *The Elgar Companion to Feminist Economics*, Northampton, MA: Edward Elgar.

Folbre, Nancy (1986) "Cleaning House: New Perspectives on Households and Economic Development," *Journal of Development Economics* 22: 5–40.

—— (1994) *Who Pays for the Kids? Gender and the Structures of Constraint*, New York: Routledge.

—— (1995) " 'Holding Hands at Midnight': The Paradox of Caring Labor," *Feminist Economics* 1(1): 73–92.

Hale, Sondra (1995) "Gender and Economics; Islam and Polygamy: A Question of Causality," *Feminist Economics* 1(2): 67–79.

Himmelweit, Susan (1995) "The Discovery of 'Unpaid Work': The Social Consequences of the Expansion of 'Work,' " *Feminist Economics* 1(2): 1–19.

—— (1999) "Domestic Labour," in Janice Peterson and Margaret Lewis (eds.) *The Elgar Companion to Feminist Economics*, Northampton, MA: Edward Elgar.

ILO (International Labour Organization) (1977) *Employment, Growth and Basic Needs*, New York: Praeger.

Jefferson, Therese and John E. King (2001) " 'Never Intended to Be a Theory of Everything': Domestic Labor in Neoclassical and Marxian Economics," *Feminist Economics* 7(3): 71–101.

Lal, Deepak (1985) *The Poverty of "Development Economics,"* Cambridge, MA: Harvard University Press.

Leonard, Ann (ed.) (1989) *Seeds: Supporting Women's Work in the Third World*, New York: Feminist Press.

Lewis, Arthur (1958) "Economic Development with Unlimited Supplies of Labour," in A.N. Agarwala and S.P. Singh (eds.) *The Economics of Underdevelopment*, New York: Oxford University Press.

Meier, Gerald M. (1984) "The Formative Period," in Gerald M. Meier and Dudley Seers (eds.) *Pioneers in Development*, New York: Oxford University Press.

—— (2001) "The Old Generation of Development Economists and the New," in Gerald M. Meier and Joseph E. Stiglitz (eds.) *Frontiers of Development Economics*, New York: Oxford University Press.

Meier, Gerald M. and James E. Rauch (2000) *Leading Issues in Economic Development*, New York: Oxford University Press.

Meier, Gerald M. and Joseph E. Stiglitz (eds.) (2001) *Frontiers of Development Economics*, New York: Oxford University Press.

Mohanty, Chandra (1991) "Under Western Eyes: Feminist Scholarship and Colonial Discourses," in Chandra Mohanty, Ann Russo and Lourdes Torres (eds.) *Third World Women and the Politics of Feminism*, Bloomington, IN: Indiana University Press.

Momsen, Janet Henshall (1991) *Women and Development in the Third World*, New York: Routledge.

Myrdal, Gunnar (1981) "Need for Reforms in Underdeveloped Countries," in Sven Grassman and Erik Lundberg (eds.) *The World Economic Order: Past and Prospects*, New York: St. Martin's Press.

Nelson, Julie (1999) "Of Markets and Martyrs: Is It OK to Pay Well for Care?" *Feminist Economics* 5(3): 43–59.

Nurkse, Ragnar (1958) "Some International Aspects of the Problem of Economic Underdevelopment," in A.N. Agarwala and S.P. Singh (eds.) *The Economics of Underdevelopment*, New York: Oxford University Press.

Rosenstein-Rodan, P.N. (1958) "Problems of Industrialization of Eastern and South-eastern Europe," in A.N. Agarwala and S.P. Singh (eds.) *The Economics of Underdevelopment*, New York: Oxford University Press.

Scheper-Hughes, Nancy (1992) *Death Without Weeping: The Violence of Everyday Life in Brazil*, Berkeley, CA: University of California Press.

Scott, Catherine (1995) *Gender and Development: Rethinking Modernization and Dependency Theory*, Boulder, CO: Lynne Rienner.

Sen, Gita, and Caren Grown (1987) *Development, Crises, and Alternative Visions*, New York: Monthly Review Press.

Spivak, Gayatri Chakravorty (1999) *A Critique of Postcolonial Reason: Toward a History of the Vanishing Present*, Cambridge, MA: Harvard University Press.

Streeten, Paul, Shahid Javed Burki, Mahbub ul Haq, Norman Hicks and Frances Stewart (1981) *First Things First: Meeting Basic Needs in Developing Countries*, New York: Oxford University Press.

Tinker, Irene (1990) "The Making of a Field: Advocates, Practitioners, and Scholars," in Irene Tinker (ed.) *Persistent Inequalities: Women and World Development*, New York: Oxford University Press.

Todaro, Michael P. and Stephen C. Smith (2003) *Economic Development*, New York: Addison-Wesley.

UNDP (United Nations Development Programme) (1995) *Human Development Report 1995*, New York: United Nations.

UNIFEM (United Nations Development Fund for Women) (2000) *Progress of the World's Women 2000*, New York: United Nations.

USAID (United States Agency for International Development) (1990) "Agency Emphasizes Women in Development," *USAID Highlights* 7(3), winter: 1–4.

Walters, Bernard (1999) "Growth Theory (Macro Models)," in Janice Peterson and Margaret Lewis (eds.) *The Elgar Companion to Feminist Economics*, Northampton, MA: Edward Elgar.

Waring, Marilyn (1988) *If Women Counted*, San Francisco, CA: Harper & Row.

Weismantel, Mary (2001) *Cholas and Pishtacos: Stories of Race and Sex in the Andes*, Chicago, IL: University of Chicago Press.

Woolley, Frances (1999) "Family, Economics of," in Janice Peterson and Margaret Lewis (eds.) *The Elgar Companion to Feminist Economics*, Northampton, MA: Edward Elgar.

Wood, Cynthia A. (1994) *Breaching the Margins of Economics*, Ann Arbor, MI: University Microfilms.

—— (1997) "The First World/Third Party Criterion: A Feminist Critique of Production Boundaries in Economics," *Feminist Economics* 3(3), fall: 47–68.

—— (2001) "Authorizing Gender and Development: 'Third World Women,' Native Informants, and Speaking Nearby," *Nepantla: Views from South* 2(3): 429–47.

—— (2002a) "Adjustment with a Woman's Face: Gender and Macroeconomic Policy at the World Bank," in Susan Eckstein and Timothy Wickam-Crowley (eds.) *Struggles for Social Rights in Latin America*, New York: Routledge.

—— (2002b) "Transforming 'Them' into 'Us': Some Dangers in Teaching Women and Development," in Mary M. Lay, Janice Monk and Deborah S. Rosenfelt (eds.) *Encompassing Gender: Integrating International Studies and Women's Studies*, New York: Feminist Press.

World Bank (2001) *Engendering Development: Through Gender Equality in Rights, Resources, and Voice*, New York: Oxford University Press.

20 The difficulty of a feminist economics[1]

Eiman Zein-Elabdin

> If some men reject the epistemology and ontology of the separative self, and women's experiences and self-understandings remain mediated by class, nationality, race, etc., our feminist endeavors must engage these complexities constructively or they will run the real and present danger of remaining woefully incomplete.
>
> (Williams 1993: 148)

Feminist economics has contributed immeasurably to challenging the core assumptions of neoclassical economics, which project a particular apprehension of economic conduct as a universal human tendency. It has uncovered gender as the social metaphor that drives much of economic theory. Yet the project of a feminist economic analysis is itself constantly challenged by the multifaceted nature of domination and difference, which both render a distinct feminist economic subject ultimately ungraspable. By difference here I do not particularly mean Derridean textual *différence* but, rather, the more generic, constantly shifting – and, indeed, deferred – sexual and social male/female difference.[2] An inherent tension lies in the fact that the recurring presence of female subordination through time and place produces a facility for making the case for a feminist economics. At the same time, however, women share their economic subalternity with a large number of men who have been historically constructed as irrational, deviant, or "less developed" and to whom the market/nonmarket divide, which many see as the root of the gender bias in economics, also applies.

Given the overlap between gender and other historical instruments of domination, for instance colonialism, the particularity of women's economic subordination can be carried only up to a point, and gender itself cannot be fully sutured as an analytical category. The difficulty of a feminist economics is thus contained in the slipperiness of difference. In this paper I would like to argue that managing this difficulty requires transcending both the paradigmatic emphasis on women and the modernist philosophy that has effected their subjugation and that of non-industrial, nonmarket cultures. Modernist philosophy – as the conglomeration of Enlightenment and post-Enlightenment European understandings of history, reason, and truth – is deeply entrenched in economics, and this invisibility powerfully operates to hide the cultural bias contained in the separative-self model so severely challenged in feminist economics. Postcolonial thinkers (e.g. Bhabha 1994) have found that because of the persistence of domination and its operation on so many different groups and levels the notion of postcoloniality can be deployed at best in a metaphorical sense. Perhaps, in a similar way, feminist economics must be only partially anchored in the plight of women.[3]

In pursuing this argument I build on a longstanding tradition of feminist scholarship that struggles with the fragility of difference (e.g. Harding 1987a, 1987b; Fuss 1989; Williams 1993; Felski 1997). Most notably, in her self-critical analysis of standpoint theory Sandra Harding (1987a) questioned the legitimacy of particularizing women's experiences and epistemologies in light of shared characteristics between women and colonized peoples. More specifically, Harding traced a "curious coincidence of feminine and African moralities" (Harding 1987b: 296), suggesting that both were socially rather than individually oriented and that they advocated cooperation more than autonomy. In fact, feminist economists have recognized that gender is always bound up with other vehicles of domination (Feiner and Roberts 1990; Nelson 1992; Strober 1994; Grapard 1995; Matthaei 1996). Nevertheless, they have not yet pushed their analyses to – as Williams put it – "engage these complexities constructively" (Williams 1993: 148). Here, I would like to move further in this direction by examining Western women and formerly colonized societies as two subaltern constituencies of European modernity, both excluded from its discourse of economic reason. My purpose is not to suggest that the two share an essential alterity or to force them into a (detestable) competitive position, but to flesh out some of the more productive possibilities of their similarities.[4]

Of course, there are also significant differences in the position of European women and colonized societies shaped by the historical location of each in empire (see, for instance, Sharpe 1993; Olson 1994; Zein-Elabdin and Charusheela, forthcoming). Nonetheless, in economics these differences are largely muted as the two are accorded a lesser rationality *vis-à-vis economic man*. Both similarities and differences are indispensable for a more adequate understanding of androcentric and cross-cultural hegemony. To the extent that the argument of this paper calls for noting the further heterogeneity of the category "women" (or "woman"), nothing is new. The point has been made by a long stream of women-of-color, from bell hooks to Audre Lorde. My argument, however, goes further, by problematizing the theoretical conception of feminist difference itself and by interrogating the cultural hegemony in which Western subalterns (such as women-of-color) may themselves be implicated.[5]

I first explore the issue of gender-centrality in feminist economics (pp. 323–5). Then I examine gender in the context of "development," the contemporary trope by which non-industrial cultures have been written out of "modernity" (pp. 325–7). The shared exclusion of Western women and these cultures from modern European discourse is discussed in the subsequent section (pp. 327–30). In the final section I briefly outline some patterns of material provisioning from contemporary Africa (the part of the world containing the majority of countries classified by the United Nations as "least developed") (pp. 330–2). These patterns exhibit the centrality of the family to provisioning, the important role of loyalty, sharing, and reciprocity, and the prevalence of obligatory over contractual relations.[6] In Western cultures these patterns are generally coded "feminine," and so far in feminist economic literature they have been largely reserved for women. The fact that in Africa they are found among many men – not as an exception, but as general cultural norm – presents a challenge in drawing up the boundaries of the subject of feminist economics and the ways in which gender and femininity are construed in relation to economic activity. The paper ends with a brief discussion of the possibility of a more complex, perhaps less gynocentric, feminist economic philosophy.

Feminist economics and gender-centrality

Feminists have contributed a necessary radical addition to economics by bringing to light the gendered nature of its malestream doctrine and the subordinate position of women (Benería and Sen 1981; Bergmann 1987; Folbre and Hartmann 1988; Feiner and Roberts 1990; Pujol 1992; Ferber and Nelson 1993; Humphries 1995; Kuiper and Sap 1995). Although most are careful to reject any hint of gender essentialism (e.g. Agarwal 1992; Strober 1994), the tendency, stemming from the inherent task of a feminist research program has been to particularize women as a distinct group. This does not invalidate feminist analysis, but, regardless of intentionality, the collective arguments imply that gender is the central bias in economics. The strong analytical emphasis on women, coupled with the profound influence of modernist philosophy (contained in the notion of development), leads to a certain treatment of non-industrial societies that overlooks patterns of immense relevance to feminist economics.[7]

Julie Nelson (1993) argued that the dualistic distinction between hard and soft approaches in economics sprang from the Cartesian separation of rationality from embodiment. She noted that the division between man and nature, which reflects a peculiarly masculinist view, underlies the gender metaphors of economics. Nelson's important contribution is to suggest that some epistemic approaches that have been devalued as feminine are worthwhile and would broaden and enrich the discipline. Thus an economics can be feminist to the extent that it identifies those "feminine" approaches while eventually transcending the dualism implied in such characterization. Nelson is clear in stressing the social construction of gender metaphors (autonomy, hardness, rigor, and logic are masculine, whereas their "opposites" – connectedness, softness, flexibility, and "illogic" – are feminine). As I demonstrate later, however, these "feminine" qualities have also been historically utilized to depict subordinate men in European colonies. Placing gender within a broader cultural context would strengthen Nelson's valuable epistemological critique of economics by showing the more extensive presence of these devalued approaches.

It would be inaccurate to claim that feminist economists have overlooked the larger context of gender oppression and the connection between the devaluation of women and that of other groups. Nelson did suggest that maybe "the defense of the privileged status of masculinity is only a part of a defense of privilege on many fronts" (Nelson 1992: 121). My contention here is that, even when mindful of these connections, feminist economic analyses have tended to approach other devalued groups as an abstract theme within the gender–race–class nexus. This tendency leads to the elision of other cultures, or at least the inadvertent use of race (an incurably ambiguous notion), as an exhaustive category for all instruments of domination beside gender and class, rendering it an easy shorthand for postcolonial societies. For example, Julie Matthaei (1996) recognizes the concomitant historical oppression of women in Europe and people in the colonies, noting that "white" women and "people of color" were both exploited servants of capitalism. But she places the emphasis on gender and race as necessary notions for understanding "capital." This emphasis allows an examination of the negative impacts of the evolution of capitalism on women and people of color. It does not extend to allow an examination of substantive similarities between women in the West and communities in other world regions that may be at odds with the assumptions of mainstream economics.

Rhonda Williams (1993) identified the homologous relation of gender and race to the dominant ideology of "Euro-America." She recognized the congruity between "feminine" and "African" worldviews, which Harding (1987b) had noted, as more than a coincidence, recalling the relegation of blacks and European women to the same lower rank through the nineteenth-century science of craniometry. Williams cautioned against falsely universalizing feminist theories and called for a racialized theorizing of gender. I have no objection. Yet, at once, I am more concerned here with the problem of falsely particularizing these theories to the effect of excluding a large number of men who share the secondary status of women within economics. Extending Williams's deconstructive critique to the development discourse, which "scientifically" relegates postcolonial cultures to pre-modernity, reveals this common predicament and allows feminist economic analyses to mobilize some of the phenomena present in culturally devalued societies as additional sources of challenge to the synthetic assumptions of neoclassical theory.

The difficulty of isolating gender can be detected in Gillian Hewitson's (1999) insightful deconstruction of Daniel Defoe's *Robinson Crusoe*, typically used in textbooks to illustrate the notion of economic man. Hewitson maps out a sophisticated reading of gender in economics, and concludes that: "'femininity,' then, is *the* 'other' of neoclassical economics" (*ibid.*: 22). This conclusion is based on the occluded presence of the "feminine," which haunts the story in the figure of Friday, Crusoe's native servant/slave, who, Hewitson argues, is feminized or denied full masculinity. This is a fair reading.[8] Nonetheless, the presence of Friday, the colonized (male) other, distinctly illustrates the extent to which the lower status of femininity is bound up with "non-feminine" forms of subalternity, in this case being of a lower race and being subject to colonialism.[9] Of course I do not think that Hewitson's emphasis on gender is meant to imply the exclusion of other categories. In fact she suggests the untangle-able relation of gender, race, and cross-cultural hegemony by noting that Crusoe "must reconstruct himself as a white, male, colonialist Englishman" (*ibid.*: 152). My point is not that culture or race is more important than gender, but, rather, that all are inextricably bound up with one another as overlapping vehicles of oppression. One could certainly establish the primacy of gender within very specific institutional contexts, but it is difficult to theorize gender or femininity as *the* generalized "other" of economics.

Men, women, and development

The presence of other subalterns in economics is demonstrated in the postwar discourse on development – understood as industry-driven heightened material accumulation similar to that which took place in the North Atlantic region. The notion of development functioned discursively as a regulated space that ultimately provided the conditions for the possibility of knowledge about and justification for political intervention in non-industrial societies (Escobar 1995). Development became the subtext that governed analyses of postcolonial societies across different schools of economics, with feminists focusing on women in the "less developed" world and drawing attention to the gender bias of development policy.[10] This, of course, has been a tremendous contribution. Unfortunately, the intense attention to women left largely untouched the underlying philosophical framework. In picking out women while putting off an epistemological critique of development feminist analysis effectively mapped the dualism of developed/less developed over the already existing binarism of man/woman.

Development economics presented the historical experience of industrial societies as an inevitable natural phenomenon. Non-industrialized countries were theoretically constituted as a set of problems and undesirable conditions that ranged from "widespread and chronic absolute poverty" to "inappropriate technologies, institutions, and value systems" (Todaro 1994: 28). The presumption of the desirability of economic growth, which draws on deeply entrenched ideas of progress and universal history in Western thought, was shared by both neoclassical and Marxian schools (Zein-Elabdin 1998, 2001). Institutionalists, otherwise sensitive to the role of hidden value premises in economics (e.g. Myrdal 1968), generally agreed. Although feminist economics arrived later in time, it was similarly constrained by this discursive space. Feminist development literature is too vast to cover here, but I think it adequately serves the purpose to mention a few field-defining works.[11]

Feminist authors have successfully challenged the presumed gender-neutrality of development-policy outcomes (Benería and Sen 1981; Benería 1982). They have also highlighted the role of the international division of labor and capitalist growth in shaping the conditions of women in non-industrialized economies. Feminists (e.g. Elson 1991) have further shown the inadequacy of the women-in-development approach, thereby moving the discussion from integrating women into preformed projects to scrutinizing gender relations as the institutional backdrop to female subordination. In general, the feminist position has been to problematize development policies as an exemplar of "male bias," namely an institutional dynamic that forced women to bear disproportionately the cost of economic growth without equally sharing in its gains (*ibid.*).[12] This is not in dispute. Decades ago Ester Boserup (1989) documented that in the course of the development of agriculture in Africa, Asia, and Latin America the productivity gap between men and women widened as men acquired a monopoly over new technology and innovations. Boserup blamed European male settlers, colonial administrators, and technical experts for transplanting their gender values to the colonies. They perceived agriculture to be a male occupation and therefore vigorously promoted men's farming over women's. The result was that men fully participated in the lucrative "modern," sector while women remained trapped in "tradition" and poverty.

Nonetheless, throughout former colonies the negative effects of the colonial encounter were shared by a large number of men. I am, of course, abstracting from the heterogeneity of both men and women in such diverse regions, but the general observation can be reasonably made. In Asia the introduction of private land ownership and the expansion of pecuniary relations contributed to the appearance of landless farmers and their conversion to wage-labor (Myrdal 1968). In southern Africa the "mineral revolution" was built on the migrant-labor system, where men were forcibly removed from villages and transported to small, closely policed compounds in mining towns (Austen 1987). Boserup herself traced the complex articulation of gender and race hierarchies in South Africa. She found that "[i] n all but one case women of the superior group earned more than men of the group below, and earnings of all non-African women were much higher than those of African men" (Boserup 1989: 147–8).

As Benería and Sen (1981) have argued, the catalyst behind the decline in the status of women relative to men in "developing" countries was an accelerated process of commodity production rather than patriarchy *ipso facto*. This process has the tendency to utilize extant social hierarchies – gender, age, or some such – that facilitate accumulation. For instance, in southern Africa European industrialists deepened the coercive patriarchal authority of local chiefs in order to ensure women's compliance with the migrant-labor system. But capitalist production also erodes or obliterates conventions that do not further accumulation. There is plenty of evidence that economic growth has led to the subversion of gender norms when it was economically opportune. A prominent example is the extensive recruitment of women in export manufacturing, as classic feminist development literature has shown (e.g. Elson and Pearson 1981).

Development favors a principle of industry-driven material accumulation that in Western economies has been institutionally effected through market exchange. This is not to suggest that patriarchy, as a theoretically separable social phenomenon, had no role in the gender asymmetry of the process of economic growth. Rather, my argument is that the internal logic of this process turns on gender only to the extent of its presence as an underlying social reality, just as race or cross-cultural hegemony are. What is more crucial to this process is the presence of an economically exploitable group, be it European women or colonized men. At a discursive level, the bias towards material accumulation results in the exclusion (or devaluation) of antithetical practices, such as sharing, loyalty, and gift-giving, whether they are exhibited by women or men, and in the ideological construction of the groups associated with such practices as irrational, less developed, or pre-modern.

Two subaltern constituencies of European modernity

The rise and expansion of industrial market culture (namely the mechanized, commodified way of life in which pecuniary relations prevail) was supported by a totality of philosophical discourse that authorized and legitimated this culture. European women and "native" men share a homologous position in this discursive space, granted that their positions are set apart by different dimensions such as the very experience of modern European cultural hegemony over other world regions.

The political framework within which originated grounding concepts of economics, such as self-interest and optimizing rationality, can be found in the liberal state. Seyla Benhabib suggests that the separative-self model historically returns to the European transition to modernity that "privatize[d] the self's relation to the cosmos" (1987: 160). In setting up the state, moral theorists (Hobbes, Locke, Rousseau) decoupled two spheres: the sphere of justice, a public arena where independent statesmen transacted; and the sphere of emotions, a private domain for love, kinship, and procreation, with which women became identified. Paula England (1993), after Benhabib, argues that the social contract implicitly relied on the assumption that women would shoulder family work and offer emotional support. This argument has been supported by extensive feminist scholarship. However, it is important to remember that, by the same move in which the modern European contract required women to volunteer their time and labor, it compelled the colonized to render theirs.

Historically, the rise of the liberal state in Europe was concomitant with the expansion of markets (Polanyi 1944). As Ann Jennings (1993) has argued, the decoupling of the public from the private was accompanied by a parallel cleft between the political and the economic, with the latter becoming identified with market exchange. The movement to a capitalist economy engendered a restriction of the roles of women in "production" as this was relocated from family to factory (Merchant 1980). Jennings points out that "it is the association of women with the family and of men with the market economy, and their dualistic separation, that has been the main foundation of gender distinction since the nineteenth century" (Jennings 1993: 122–3). This remark suggests to me that the gender bias in economics is derivative from the theoretical bias toward market exchange as it evolved in modern Europe. The key in the basic neoclassical model is the theoretical construction of the economic agent rather than his/her gender. The notion of a separative self thus equally excludes all men who have not been socialized in economic relations characterized by autonomy, opportunism, and dispassion.

The discourse of European modernity was grounded in an exclusive claim on the idea of rationality, largely interpreted as the Enlightenment notion of instrumental reason.[13] In economics, rationality took on the even narrower meaning of individual welfare maximization, which effectively precluded all non-self-centered conceptions of economic action. The ideological service of the concept of rationality cannot be underestimated. Its role in the discursive exclusion of women from modern history was effected through the deployment of cognitive dualisms such as rational/emotional, objective/subjective, individual/social, and competitive/nurturant (Jennings 1993), with men being accorded the valorized qualities of rationality, objectivity, individuality, and competition.[14] Not all men, however. "Native" men were constructed as irrational, pre-logical, and savage. This construction was cemented by extensive anthropological research, generating the taxonomy of civilized/primitive, modern/traditional, and developed/un(der/less)developed. In *How Natives Think*, for example, Lévy-Bruhl, the influential French philosopher and social anthropologist, claimed that the mental activities of "natives" lacked a logical character. Unlike Europeans, he argued, "[t]he slightest mental effort involving abstract reasoning, however elementary it may be, is so distasteful to them that they immediately declare themselves tired and give it up" (Lévy-Bruhl 1985: 115).

The common subalternity of native man and European woman is crystallized in that femininity seems to be the preferred metaphor for conquered men – recall Defoe's feminized Friday (Hewitson 1999). Many colonial administrators likened Asian and African men to women, not only in mental faculties, but in body qualities as well. Here is the (in)famous Thomas Macaulay, arguing the benefits of physical education in India:

> The physical organization of the Bengalee is feeble even to effeminacy. He lives in a constant vapour bath. His pursuits are sedentary, his limbs delicate, his movements languid. During many ages he has been trampled upon by men of bolder and more hearty breeds.
>
> (Macaulay 1843: 99)[15]

In fact, many men in the colonies embraced their association with femininity as part of a defiant anti-colonial identity. A prominent case was Léopold Senghor, the former president of Senegal and one of the articulators of negritude, a pan-African movement that emerged in the first half of the twentieth century. Senghor's negritude manifesto *On Negrohood* (1962) claimed that the essence of the African negro was *his* emotionality – in his judgment, an antithesis of European rationality. He particularly reveled in the fact that during World War II the French were astonished to find that Senegalese conscripts had the "sensitivity of women" (*ibid.*: 1).

Women, devalued cultures and various social groups have all been discursively constructed as symbols of deficiency and lower humanity. This is not a novel finding. In *Victorian Anthropology*, George Stocking (1987) notes:

> Along different lines – of domestic life (woman, child), of socioeconomic status (laborer, peasant, pauper), of deviancy (criminal, madman), and of "race" (Celtic Irish-man, black savage) – they all stood in a subordinate hierarchical relationship to those who dominated the economic life, who shared the political power, or who most actively articulated the cultural ideology of mid-Victorian Britain.
>
> (Stocking 1987: 229–30)

Stocking further notes the debasement of women's cognitive faculties. He quotes Herbert Spencer, stating that

> the intellectual traits of primitive man were especially evident in "women of the inferior ranks" of our own society – who "quickly form very positive beliefs"; whose thoughts, "full of personal experiences," lacked "truths of high generality"; who could never detach an "abstract conception" from a "concrete case."
>
> (Stocking 1987: 229)[16]

Notice the agreement between Spencer and Lévy-Bruhl.

Of course, the similarity between European women and colonized men does not mean that their subordination is interchangeable. Western women have participated in imperial domination in capacities ranging from housewife to colonial administrator (Callaway 1987). This historical complicity was documented in travel writing, much of which consisted of protest against exclusion from more effectively partaking in colonial tasks (Sharpe 1993). Boserup's (1989) note of the superior status of European women to native African men in South Africa also points to the divergent position of these two constituencies. Nonetheless, in economics these differences are theoretically subsumed under the general status of lacking the market rationality of a homo economicus. This subsumption may be more easily grasped if one recalls the facility with which femininity slips into savagery or vice versa in the literature (as in Spencer's principles of psychology), a tendency rooted in the long tradition of associating women with "nature" in European thought (Merchant 1980). Gender itself operates on multiple levels, for example as a symbol (e.g. masculinity for conquest) or as a relationship.[17] As a group relationship, gender may specify different spheres or patterns of economic activity. All levels, however, are culturally specific and therefore can be comprehended only in institutional context (Zein-Elabdin 1996; also see Charusheela 2001).

The gender of provisioning: examples from Africa

In this section I would like to discuss economic patterns from two postcolonial African societies that reveal remarkable congruity with those currently emphasized in feminist economics. The patterns indicate the centrality of the "family" to material provisioning, sharing, and reciprocity, and the predominance of obligation over contract relations.[18] Space does not allow me to examine these in depth but only enough to suggest that they raise questions regarding the model of autonomous choice that should attract the attention of feminist economists. Further investigation, including the extent of the pervasiveness of such practices, must remain a task for future work. For the moment, the fact that these patterns are not gendered feminine – as they have generally been in Western contexts – but are commonly found among men suggests the need for a broader, different type of feminist economic philosophy.

Not surprisingly, much of the evidence comes from outside of economics. Anthropologists have long recognized the role of kinship in material provisioning across a wide range of African societies, including the Hausa in Nigeria, the Lugbara in Uganda, the Herero and Tonga in southern Africa and pastoralists in northern Somalia (Bohannan and Dalton 1962). Indeed, the general motif of economic relations in contemporary Africa has been summarized by Göran Hyden – a political scientist – as *the economy of affection*, defined as "a network of support, communications and interaction among structurally defined groups connected by blood, kin, community or other affinities, for example, religion" (Hyden 1983: 8), driven largely by mutual obligation and personal commitment. Given space limitations, I will briefly outline two studies of such relations: Per Trulsson's (1997) analysis of entrepreneurs in the northwest region of Tanzania and Janet MacGaffey's (1991) ethnography of *the second economy* in Zaire. The two studies examine different contexts, but both support the feminist critique of the assumptions of narrow self-interest and independence of individual and social welfare.[19]

Trulsson employs a new institutional economic approach to identify the impact of constraints such as infrastructure, finance, technology, and labor on the business practices of Tanzanian entrepreneurs. In examining decisionmaking among businesses engaged in a variety of industrial ventures, including food processing, textiles, printing, and construction, he was particularly interested in explaining why African entrepreneurs "appear irrational to a Western observer" (Trulsson 1997: 44). Trulsson's study is particularly significant because his sample of 26 included only one woman. His findings show that social obligation, particularly commitment to family and kin, was the primary cause of shortage of liquidity among firms. An extreme case is a producer of plastic containers who financed the education of 35 children in his "extended" family. Furthermore, Trulsson found that employing members of the family is an integral aspect of the labor market. He demonstrated that strong obligation to relatives, neighbors, and friends goes to explain apparently irrational behavior such as investing in costly labor-saving machinery while maintaining a seemingly redundant number of workers.

Janet MacGaffey (1991), an anthropologist, investigated what she designated as the second economy in three border regions of Zaire (now the Democratic Republic of Congo), where the "informal sector" is estimated to be three times as large as official gross domestic product (GDP). MacGaffey defined the second economy as encompassing all non-monetized production for one's own consumption and monetized but unrecorded, unmeasured, or illegal activities. Her study reveals the role of mutual obligation and the bond of kinship both in basic survival and in business ventures. She documents pervasive reciprocity between families, clans, and trading partners. In particular, "delayed reciprocity" allows non-monetized exchange to play an important role in the movement of food supplies between rural and urban areas. An extensive list of food items, in addition to other vital goods such as pharmaceutical products and fuel, was regularly transported by relatives traveling back and forth. Household help, childcare, and unpaid labor – in general – were some of the services most commonly provided in return for assistance rendered in business.

The purpose of these examples is not to idealize such practices as an antidote to market exchange. The examples, in fact, point to the artificiality of the dichotomy between market and nonmarket spheres. The transactions identified in MacGaffey's study are not barter exchanges removed from a "market economy." Nor do they represent a "moral economy" characteristic of all "traditional" societies. They are imbricated in complex settings that amalgamate market and nonmarket relations. The purpose, rather, is to bring to light "non-feminine" economic patterns that significantly coincide with feminist economic arguments and to highlight the cultural bias of the assumption of a separative self. In development economics such patterns are typically left unexamined because they are taken as inevitably disappearing attributes of pre-industrial cultures. Feminists, too, may overlook these patterns as a result of the conceptual division of labor between general and development literature in economics.

Although the examples are brief, the parallels to feminist economics can be detected. Folbre has suggested the notion of caring labor: "undertaken out of affection or a sense of responsibility for other people, with no expectation of immediate pecuniary reward" (Folbre 1995: 75). Without denying the gender specification in Tanzania or Zaire that compels women to perform a disproportionate share of household work, the idea of caring labor can theoretically also describe much of the behavior of the business*men* in Trulsson's study. After all, paying for the education of 35 children does require additional labor – if not within the confines of the household – and a significant degree of selflessness. Folbre has not missed this possibility, as she makes clear that caring labor can apply to both women and men.[20] The point to be explored further is what this implies for a feminist economic theory. A second parallel to the examples cited above in feminist economics is the idea of an "other economy...concerned with the direct production and maintenance of human beings as an end in itself" (Donath 2000: 115). This idea clearly echoes Hyden's economy of affection as well as MacGaffey's second economy which caters primarily to provisioning and maintenance. Caring labor, the other economy, or the economy of affection all underline the inability of the separative-self model to capture such pervasive economic habits and rationalities.

Conclusion: a feminist philosophy of economics?

What, then, should come out of this discussion as far as feminist analysis is concerned? I would argue that these shared experiences complicate the project of feminist economics, but they also add to its productive potential. If economics is understood as a culturally embedded study of provisioning as well as wealth accumulation, and if one concedes that some cultures have been ideologically devalued by the metaphysics of modernism in a parallel manner to the way in which women have been devalued in economics, then feminist economics should be able to invoke relevant phenomena from societies that have so far been framed as irrational or less developed to support its critique of neoclassical theory.

The evidence from Africa problematizes the centrality of gender in feminist economics because it indicates that qualities such as gifting, obligation, and loyalty cannot be easily theorized as feminine. On the other hand, however, the evidence strengthens the feminist critique because it supports many themes that feminists have raised, for instance the complexity of care (Folbre 1995) and the human condition as often a "state of helplessness and unchosen dependency" (Strassmann 1993: 63). Feminists have argued that confining the definition of economics to market exchange excludes household and other non-choice-based activities (Nelson 1993). This argument can be fortified by showing the extent to which these are more often norms rather than exceptions to self-centered maximization.

The task(s) of a feminist economics have been articulated in various overlapping ways: more equity for and improvement in women's conditions (Bergmann 1987; Strober 1994); less androcentric economic analysis (Humphries 1995); a better model of the family and reproduction (Folbre 1995); an epistemological transformation to produce "better accounts of economic reality" (Seiz 1995: 111; Waller and Jennings 1990; Pujol 1992); and "describing and analyzing the other economy" (Donath 2000: 117). As feminist economists have realized, this multiplicity of goals necessarily intersects with almost every other facet of human sociality. What remains is more substantial incorporation of this awareness – that is, moving beyond the general observation of commonalties between women and other devalued groups to more systematically examine and employ these commonalties to produce new interpretations of economic phenomena.

I would like tentatively to suggest a general framework for a feminist economic philosophy, which I would characterize as a *philosophy of hybrid subalternity*. I define hybrid subalternity as subordination deriving from heterogeneous sources rather than a single axis such as gender or colonial subjectivity.[21] This framework remains feminist to the extent that it is partially anchored in a concern for women's welfare; however, it is paradigmatically guided by the multiformity and instability of difference, and is deeply aware of its own complicity in the cultural hegemony of economic discourse. A feminist economic philosophy – which by definition speaks to a contemporary global constituency – cannot take European modernity, with its essentialist and hegemonic tendencies, as its starting point. Instead, it must be a *non-modernist philosophy grounded in a self-critical approach and an ethical sensitivity to subaltern difference in all its illusive forms*. This requires transcending an implicitly essentialist notion of gender, such that it holds no presumption that gender underlies economic processes except in culturally specific, path-dependent ways (see Zein-Elabdin 1996). It also requires that it transcend the modernist historicism that fuels assumptions about the inevitability and cultural superiority of industrial modernity, and instead conceives the economy as culturally instituted habits for material provisioning and accumulation. The slipperiness of difference requires scrutiny of highly specific institutional contexts and constant transformation in the subject of feminist inquiry. This may diminish the difficulty of a feminist economics.

Notes

1 This chapter is partly based on "Economic Heterodoxy and Subaltern Cultures: The Case of Feminist Economics," a paper I presented at Marxism 2000, University of Massachusetts,

Amherst, in September 2000. I am very grateful to Tony Maynard, S. Charusheela, Michael Billig, Antonio Callari, Steve Gudeman, and Julie Nelson for helpful comments, and to Drucilla Barker and Edith Kuiper for very constructive suggestions.

2 I do not think that a stated rejection of essentialism is necessarily sufficient for maneuvering this problem. See Felski (1997) for an insightful treatment.

3 The term "postcolonial" refers both to contemporary societies formerly colonized by Europeans and to a certain critique of the colonial experience and its extension in the current hegemony of Northern industrialized countries. This critique censures Western – and all forms of – domination, but equally recognizes the Western dimensions of postcoloniality. The term "subaltern" here means subordinate, inferior. Postcolonial authors have borrowed it from Antonio Gramsci (1975), who used it to refer to lower-ranking social classes in Fascist Italy. For a review of postcolonial thought, particularly in relation to feminist economics, see Zein-Elabdin and Charusheela (forthcoming).

4 I am aware of the flaws associated with large terms such as modern, Western, European, developed, and their counterparts – non-modern, non-Western, non-European, less developed. Many men within the Western world have been relegated to an inferior position and many women hold social positions of privilege over other women. I use these terms in an ideal-typical way to denote very broad historical and politico-economic cartographies, hopefully without minimizing their complexity. The terms are interchangeable but each carries a certain emphasis. "European" highlights the historical role of Europe, "Western" has a more contemporary significance. For a postcolonial perspective on the problem of modernity, see Zein-Elabdin (2001).

5 For an example of relevant discussions in postcolonial feminist literature, see Narayan and Harding (2000).

6 I am not claiming a uniformity of African attitudes in this regard, but merely pointing out a contingent social phenomenon. It is worth noting that Harding's (1987b) observation regarding the convergence of African and feminist moralities was prompted by the work of Vernon Dixon (1970), who argued that African-Americans had a more intimate, less distant relation to the external world than did European-Americans, and that they acted in a communal manner. He thus made his proposition for a "black economics." This interpretation seems to assume – I think mistakenly – an essential, stable "black" character. Also, see Ferber and Nelson (1993: introduction) for a comment on the Harding–Dixon exchange.

7 In this section I only examine feminist contributions in the field of theory, leaving aside the large body of scholarship in areas such as empirical analysis of the family and labor markets. Hewitson (1999) provides a substantial review of the literature.

8 Although the argument that Friday is feminized is somewhat tenuous since Crusoe insists on his "masculinity," describing him as having "*something very manly in his face*" (Robinson Crusoe, cited in Hewitson 1999: 155; emphasis added). Grapard (1995) offers another subversive reading of *Crusoe*.

9 The split between race and colonial domination is indicated by the subjectivity of European settlers in the colonies to metropolitan imperial powers. For a discussion of instances of divergent economic interests of European settlers and colonial governments in southern Africa, see Austen (1987).

10 The development literature is extensive, but Todaro (1994) offers a useful textbook coverage. For the continuity between colonialism and development, see Austen (1987) and Escobar (1995).

11 For a survey, see Visvanathan et al. (1997). See Barker (1998) for a critical review of dualism and development in feminist literature. Additional treatment of development feminism can be found in Zein-Elabdin and Charusheela (forthcoming).

12 DAWN (Development Alternatives with Women for a New Era) criticized the dominant development path and offered a "Southern" woman's perspective (Sen and Grown 1987). Instead, however, they projected the impoverished "third-world-woman" as the final site of oppression and hence agency for formulating alternative visions. Although this conception merely reverses the hierarchy of domination, DAWN's critique offered an entry point to the task of challenging the authority of Western prescriptions. For other feminist critiques of development, see

Harcourt (1994) and Olson (1994). Olson gives an institutionalist perspective, drawing on the postcolonial notion of orientalism.

13 Max Weber attributed to rationality a critical role in the evolution of capitalism:

> In the last resort the factor which produced capitalism is the rational permanent enterprise, rational accounting, rational technology and rational law.... Necessary complementary factors were the rational spirit, the rationalization of the conduct of life in general, and a rationalistic economic ethic.
>
> (Weber 1961: 260)

14 To be sure, there is an old association of men with reason and women with emotion. In Platonic and neo-Platonic symbolism ideas were masculine, matter was feminine. For Aristotle, reason (characteristic of men) was to rule over appetites (predominant in women) (Merchant 1980). That this distinction was also drawn between free and slave men again points toward the concurrence of female and male oppression.

15 Thomas Babington Macaulay (1800–59) was a prolific English essayist who served as a public officer in a number of posts, including the Supreme Council of India from 1833 to 1837 (Pinney 1982).

16 From Spencer's *Principles of Psychology*, published in 1890.

17 I am indebted to the editors for prompting me to include this important point. Limited space, unfortunately, precludes further elaboration.

18 The term "reciprocity" has been used in various ways in anthropology, mainly drawing on Polanyi's definition as "movement between correlative points of symmetrical groupings" (Polanyi 1957: 149). Here it may be taken to include all movement of goods, resources or money that does not necessarily involve an expectation of a return, and implies no equivalence of value.

19 For further discussion of similar phenomena, see Lopes (1994).

20 Folbre's notion of "long-run reciprocity" (1995: 76) – as an element of caring labor – also parallels MacGaffey's delayed reciprocity in Zaire. See Chapter 17 for an additional discussion of caring labor.

21 In postcolonial discourse the idea of hybridity *generally* marks the cultural fusion resulting from the process of colonialism (see Bhabha 1994; Zein-Elabdin and Charusheela, forthcoming). Here, I also use it to indicate a multifaceted and unstable condition.

Bibliography

Agarwal, Bina (1992) "The Gender and Environment Debate: Lessons From India," *Feminist Studies* 18(1), spring: 119–58.

Austen, Ralph A. (1987) *African Economic History: Internal Development and External Dependency*, London: James Currey.

Barker, Drucilla K. (1998) "Dualisms, Discourse, and Development," *Hypatia* 13(3), summer: 83–94.

Benería, Lourdes (ed.) (1982) *Women and Development: The Sexual Division of Labor in Rural Societies*, New York: Praeger.

Benería, Lourdes and Gita Sen (1981) "Accumulation, Reproduction, and Women's Role in Economic Development: Boserup Revisited," *Signs* 7(2), winter: 141–57.

Benhabib, Seyla (1987) "The Generalized and the Concrete Other: The Kohlberg–Gilligan Controversy and Moral Theory," in Diana T. Meyers and Eva Feder Kittay (eds.) *Women and Moral Theory*, Totowa, NJ: Rowan & Littlefield.

Bergmann, Barbara R. (1987) "The Task of a Feminist Economics: A More Equitable Future," in Christie Farnham (ed.) *The Impact of Feminist Research in the Academy*, Bloomington, IN: Indiana University.

Bhabha, Homi K. (1994) *The Location of Culture*, London: Routledge.

Bohannan, Paul and George Dalton (eds.) (1962) *Markets in Africa*, Evanston, IL: Northwestern University.

Boserup, Ester (1989) *Woman's Role in Economic Development*, New York: St. Martin's Press; first published in 1970.

Callaway, Helen (1987) *Gender, Culture, and Empire: European Women in Colonial Nigeria*, Urbana, IL: University of Illinois.

Charusheela, S. (2001) "Women's Choices and the Ethnocentrism/Relativism Dilemma," in Stephen Cullenberg, Jack Amariglio and David Ruccio (eds.) *Postmodernism, Economics and Knowledge*, London: Routledge.

Dixon, Vernon, J. (1970) "The Di-Unital Approach to 'Black Economics,'" *American Economic Review* 60(2): 424–9.

Donath, Susan (2000) "The Other Economy: A Suggestion for a Distinctively Feminist Economics," *Feminist Economics* 6(1), March: 115–23.

Elson, Diane (ed.) (1991) *Male Bias in the Development Process*, Manchester: Manchester University Press.

Elson, Diane and Ruth Pearson (1981) "Nimble Fingers Make Cheap Workers: An Analysis of Women's Employment in Third World Export Manufacturing," *Feminist Review*, spring: 87–107.

England, Paula (1993) "The Separative Self: Androcentric Bias in Neoclassical Assumptions," in Marianne A. Ferber and Julie A. Nelson (eds.) *Beyond Economic Man: Feminist Theory and Economics*, Chicago, IL: University of Chicago.

Escobar, Arturo (1995) *Encountering Development: The Making and Unmaking of the Third World*, Princeton, NJ: Princeton University.

Feiner, Susan F. and Bruce B. Roberts (1990) "Hidden by the Invisible Hand: Neoclassical Economic Theory and the Textbook Treatment of Race and Gender," *Gender and Society* 4(2), June: 159–81.

Felski, Rita (1997) "The Doxa of Difference," *Signs* 23(1): 1–21.

Ferber, Marianne and Julie Nelson (eds.) (1993) *Beyond Economic Man: Feminist Theory and Economics*, Chicago, IL: University of Chicago.

Folbre, Nancy (1995) "'Holding Hands at Midnight': the Paradox of Caring Labor," *Feminist Economics* 1(1), spring: 73–92.

Folbre, Nancy and Heidi Hartmann (1988) "The Rhetoric of Self-interest: Ideology and Gender in Economic Theory," in Arjo Klamer, Donald McCloskey and Robert Solow (eds.) *The Consequences of Economic Rhetoric*, Cambridge: Cambridge University Press.

Fuss, Diana (1989) *Essentially Speaking: Feminism, Nature, and Difference*, London: Routledge.

Gramsci, Antonio (1975) *The Prison Notebooks*, vols. I and II, trans. and ed. Joseph Buttigieg, New York: Columbia University.

Grapard, Ulla (1995) "Robinson Crusoe: the Quintessential Economic Man?," *Feminist Economics* 1(1), spring: 33–52.

Harcourt, Wendy (ed.) (1994) *Feminist Perspectives on Sustainable Development*, London: Zed Books.

Harding, Sandra (1987a) "The Instability of the Analytical Categories of Feminist Theory," in Sandra Harding and Jean F. O'Barr (eds.) *Sex and Scientific Inquiry*, Chicago, IL: University of Chicago.

—— (1987b) "The Curious Coincidence of Feminine and African Moralities: Challenges for Feminist Theory," in Diana T. Meyers and Eva Feder Kittay (eds.) *Women and Moral Theory*, Totowa, NJ: Rowan & Littlefield.

Hewitson, Gillian J. (1999) *Feminist Economics: Interrogating the Masculinity of Rational Economic Man*, Northhampton, MA: Edward Elgar.

Humphries, Jane (ed.) (1995) *Gender and Economics*, Brookfield, VT: Edward Elgar.

Hyden, Göran (1983) *No Shortcuts to Progress: African Development Management in Perspective*, Berkeley, CA: University of California.

Jennings, Ann (1993) "Public or Private? Institutional Economics and Feminism," in Marianne A. Ferber and Julie A. Nelson (eds.) *Beyond Economic Man: Feminist Theory and Economics*, Chicago, IL: University of Chicago.

Kuiper, Edith and Jolande Sap (eds.) (1995) *Out of the Margin: Feminist Perspectives on Economics*, London: Routledge.

Lévy-Bruhl, Lucien (1985) *How Natives Think*, Princeton, NJ: Princeton University; first published 1910.

Lopes, Carlos (1994) *Enough is Enough! For an Alternative Diagnosis of the African Crisis*, Uppsala: Scandinavian Institute of African Studies.

Macaulay, Thomas Babington (1843) "Warren Hastings," in *Critical and Miscellaneous Essays*, vol. IV, Philadelphia, PA: Carey & Hart.

MacGaffey, Janet, with V. Mukohya, R. Nkera, B. Schoepf, M. Beda and W. Engundu (1991) *The Real Economy of Zaire: The Contribution of Smuggling & Other Unofficial Activities to National Wealth*, Philadelphia, PA: University of Pennsylvania.

Matthaei, Julie (1996) "Why Marxist, Feminist and Anti-Racist Economists Should Be Marxist-Feminist-Anti-Racist Economists," *Feminist Economics* 2(1), spring: 22–42.

Merchant, Carolyn (1980) *The Death of Nature: Women, Ecology, and the Scientific Revolution*, San Francisco, CA: HarperCollins.

Myrdal, Gunnar (1968) *Asian Drama: An Inquiry into the Poverty of Nations*, vol. I, New York: Twentieth Century Fund.

Narayan, Uma and Sandra Harding (eds.) (2000) *Decentering the Center: Philosophy for a Multicultural, Postcolonial and Feminist World*, Bloomington, IN: Indiana University.

Nelson, Julie A. (1992) "Gender, Metaphor, and the Definition of Economics," *Economics and Philosophy* 8(1), April: 103–25.

—— (1993) "The Study of Choice or the Study of Provisioning? Gender and the Definition of Economics," in Marianne A. Ferber and Julie A. Nelson (eds.) *Beyond Economic Man: Feminist Theory and Economics*, Chicago, IL: University of Chicago.

Olson, Paulette (1994) "Feminism and Science Reconsidered: Insights from the Margins," in Janice Peterson and Doug Brown (eds.) *The Economic Status of Women Under Capitalism: Institutional Economics and Feminist Theory*, Brookfield, VT: Edward Elgar.

Pinney, Thomas (ed.) (1982) *The Selected Letters of Thomas Babington Macaulay*, Cambridge: Cambridge University Press.

Polanyi, Karl (1944) *The Great Transformation*, New York: Rinehart & Company.

—— (1957) "The Economy as Instituted Process," in K. Polanyi, Conrad M. Arensberg and Harry W. Pearson (eds.) *Trade and Market in the Early Empires: Economies in History and Theory*, Glencoe, IL: Free Press.

Pujol, Michèle A. (1992) *Feminism and Anti-Feminism in Early Economic Thought*, Brookfield, VT: Edward Elgar.

Seiz, Janet A. (1995) "Epistemology and the Tasks of Feminist Economics," *Feminist Economics* 1(3), fall: 110–18.

Sen, Gita and Caren Grown (1987) *Development, Crises, and Alternative Visions: Third World Women's Perspectives*, New York: Monthly Review Press.

Senghor, Léopold Sédar (1962) "On Negrohood: The Psychology of the African Negro," *Diogenes* 37, spring: 1–15.

Sharpe, Jenny (1993) *Allegories of Empire: The Figure of Woman in the Colonial Text*, Minneapolis, MN: University of Minnesota.

Stocking, George W. (Jr.) (1987) *Victorian Anthropology*, New York: Free Press.

Strassmann, Diana (1993) "Not a Free Market: The Rhetoric of Disciplinary Authority in Economics," in Marianne A. Ferber and Julie A. Nelson (eds.) *Beyond Economic Man: Feminist Theory and Economics*, Chicago, IL: University of Chicago.

Strober, Myra (1994) "Rethinking Economics Through a Feminist Lens," *American Economic Review Papers and Proceedings* 84(2), May: 143–7.

Todaro, Michael P. (1994) *Economic Development*, New York: Longman.

Trulsson, Per (1997) *Strategies of Entrepreneurship: Understanding Industrial Entrepreneurship and Structural Change in Northwest Tanzania*, Linköping, Sweden: Linköping University.

Visvanathan, Nalini, Lynn Duggan, Laurie Nisonoff and Nan Wiegersma (eds.) (1997) *The Women, Gender, and Development Reader*, London: Zed Books.

Waller, William and Ann Jennings (1990) "On the Possibility of a Feminist Economics: The Convergence of Institutional and Feminist Methodology," *Journal of Economic Issues* 24(2), June: 613–22.

Weber, Max (1961) *General Economic History*, New York: Collier Books.

Williams, Rhonda (1993) "Race, Deconstruction, and the Emergent Agenda of Feminist Economic Theory," in Marianne A. Ferber and Julie A. Nelson (eds.) *Beyond Economic Man: Feminist Theory and Economics*, Chicago, IL: University of Chicago.

Zein-Elabdin, Eiman (1996) "Development, Gender and the Environment: Theoretical or Contextual Link? Toward an Institutional Analysis of Gender," *Journal of Economic Issues* 30(4): 929–47.

—— (1998) "The Question of Development in Africa: A Conversation for Propitious Change," *Journal of African Philosophy* 11(2), December: 113–25.

—— (2001) "Contours of a Non-modernist Discourse: the Contested Space of History and Development," *Review of Radical Political Economics* 33(3), September: 255–63.

Zein-Elabdin, Eiman and S. Charusheela (forthcoming) "Feminism, Postcolonial Thought, and Economics," in Julie A. Nelson and Marianne A. Ferber (eds.) *Feminist Economics Today: Beyond Economic Man*, Chicago, IL: University of Chicago.

Index

Abbott, Edith 25
absolutism and relativism 122–30
Adam Smith's Daughters (Thomson and Polkinghorn) 4
Adams, Jane 137
adaptation 250; micro model of adaptive approach 252–7
affection, economy of affection 330, 332
affirmative action 90–2
Africa: African morality 322, 324, 334n; provisioning 330–2
Agarwal, Bina 93, 295, 296
agential reality 116
agriculture: agrarian policy and intrahousehold bargaining 299n; and development 326
Akerlof, G. A. 271, 278
Albelda, Randy 98
Alborn, Timothy L. 174
Alcoff, Linda 138
Althusser, Louis 183
altruism, caring 216, 248
Anderson, Elisabeth 113
anxiety: defense against 186; separation anxiety 187–9
Aristotle 34n, 335n
Army Sanitary Commission 173
Asia, introduction of private land ownership 326
assumptions, core assumptions and ontology 109–10
asymmetry, dependency relation in caring labor 231–43
autonomy: autonomous agents 59; and caring 232–3; fantasy of 189; mother-child relationship and drive for autonomy 187–8; object relations theory 276, *see also* dependency

Badgett, M. V. Lee 100n
Barad, Karen 116
bargaining: agrarian policy, intrahousehold bargaining 299n; division of labor, bargaining power 270–1; education, intrahousehold bargaining 292, 300n; intrahousehold bargaining models 287–98; wage-labor, intrahousehold bargaining 287–90, 291, 295–8
Barker, Drucilla K. 1–15, 59, 125
basic needs, social development 310–12
Bateman, Bradley W. 140n
Bauman, Zygmunt 196
Beasley, C. 268
Becker, Gary S. 5, 38, 51, 59; biological deviants 276, 278; home economics 269, 270; nonmarket production 63; sexual pay differential 218, 222; unpaid domestic labor 318n
Beecher, Catherine 47–8
behavior: adaptation 250; biology, modes of behavior and evolution 258–9; caring, modes of behavior 258–63; micro model of adaptive approach 252–7; modes of behavior, caring, evolutionary approach 257
Benería, Lourdes 70–1, 76, 95, 311, 326
Benhabib, Seyla 327
Bennington, G. 207n
Bergeron, Suzanne 299n
Bergmann, Barbara: crowding hypothesis 218; danger of romanticizing care 223, 225; gender inequality 220–1

Beyond Economic Man 99–100, 108
biology: biological deviants 276, 278; competitive mechanism 264n; domestic labor and gender identity 268–70; modes of behavior and evolution 258–9
Blank, Rebecca M. 99–100
blood donation 215
Bodichon, B. L. Smith 30
Booth, Charles 171
Bordo, Susan 189; anxiety 186; dependency and drive for autonomy 187–8; loss and repudiation 180
Boris, Eileen 81
Boserup, Ester 313, 326, 330
Bragstad, Torunn 221
Brandeis, Elizabeth 80
Braunstein, Elissa 59
Brown, Murray 287
Bush, Barbara 175
Butler, Judith: category of universality 208n; heterosexual hegemony 281n; sex and gender 278, 280

Cadbury, Edward 25
Cambridge University, admission of women 34n
Cannan, E. 30
Capital (Marx) 72
capitalism: evolution of 324; evolution of and rationality 335n
Cappelli, Peter 97
caring 12–13, 97–8, 213–27, 231–43; asymmetry in dependency relation 231–43; care economy 59; caring deficit 257; caring situation, motivation, work and resource components 236–8; childcare, efficiency 61; childcare facilities, working mothers 27–8; choice, preferential and other-regarding 232–4; as constitutive act 235–6; definition 214–15; division of labor 268–72; equality and difference 223–4; evolutionary approach 247–63; macro model of evolutionary approach 257–63; micro model of evolutionary approach 252–7; modes of behavior 258–63; motivation 216–17, 234–5; power 242; public policies 224–7; relatedness 239–40; split functions 242; unpaid domestic labor as caring labor 267–8; value of 217–24, 225–6, *see also* childcare; domestic labor; family
Catholic Church, medieval Europe 182
census, classification of families 170–4
Chadwick, Clint 97
change 247–8; and culture 250–1; technology 251, *see also* evolutionary approach
Chanter, Tina 277
Charusheela, S. 287–98
childcare *see* caring; domestic labor
Chodorow, Nancy 182, 221; caring 273; heterosexuality 281n; men's institutionalization of defences 275; mother-child relationship 180–1
choice: caring as result of other-regarding choices 233–4; caring as result of preferential choice 232–4; freedom of choice 40–4, 203; Kyrk's theory of consumption 40–4
civilization, classifying populations 166–70
Clark, Alice 25
Clark, John Bates 73
classification: census 170–4; social classification and facts of difference 161–77
Cloud, Kathleen 95
Coleman, James 219
colonialism: and race 325, 334n; rationale for 14, *see also* neocolonial projects; postcolonial
commercial man, as feminine 145
commitment, caring 233–4
commodity production: developing countries 326–7, *see also* noncommodity sector
Commons, John R. 137
competition: interference and exploitation competition 264n; Kyrk on fair competition 41; modes of behavior 258–62
componenent concept, caring situation 236–8
Connell, R. W. 74
Constantine, Jill 97
constitutive act, caring as 235–6
constructionism 92
consumption: and education 50;

institutional economics 48–9; Kyrk on 38–52; waste 40–4
Cooper, Brian P. 161–77
critical realism 110–12, 119*n*
crowding 30; crowding hypothesis, sexual division of labor 218–19
culture: and change 250–1; economics as culturally embedded 332; knowledge and beliefs 123; religion, cultural assumptions 131*n*; and science 128–9
'customary wage' 30

Dale, Kristen 221
Dallery, A. 185
Darity, William 59
Darwin, Charles 128
daycare centres, caring labor 219–20
Defoe, Daniel 164, 328
demand and supply (law of): and infant dependency 188, 192*n*; wage setting 74; wages 30
dependency: caring labor 240–2; dependants, caring labor 239–40; infant dependency 186, 188, 192*n*; mother-infant relationship and the market 185–7; women as dependent 23–6, *see also* autonomy
depressive position 190, 192*n*
developing countries: Africa, provisioning 330–2; African morality 322, 324, 334*n*; commodity production 326–7; effects of family structure on labour-market outcomes 97; marginalization of domestic labor 304–17; Third World, marginalization of domestic labor 304–17; third-world woman 334*n*
development: basic needs 310–12; defining economic activity 307–10; and domestic labor 294–5, 300*n*, 304–17; and gender 313–14; as industry-driven 325–7; neoliberal economics 312–13
Development Alternatives with Women for a New Era (DAWN) 334*n*
deviance: biological deviants 276, 278; difference as 295–6
Dewey, John 41, 49–50, 137
difference: bargaining models 295–7; and equality 222–4; facts of difference 161–77; and identity 200
Dimand, Mary-Ann 4, 57, 58, 61

Dimen, Muriel 184
disease, sanitary reforms 173, 175–6
division of labor 3; bargaining power 270–1; domestic labor 268–72; gender 59–61; object relations theory 272–8; sexual 218–19, *see also* domestic labor
Dixon, Vernon 334*n*
domestic labor 61, 318*n*; and development 294–5, 300*n*; and development economics 304–17; gender identity 266–80, *see also* caring; division of labor; family
domination 15, 322
Donath, S. 268
dual economy model, nonmarket sector 307
duty, and nonmarket production 63

Economic Journal 5, 25
Economic Problems of the Family (Kyrk) 44–5, 47
'Economic Risks of Being a Housewife, The' (Bergman) 221
economics: as culturally embedded 332; economic activity, definition 307–10; storytelling 203–4, *see also* home economics; institutional economics; neoclassical economics; neoliberal economics; political economy
Economics and Utopia (Hodgson) 52
ecos 184, 189
Edgeworth, F.Y. 4, 21, 34*n*; consequences of women in the workforce 23; opposed allowances for mothers 30; wages 28, 31
education: and consumption 50; and efficiency 60; intrahousehold bargaining 292, 300*n*
efficiency 82, 83*n*; Gillman on 58–67; macro-efficiency and micro-efficiency 76, 83*n*; as minimization of waste 60–2; nonmarket production 60, 63–5, *see also* waste
egalitarian fallacy 207*n*
ego, development of 147
Elson, Diane 59, 60, 93, 313, 317*n*
Elster, Jon 248
emancipation: and epistemology 195, 198–200; and labor 287, 288

emotionality: compulsory emotions 299*n*; 'native men' 329
empirical methodology 89–100
employment: development and domestic labor 294–5; employment options 292–4; as empowerment, critique of 287–98; independence, and opposition to women's employment 25; labor market, determinants of women's entry into 290–2; location of in household bargaining models 287–90; paid labor 14; race, employment options 292–3; workforce, women in 23–6, 34*n*, *see also* labor
Engels, Friedrich 34*n*
Engendering Development (World Bank) 95, 290
England, Paula 221, 273–4, 327
Enlightenment 130
epistemology: and emancipation 195, 198–200; and ontology 8–9, 105–18
equality: and difference 222–4; race, income inequality 326
ethics: Dewey and Kyrk 49–50, *see also* values
'European' 334*n*
European modernity 327–30
evolutionary approach 247–63; macro model 257–63; micro model 252–7
exchange 181; denial of sharing 187–90; market exchange, gender bias 328; and sharing 184–5, *see also* market
exit, as uncaring behaviour 241–2
experience, process ontology 136
extra-household environmental parameters (EEP) 296, 297

Fabian Women's Group 25
Factory Acts 24, 28; as discriminatory 25–6
facts: facts of difference 161–77; and values 105
fairness 74
fallibilism 131*n*
family: effect of family structure on labor-market outcomes 96–7; family life, penetration of market 257; family obligations, Tanzania 331; family wage 24, 25, 26; Kyrk on economic problems of 44–5; social classifications 170–5, *see also* caring; domestic labor
Farr, William 163, 171–4
father, Adam Smith on identification with 152–5
Fawcett, M. Garrett 30
Feiner, Susan F. 180–91
feminine: Adam Smith on passions 151–2; femininity 325; *see also* gender
Feminism and Anti-Feminism in Early Economic Thought (Pujol) 4
feminist: economics, conceptualization of 2–3; feminist empiricism 91
Feminist Economics 5, 89
Ferber, Marianne A. 90, 91
Ferguson, Ann 221
fertility 291, 299*n*
fiction 203; Charlotte Gilman 56–8, 61–2, 64–6
Field, James Alfred 39
Figart, Deborah M. 70–83
Flax, Jane 116, 186; knowledge 199
Folbre, Nancy 95, 332; caring labor 213–27, 268; caring motivation 234–5; gender division of labour 59; long-run reciprocity 335*n*
Foucault, Michel 124, 127
Frederick, Christine 47–8
freedom of choice 203; Kyrk's theory of consumption 40–4
Freeman, John 263*n*
Freud, Sigmund 154, 183; Catholic Church 182; love object 192*n*; splitting 189
Frey, Bruno 63
Friday (*Robinson Crusoe*), feminization of 324–5, 328, 334*n*
Friedan, Betty 288, 289; US feminist movement 298–9*n*
Fuchs, Victor 218

game theory 300*n*; household interaction 287–8, 298*n*; oversupply of labor 291
Garrett, Nancy 95
Gatens, M. 279–80
gauchos (South America), and civilization 167
gender: definition 281*n*; gender analysis 2; gender compass 273; gender and development (GAD) 13; gender identity 266–80; gender-centrality

323–5; and sex 276–80; wounded man narrative 274, *see also* feminine; identity; masculine
gentlemen, social classification 164, 166
Gershwin, Ira and George 213, 223
gift economy 216
Gilman, Charlotte Perkins 5, 56–67
Gilroy, Paul 287
globalization 3, 97, 290, 299*n*
goals, importance of in judging practices 124–5
God, and Nature 186
Godwin, R. 181
Gramsci, Antonio 334*n*
Grapard, Ulla 56, 57, 58, 60, 117–18
gross domestic product (GDP), and efficiency 58
gross national product (GNP) 95; and caring labor 225
Grossbard-Shechtman, Shoshana 98, 218
growth *see* development

Hacking, Ian 124
Hampton, Jean 140*n*
Hannan, Michael T. 263*n*
Haraway, Donna 130*n*, 138, 201, 207*n*
Harding, Sandra 91, 322, 334*n*; epistemology 118*n*; knowledge 114–16; objectivism and realism 122–30
Hartmann, Heidi 46
Hartshorne, Charles 138
Haveman, Jon D. 97
Head, Francis B. 167
Heather-Bigg, Ada 25
Held, Virginia 216
Herland (Gilman) 64–5, 66
heterosexuality: compulsory heterosexuality 278–80, 281*n*; object relations theory 281*n*
Hewitson, Gillian J. 56, 266–80; femininity 324–5
Hill, Georgiana 25
Hill, M. 182
Himmelweit, Susan 235, 247–63, 268
Hirschfeld, Mary 38, 46, 49
history 203; and knowledge 126; rereading 3–6
Hodgson, Geoffrey 51, 52
Hogg, M. H. 25, 34*n*

home economics: Kyrk on 47–8; unpaid domestic labor 268–70
Home, The (Gilman) 60, 61, 63
homo economicus, fantasy mother of the unconscious 185, 191*n*
hooks, bell 322
hours, effects of family structure on hours worked 96–7
households: household production, efficiency 63–5; intrahousehold dynamics and resource allocation 95–6, *see also* caring; domestic labor; nonmarket production
How Natives Think (Lévy-Bruhl) 328
human capital 32, 73, 292, 293
Human Development Report (United Nations) 97
Humboldt, Alexander, Baron von 167
Humphries, Jane 82
Hutchins, Elizabeth 25
Hutchinson, Emilie 78, 79
hybrid subalternity 333, 335*n*
Hyden, Göran 330, 332

ideas: marketplace of 204; as masculine 335*n*, *see also* knowledge; science
identity 194–206; and difference 200; domestic labor 266–80; domestic labor and gender identity 268–70; gender identity 266–80; identity politics 200–1; masculine identity 145–57, 186; object relations theory 155, 273–8; separation, gender identity 273–4, *see also* gender
If Women Counted (Waring) 94
imagination: Adam Smith on 149–51, 154; literary imagination 66
impartial spectator, Adam Smith on 153–4
independence, and opposition to women's employment 25
individualism 181
Industrial Democracy (Webb and Webb) 76
industry-driven, development 325–7
inefficiencies 61, *see also* efficiency; waste
infancy: dependence 186, 188, 192*n*, *see also* mother-child relationship
infant mortality 26–7, 29
institutional economics: caring labor 220–2, 224; Kyrk on consumption 48–9, 51

International Association for Feminist Economics (IAFFE) 89
International Labour Organization (ILO), contribution of rural women 311
International Monetary Fund (IMF) 13

Jacobsen, Joyce P. 89–100
James, William 137
Jennings, Ann 328
Jevons, S. 4, 21; Factory Acts 28; mothers in the workforce 26–7, 28; women in the workforce 23–4
Jochimsen, Maren A. 224, 231–43
Justman, Stewart 145, 158n

Katz, Elizabeth 296–7
Kaufman, Michael 273, 274
Kaul, Nitasha 194–206
Keller, Catherine 138
Keller, Evelyn Fox 148
Kestenberg, Judith S. 186
Kilbourne, Barbara 221
Kim, Marlene 93
Kimmel, Michael S. 273, 274
kinship, African societies 330
Klamer, Arjo 9
Knight, Frank 50
Knobloch, Ulrike 224
knowledge 6; as adding to reality 137; epistemology and ontology 8–9, 105–18; insitutionalized storytelling 203; and language 123–4, 130n, 204; and lived experience 134; McCloskey, Deirdre 112; post-positivism 126–9; and practice 116–17; relativism and absolutism 122–30; social influences on 112–14; and social movements 130–1; statistics 165, see also science
Kranton, R. E. 271, 278
Kuhn, Thomas 7, 115, 123, 124, 126, 128, 131n
Kuiper, Edith 1–15, 145–57
Kyrk, Hazel 5, 38–52, 59

La Plata Federal Union 168, 169
labor see employment
Lancaster, Kelvin 51
Lane, Ann 57
language, and knowledge 123–4, 130n, 204

Lawson, Tony 8, 106, 112, 114, 115; critical realism 110–12, 119n
Lévy-Bruhl, Lucien 328
Lewis, Margaret 57
Lewis, W. Arthur 306, 307, 308, 314
liberal state, social contract 327–8
life, wanting and needing 184
living wage 71–3, 78, 79; definition 76; gender 77–9; living-wage movement 72–3; race 80–1
Lloyd, Genevieve 9
Long, David 98
Longino, Helen E. 90, 99
Lorde, Andre 322
loss: and repudiation 180, see also separation
love: and nonmarket production 63; and self-command, Adam Smith on 155–6, 158n, see also caring
Lundberg, S. 270, 278
Lyotard, Jean-François 196

Macaulay, Thomas Babington 328–9, 335n
McCloskey, Deirdre 6, 105–6, 114; knowledge 112; methodological rules 107–8; rhetoric 109, 110, 117; *Sprachethik* 108, 112, 117, 119n
McCloskey, Donald N. 202
McCulloch, J. R. 169–70
McElroy, Marjorie 296
MacGaffey, Janet 331, 332
McMahon, A. 274, 276
McNay, L. 276
Madrick, Jeff 95
Mäki, Uskali 106, 112; ontology 109–10, 114, 115
Malthus, Thomas R. 165, 166–7
Manser, Marilyn 287
marginal productivity theory of wages 73
marginalization, domestic labor in Third World 304–17
market: Law of Markets 188; market economy, reward for pursuit of self-interest 223–4; market exchange, gender bias 328; as setting wages 73–4, 82; symbolism of 185–9, see also exchange
married, women as 23–6
Marshall, A. 4, 21, 44; mothers in the workforce 26, 27–8; rationality 32;

wages 28; women in the workforce 23–4
Marshall, Judith 96
Martineau, Harriet 171
Marx, Karl 34n, 138, 183; labor power 83n; market as Eden 185, 188; production 215; wages 72
masculine: ideas as 335n; infant dependency and masculine identity 186; masculine identity, Adam Smith's *Theory of Moral Sentiments* 145–57; men caring 262; scientific as 184–5, *see also* gender
Matheson, M. Cecile 25
Matthaei, Julie 324
'meaningful efficiency' 60
men *see* gender; identity; masculine
metanarratives 196
methodology, empirical methodology 89–100
Miers, John 168
Mill, James 165
Mill, John Stuart 30, 34n, 171
Mincer, Jacob 24, 218
mineral revolution, South Africa 326
Mirowski, Phillip 300n
Mitchell, Wesley 48–9, 137
modernity, European modernity 327–30
modes of behavior, caring, evolutionary approach 257–9
Mohanty, Chandra 315, 316
Monroe, Day 44
morality: African morality 322, 324, 334n; caring 234; moral and economic split 134–9; moral obligation, motivation 248
Morgan, Mary S. 140n
mortality rates, sanitary reforms 173
mother-child relationship 147, 180–1, 183, 190; dependency and drive for autonomy 187–8; and the market 185–7; supply and demand 188, *see also* caring
motherhood 60; 'motherhood allowance' 29; women as mothers 26–30
motivation: caring as constitutive act 235–6; caring labor 216–17, 234–5, 268; motivation component, caring situation 236–8; and self-interest 248
Mutari, Ellen 70–83

Muth, Richard 51
mutualism, modes of behavior 260–1

Nathan, Maud 79
National Consumers' League 79, 83
'native men': feminization 328–9; social contract in European modernity 327–8
Nature: and God 186; scientific view of 185
necessity, and nonmarket production 63
needs: caring labor 239–40, *see also* wants
Nelson, Julie A. 90, 91, 93, 226, 231; gender compass 273–4; gender metaphors 323–4; moral and economic split 134–9; motivation/activity dualism in caring 235, 236; provisioning 60
Nelson, Lynn Hankinson 91
neo-institutionalism 140n
neoclassical economics 21–2; caring labor 218–20, 224; mothers in the workforce 26–30; productivity 30–2; psychoanalytic reading of 180–91; rationality 32–3; women in the workforce 23–6
neocolonial projects: sexualized and/or servile labor 300n, *see also* colonialism; postcolonial
neoliberal economics, development 312–13
Netz, Janet S. 97
New Deal, Kyrk's involvement with 46
Nightingale, Florence 173
nonmarket production: development economics 307; efficiency 60, 63–5; Tanzania and Zaire 331, *see also* caring; domestic labor
nontradeable goods 94–5
Nozick, Robert 119n
Nuñez, Ignacio 168
Nurkse, Ragnar 306
nurturing: women as having a comparative advantage 29, *see also* caring; mother-child relationship
Nussbaum, Martha 51–2, 66

object relations theory 146, 147–8, 191n; caring 221, 273; identity 155, 273–8
objectivity: flight to 190; strong objectivity

114, *see also* knowledge; rationality; science
obligation, caring labor 217
O'Brien, Ellen 225
O'Donnell, Margaret 57, 58
omnipotence, fantasy of 189–90
On Negrohood (Senghor) 329
ontology 8–9, 105–18; and epistemology 8–9, 105–18; process ontology 136–7
oppression, and caring 222
Ortner, Sherry 74
over-crowding 173, 177n
overseas contract workers (OCWs) 293

Papanek, Hanna 299n
parasitic industries analysis 75 7, 78, 81, 82
parasitism, modes of behavior 260–1
parenting deficit 257, 262, *see also* mother-child relationship
Pareto optimality 58, 59, 63, 66
Pareto, Vilfredo 58
patriarchy, and commodity production in developing countries 326–7
pay *see* wages
pecuniary emulation 48
Peirce, Charles Saunders 140n
perceived contribution, household bargaining 289
persuasion 108, 109
Peter, Fabienne 105–18
Petty, William 164
Philippines, overseas contract workers 293
Pigou, A. C. 4, 21; allowances for mothers 30; mothers in the workforce 23–4, 26, 27, 28; productivity 30; wages 28, 31–2; widows 30, 34n; women's dependence 23
pin money 25
Pocock, John G. A. 145
Polachek, Solomon W. 24, 93, 218
Polanyi, Livia 22–3
political economy, wage setting 70–83
Polkinghorn, Bette 4
Pollack, R. A. 270, 278
population: and civilization in 1820s South America 166–70; evolutionary approach to economics 249–50
post-positivism 126–9
postcolonial 334n; postcolonial sentiment 205; postcolonial thinkers 322, *see also* colonialism; neocolonial projects
post'isms 194–206
postmodernism 196
poststructuralist feminism 202–4
poverty: infant mortality 27; intrahousehold resource allocation 96
power, caring situations 242
Power, Marilyn 70–83
practice 105–18; goals, importance of 124–5; impact of feminist economics on 98–100; and knowledge 116–17; practice theory 74–5
Prasch, Robert 57, 61
praxis, and theory 199
predation, modes of behavior 260–2
price, wages as 73–4
Prigogine, Ilya 138
process thought 136–9
production 215; commodity production in developing countries 326–7; gender bias 328; nonmarket production 60, 63–5
productivity 30–2
Progressive Era, USA 77
provisioning 60, 72
psychic income, caring labor 219
psychoanalysis *see* object relations theory
public policies, caring labor 224–7
Pujol, Michèle 4, 21–33

Quetelet, Adolphe 162, 164, 170, 174
Quine, W. V. O. 7, 126, 128

race: and colonial domination 334n; employment options 292–3; and gender 325; income inequality 326; living wage 80–1; social classification 165
Raphael, D. D. 153–4, 158n
Rathbone, Eleanor 25, 29
rationality 32–3, 263n; and evolution of capitalism 335n; rationalism and relativism 112–13; and social norms 248, *see also* knowledge; objectivity; science
Rawls, John 119n
realism, and rhetoric 107–12
reality, and theory 204

reason 335n, *see also* objectivity; rationality; science
reciprocity 330, 335n; caring labor 215; long-run reciprocity 335n
Redmount, Esther 100n
Reid, Margaret 5, 38, 44; efficiency 58–9; nonmarket production 60, 63
reification (scientific knowledge), and relativism 106
relatedness, caring labor 239–40
relativism 114, 201, 207n; and absolutism 122–30; and rationalism 112–13; and reification of scientific knowledge 106
religion: cultural assumptions 131n, *see also* culture
reproduction: reproductive work 317n; and wage-labor 291
repudiation, and loss 180
resource allocation, intrahousehold 95–6
resource component, caring situation 237–8
rhetoric, and realism 107–12
Richards, Ellen 47–8
Richardson, D. 281n
Rickman, John 170–1
Robinson Crusoe (Defoe) 56, 324–5, 334n
Robinson, Joan 194
Rorty, Richard 140n
Rosenstein-Rodan, P. N. 306
Rostow, Walt 306
Rouse, Joseph 116, 124, 130n
Rowntree, Seebohm 34n
Rubery, Jill 82
Rutherford, Malcolm 140n

sanitary reforms, mortality rates 173
Sawyer, Malcolm 83n
Say, Jean-Baptiste 188
scarcity, and separation in mother-infant relationship 187, 190
Schumpeter, Joseph A. 158n
science: and culture 128–9; scientific knowledge as socially constructed 105–7; scientific as masculine 184–5; social nature of 6–9, 15; social sciences, critical realism 111, *see also* knowledge; objectivity; rationality
Scott, Catherine 306
Sebberson, David 57
second economy, Zaire 331, 332

Seigfried, Charlene 138
Seitz, Janet 106
self-command, Adam Smith on 155–6
self-interest 248; modes of behavior 258; rewards for pursuit of 223–4
Sen, Amartya 52, 71, 222, 296; commitment 233–4; perceived contribution 289
Sen, Gita 311, 326
Senghor, Léopold 329
Senior, Nassau W. 162
separation: gender identity 273–4; mother-infant relationship 187, 190; separation anxiety, denial of 187–9
separative self 273–4, 321, 327
sexuality 100n; compulsory heterosexuality 278–80, 281n; heterosexuality, object relations theory 281n; sex and gender 276–80
sexualized labor 293, 300n
Shann, George 25
Shapiro, Michael J. 203
sharing 180–91; denial of 187–90
Sheth, Falguni 57, 61
Sidgwick, E. M. 34n
Sklar, Katherine Kish 79
Smart, William 30
Smith, Adam 10; masculine identity in *Theory of Moral Sentiments* 145–57; progress 177n; wage setting 72
Smith, Ellen 34n
social contract, liberal state 327–8
social development, basic needs 310–12
social good 15
social institution, economics as 3
social movements, and knowledge 130–1
social norms: division of labor 270–1; micro model of adaptive approach 252–7; and rationality 248
social practice, wage setting as 72, 74–5, 79–81
social sciences, critical realism 111
South *see* developing countries; development; Third World
South Africa, income inequality 326
South America, social classification 166–70
Spelman, Vicki 34n
Spencer, Herbert 329
Spivak, Gayatri Chakravorty 205, 208n
Sprachethik 108, 112, 117, 119n

Staab, Josephine 52
state intervention, Kyrk's theory of consumption 41
statistics, and facts of difference 161–77
status, subalternity of native man and European woman 327–30
Stengers, Isabelle 138
Stiglitz, Joseph 220
Stocking, George 329
storytelling, economics 203–4
Strassmann, Diana L. 6, 22–3, 108, 202; core assumptions 109–10
strategic essentialism 208n
Streeton, Paul 311–12
Strober, Myra 223
strong objectivity 114
structural adjustment policies 313
Stuart, Frank 34n
subalternity 334n; hybrid subalternity 333; native man and European woman 327–30
subsidy, parasitic industries 76–7
subsistence 73; subsistence economy, nonmarket sector 307
supply and demand *see* demand and supply
Swartz, Maud 78
sympathy, Adam Smith on 149–51

Tanzania 330–1, 332
Taylor, Harriet 30
technology, change 251
text 207n; economics as 202–4; postcolonial sentiment 205
theory: and critique 197–8; practice theory 74–5; as producing reality 204; as productive enterprise 195; theory of consumption 40–4, *see also* game theory; object relations theory
Theory of Consumption, A (Kyrk) 40–4
Theory of the Leisure Clas, A (Veblen) 42
Theory of Moral Sentiments, The (Smith) 10, 145–57
Third World: marginalization of domestic labor 304–17; third-world woman 334n, *see also* developing countries; development
Thomson, Dorothy L. 4
Thurow, Lester 219
time: domestic labor 61; modes of behavior 259, 260; process ontology 137
Titmuss, Richard 215
training, and productivity 31
Treatise on Domestic Economy (Beecher) 47
Tronto, Joan 214, 217, 222, 239
Trulsson, Per 330–1
Tuana, Nancy 91
Tufts, James 42–3

unconscious 183
United Nations 13, 97; United Nations Development Programme (UNDP) 317
universality, category of 208n
Unremunerated Work Act (1993) (USA) 225
USA: census 175; implementation of living wage 79–81; labor regulations 77; living-wage movement 72–3; Progressive Era 77
USAID, investing in women 312

values: and facts 105; Kyrk's theory of consumption 42–3, *see also* ethics
Van Fraassen, Baas 109
Van Kleeck, Mary 80, 83n
Van Staveren, Irene, fiction 56–67
Van Velzen, Susan, consumption 38–52
Vaughan, Genevieve 216
Veblen, Thorstein 42, 45, 48, 57
Victorian ideology 21
violence, domestic violence 281n
vulnerability, asymmetry in caring 231–43

wages 5; below-subsistence 28; caring labor 218–20; effect of family structure 96–7; gendering living wage 77–9; living wage 71–3, 77–81; neoclassical economics on 24; parasitic industries 76–7; pay equity, caring labor 225; political economy of wage setting 70–83; as price 73–4; productivity 30–2; social practice, wage setting as 72, 74–5, 79–81; USA, implementation of living wage 79–81; women's 'comparative advantage' 29; women's entry into labor market 290–2, *see also* employment
Wagman, Barnet 95

Walters, Bernard 317*n*
wants, market as Garden of Eden 184–7
Ward, Benjamin N. 202
Waring, Marilyn 94
waste 40; efficiency as minimization of 60–2; Kyrk's theory of consumption 40–4, *see also* efficiency
Webb, Beatrice 76–7, 78, 82
Webb, Sidney 76–7, 78, 82
Webb-Potter, Beatrice 30
Weber, Max 263*n*, 335*n*
Weisskopf, Thomas 234
Welldon, E. 187
'Western' 334*n*
Wheeler, Roxann 165
Whitehead, Alfred North 137, 140*n*
widows 34*n*
Williams, Rhonda 321, 322, 324
Wilson, Woodrow 39, 41
Winnicott, D. W. 183
Woman's Role in Economic Development (Boserup) 313
'women', as category 1–2
women and development (WID) 13
Women and Economics (Gilman) 57, 60, 61
Women and Human Development (Nussbaum) 51–2
Women of Value (Dimand et al) 4
Women's Bureau, economies of family life 80, 81
Wood, Cynthia A. 304–17
Woolf, Virginia 66
Woolley, Frances R. 92, 96, 98
words *see* language
work component, caring situation 237–8
workforce *see* employment
World Bank 13, 95, 97, 290; structural adjustment 313
World Development 95

Yellow Wallpaper, The (Gillman) 61–2, 66
Young, Arthur 165

Zaire 331, 332
Zein-Elabdin, Eiman 321–33